ONE THOUSAND BUILDINGS OF
LONDON

Photographs by John Reynolds

Text by Gill Davies

One Thousand New York Buildings

One Thousand Buildings of Paris

ONE THOUSAND BUILDINGS OF
LONDON

PHOTOGRAPHS BY JOHN REYNOLDS

TEXT BY GILL DAVIES

BLACK DOG
& LEVENTHAL
PUBLISHERS
NEW YORK

ISBN-10: 1-57912-587-5
ISBN-13: 978-1-57912-587-5

Library of Congress Cataloging-in-Publication Data on file at the offices of the publisher.

Permission to depict specific buildings is outlined on page 576, which constitutes an extension of this copyright page.

Text by
Gill Davies

Book cover design and maps
Sheila Hart Design Inc.

Building selection, interior design, and production
Playne Design Limited, London
Designers
Kieran Fairnington
Clare Playne
Research and technical
Simon Hack
The Tin Limited
Playne Books Limited, Pembrokeshire UK
Designers
Richard Cotton
Geraint Jones
David Playne
Research and editorial assistants
Aureole Communications
Sheila Jones
Chris Kilvington
Rupert Matthews
Christine Skinner

Published by
Black Dog & Leventhal Publishers, Inc.
151 West 19th Street
New York, New York 10011

Distributed by
Workman Publishing Company
708 Broadway
New York, New York 10003

b   d   f   h   g   e   c   a

Manufactured in China

CONTENTS

INTRODUCTION

Sir, if you wish to have a just notion of the magnitude of this city, you must not be satisfied with seeing its great streets and squares, but must survey the innumerable little lanes and courts. It is not in the showy evolutions of buildings, but in the multiplicity of human habitations which are crowded together, that the wonderful immensity of London consists.

—Samuel Johnson, 1709–84

Arriving in London is always an unforgettable experience. Arriving there for the very first time, raw from school, to take up an editorial role in a publishing house was particularly exciting. Each evening, I left my desk in High Holborn and set out to explore—walking, staring, gazing all around, wildly enthusiastic about being in such an exhilarating city—and stepping out alone, all the better to absorb the architecture and history that presented itself around every corner.

With the passage of time, some streets and sights are rather more familiar to me now but the city remains just as exciting. I no longer live there. I have become a visitor, with my palate refreshed and ready for new experiences. Researching and writing this book has been a hugely satisfying undertaking. I have learned so much and discovered many, many more of the city's secrets. London is a veritable kaleidoscope of images and stories, many of which are encapsulated in the buildings—the Tower of London, the Houses of Parliament, the busy streets and shops, the splendour of Royal London, Georgian terraces, neat little semi-detached houses, inns where Charles Dickens and Doctor Johnson rested a while before taking up their pens again. . . .

I must thank so many people involved in this exploration: the photographer, John, whose enthusiasm and energy was so infectious; J.P. Leventhal for believing we could achieve his dream; editors Laura Ross and Iris Bass for keeping our feet on the ground and making sure we did so; the diligent teams at both Playne Design and Playne Books for tremendous support, input, organisation—and patience when my scatter-brained intoxication with this wonderful city needed to be channelled.

Thank you all . . . and may I propose a toast to London, to the thousand faces encapsulated here and the many more besides . . . to quote from the venerable Doctor Johnson once again: "Sir, when a man is tired of London, he is tired of life; for there is in London all that life can afford."

Gill Davies

AUTHOR'S NOTE

London is a huge city with many areas and divisions—geographical and political. The decision was made to use the postal codes as the 'boundaries' for each chapter as these encompass well-known, established zones such as Kensington. Moreover, no numbered postcode crosses the natural boundary of the river Thames (which also helped the photographer's schedule!). Eight new postcodes were created in the 1960s based on a system first introduced under Sir Rowland Hill in 1858. The postal codes in Central London—West Central (WC) and East Central (EC)—are numbered according to their centrality; the other sectors are numbered by assigning Number 1 to the district closest to the centre and allowing the rest of the numbers to follow alphabetically, according to the name of the location. (There are no London postal districts labelled NE or S and the television soap opera *East Enders* is set in the fictional postal district of E20.) Please note that EC includes the City of London, and SW1 the City of Westminster.

While the buildings that have been photographed do cover a wide area of London, there are just a few postcode areas that have escaped the privilege of inclusion in this book, and the contents list reflects this.

All the photographs are new, taken specifically for this book, and so certain notable buildings have, unfortunately, had to be omitted because they are under scaffolding at present—such as Unilever House and the Royal Festival Hall. The titles used for the buildings may be the actual house names, but often they are of my own devising, in particular to avoid duplication when the address appears above. There are many mentions of ghosts. While the veracity of such apparitions may or may not be accepted, for reasons of space this has not been questioned or prefaced by doubts or explanations.

The Great Fire of 1666 impacted on so many buildings that, again for reasons of space, the date is often omitted, and sometimes it is referred to simply as 'the Fire.'

London has many ancient buildings and it has been quite a challenge to discover all the relevant information but it is amazing just how much is known and recorded. Nonetheless, certain dates and architects have proved elusive, despite vigorous research. I apologise for any such omissions and would welcome this information so that it may be included in future editions.

PHOTOGRAPHER'S NOTE

I remember my first visit to London very clearly. It was 1994; I'd just finished college and had come down to a studio in Soho to shoot some stilllifes for a design agency. I went for a walk along Regent Street and I remember thinking, as I looked up at the buildings, that they must have been, by and large, the same buildings that my parents (both originally Londoners, who had died several years earlier) used to look up at, too. In that moment, it was as though the fibre of the buildings had drawn up all of the history and life that had unfolded in and around them, and the buildings themselves were gently resonating with it.

I made it a goal, whenever I took photographs here, to try and capture some of this energy, along with some of the spirit in which the buildings were originally designed and built. Just like people, some buildings have been loved and looked after whilst others have been the victims of neglect. Some will stand to a ripe old age and others will be torn down after only a few years, to be replaced by another cycle of change.

Within months of my first trip to this amazing capital I'd become a Londoner myself, and it has been my home ever since. London is great for that—no matter what your ethnic background or religious persuasion, if you decide to take up residence, you can call yourself a Londoner and nobody will question you about it; you're a member of the club.

I have really enjoyed working on this project—it has been the most satisfying and fulfilling job I have ever done. It has taken me to places in London that, in my twelve years of residency, I had never visited, and some that I'd never even heard of, but now I shall remember all of them, and if ever I need a change of career, I'm sure that I'll be able to find a job as a London cabbie!

During the course of this project, I travelled over two-and-a-half thousand miles on a borrowed 125cc Vespa (thanks Clare!) draped in all kinds of exotic photographic equipment. During this time I wore out three scooter tyres, one pair of boots, and the shutter in my wide-angle lens. I broke shutter release cables too numerous to mention. I picked up only two parking tickets. I lost a stone in weight.

I was stopped and searched by the police under the Prevention of Terrorism Act three times. I plotted the position of every building to be shot on a nine-sheet London map. I wore the scooter's brake shoes down to the metal. I made countless lists of important things to do.

I should like to dedicate this book to my wife Katie, for without her constant support, love, and enthusiasm, I simply could not have taken on such a mammoth project. Whilst holding down her own very successful career, she still found the time and the energy to look after me and make me her priority.

I'd also like to thank Mark and Olpha Gibbon and Bob and Margaret O'Donnell for all their support and love. I'd like to thank Alan Simpson for firing my enthusiasm for photography in the first place, and providing answers to all my questions with a wry smile and a rare wit. Thanks must also go to Theo Cohen for well-timed and well-chosen words of encouragement and wisdom; Jenny, Lawrence, and Steve at Teamwork; and Paula Pell-Johnson at Linhof and Studio, for guiding me around the equipment needed for such a very technically challenging and demanding project. Thanks, too, to Clare Playne, Simon Hack, and Kieran Farnington of Playne Design and to David Playne of Playne Books for giving me the opportunity to work on such a fine project, and thanks to Gill Davies for such a superb piece of research and writing. Finally, a big thank-you to all the people who kindly provided access and gave the permission that enabled this book to be. It is greatly appreciated.

John Reynolds

Technical Note
The images were shot using a Phase One P25 digital back on an Alpa 12 SWA, with Schneider and Rodenstock digital lenses. The images were processed on an Apple G5 2.0ghz Dual processor using C1 Pro and Adobe Photoshop. It was all viewed on a Lacie electron blue IV CRT monitor with Gretag Macbeth calibration.

WEST LONDON (W)

London's 'west side story' begins in Mayfair and Soho and then runs along to Kensington, Paddington, Notting Hill, and Shepherds Bush; and thence to Chiswick, Hammersmith, and Ealing. Its central zone includes theatres, cinemas, and night clubs—plus the busiest shopping district.

Today, Mayfair is a most prestigious address. The area was originally developed in the early 1700s by wealthy landowners (the Grosvenors and the Berkeleys) but was, in fact, named after a notorious bawdy fair held here until the early 1700s, when it was finally banned because it invited, 'drunkenness, fornication, gaming and lewdness.'

Famous architect John Nash designed Regent Street in 1812 and, in doing so, divided the upmarket areas of Mayfair and St James's from rather sleazier Soho. The street's lovely arcades were designed to protect shoppers from the muddy, dung-filled roads.

Oxford Street was originally the main Roman route to Oxford, hence its name. By the 1700s, it was part of the route along which prisoners were taken to Tyburn Gallows at Marble Arch.

Meanwhile, Soho grew apace on open fields through which many hunts rode, and acquired its name from the hunting call of 'Soe Hoe.' Charles Gerrard, Sir Francis Compton, and Richard Frith helped to develop the area in the late 1600s and have streets named after them.

Further west are the lush, green acres of Hyde Park, Kensington Gardens (with the Palace), Holland Park, and, beyond, the riverside village of Chiswick where Hogarth once lived.

W1

Devonshire

Weymouth St

Baker Street

Gloucester Place

Seymour Place
Wyndham
Montagu
Square

George St.

Seymour Street
Bryanston Street

Oxford Street

Portman Square

Manchester Square

Wigmore Street

Duke St.

Stratford

New Cavendish St.

Mansfield

Portland Pl.

Great Portland St.

Langham

Cavendish Square

Margaret Street

Mortimer Street

Cleveland St.

Fitzroy Square

Tottenham Ct Rd

Howland St.

Charlotte

Great Marlborough St.

Wardour St.

Regent St.

Hanover Square

Newport Street

Brook

Grosvenor Square

Upper Brook St.

Mount Row

Mount St.

Carlos

Berkeley Square

Audley St.

South Audley St.

Park Lane

Park Lane

Chesterfield

Clarges St.

Curzon St.

Piccadilly

Hyde Park Corner

Burlington Gardens

Argyll

Soho Square

Greek St.

Dean St.

Berwick St.

Shaftsbury Ave.

Golden Square

Old Bond St.

Savile Row

Athenia

| 1 | 2 | 3 | 4 | 5 | 6 | 7 | 8 | 9 | 10 | 11 | 12 | 13 | 14 | 15 | 16 | 17 | 18 | 19 | 20 | 21 | 22 | 23 | 24 | 25 | 26 | 27 | 28 | 29 | 30 | 31 | 32 | 33 | 34 | 35 | 36 | 37 | 38 | 39 | 40 | 41 | 42 | 43 | 44 | 45 | 46 | 47 | 48 | 49 | 50 | 51 | 52 | 53 | 54 | 55 | 56 | 57 | 58 | 59 | 60 | 61 | 62 | 63 | 64 | 65 | 66 | 67 | 68 | 69 | 70 | 71 | 72 | 73 | 74 | 75 | 76 | 77 | 78 | 79 | 80 | 81 | 82 | 83 | 84 | 85 |

Cavendish

ord St.

W1   Mayfair
W2   Bayswater
W3   Acton
W4   Chiswick
W5   Ealing
W6   Hammersmith
W7   Hanwell
W8   Kensington
W9   Maida Vale
W10 Ladbroke Grove
W11 Notting Hill
W12 Shepherd's Bush
W13 West Ealing
W14 West Kensington

MARBLE ARCH

I   WI

1828 JOHN NASH

Marble Arch, reputedly inspired by the design of the Arch of Constantine in Rome, was originally located in front of Buckingham Palace, and was intended to be the building's main entrance for royalty. It was moved to its present site when the palace was extended in 1851. Today, it serves as a gateway between Bayswater and Marylebone but only senior members of the royal family, Royal Horse Artillery, and King's Troop, are allowed to pass beneath. It has three archways of Corinthian columns with sculpted reliefs that represent England, Scotland, and Ireland. Once upon a time, Tyburn Gallows stood here and, from the twelfth century, was where criminals, thieves, and political prisoners were hung in public executions that continued until 1783. A condemned man was permitted one last drink at an ale house on the road to the gallows, hence the popular phrase, 'one for the road.' One of the guards was left in charge of the cart and not allowed to drink, so the saying 'on the wagon' also arrived!

2

THE INCOMPLETE CIRCUS

2   W1

1700s

This 1700s crescent is the only curved
section of road realised of the intended circus
originally planned here. It was named for
George II's son, William, Duke of Cumberland,
who was known as the 'Butcher of Culloden'
after the battle he fought there with Bonnie
Prince Charlie and the Scots. The sweep of
crescent is graced with beautiful, elegant lamp
holders and railings. Today, the central portion
is occupied by a synagogue.

WYNDHAM PLACE

ST MARY'S

3   W1

1821–24 SIR ROBERT SMIRKE

Sir William Portman, Lord Chief Justice,
bought the land here in 1553. The names of
many streets in the area are associated with
the family, including one Anne Wyndham who
married Henry William Portman. This splendid
church was built to the designs of Sir Robert
Smirke, who revelled in Greek Revival style.
Some fifty years on, the church was altered
by Sir Arthur Blomfield (1875) and it was
redecorated by Sir Albert Richardson after
World War II. Its glorious semicircular portico
is set on a paved forecourt and graced with
Ionic columns, above which rise a delicate
round stone tower and cupola. Its square body
is built of stock brick, with two-tier windows.
The interior has a gallery and Doric columns
that rise to a gently curved, coffered ceiling.
This Grade I-listed building has recently had a
£3.7-million renovation to restore the original
Georgian splendour .

3

4

5

6

HOME TO THE BEATLES

1811 DAVID PORTE

Montagu Square, named after literary hostess Mrs Elizabeth Montagu, is now the only square left in Westminster that is purely residential. It has a peaceful, shady garden. Here the houses, some with shallow bay windows, form a narrow oblong of brick terraces. Ringo Starr lived here in 1965–69 (he also rented the house to Jimi Hendrix), and John Lennon and Yoko Ono first lived together here at number 34, the location for their nude *Two Virgins* album cover. This is also where Paul McCartney wrote and, in a temporary studio, recorded a demo version of *Eleanor Rigby*. Mick Jagger lived in the nearby Bryanston Mews East. In earlier times, novelist Anthony Trollope lived from 1815–82 at number 39—now turned into flats.

GLOUCESTER PLACE

A LONG GEORGIAN STREET

MAINLY EARLY 1800s JOHN ELWES AND OTHERS

Running roughly south from Hyde Park, this very long (it has two postcodes) and relatively intact Georgian street has many grandiose houses. Much of it was built by John Elwes, and the street was named after William, Duke of Gloucester and brother of George III. Its residents have included Mary Anne Clark, a bricklayer's daughter who, as mistress of the 'Grand Ole' Duke of York (commander in chief of the army) occupied number 62 from 1803 for some seven years. Here she kept many fine carriages, ten horses, three cooks, twenty servants, and much gold plate—until the duke deserted her on the discovery that she had been relieving army officers of cash in exchange for promises of promotion. Number 99 was Elizabeth Barrett's first London home from 1836–38 (from when she was thirty) before the family moved to Wimpole Street, and Wilkie Collins wrote *The Moonstone* at number 65, where he lived 1867–88.

BRYANSTON SQUARE

GRAND HOUSES

1811–21 JOSEPH PARKINSON

In an area of meticulously laid-out streets and some grand old houses, this square is home to splendid old London plane trees, camellias, rhododendrons, azaleas, and roses as well as an 1863 memorial drinking fountain and a cast-iron water pump from the early 1800s. The buildings were meant to create the effect of a grand design of two fine palaces, with stuccoed end pavilions and vast Ionic columns and pediments. Sadly, the houses in the centre west section have been replaced with a neo-Georgian apartment building. However, the original Parkinson houses have survived on the east side and at the four corners. In 1839, Mustapha Pasha Reschid, the Turkish statesman, reformer, and ambassador, lived at number 1.

HAMPDEN GURNEY

1995–2002 BUILDING DESIGN PARTNERSHIP

Built on a wartime bomb site and replacing an earlier low-rise 1950s school, this steel-framed building incorporates levels set high above the streets. Its roof springs from a steel truss, with a lightwell below, and part of this serves as a 'technology garden.' Thus the radical, flexible design incorporates open air teaching — and play areas connected to the classrooms by bridges. The building revels in transparency and lightness. The architecture of this primary school has a 'vertical' theme, with classrooms set on three levels; the children literally 'move up' the school as they grow older, rising from ground-floor nursery level to the top storey by the time they are the most senior pupils here.

7

8

HERTFORD HOUSE, MANCHESTER SQUARE
THE WALLACE COLLECTION

8   WI

1776 DUKE OF MANCHESTER AND 1882 SIR RICHARD WALLACE

Manchester Square is small but has many grand houses. It was developed and named for the Duke of Manchester, who raised a fine edifice on the north side in the 1770s, when the square was conveniently close to good duck-shooting country. A century later, this house was altered to its present form by Sir Richard Wallace, an illegitimate but favoured heir. It has a lovely pillared entrance with semicircular windows above and a very pleasing simplicity of form. Wallace owned a vast and impressive collection of paintings and decorative art—including the *Laughing Cavalier* by Fans Hals and works by Rembrandt, Rubens, Watteau, and Poussin—plus porcelain, furniture, and armour. When he died in 1890, Wallace left these treasures to his wife—who later bequeathed them all to the nation. The Wallace Collection, one of the finest private collections assembled by one family, is now a national museum but the house still largely retains the 1800s room layout of Sir Richard's day. In 1998, a new glazed roof was added to the courtyard.

9

10

11

THISTLE HOTEL

9   WI

1932-33 SIR JOHN BURNET, TAIT AND PARTNERS;
DESIGNED BY FRANCIS LORNE

This 1930s hotel is set discreetly behind shops on its Oxford Street façade with its entrance on the other side in Bryanston Street. The unusual design incorporates light wells, streamlined Dutch styling, sweeping lines, and nicely rounded corners, and manages to assimilate nearly 700 bedrooms. The Mount Royal has now undergone a major refurbishment, retaining the best of its original features but introducing modern technology and facilities. There are spacious public rooms, a bar, and a brasserie.

PORTMAN SQUARE

ELEGANT HOUSES

10   WI

1775-77 ROBERT ADAM AND JAMES WYATT

The square was first developed in the eighteenth century by Henry William Portman, on meadowland passed down from a Tudor ancestor. Numbers 20 and 21 are particularly fine properties. Home House is one of only two remaining great houses in London designed by Robert Adam. (The other is Chandos House in Chandos Street—*see page 27*). Adam developed a continuous sequence of rooms for the London base of the Countess of Home, with appropriate designs and styles that included some fine delicate, linear decoration. The elegant drawing rooms and Music Room are particularly lovely. Adam led the classical revival in England for both architecture and interior decoration. Sadly, these buildings were unoccupied from the late 1980s and ended up on the Buildings at Risk Register until a full restoration programme rescued the fine rooms and re-roofed the entire building. The wilderness gardens, laid out in about 1780 with a moveable temple built by the Turkish ambassador, were also restored in 2005. Home House is now used as a private club.

NORTH AUDLEY STREET

ST MARK'S

11   WI

1824–28 J. P. GANDY-DEERING

Set within the Mayfair Conservation Area, St Mark's is a fine Grade I-listed building and a good example of both late Georgian and high Victorian ecclesiastical architecture and decoration. Built as a chapel-of-ease to St George, Hanover Square, the front has a high Greek portico and tall Ionic columns; apertures in the pretty octagonal lantern let light into the building. Its interior was extensively remodelled by Sir Arthur Blomfield in 1878 to give it a Norman flavour. Sadly, in 1974, the church was declared redundant and lay empty for twenty years. The Commonwealth Church has occupied it since 1994 but the building has continued to deteriorate with water ingress and dry rot.

SELFRIDGES

I2   WI

1907-28 R. F. ATINSON (WITH DANIEL BURNHAM UNDER SIR JOHN BURNET)

When Selfridges opened in 1909, women had just gained the freedom to go out alone, without gentleman escorts; 90,000 people visited the largest store ever designed as a single shop. It had eight floors, nine passenger lifts, and one hundred departments. The first public demonstration of television was made here by John Logie Baird, in 1925. There was a silence room where the sign today still orders, 'Ladies Will Refrain From Conversation.' A recent £300-million development plan encompasses a new five-star hotel. It remains one of London's grandest shop façades with its huge, richly decorated Ionic columns. The store probably originated the saying 'The customer is always right.'

UKRANIAN CATHEDRAL

I3   WI

1889-91 ALFRED WATERHOUSE; 1967 CONVERTED INTO ITS PRESENT ROLE

This Ukranian Catholic Cathedral of the Holy Family in Exile was formerly a Congregational chapel. Alfred Waterhouse, the son of wealthy mill-owning Quaker parents, was a highly successful Victorian architect. Typical of his work, this building presents an interesting mix of Gothic and free Romanesque styles, with some lovely brick and buff terracotta tiles. The interior space is basically oval, with a splendid gallery carried on iron piers and covered in yet more terracotta.

STRATFORD PLACE, OFF OXFORD STREET, FORMERLY DERBY HOUSE
STRATFORD HOUSE

I4   WI

C. I773 RICHARD EDWIN 1909 G. H. JENKINS AND SIR CHARLES ALLOM

This magnificent Adam-style mansion was built for Edward Stratford, the second Earl of Aldeborough at the north end of the close. It is a rather splendid stone-faced classical building with dignified Ionic pilasters and a central pediment. An east wing with a ballroom was added in 1909. The house was occupied in the early 1900s by the seventeenth earl, who was war secretary in 1916–18 and ambassador to France in 1918–20. After World War II, the publishers Hutchinson took up residence, but it is now the Oriental Club.

41, 43, 66-76 BROOK STREET
GEORGIAN HOUSES

I5   WI

1720-25

Number 76 was once the residence of Colen Campbell, editor of *Vitruvius Britannicus* and architect of the original south side of Grosvenor Square. Today, many of the houses in this area are listed buildings. Some ten or so of the Georgian houses have been linked internally to create a flow of office space. In 1735, Robert Seymoure noted that Brook Street was 'nobly built and inhabited by people of quality.' In those days, the Tyburn watercourse flowed alongside, but this was covered over in the 1720s. A cobbled footway descends into White Lion Yard, near where the White Lion Inn stood in the 1700s. Alas, the old inn was demolished and only the yard now remains.

25 BROOK STREET
HANDEL'S HOUSE

I6   WI

1720-5

From 1723, this was the residence of composer George Frideric Handel (1685–1759), who wrote *The Messiah*, *Zadok the Priest*, and the *Royal Fireworks Music* here. On his death, the tenancy passed to his servant, who purchased Handel's remaining chattels for £48. In about 1790, a bow-window block replaced closets at the rear. In the 1830s, the garrets were raised to full-storey height. By 1905, the house was a shop but, from 1969–70, rock star Jimi Hendrix lived upstairs; blue plaques now honour both these 'poles-apart' musicians. Today, meticulous restoration has restored the fine, early Georgian interiors and the house (with number 23) hosts a museum celebrating Handel's life and works.

28 BROOK STREET
KENZO

I7   WI

1990 DAVID CHIPPERFIELD ARCHITECTS

David Chipperfield began his career working for Richard Rogers and then Norman Foster, and is renowned for his modernist creations that may be restrained and austere but are always appropriate. Here, there is interesting use of both natural light and artificial lighting, and interesting subtle changes of floor level. To its east, a smaller shop at number 26, called Equipment, was also designed by Chipperfield and opened one year later. His practice, founded 1984, undertakes a wide range of projects—from high-rise buildings and museums to interior design and made-to-order furniture.

12

013

14

15

16

17

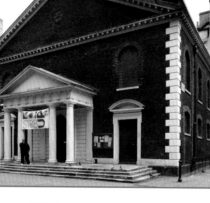

18

19

CAVENDISH SQUARE
ST PETER'S

18   W1

HANOVER SQUARE
ST GEORGE'S

19   W1

1721–24 JAMES GIBBS

The building of Cavendish Square began in
1717, but this work was interrupted in 1720
when the bursting of the South Sea Bubble
created financial chaos. Lady Mary Wortley
Montagu, the famous traveller and letter-
writer, lived at number 5 from 1723–38, and
Lord Nelson was in residence here in 1791.
The Wren-inspired chapel is set on an island
site and has decorative brickwork, a fine
porch with pillars and pediment, and a small,
double-cupola tower. Inside are a curved
ceiling, huge columns, and decorative
plasterwork. It was designed by the very
talented James Gibbs who studied in Rome,
the first English architect to do so—with Carlo
Fontana. Gibbs is probably most famous as
the architect of St Martin-in-the-Fields.

1721–24 JOHN JAMES

In the late 1600s, as new suburbs spread
westward, parish boundaries changed and
many new churches were raised. In 1711,
Parliament passed Queen Anne's act for the
erection of fifty new churches in and around
the City and Westminster. This is one of them;
its new parish stretched from Regent Street to
the Serpentine and south to include Mayfair,
Belgravia, and Pimlico. The first stone was laid
on June 20, 1721, and it took three and a half
years to complete, at a total cost of £10,000.
The architect, John James, was one of Sir
Christopher Wren's assistants. The church was
consecrated by Edmund Gibson, bishop of
London, in 1725. The west front has a large
Roman temple–style portico with an elegant
steeple set behind. The interior was restored
by Sir Arthur Blomfield in 1894. Here the
Grinling Gibbons reredos frames a 1724
painting of *The Last Supper*, by William Kent.
The windows contain early 1500s Flemish
glass (from Antwerp). George Frideric Handel
was a regular worshipper at St George's—
which now hosts Great Britain's annual Handel
Festival. St George's is presently the parish
church of Mayfair.

20

21

11-14 CAVENDISH SQUARE

STONE-FACED HOUSES

20   WI

200 OXFORD STREET

SHOP AND OFFICES

21   WI

c. 1771 TUFFNELL

This once stately square is now overshadowed by department stores; the trees in the middle were removed in the 1960s when a vast underground car park was built. But this spacious square must have been very regal in its day, laid out by John Prince for Edward Harley, Second Earl of Oxford, and named after his wife, Lady Henrietta Cavendish Holles. It still retains two glorious stone-faced houses, dating from about 1770. There was a pause in building progress when the bursting of the South Sea Bubble created economic chaos in 1720. Numbers 11 to 14 were eventually completed by one Mr Tuffnell. Today, joined by an arch, they house the Convent of the Holy Child and have a 1950s *Madonna and Child* sculpture created by Jacob Epstein.

A plaque on the wall explains that from 1942 to 1957, this building served as the headquarters of the BBC Overseas Services during World War II. Broadcasts were made directly to America from the roof, even during air-raids. Under one of the 'small talks' studios, immediately below a manhole cover in the cubicle floor, ran the River Fleet and the sound of running water could often be heard in the background. Eminent speakers here include Salvador Dali and J. B. Priestley. When this closed in 1957, all services were transferred to Bush House and the building became a shop.

22

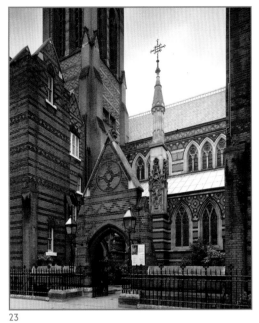

23

24

25

26

27

WELSH BAPTIST CHAPEL

22   W1

c. 1889

Formerly known as Castle Street East, after a nearby inn, the name of this street was changed in 1918. The first council rates were levied here in 1723. It is now full of small wholesale fashion showrooms and galleries but is also the setting for this elegant chapel with tall pillars and lovely balustraded staircases set each side of the central ornate entrance—creating a rather theatrical appearance. As well as serving as a place of worship, the Capel Bedyddwyr Cymreig is also used for the rehearsals of an amateur choir and orchestra, mostly comprised of lawyers.

ALL SAINTS

23   W1

1849-59 WILLIAM BUTTERFIELD

William Butterfield had a grand opportunity here to express both his religious and architectural ideas, and created one of the most influential urban churches of its era—in early High Victorian, Gothic Revival style. The narrow plot would prove quite a challenge but Butterfield also created two houses for clergy, a choir school, and a small courtyard. The soaring tower and steeple reach nearly 70 metres (227 feet). The church interior revels in chequered patterns, polished granite piers, rich stained glass, marble, alabaster, and coloured tiles. John Ruskin said it was, 'the first piece of architecture I have seen built in modern days which is free from all signs of timidity.'

GRANGE LANGHAM COURT HOTEL

24   W1

1885

Langham Street was laid out in the early 1800s and takes its name from Sir James Langham, a local, wealthy, eminent man. Scholar and editor Edward Malone lived at number 40 from 1779–1812. Today, the Grange Langham Court Hotel offers a tranquil haven in a central location in a rather unusual building. Although completely rebuilt in 1989, the splendid Victorian styling has been retained—including its façade of shiny, white, glazed brick, with lovely diamond patterning, striped decoration around the window arches, and elegant balustrades and chimneys.

ALL SOULS

25   W1

1822-24 JOHN NASH, RESTORED AFTER WORLD WAR II

This was part of John Nash's grand scheme for the area and, by the entrance, his bust gazes down Regent Street. The church gives Regent Street a fine flourish, despite the difficult angles of the site; the front circular portico acts as a pivot to the flow of roads. The conical spire mimics the larger portico below (a feature ridiculed at the time), and the church is faced with Bath stone. Winged cherub heads on the columns are based on Michelangelo's designs. Inside, a flat coffered ceiling is set above Corinthian columns and galleries, and there is bright blue and gold decoration. The altarpiece was a gift from King George IV. The BBC used the church to broadcast its daily service from 1951–94.

CHANDOS HOUSE

26   W1

1769-71 ROBERT (AND JAMES) ADAM

This very simple but pleasing stone-fronted house (now Grade I–listed) was first occupied by James Brydges, Duke of Chandos. The façade is of Craigleath stone with a lovely, porticoed entrance and a single band of carved wave decoration. After the death of the duke in 1789, the duchess, Anna Eliza Brydges, was declared a lunatic and confined to the house, losing control of her estates. Later, the lease was sold to the Austro-Hungarian embassy and wild, extravagant parties were sometimes hosted here by ambassador Prince Esterhazy. In 1871, the Duke of Buckingham and Chandos (a descendant of its original owner) leased the property; it remained in the family until 1905.

BROADCASTING HOUSE

27   W1

1931 VAL MYERS AND WATSON-HART

The 'Beeb's new headquarters, Broadcasting House, was officially opened in May 1932. This heroic building was soon a symbol of national unity during World War II, with its towering Portland stone façades, sculptures by Eric Gill, and a vast rounded frontage that resembles the prow of a ship. Inside, the demands of soundproofing, artificial lighting, air-conditioning, and new technical innovations have impacted on the original architecture but greater changes are underway. Soon, a new state-of-the-art centre for BBC national and international radio, television, and online services will transform Broadcasting House into a fine modern centre for global broadcasting.

28

29

4-I5, I8, 20-22 MANSFIELD STREET
ROBERT ADAM HOUSES

28   WI

PORTLAND PLACE
A GRAND I700s STREET

29   WI

I770s ROBERT ADAM

Robert Adam, the son of a stonemason, studied classical Roman ruins on the Grand Tour of France and Italy, and eventually had an enormous impact on Georgian art and architecture. Built on the site of a reservoir and named after Viscount Mansfield, Duke of Newscastle, this very pleasing row contains substantial houses. They are plain but fine, with railings and balconies, and have pretty fan-topped doorways and light, well-proportioned lines in neo-classical style. They exude elegance. Inside are lovely decorated ceilings. Architects John Loughborough Pearson and Sir Edwin Lutyens both lived at number 13 (from 1881–97 and 1919–44, respectively); the inventor and reformer Charles, third Earl of Stanhope, lived at number 20 from 1787–95.

I776-80 JAMES ADAM

This was planned as a single, very wide street. It was named after the ground landlord, the Duke of Portland, and owes its breadth to a mandate given by the planners to Lord Foley that the view northwards from the windows of his house, at the southern end of the street, should never be obscured. Today, with all the rebuilding since its inception and World War II bomb damage, it is hard to visualize the original grand plan. Later, the road became part of Nash's grand route from Carlton House to Regent's Park, with the half-circus of Park Crescent crowning Portland Place. There is a fairly complete section of original houses on the east side, between Weymouth Street and New Cavendish Street. Here the brick house-fronts have fine stucco pilasters and sunken panels decorated with honeysuckle. Famous residents include: Admiral Lord Radstock, who died at number 10 in 1825 (the site is now covered by Broadcasting House); Anne Isabella Milbanke, who was courted at number 63; authors John Buchan (who lived at number 76) and Frances Hodgson Burnett (who wrote *Little Lord Fauntleroy* and lived at number 63); and Admiral Jellicoe, resident of number 80.

1812 JOHN NASH

This remarkable curve of buildings marks the formal entry to Regent's Park. It was originally planned as a complete circus, the largest in Europe, but, in the event, became a beautiful sweeping crescent that just tips the base of the park. Single-storey colonnades of paired Ionic columns run the length of the wide quadrants, and act as a screen set before the individual doorways—so creating uniformity and flow. Lord Lister, the surgeon, lived at number 12 from 1877–1912, and Joseph Bonaparte stayed for a short while at number 23. Today, the crescent is home to many learned societies and important bodies. With its grace, proportion, and elegant simplicity, Park Crescent remains one of the finest architectural set-pieces in London.

30

31

ROYAL INSTITUTE OF BRITISH ARCHITECTS

31   WI

1932–34 GREY WORNUM

RIBA was founded in 1834 as the Institute of British Architects. Its Royal Charter was granted by William IV in 1837 and, in 1866, the title was conferred by Queen Victoria. Its presidents have included architects C. R. Cockerell, Sir George Gilbert Scott, Charles Barry, Alfred Waterhouse, Sir Reginald Blomfield, H. S. Goodhart-Rendel, Sir Edwin Lutyens, and Sir Basil Spence. Here, very appropriately, the architect for the building was chosen through a competition. The impressive Grade II–listed structure that resulted is a sturdy edifice in Portland stone that encloses a complex interior, created with much decorative craftsmanship. The building functions as a learned institute—with one of the best architectural libraries in the world, lecture theatres, committee rooms, and a club for members. There is a café with an outdoor terrace, galleries hosting exhibitions, and a good architectural bookshop.

32

A RING OF HOUSING

CLIPSTONE STREET

32   WI

1966–71 FREDERICK MCMANUS AND PARTNERS

Clipstone Street was first built from about 1720–50, and was named after the Duke of Portland's estate located at Clipstone, in Nottinghamshire. Painter and sculptor George Frederic Watts (one-time husband of actress Ellen Terry) lived at number 1 in 1838 and at number 14 in 1840. The present, 1960s six-storey building in Clipstone Street is, in fact, built in a ring formation with homes for some eight hundred people; it has a courtyard within that is surrounded by balconies. The building has a painted, concrete-frame exterior; its façade of windows and divides creates a pleasing, striped effect.

33

34

CLIPSTONE STREET

COLLEGE OF ENGINEERING AND SCIENCE

33   W1

FITZROY SQUARE

AN ELEGANT SQUARE

34   W1

1970 LYONS ISRAEL AND ELLIS

Historically, this first polytechnic played a huge role in the popularisation of science, and was a tourist attraction in Victorian London. In 1839, it was the first institution here to demonstrate photography.
Prince Albert became patron to the Royal Polytechnic Institution in 1841 and, in 1848, its new theatre held spectacular magic lantern shows. Quintin Hogg founded the next polytechnic in Regent Street in 1881 and here Professor John Pepper invented the popular theatrical illusion known as Pepper's ghost.
In 1896, the United Kingdom's first public moving picture show was held in the Polytechnic Theatre (later a cinema). The Polytechnic of Central London was one of thirty new polytechnics. The building shown here, with its many towers, opened in 1970, offering lecture theatres, offices, laboratories, and a spectacular entrance hall with flying galleries. In 1992, the Regent Street polytechnic became the University of Westminster headquarters.

1793–98 (EAST), 1794 (SOUTH), 1827–35 (NORTH AND WEST)
ROBERT ADAM

Henry Fitzroy was the son of Charles II and Barbara Villiers, and it was one of his descendants that built this square, regarded by some as London's finest. It was planned in its entirety but the buildings arrived in several bursts. The east side is a streamlined palazzo of individual houses in Portland stone with unfluted columns. The south side was destroyed in World War II but has been replaced. The north and west sides have stuccoed fronts—using stone for homes was then unusual in London. Blue plaques record that writer-artist William de Morgan and Prime Minister Lord Salisbury lived here. Virginia Woolf and George Bernard Shaw lived at number 29 (at different times); at number 37, Ford Madox Brown entertained fellow artists Rossetti, Holman Hunt, William Morris, Swinburne, and Whistler. In 1913, artist and art theorist Roger Fry gathered many brilliant, creative people here and opened the Omega Workshops to produce ceramics, painted furniture, textiles, glass, and jewellery—all marked with Ω, the Greek letter Omega. The square is now a pedestrian precinct.

THE BRITISH TELECOM TOWER

35   W1

1963–66 ARCHITECTS' SECTION OF THE MINISTRY OF WORKS: MAIN ARCHITECT ERIC BEDFORD

At 174 metres (580 feet) high — plus a mast and weather radar aerial that extends it to 188 metres (620 feet) — this was the tallest building in London until the National Westminster Tower (now Tower 42) arrived in 1981. Its construction cost over £2 million. The tower is made of 13,000 tonnes of concrete, plus steel, and is clad in glass with a special tint to prevent heat build-up. Its circular shape reduces wind resistance and lends it both stability and grace. The tower initially transmitted microwave telephone, radio, and television — and today incorporates fibre optic links and Internet transmission. Many enjoyed the view from the observation gallery until this was closed after a bomb exploded on the 31st floor in 1971. The revolving restaurant was closed, except for corporate events, in 1980, but not before over 4.5 million people had visited the tower. Two internal high-speed lifts travel at 6 metres (over 2 yards) per second, and take just thirty seconds to reach the top. An Act of Parliament was required to change fire regulations, allowing this to be the only building in the United Kingdom that can be evacuated by lifts (the only means of exit). Despite its very obvious presence, it was, curiously, classed as an 'official secret' until the mid-1990s; the tower was omitted from Ordnance Survey and other official maps and taking its photograph was technically an offence! It was Grade II listed in 2003.

1916 SMITH AND BREWER

Heal's has been famous for its stylish, modern designs ever since it opened its first store nearly two hundred years ago. John Harris Heal came to London in 1805 to work with a feather-dressing firm and in 1810 set up his own business. In 1893, Ambrose Heal Junior, a cabinet maker, joined the family firm and soon the company's simple oak Arts and Crafts vernacular furniture proved enormously popular. The building has been extended but the original store's façade reflects the functional, craft-based lines. Stone casings run the full height of the store, divided by blue spandrels depicting the tools of the trade. Today the store offers high-quality furniture, rugs, fabrics, bed linens, and home accessories, and has continued to reflect the fashions of the day—whether Art Deco, Pop Art, or Flower Power.

1766

Colville Place stands near the site of an eighteenth-century windmill on what was, in much earlier times, called Crabtree Field. Coleville Place derives its name from John Colville, a builder and carpenter who was contracted to build the first streets and houses here. It is a rare example of a surviving Georgian court—a small alley of houses, and shop fronts. Today, this is a quiet corner, where ornamental stone pots and urns overflow with plants. There is a stone flagged pavement, plus a line of trees and a green park on the southern side.

36

37

SOHO SQUARE

ST PATRICK'S CHURCH

38   WI

1891–1903 JOHN KELLY AND BIRCHALL

Soho Square was once graced by ambassadors and aristocrats. A chapel opened here to serve settlers in 1791 in an area 'inhabited principally by the poorest and least informed of the Irish . . . .' St Patrick's stands on the site of Carlisle House, in 1690 the residence of Mrs Cornelys, an opera singer from Venice, who had a child by Casanova. The house became the hub of London society, with masquerade balls, concerts, and operas, until Mrs Cornelys was imprisoned for bankruptcy. Today's church has a strong Italian flavour, with a redbrick exterior. A relic of Tyburn martyr Blessed Oliver Plunkett is housed here. Entertainer Danny la Rue was an altar server for many years and numerous celebrities have been married here, including Tommy Steele.

38

21 DEAN STREET

SOHO THEATRE

39   WI

1996–2000 PAXTON LOCHER ARCHITECTS

Obliged to quit the Cockpit Theatre in 1995, a small theatrical company set about converting a former synagogue, helped by an £8 million Lottery grant from the Arts Council. A lightweight canopy marks the street entrance. The ground floor and basement house the box office, bar, and restaurant while the new, 200-seat auditorium, with its steeply raked bench seating, is set at first and second floor level. The third floor is used for rehearsal and administrative space and, above all this, apartments occupy the top three floors. This has been a highly successful new project. The theatre company has grown from just five people with a turnover of £250,000 to have twenty-two full-time staff and a turnover closer to £2 million.

39

WARDOUR STREET

ST ANNE'S, SOHO

40   WI

1686, 1801–03, 1991 S. P. COCKERELL; THE WESTWOOD PRACTICE

The original 1686 church was the work of Wren (or William Talman). The church was renowned for its 'singing boys' and, in 1886, the choir was summoned to Windsor Castle to sing for Queen Victoria. In the 1920s, St Anne's presented the first religious service with music broadcast on the radio. Essayist William Hazlitt was buried here in 1830 and the St Anne Society included such names as T. S. Eliot, Agatha Christie, Arnold Bennett, C. S. Lewis, and churchwarden, Dorothy L. Sayers (who is buried here). Four clock faces are set into the yellow brick tower with its tall steeple. World War II bombs took a vigorous toll; only the outer walls and tower survived. In 1991, St Anne's re-opened—incorporated into a new development of offices and flats. The old church tower is now set in a tiny park and garden.

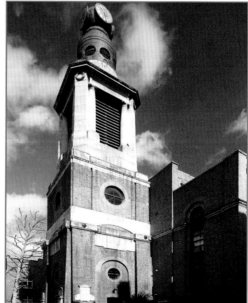

40

41

1924 AND 1926 E. T. AND S. E. HALL

Arthur Lasenby Liberty began by importing shawls from India and opened his first shop in 1875, selling soft silks, and goods from Japan, Java, Indochina, and Persia. By 1883, he had acquired two more shops. In time, he owned all of 140–150 Regent Street. In 1881, Gilbert and Sullivan enhanced Liberty's fame by using their fabrics for costumes in *Patience*. Liberty's went on to pioneer the sale of Art Nouveau. Customers included Ruskin, Charles Keene, Rossetti, and Whistler. In time the shop sold furniture, silver, pewter, jewellery, and wallpapers. The Tudor House building was built in 1924 (at the height of the 1920s Tudor revival) so that trading could continue while the Regent Street shop was renovated. The two buildings are linked by a three-storey bridge over Kingly Street. Built with the timbers of two battleships, the HMS *Impregnable* and HMS *Hindustan,* the opulent building has handmade roof tiles, linen-fold panelled lift doors, leaded lights, and stained glass made by Liberty's craftsmen and Italian master carvers. The central well was surrounded by galleries on which exotic rugs and quilts were displayed in intimate 'rooms' with fireplaces. The shop's Regent Street façade (1926) is neo-classical, and features a vast screen of columns above a rectangular base, with a group of figures and Britannia on top. Some figures peep over the parapet, on which a frieze portrays exotic goods being transported by sailing ship, camel, and elephant. The shop was famous for dress fabrics — including dainty, floral Liberty Prints and Tana Lawn. Liberty has continued to be at the forefront of fashion, promoting craftsmen and designers (including Mary Quant and Yves Saint Laurent). In 1975, the store celebrated its centenary with an exhibition at the Victoria and Albert Museum.

42

1928 RAYMOND HOOD; 1935 ADDITIONS BY GORDON JEEVES

This was originally designed as a showroom for the American Radiator Company. Its American architect, Raymond M. Hood, was educated at Brown University, MIT, and the École des Beaux-Arts in Paris, and became renowned as a New York skyscraper pioneer who worked in the Art Deco style. Here, the sheer, polished, black granite façade has simple window openings. There is an Egyptian cornice plus decorative floral tiles, inlaid gilt, and other Moorish-, Mexican-, and Persian-inspired features. Today the ground level part of the building is occupied by Caffe Uno and Garfunkels.

43

44

34 KINGLY STRRET; FORMERLY THE BRICKLAYERS ARMS	117-127 REGENT STREET
THE CLACHAN	**WESTMORLAND HOUSE**
43 W10	44 W1

1898

The 1924 Liberty store expansion involved a mock-Tudor extension and the Bricklayers Arms was incorporated into this grand plan. For some sixty years, it remained a part of the complex and Liberty's holdings but, in 1983, was sold and became a Nicholson Inn (pubs of historical or architectural interest). It was renamed the *Clachan*, which, in Scotland, means 'a small village'. Built in mellow brick, the pub has a marble fascia, huge carved stone window cases, ornate dormers, and a turret and dome. Within are rich wood carving, interesting structural ironwork, copious old prints and sepia photographs. The cosy, raised seating area at the back was probably once the landlord's parlour.

1920–25 SIR JOHN BURNET FRIAS, RSA, RA, THOMAS TAIT

The rebuilding of Nash's Regent Street and Quadrant had been interrupted by World War I but, by the 1920s, was once again surging ahead. Just north of Blomfield's contemporary Quadrant on the acute corner of Vigo Street, Westmorland House was Burnet and Tait's first post-war commission and is an example of their renowned use of end pavilions enclosing plainer, classical building. Its rounded ends, decorated with columns and copper-covered domes, enclose six storeys of shops and offices. Sir John James Burnet was awarded the Royal Gold Medal for the promotion of architecture in 1923; this coveted annual award, made by the Sovereign, honours an architect (or practice) for excellence or advancement of architecture.

3-17 SAVILE ROW
BEATLES, BURLINGTON, BRIGHT
45   W1

EARLY 1700s

This street, most famous as the headquarters of London's tailoring trade, is now also known as the place where the Beatles gave their last performance, on the roof of their offices here in 1969. Laid out soon after Burlington House was built, the streets north of this were inhabited by many of Burlington's circle. Numbers 3–17 are the only surviving original buildings of which numbers 1 (although altered), 3, 11–14, 16, and 17 contain work by William Kent. Richard Brinsley Sheridan, dramatist and politician, lived at number 14 from 1813–16, and Richard Bright, who identified Bright's disease, lived at number 11 from 1830–58. Number 1 was occupied by the Royal Geographical Society from 1870–1911, and here, in 1874, lay in state the body of Dr Livingstone, before being taken to Westminster Abbey.

45

GOLDEN SQUARE
WHERE GELDINGS GRAZED
46   W1

1670–1700s VARIOUS, PLANS PROBABLY BY SIR CHRISTOPHER WREN

The name Golden derived from the geldings that once grazed here. In the early 1700s, it became highly fashionable, described by Strype as 'a very handsome place railed round and gravelled with many very good houses inhabited by gentry on all sides.' Residents have included Barbara Villiers, Duchess of Cleveland, Swiss painter Angelica Kauffman, painter Martin Archer Shee (president of the Royal Academy) and Scottish surgeon and collector John Hunter. Mrs Jordan, actress and mistress of the Duke of Clarence (later King William IV), took number 30 for her three daughters. When Dickens wrote *Nicholas Nickleby*, he placed Ralph Nickleby's rather gloomy house here. By the 1860s, there were boarding houses here, plus musical instruments makers, architects, engineers, and solicitors. Numbers 11 and 21 are original.

46

PICCADILLY AND BURLINGTON GARDENS; FORMERLY MELBOURNE HOUSE
THE ALBANY
47   W1

1770–1804, 1803–4 SIR WILLIAM CHAMBERS, HENRY HOLLAND

First built for Lord Melbourne, this Parisian hotel–style, Palladian building is set behind a formal gateway and long forecourt. Low nine-bay buildings are set on each side of the main seven-bay façade. The Duke of York wanted this as his London residence after his marriage and, from 1793, the royal pair lived here for eight years—by which time not only was the building mortgaged to Thomas Coutts, the banker, but the duke had run up countless debts. He had to dispose of his small palace. It was sold and converted it into bachelors' chambers, renamed after the Duke of York's second title, the Duke of Albany. Two new parallel rows of chambers lead to a gated entrance and the paved, covered Rope Walk to the lodges. Residents have included Lord Palmerston, Sir Robert Smirke, George Canning, and Lord Byron.

47

48

THE WEST END'S MEETING PLACE

48   WI

1819 JOHN NASH 1905–30 R. NORMAN SHAW, ASTON WEBB,
ERNEST NEWTON, AND SIR REGINALD BLOMFIELD

Piccadilly Circus is a plaza and traffic intersection in the
West End of the city, formed when John Nash created
Regent Street and the Quadrant in the early 1800s. Its
name derived from the pickadills (shirt frills) sold in this
area in the 1600s. In 1905, the Treasury authorised the
Commissioners of Woods and Forests to employ architect
Richard Norman Shaw to finalise the detailed designs
for the rebuilding of Nash's Quadrant, the north side of
Piccadilly and Piccadilly Circus. Some of Shaw's plans had
to be modified to keep disgruntled shopkeepers happy
and, in 1916, Webb, Newton and Blomfield collaborated
on new plans, Blomfield dominating the Regent Street
designs. Today, Piccadilly is renowned for its exciting
night illuminations, with neon lights that began with the
Bovril and Schweppes signs in 1910, followed by huge
advertising on the London Pavilion facades in 1923, and
finally, today's ever-changing spectacle of words, images,
and colour.

49

PICCADILLY CIRCUS; FORMERLY SWAN AND EDGAR

VIRGIN MEGASTORE

49   W1

1910–20 EXTERIORS SIR REGINALD BLOMFIELD; 2003 COLLET & BURGER

This is a store that has had many faces. During Blomfield's rebuilding of Regent Street Quandrant, much of the John Nash's original mid-1800s vision was lost, but Blomfield did at least recapture the Baroque style in the street — albeit French rather than English. Here, Swan and Edgar ran their famous haberdashery shop. William Edgar had progressed from a stall in St James Market to join forces with Mr Swan and, after the redevelopment of Piccadilly Circus, the two moved premises from Ludgate to number 20 Piccadilly in 1812–14 — and then, after the redevelopment of Piccadilly Circus, arrived at 49 Regent Street. By 1841, a new shop front had appeared in Piccadilly Circus. The store flourished, patronised by the Royal Family, and by 1848, occupied numbers 45–51 the Quadrant, plus a good part of the Piccadilly Circus corner. The shop front was one of the businesses targeted by window-breaking suffragettes in November 1911. The premises were rebuilt in 1910–20 to Sir Reginald Blomfield's design. The store was hit during London's last zeppelin raid in 1917. By 1927, it had been taken over by the Drapery Trust, and was later absorbed by the Debenham Group. It was bought by Richard Branson of the Virgin Group in 2003 and is now a Virgin Records Megastore, transformed by French architects Collet & Burger into an 'entertainment emporium,' with many exciting new design features.

BUSY SHOPPING STREETS

Oxford Street began to develop into a major shopping centre in the early 1900s (the first big store to arrive here was Waring and Gillow, in 1906) and now, with one of the highest concentrations of shops in the world, this is possibly Britain's busiest street. As well as the flagship branches of famous stores, there are many small specialist retailers, and over three hundred shops sell everything from souvenir gifts to haute couture. Some nine million tourists visit each year and up to sixty thousand people can be working in Oxford Street at any one time.

Selfridges, one of the most famous shops here, opened in 1909 and attracts over seventeen million shoppers every year. It also served a military role in World War II, when a decoder using early digital technology was hidden in the basement; so when Winston Churchill telephoned President Roosevelt or the Allied Command in Europe, his call went via the store!

Regent Street has many prestigious shops such as Burberry—founded in 1856 and renowned for its distinctive checked fabric. Hamley's, the famous toyshop, has been flourishing for over some two and a half centuries, with seven floors of toys, games, and models–including its vast model railway. Liberty, a most beautiful shop, was founded in 1875. Specialising in ornaments, fabrics and objets d'art from Japan and the Far East, it attracted Pre-Raphaelite artists such as Rossetti.

Meanwhile, Jermyn Street was developed by Henry Jermyn, at one time Earl of St Albans, and became a popular residential location for gentlemen and bachelors; it still bustles with barbers, shirt makers, tailors, tobacconists, and wine merchants.

Some of London's specialist shops include Anything Left-Handed in Brewer Street and jewellers Asprey & Garrard—Crown Jeweller for 150 years, with a heritage stretching back some five centuries. Many of the diamond necklaces, rings, bracelets, and pins that adorn the Oscar stars come from Asprey & Garrard.

50

51

50–52 PICCADILLY CIRCUS

RUSTICATED GRANDEUR

50   W1

63–65 PICCADILLY

NATWEST BANK

51   W1

1906 R. NORMAN SHAW

Once an insurance office and then the County Fire Office, this building on the north of Piccadilly Circus is a most impressive feature, in monumental style with a grand arcade, and enormous archways that open onto the adjoining streets. It has splendid frontages on all aspects and echoes the stately east front of the former Swan and Edgar store across the road (now a Virgin Megastore). The curved intricacy of the balconies seems especially delicate in this robust setting.

1922–23 WILLIAM CURTIS GREEN

There is quite a concentration of banks in this area. Occupying a corner site on Piccadilly and Albemarle Street, this one by renowned architect William Curtis Green has a plethora of columns and arches that create interesting curves at all floor levels. At the top, a loggia of two storeys is placed behind slender Ionic columns under the green slate roof, and there are interesting runs of balconies at two levels. NatWest Bank (formerly the National Westminster bank), with its now familiar three-arrowheads logo, commenced trading in January 1970. It owes its origin to National Provincial Bank (established 1833) and Westminster Bank (established 1836), which can trace their histories back to the 1650s.

157-60 PICCADILLY; FORMERLY WOLSELEY MOTORS
CHINA HOUSE

52   W1

1922-26 WILLIAM CURTIS GREEN

Set on the south side of Piccadilly (at the corner of Arlington Street), this design was inspired by a bank in Boston, but initially it served as an elegant Edwardian showroom for Wolseley Motors Limited, whose automobiles were displayed on marble floors. The showroom was sold to Barclays Bank and then Curtis Green undertook its conversion in 1926, adding extra ironwork and bronze doors. Arches on the ground floor, decorated with glorious ironwork, support giant Corinthian columns. The interior was enriched with lacquered Japanese-style decorations and Venetian red paint (said to be some twenty-six coats thick) on the banking hall columns. Now, a glossy noodle bar serves its delicacies here, surrounded by red lacquer, massive pillars, dramatic chandeliers, and vaulted ceilings.

52

PICCADILLY; FORMERLY PICCADILLY HOTEL
LE MERIDIEN

53   W1

1905-08 R. NORMAN SHAW

Shaw was a highly influential British architect who pioneered Old English and Queen Anne styles and also designed country houses, commercial buildings, and churches. This robust, large-scale hotel, in his late, heavy baroque style, was part of his scheme for the redevelopment of Piccadilly Circus. The frontage sports giant, triple-height, Ionic columns, with the bedrooms set back from a screen of columns. It is decorated in classic Edwardian style, and has nine floors and some 260 luxurious bedrooms—plus a vast indoor swimming pool. This grand hotel was renovated in 2001, and today its Edwardian details blend with contemporary styling; there are light marble floors, dark ash furnishings, fan-shaped windows, friezes, and leaded-glass domes.

53

BETWEEN PICCADILLY AND BURLINGTON GARDENS
BURLINGTON ARCADE

54   W1

1815-19 SAMUEL WARE; 1911 AND 1931 (END FAÇADES AND ENTRANCE) E. BERESFORD PITE

Set on a strip of Burlington House garden, this was built for Lord George Cavendish—to prevent passers-by from throwing debris into his garden. It became the fashionable place to purchase jewellery and luxury items in its tiny, neat shops, set under a lovely arched glass roof. The arms of Lord Chesham were placed over the Piccadilly entrance but, in 1926, the Chesham family sold the arcade to the Prudential Assurance Company for £333,000 and, in 1931, the entrance was redesigned. Former soldiers of the Tenth Hussars, Lord Chesham's regiment, used to act as beadles—to maintain order: to deter running, singing, and the carrying of open umbrellas or large parcels. Now reliable ex-serviceman from any regiment maintain this role. H. Simmons, the tobacconist, was founded in 1838.

54

55

196a PICCADILLY; FORMERLY HSBC / MIDLAND BANK
HAUSER & WIRTH GALLERY

55   W1

1922 SIR EDWIN LUTYENS

Edwin Lutyens designed over thirty-six major English country houses. He also worked with Gertrude Jekyll to create more than a hundred gardens. His works include the Cenotaph in Whitehall, the British Embassy in Washington, D.C.—and Queen Mary's Dolls' House. Here, the almost square façade of this very attractive, 'designer bank,' is in redbrick and Portland stone with many ornate details and a strong sense of symmetry. Arches curve over the sturdy doors to enclose oval features; there are multi-paned windows, and pretty carved ornamentation adds interest to the top storey. Inside is the single, and well-preserved, banking hall. Since 2003, this has served as an art gallery, located just across the road from the Royal Academy of Art, and close to fine-art dealers and auction houses.

56

6 BURLINGTON GARDENS; FORMERLY BURLINGTON HOUSE AND MUSEUM OF MANKIND
THE ROYAL ACADEMY OF ARTS

56   W1

1866–69 SIR JAMES PENNETHORNE; 2004–7 MICHAEL HOPKINS AND PARTNERS

This building is in an Italianate style, with many pillars, towers, and splendid statues. In 1854, the government bought the Burlington estate from the Cavendish family, and leased Burlington House and a part of the garden to the Royal Academy for 999 years. From 1902 until 1970, it was used by the civil service; and then the Museum of Mankind (part of the British Museum) occupied the elegant building, exhibiting collections and treasures from many indigenous peoples, and both ancient and modern cultures. The Royal Academy is presently developing this newly acquired £5-million site, into a complex for the visual arts—with lecture theatres, workshops, conference rooms, and a new large gallery. At last the public will be able to visit the historic vaults of Burlington House.

57

PICCADILLY
BURLINGTON HOUSE

57   W1

1664–65 SIR JOHN DENHAM, 1700s–1800s EXTENDED AND REMODELLED COLEN CAMPBELL, BANKS AND BARRY, AND OTHERS, 1991 FOSTER ASSOCIATES

The third Earl of Burlington, inspired by a visit to Italy in 1714–15, had the façade of this great mansion remodelled, with a splendid curved colonnade mutating from Baroque to Palladian. In Portland stone, his façade has Ionic columns and Venetian windows. In 1815, the house was bought by Lord Cavendish, and the grand staircase arrived. The splendid saloon has a magnificent ceiling. From the mid-1800s until 1982, the building was the headquarters of the Royal Academy. The arched Italianate front was added in 1873. Exhibitions include the celebrated summer exhibitions of some 1,200 new works by living British artists. The new 1991 Sackler Galleries provide three top-lit vaulted rooms, reached by a new glass lift and stair set in a light well.

58

WATERSTONE'S

1935–36 JOSEPH EMBERTON; 1960s ARCHITECTS CO-PARTNERSHIP

This pioneering store design, now a listed building, used the combined energies of architect Joseph Emberton, structural engineer Felix Samuel, and designer László Moholy-Nagy. The Piccadilly façade has horizontal strip windows with a canopy projecting over the top storey. Its welded steel structure implemented huge girders in the upper storeys. There is some fine external metalwork and, internally, the store has the feel of a large house, with cosy rooms rather than the vast open areas common to most department stores. Two storeys were added in the 1960s. Today, this is Europe's largest bookstore, with a vast selection of books, comfortable sofas and chairs for a rest and a read—plus a gift shop, art gallery, coffee bars, a good French restaurant, and a café in the basement.

THE ROYAL ARCADE

1879

The High Victorian Royal Arcade has a pretty glass roof running its full length—echoed by the glass of the shop fronts that are faceted at the corners with black-painted window frames and columns of gold piping. Built in 1879, the neo-Gothic arcade is 40 metres (132 feet) long with expensive shops lining both sides, selling cashmere jumpers, golfing knickerbockers, hunting jackets, and specialities such as pipe tobacco and chocolate. Each shop is separated by arches, with an open pediment above. The arcade connects Brown's Hotel and Bond Street and was, at first, simply called the Arcade (as stated on its entrance pediment), but, in 1882, it received royal patronage when Queen Victoria patronised H. W. Brettel's (hosiers and shirt-makers), buying her riding skirts and shirts, handkerchiefs, undervests, and wool here. The shop is still in business, at number 12. The Folio Society showrooms are at number 5. Today chocolate manufacturers Charbonnel et Walker Ltd, at number 1 (famous for its chocolate-covered strawberries) is patronised by Queen Elizabeth II.

60

61

THE RITZ HOTEL

60   WI

1906 MEWÈS AND DAVIS
(INTERIORS EXECUTED BY WARING AND GILLOW)

This first steel-framed building in London, in French château style, was built for Swiss hotelier César Ritz. (The architects had already built his Paris Ritz.) In fine Norwegian granite and Portland stone, it is crowned by a two-storey roof; here large copper lions add stature to the corners while tall chimneys and dormers soar behind. The interior is in Louis XVI style. A long vaulted gallery with marble floors and crystal chandeliers runs its entire length. The restaurant has glorious chandeliers linked by gilt bronze garlands. Some former famous guests are depicted in murals in the foyer; the hotel has been patronized by King Edward VII (as Prince of Wales), King Alfonso of Spain, the Aga Khan, and Paul Getty. Here, Pavlova danced, Noel Coward wrote songs, and Churchill, de Gaulle, and Eisenhower held summit meetings during World War II. In 1921, Charlie Chaplin needed forty policemen to escort him inside through ranks of fans and, in the 1950s, Tallulah Bankhead sipped champagne from her slipper here. The Palm Court has remained a popular place for tea. In 1995, the Ritz was restored—at a cost of over £50 million. In 2002, it received a Royal Warrant from the Prince of Wales. The terms 'ritzy' and 'putting on the ritz' sprang from this opulent, glamorous setting that oozes Edwardian elegance.

THE BISHOP OF ELY'S HOUSE

61   WI

1772 SIR ROBERT TAYLOR

Famous Dover Street residents have included diarist John Evelyn, poet Alexander Pope, brewer and politician Samuel Whitbread, architect John Nash, and composer Frédéric Chopin. The London residence of the acting bishop of Ely moved from Ely Place to the newly built Ely House (built for and by Edmund Keene, then the bishop of Ely, as his town residence) in 1772—and this remained their official London home until 1909. The street name derives from Henry Jermyn, Earl of Dover, and has several large mid-Georgian houses; this tall house is considered the finest. The central medallion between the first and second floors carries the bishop's coat of arms. It has a very high first floor and its precise architectural features are emphasised by the simple façade. The three-bay stone-faced front is a superb example of Palladianism and, despite considerable alteration for the Albemarle Club in 1909, the interior still has some fine features. Sir Robert Taylor was a notable English architect who in due course was appointed architect to the Bank of England.

62

63

OLD BURLINGTON STREET

62   WI

TIME & LIFE BUILDING

63   WI

1718–30

Richard Boyle, Earl of Burlington, laid out this street—the main one on the Burlington estate—and here his favoured artists, Colen Campbell and William Kent, lived at one time. The finest house was the small, Palladian palazzo at number 29 — sadly, demolished in 1935. Today, the street is dominated by modern office blocks and tailors' shops. However, numbers 31 (above) and 32 (designed by Campbell and built in 1718–23) are part of a row of four houses that may have been the inspiration for the 1700s terraces so prevalent in Georgian London. Number 31 is original and shows some good, early-Georgian touches, with a magnificent lampholder and doorway ironwork, while the windows at number 30 have Victorian stucco surrounds. Henry Palham, later prime minister, lived at number 32 in 1722–32, and the memoir-writer John, Lord Hervey, at number 31. Major-General Edward Wolfe (father of General James Wolfe), and the first Marquis Cornwallis, commander of the British force at Yorktown, lived here, too—but, sadly, their homes have long since vanished.

1952 MICHAEL ROSENAUER

The architect for this was Viennese Michael Rosenauer who, on the strength of his experience of low-cost housing, was invited to England in 1927—initially to advise the London County Council and the Ministry of Health on slum clearance. The building also involved the work of many artists and designers. Rosenauer commissioned works from contemporary artists, which include a mural painting by Ben Nicholson and a cafeteria design by Casson and Neville Conder. Henry Moore produced four carvings in Portland stone that create a frieze across part of the second-floor frontage, and a reclining figure graces the terrrace. The acclaimed young sculptor Geoffrey Clarke made interesting abstract metalworks for the building. Its exterior has a five-storey façade in Portland stone set on a marble plinth.

MOUNT STREET

64   WI

c. 1885 SIR ERNEST GEORGE, W. H. POWELL (1889) J. T. SMITH (1886), A. T. BOLTON (1893), ISAACS AND FLORENCE (1901)

This is a street that has a plethora of buildings with richly decorated, red terracotta tiles, largely by Sir Ernest George (an eminent nineteenth-century architect). There are excellent ornate tile examples by several others, including the Connaught Hotel (Isaacs and Florence). From Carlos Place, the street becomes more regular, and there are fine gabled and three-storeyed houses. Two gated entrances to St George's Gardens are set on the south side of the street. Number 41 is an immaculate late Victorian pub, the Audley, clad in pretty pale pink terracotta tiles, its interior in the style of a gentlemen's club, with dark wooden panelling plus some intricate carving, glazed tiles, and original crystal chandeliers.

64

116-21 MOUNT STREET

HOUSES WITH ORNATE TILING

65   WI

1886 J. T. SMITH

This was ever a busy place with both shops and houses. A poulterers, John Baily and Son, had been established at number 116 in 1720, but then the first Duke of Westminster (the Most Noble Hugh Lupus Grosvenor) had this whole street rebuilt in 1880–1900. By the time of his dukedom, the family's property in Mayfair, Belgravia, and Pimlico had made the Grosvenors the richest family in the United Kingdom. Here, much use was made of the pinkish red terracotta that the duke so approved. J. T. Smith's work on numbers 118–121 shows wonderful ornate examples of this tiling, in a street that has many fine examples. There were luxury shops at one end, with accommodation above, and fine, large, private houses towards the other end.

65

MOUNT STREET

CONNAUGHT HOTEL

66   WI

1901 ISAACS & FLORENCE

Originally a 'home from home' for the landed gentry of England when visiting the capital, this hotel was rebuilt and named the Coburg Hotel in 1896, after Prince Albert of Saxe-Coburg. When World War I broke out, it was renamed to avoid any German associations, and became the Connaught (after Queen Victoria's third son, Arthur, first Duke of Connaught). It served as the London home for landed families, many of whom had permanent suites here and, in World War II, was the London headquarters of General de Gaulle. Its handsomely proportioned interior has a majestic mahogany winding staircase and exquisite pieces of antique furniture. In 1956, the hotel was acquired by the Savoy Group. It is popular with film stars, and its Terrace Restaurant is run by superchef Gordon Ramsay (with Angela Hartnett).

66

6-10 MOUNT ROW
TUDOR-STYLE HOUSE

67   W1

1929-31 FREDERICK ETCHELLS

The row takes its name from Mount field, where there was once a small earthworks called Oliver's Mount, a Civil War fortification. The street arrived about 1720–40 with small, unpretentious houses, a parish workhouse set on its south side, plus shops and respectable lodging houses. In 1880–1900, the whole street was rebuilt under the first Duke of Westminster, with many pink terracotta Queen Anne-style houses (the workhouse moved to Pimlico). Soon luxury shops and substantial private houses sprang up. This little group of offices takes the form of an Elizabethan house with overhanging eaves, a Tudor-arched entrance with windows projecting above, and a rear court with decorative plasterwork trees. Architect Frederick Etchells was also a notable artist.

67

FARM STREET
CHURCH OF THE IMMACULATE CONCEPTION

68   W1

1844-49 J. J. SCOLES, HIGH ALTAR BY AUGUSTUS WELBY PUGIN

This Jesuit street in the Mayfair district took its name from Hay Hill Farm which, in the 1700s, extended from the present Hill Street eastward across Berkeley Square and beyond. The church raised on the Berkeley estate has a fairly simple exterior but those who cross its threshold discover a vast and beautiful Gothic interior. Its gracious nave has eight bays, with red granite columns buttressing to create polygonal chapels, tall clerestory windows, and a fine rose window at the west end. The white ceiling has a delicate geometric structure. The church may be entered from Mount Street (through the gardens) as well as from Farm Street.

68

125-29 MOUNT STREET
HOMES FOR 'PERSONS OF QUALITY'

69   W1

1889 W. H. POWELL

These buildings have superb terracotta tiles by W. H. Powell. The rebuilding was undertaken on behalf of upholsterers Allen and Mannooch, stationers Henningham and Hollis, saddlers Miller, Owen, and Company, and D. A. Lewis—linen-draper. Number 129 was planned as a model 'sanitary house' on behalf of the National Health Society but this project never reached fruition due to lack of funds. W. H. Powell, chosen as the architect in 1885, produced a disciplined Queen Anne-style design with straight gables and tall chimneys. The facing, in bands of yellow brick with buff Doulton's terracotta, has sometimes been referred to as 'streaky-bacon style.' The construction cost about £20,000 and was home to 'persons of quality.'

69

70

71

72

73

74

75

GROSVENOR HOUSE HOTEL

1926–28 WIMPERIS, SIMPSON & GUTHRIE, CONSULTANT SIR EDWARD LUTYENS

This grand hotel by stately Hyde Park was built on the site of Lord Grosvenor's 1800s mansion. It has luxurious suites, clubs, restaurants, a splendid Edwardian wood-panelled library, the Bollinger Bar (a renowned champagne house), and the largest ballroom in Europe, the Great Room, which has hosted many gala events—especially in the 1930s. The hotel has a massive base, square-roofed pavilions, and a screen of huge Corinthian columns. Recent renovations cost £35 million. Guests who stay in Le Royal Club bedrooms have a valet who unpacks suitcases, presses suits, and shines shoes; they receive temporary business cards printed with this London address.

GROSVENOR ESTATE HOUSES

1724–41

This was one of the main streets on the Grosvenor Estate and was begun in about 1724, with Upper Grosvenor Street dating from the 1760s. The houses are original, but a good number have stone fronts dating from 1905–14. Grosvenor House was the town residence of the Grosvenor family from 1808 to 1916—one of the finest residential properties in Mayfair. Today, the United States Embassy and Grosvenor House Hotel rather dominate the scene and many of the houses serve as offices. Famous residents include Sir Robert Peel (father of the prime minister) in 1800–22 and Captain David Beatty (later Earl Beatty), an admiral of the fleet from 1903–1910.

DUDLEY HOUSE

1824–28 WILLIAM ATKINSON

Dudley House is a small property on prestigious Park Lane, with an Ionic colonnade and a lovely first-floor glazed iron loggia. It survives as the only aristocratic dwelling left here where once there were so many. The Dudley family had already been associated with the site for some two centuries when the Earl of Dudley added a wonderful ballroom and picture gallery in 1855–58. The building survived bombing in 1940 and was remodelled by Sir Basil Spence in 1969–70 for the Hammerson group of companies. In January 2006, it sold for £37.4 million to a private investment company controlled by a Middle Eastern investor.

33 UPPER BROOK STREET

C. 1765 SIR ROBERT TAYLOR

Brook Street is a principal street on the Grosvenor estate, built from 1721 with houses in this salubrious area occupied by titled folk. Upper Brook Street was almost entirely residential until 1939, and many eighteenth-century houses survive. Several houses have been given new frontages—some with stone façades. Today, most of the buildings serve as offices or house foreign diplomats and Georgian-style apartment blocks have arrived recently. Number 33, Sir Robert Taylor's first London town house, is vast; its splendid façade seems to dwarf its neighbours. Elaborate ground-floor arches are arranged in recessed layers, with the main arches on Tuscan columns.

A COLLECTION OF FINE HOUSES

REBUILT 1823–27 (NUMBER 95 RECONSTRUCTED 1842–44)

Park Lane is renowned as one of the most exclusive parts of London and, from the 1820s, was much sought after by the rich and titled. Together with Mayfair, it is the most expensive option on the Monopoly board! It was originally lined with fine detached houses built for aristocrats along the edge of Grosvenor estate. This particular group are a magnificent clutch set back from the road. They ooze elegance and extravagance, with their curved projecting frontages, verandas, balconies, and Regency bay windows. Benjamin Disraeli lived at number 93 from 1839–72.

ROYAL HOMES

1845 MANY INCLUDING EDWARD SHEPHERD

This street was named after Hugh Audley, whose heirs acquired the estate in 1677. In about 1720, larger properties were built at the south end, many with fine Georgian plasterwork inside. Charles X of France lived at number 72 and Prime Minister John Stuart at number 75 in 1754–92; this became the Egyptian Embassy in 1927. In 1969, a ceiling painting proved to be a Tiepolo and was sold to the National Gallery. The street's architecture is a mixture of calm Georgian façades and vigorous Victorian implants. James Boswell often stayed at a house here , and Queen Caroline, wife of King George IV, lived at number 77 for a short while in 1820.

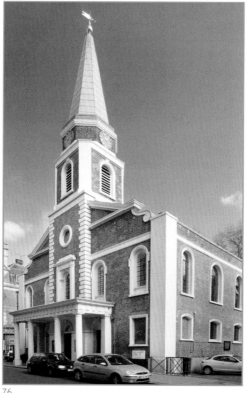

76

77

SOUTH AUDLEY STREET
GROSVENOR CHAPEL

76   W1

1739 BENJAMIN TIMBRELL

This modest little chapel in brown brick, with
St George's Gardens set behind, was built to
serve the newly developed Grosvenor Square
estate to the north. In 1831, it became a
chapel-of-ease to St George, Hanover Square.
Set before its small park, the chapel evolved
through the labours of its craftsmen rather
than a grand architectural scheme. It has a
certain flavour of New England and, indeed,
was used by American armed forces in World
War II. Its renowned organ was built by
Abraham Jordan in 1732. Here are buried the
Duke of Wellington's parents, as well as Lady
Mary Wortley Montagu and John Wilkes—
a flamboyant, rakish, ugly but charming
politician—and Lord Mayor of London.

CHESTERFIELD AND CHARLES STREETS
GEORGIAN HOUSES

77   W1

1740 VARIOUS

Here is probably the least altered eighteenth-
century street in the whole of Mayfair. Both
sides of Chesterfield Street have remarkably
intact Georgian terraces (as does Charles
Street at its top end) with all but one of the
houses (number 10) classic dwellings from
the 1700s with fine decorative features. Those
houses on the west side originally backed
on to the garden of Chesterfield House.
Playwright and novelist Somerset Maugham
lived here, at number 6, in 1911–19. Charles
Street, at the top end of Chesterfield Street,
extends from Berkeley Square to Waverton
Street and also has many lovely houses from
the same period. This street was probably
named for the Berkeleys; it lay on Lord
Berkeley's estate and Charles was a name
commonly used in the family.

LONDON HILTON

79   W1

1963 LEWIS SOLOMON KAYE AND PARTNERS
AND WILLIAM B. TABLER

Replacing a row of houses—one, from 1847, in Perpendicular Gothic style—this twenty-eight-storey hotel towering above Hyde Park was one of the earliest 'skyscraper-style' buildings in London, with a rooftop restaurant and bar by Casson, Conder & Partners. The Hilton's flagship property, it commands superb views over London's Hyde Park. The building presents interesting angles, with a mix of curved and straight surfaces, and contains nearly 450 luxurious rooms and 55 individually designed suites. It is 101 metres (331 feet) tall.

78

79

PARK LANE AND CURZON STREET

45 PARK LANE

79   W1

1963–65 COTTON BALLARD AND BLOW
WITH WALTER GROPIUS, BENJAMIN THOMPSON
AND LLEWELYN DAVIES AND WEEKS

This is the site of the famous Playboy Bunny Club in the 1960s. Gropius (founder of the Bauhaus, and famous for his New York Pan Am Building—now Met Life) collaborated with several other architects to create this eight-storey building with a pre-cast concrete façade and a rounded end facing Stanhope Gate. Here, the arrival in London of Hugh Hefner's bunny girls caused a huge stir in the Swinging Sixties. (Hugh Hefner conceived the idea for *Playboy* while he was in college and plans to be buried in a crypt next to Marilyn Monroe in the USA.) The Playboy Club opened here in 1966 but soon came under attack from the emerging feminist movement, led by such women as Germaine Greer. In due course, the club became the preserve of the rich and famous—from pop stars (and some criminals) to businessmen and politicians. In 1989, a brother of the sultan of Brunei, the world's richest man, was accused in the High Court of keeping prostitutes in the former Playboy Club in London, where he had bought the upper floors for £21 million.

PARK LANE

DORCHESTER HOTEL

80   W1

1930 WILLIAM CURTIS GREEN

In the eleventh century, William the Conqueror gave this site (in the manor of Hyde) to Geoffrey de Mandeville. Dorchester House was raised in 1751 and renamed later after its owner became Earl of Dorchester in 1792. In 1928, Sir Robert McAlpine and Sons and Gordon Hotel Ltd built a hotel here—a modern, progressive piece of architecture. The building rose quickly—one floor each week—and 40,000 tons of soil were excavated to create space below for kitchens, garages, and Turkish baths. The exterior façade is faced in faience with octagonal window towers. A thick raft of concrete over the public rooms supported eight floors of bedrooms. The new reinforced concrete allowed vast public spaces to be uncluttered by pillar supports and this sturdy structure encouraged General Eisenhower to choose it as his headquarters during World War II. The vast, pillarless ballroom has mirrored walls set with sparkling studs. Examples of cocktails created by one barman, famed for his cocktail-shaker expertise, were later sealed into the wall of a new bar. In the 1950s, the hotel was extended; Oliver Messel, a celebrated theatre designer, created extravagant floral themes, including an enchanted-forest penthouse suite. Illustrious hotel guests have included Alfred Hitchcock, Laurence Olivier and Vivien Leigh, Richard Burton and Elizabeth Taylor, Brigitte Bardot, Danny Kaye, Noel Coward, Marlene Dietrich, Cecil Beaton, Judy Garland, Duke Ellington, Sir Winston Churchill, Somerset Maugham, the Beatles, James Mason, Charlton Heston, Yul Brynner, Julie Andrews, Warren Beatty, Peter Sellers, Tom Cruise and Nicole Kidman, Arnold Schwarzenegger, and Kim Basinger. In 1977, the hotel was sold to an Arab consortium and, by 1990, the building had been refitted, with superb new facilities and restaurants plus all the latest entertainment and business technology.

80

81

CURZON CINEMA

81   W1

1963 SIR JOHN BURNET, TAIT AND PARTNERS

Originally, in 1935, this was a single-storey building, but in 1963 it was reconstructed by the same architects to include offices, a shop, flats, and an underground car park—as well as the cinema. Today, the Curzon Mayfair is an exclusive—and very stylish—place of entertainment. Boasting two screens (one of which is among the largest screens in London), it has been voted one of London's top twenty cinemas.

82

83

SHEPHERD MARKET

82   W1

1735 EDWARD SHEPHERD

This development of small shops was originally built to serve the grand residences of Piccadilly. Now, the charming enclave is busy with outdoor cafés, shops, pubs, restaurants, and people thronging the thoroughfares. It is named for architect Edward Shepherd, who lived in nearby Crewe House. Mr Shepherd received a royal grant for a cattle market in 1738 and by the 1760s the fair bustled with jugglers, prize fighters, fire eaters, merry-go-rounds, bull-baiting, eel-divers, and Tiddy-Dol, the Gingerbread Man, who dressed in white satin and sang to attract customers. The fair ended in 1764 when the Earl of Coventry objected to the noise and disturbance near his premises—but the market still continues.

MID-EIGHTEENTH-CENTURY HOUSES, INCLUDING . . .

45 AND 46 BERKELEY SQUARE

83   W1

1744 VARIOUS ARCHITECTS, INCLUDING JOHN DEVALL

First laid out in the 1730s, Berkeley Square began as a series of large houses on the east and west sides, mainly built by Edward Cock and Francis Hillyard. None of the original houses survived on the east side, where Berkeley Square House showrooms and offices now hold sway. However, on the west side, numbers 42 to 46 and 49 to 52 are all rather lovely mid-eighteenth-century houses. In particular, numbers 45 and 46 are a splendid rusticated stone-faced pair, dating from 1744 and set behind wrought-iron railings. Number 45, probably built by mason John Devall in about 1744, was the residence of the renowned soldier and administrator, Clive of India, from 1761 until his death from an overdose of laudanum in 1774. The square was recently bought by a consortium of Middle Eastern investors, who plan to restore and regenerate both the square and surrounding area.

84

85

44 BERKELEY SQUARE
HOUSE OF LADY FINCH

84   WI

50, 51, AND 52 BERKELEY SQUARE
STATESMEN AND BOOKS

85   WI

1744–45 WILLIAM KENT

Some have called this the finest terrace house in London—others describe it as a fascinating haunted house! Built for Lord Burlington's cousin—maid of honour to George II's sister, Amelia—it has a relatively simple Palladian façade with very elegant proportions. Pediments are set above the three tall first floor windows, with pretty square windows marking the top, third storey. A large rusticated surround creates a gracious entrance. Inside are many palatial rooms. Horace Walpole said that the main Baroque staircase was 'as beautiful a piece of scenery and…of art as can be imagined…' In the fine drawing room, Lady Isabella welcomed many of the luminaries of her age. Later, the house belonged to Lord Clermont, who entertained the Prince Regent, the future George IV, here. In 1959, the Clermont Club took over occupancy only to find the house haunted by Lady Finch's major-domo in his smart green livery and powdered wig. They say he flits up and down the grand staircase and watches the games of roulette and backgammon in the grand salon before melting through one of the staircase doors.

1730s

This beautiful square, with magnificent plane trees over two hundred years old, is the setting for these lovely Georgian townhouses with elegant entrances, plant-filled balconies, and sash windows. Established in 1853, Maggs Brothers Rare Books occupies number 50, with many antiquarian volumes and first editions. Statesman, twice foreign secretary, and finally prime minister in 1827, George Canning lived here—one of the first prominent politicians to use the term Tory openly (in the 1790s), and then the word Conservative (in 1824). He died in Chiswick, in the house of the Duke of Devonshire, in the very room in which politician Charles Fox had died some two decades before.

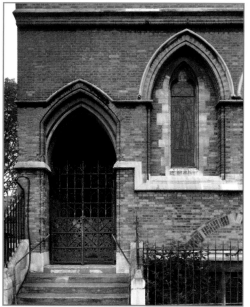

86

1868–78 GEORGE EDMUND STREET

This is one of the loveliest Gothic Revival churches in London, with a soaring slender spire, smaller turrets, and a pretty belfry. The exterior has stripes of stone and dark brown brick—a theme repeated inside, too. Here there is a high nave and some excellent use of diagonal pink and green tiles as decoration. The architect was a member of the congregation here, a professor of architecture at the Royal Academy in 1879, and an author of several books on Spanish and Italian architecture. Street loved the Gothic style and used it on many churches as well as the Royal Courts of Justice (1868–81) in the Strand.

87

1981 QUINLAN TERRY

Built in eighteenth-century style, in vernacular, classical Georgian, this church hall is actually a 1980s building. It has fine old bricks, reconstructed stone windowsills, lovely figures set in niches each side of the door, and decorative brick quoins at the corners. Quinlan Terry had already worked on the restoration of the church in 1974. He is sometimes described as Prince Charles's favourite architect because of his preference for classical styles and Palladianism. He also remodelled the interior of 10 Downing Street in the 1980s, and designed a series of villas, built from 1994–2003, northwest of Regent's Park.

88

1933–35 P. E. CULVERHOUSE

This recently restored steel-framed and clad building was designed by P. E. Culverhouse of the Great Western Railway Chief Civil Engineers office. It is a remarkable and rare example of a *moderne* office building—tall, bold, and dignified. It assumed its new name in 1987. The road name has changed, too, from Arrivals Road—which ran right through the station to link up with Praed Street. Large lettering proclaims G.W.R. Paddington at the parapet level.

89

PADDINGTON GREEN

ST MARY

89 W2

1788–91 JOHN PLAW; 1970s RESTORED BY ERITH AND TERRY

This rather charming, small church is built of yellow brick with white stone dressings in a Greek cross plan. Its square centre is set below a shallow dome above four main columns that branch out to encompass segmental curves and vaults to form a chancel, Venetian window, and a three-sided gallery. The church's main façade has a grand Tuscan portico. Above the small dome rise a clock tower and cupola. Nearby, a glass canopy covers the grave of Sarah Siddons, the actress who rose to great acclaim in Drury Lane Theatre in the late 1700s and early 1800s. Napoleon's surgeon, Barry O'Meara (1786–1821), is also buried here.

90

PRAED STREET

ST MARY'S HOSPITAL

90 W2

1851 HOOPER AND WYATT

In 1837, Brunel's Great Western Railway had its terminus at Paddington. As the area thrived, a voluntary hospital sprang up—soon called St Mary's after the adjacent church. Prince Albert laid the foundation stone, but the contractors went bankrupt and did not open until 1851. Over the years, more wards and wings arrived and, in 1988, its medical school merged with Imperial College. It was in St Mary's laboratories in 1928 that Alexander Fleming discovered penicillin; this new medicine soon helped to save many of the wounded in World War II and countless lives since. A small museum contains Fleming's worktable, petri dishes, and books.

91

146 PRAED STREET; FORMERLY GREAT WESTERN ROYAL HOTEL

HILTON LONDON METROPOLE

91 W2

1854 PHILIP CHARLES HARDWICK; 2001–02 RESTORED MUIRGOLD LIMITED

This gracious hotel was set at the front of Paddington Station, with decorative twin towers rising above its ornate white façade. A pediment by John Thomas illustrates Peace, Plenty, Industry, and Science. This was one of Victorian London's grandest hotels—refurbished in the 1930s. Today, after a £60 million restoration of its Art Deco interiors, it offers luxurious bedrooms, a swimming pool, and many other facilities including an Executive Floor with both bedrooms and suites. Passengers can take the escalator from Paddington Station concourse straight into the lobby.

92

93

26 SALE PLACE

ROYAL EXCHANGE

92   W2

INCLUDING CONNAUGHT SQUARE, CONNAUGHT STREET,
HYDE PARK SQUARE, WESTBOURNE TERRACE

TYBURNIA

93   W2

1820s–30s

This single-bar, family-run pub is tucked away down a side street, just five minutes' walk from Paddington Station. Many new buildings arrived here in the 1820s, in the wake of the Grand Junction Canal. The pub could well have acted as a veritable builders' canteen while the surrounding houses were under construction. It may have been named after the City monetary institution . . . or after the royal mail-coach whose guards collected and exchanged mail from hooks mounted by the road . . . or after King Richard III, famous for wanting to exchange his kingdom for a horse on the battlefield at Bosworth. The hapless king is, in fact, depicted on the pub sign. This is a nice old-fashioned, traditional pub that has escaped the drastic modernising which has spoiled so many others.

1828–35 S. P. COCKERELL AND GEORGE GUTCH

Hyde Park Estate was built on land owned by the bishop of London and later, starting with Connaught Square in the 1820s, by church commissioners. The name Tyburnia derived from the River Tyburn and the notorious Tyburn Tree—the king's gallows, where many met a grisly end from 1196–1783. Up to twenty-four prisoners could be hung at once, watched by huge numbers (200,000 on one occasion). By the early 1800s, Tyburnia referred to the south-eastern corner of the parish, the first part of the Paddington Estate to really develop. City merchants and artists had already discovered the area but the arrival of Paddington Station in 1838 really boosted its growth. Here is a fascinating tapestry of domestic streets, wider avenues, strips of green and squares (some exclusive and gated), and many eighteenth-century buildings. Westbourne Terrace was possibly London's most elegant street in the 1850s and now PM Tony Blair has bought a house in the area where Winston Churchill grew up— Connaught Square.

94

EASTBOURNE TERRACE AND PRAED STREET
PADDINGTON STATION

94   W2

1850–54 ISAMBARD KINGDOM BRUNEL, MATTHEW DIGBY WYATT, OWEN JONES

In 1842, Queen Victoria arrived here after her very first railway journey. Reputedly, the speed of 70 kilometres per hour (44 mph) provoked Prince Albert to say, 'Not so fast next time, Mr Conductor.' In 1851, the Great Western decided to build a new station a little further east and it was designed by the renowned engineer, Isambard Kingdom Brunel. Wyatt and Jones added the architectural decorations. The magnificent triple barrel-vaulted roof of wrought iron and glass is supported on elegant cast-iron columns—with ironwork decoration on both roof and capitals. A fourth aisle was added to the north side when the station was extended in 1909–16, making the total area 13 acres. A plaque by Platform One marks the station's 1954 centenary, and depicts Brunel, wearing his signature stovepipe hat. The children's book character Paddington Bear was named after this splendid station and Paddington itself was named after Padda, an Anglo-Saxon chieftain.

HALLFIELD HOUSING ESTATE
95   W2

1951-59 TECTON, DRAKE AND LASDUN

Much of Bayswater is made up of Victorian mansion blocks, many of which have been divided up into flats, with some purpose-built apartment blocks dating from the thirties and forties. Then a large area by Bishops Bridge Road was cleared and redeveloped as the Hallfield Estate—a large council estate, with some eight hundred apartments constructed as fifteen huge slab blocks. Most of the flats have now become private residences and are listed buildings. The Hallfield primary school (1951–54), with its ramped entrance from Inverness Terrace, is also one of Lasdun's pieces.

1930s MODERNIST HOUSE
96   W2

1938 SIR DENYS LASDUN

This fine street, first built in the 1850s, is lined with charming mid-Victorian villas. Raised nearly ninety years later, number 32 is a very different structure, a Grade II–listed building, now well screened by trees. This is an early design by the controversial Modernist architect, Denys Lasdun—made when he was only twenty-four years old—and it is clearly influenced by Le Corbusier's work. Lasdun was awarded the RIBA Royal Gold Medal in 1977.

1960s MAISONETTES
97   W2

**1964–73 DOUGLAS STEPHEN AND PARTNERS
(ASSISTANT ARCHITECT KENNETH FRAMPTON)**

In the 1730s, descendants of the First Earl of Craven (after whom the gardens are named) moved a pest (quarantine) house here from Soho—where it had been built after the 1665 plague. Despite this macabre start, the area became popular. During the 1830s, Unitarian minister William Fox lived at number 5 with housekeeper, Eliza Flower, a friend of Robert Browning. The forty-eight dwellings cross over and under central access corridors so that the living rooms all face the street and the bedrooms and their balconies face the garden. The painted concrete façades create a neat chequered pattern.

FOUNTAINS ABBEY
98   W2

1824; 1880s–'90s

A huge Victorian green tiled fireplace here has portraits of stern gentlemen—one of whom has turned his back on the pub's carousers. Named after nearby wells, and Westminster Abbey (whose monks owned the land here), this pub claims to have helped the discovery of penicillin! In 1928, Sir Alexander Fleming (a regular here) left dishes of bacteria culture beside the open laboratory window and later found that fungus spores had destroyed the bacteria. The window was opposite the pub and so the spores might have come from its cellars, although they probably drifted from the lab below his, where a mould specialist was experimenting.

THE VICTORIA
99   W2

1864

On the corner of a smart terrace, this grand, ornate, early Victorian curved façade screens a relatively small interior. Apart from the old partitions—removed to give patrons more elbow room—most of the original features survive, including a small, delicate fireplace with marquetry banding. A frieze of painted panels depicts British army redcoats in action while there are mirrors with an incredible, gothic mass of intertwining fleurs-de-lys in gold, ruby, and deep blue, with Tudor rose roundels above. At the top of steep, twisting stairs is a comfortable, panelled library room, with gilt-framed paintings of venerable Victorian gentlemen, and the Theatre Bar with fittings from the Strand's Gaiety Theatre.

THE SWAN
100   W2

c. 1721

This very old pub appears in a list of licensed victuallers of 1721. From 1790, it was a tavern for the Floral Tea Garden on the site of a physic garden set up by apothecary and herbalist Sir John Hill (a favourite of George III.) The pub claims to have been (but probably was not!) a coaching inn and a haunt of highwayman Claude Duval, who, afters ten years as a robber, swindler, card-sharp, and lover, was hanged at Tyburn in 1620. Before being hung at Marble Arch, prisoners were allowed a final drink in this pub while the vehicle waited outside to take them where no more drinks would be forthcoming!

95

96

97

98

99

100

101

102

4 BATHURST STREET	24 CRAVEN TERRACE
THE ARCHERY TAVERN	THE MITRE
101 W2	102 W2

1840

In 1818, Thomas Waring—manufacturer of bows, arrows, and related sundries—rented four acres of land here from the Bishop of London and, under the Royal Toxophilite Society, established the butts. The Archery Tavern was built as part of the Regency street on this site. A rustic tavern, it has ever been frequented by those who work in the stables in the mews behind the pub. The archery theme continues, with old prints, the sheet music for the Robin Hood theme, and an old bow on display. Film buffs should note that, nearby, number 42 Bathurst Mews was the location for Chrisine Keeler's flat in the movie *Scandal*, and that the Royal Lancaster Hotel was where *The Italian Job* crooks gathered in the original 1969 film.

1850s

This Grade II–listed pub was originally built to slake the thirsts of the servants and tradesmen, butlers and higher-class grocers who served the mansions fronting Hyde Park. It has an elegant marble frontage—a marked contrast to its rather dubious surroundings today. There are fragments of original etched glass and some fine marble fireplaces. A little snug, originally meant for women only, has survived with decorated glass, a moulded timber door and 1880–90s window cases.

103

104

---

17 LEINSTER TERRACE

THE LEINSTER ARMS

103   W2

1830s–'40s

Whether or not this Victorian pub was once a coaching inn is debatable, but it does possess a coach arch, leading on to a long mews where local gentry once kept their private carriages and teams. This was probably a pub for servants and tradesmen. Today it is a cosy place to down a pint. It has bare floorboards and a low ceiling covered in pressed paper from about the 1890s. USAAF memorabilia, with some framed shirts and ties and photos, marks the pub's wartime popularity with American aircrew. Playwright J. M. Barrie lived just around the corner and wrote *Peter Pan* in the summerhouse there in 1904.

3–5 PORCHESTER TERRACE

A DETACHED ILLUSION

104   W2

1823–24 J. C. LOUDON

John Claudius Loudon was a famous landscape architect and city planner who lived at number 3 until his death in 1843. He recommended the now-familiar plane tree for London streets and squares, and was one of the first planners to envision how green places in cities would improve the city air. This villa appears to be a detached, independent dwelling but that is an illusion: the verandas and dummy windows disguise party walls and there is more than one home here. The lovely, central, domed conservatory, flanked by the verandas, is a very pretty feature. Some later Victorian impositions were removed in 1972, allowing the original design to emerge once again.

105

106

DEPARTMENT STORE, QUEENSWAY	10 SALEM ROAD
WHITELEYS	**PHILLIPS WEST 2**
105 W2	106 W2

1908-12, 1989 BELCHER AND JOASS
BUILDING DESIGN PARTNERSHIP

Young William Whiteley arrived in London with only £10 in his pocket. He worked hard, studying the retail market until he had saved £700 to buy a small shop in Bayswater. By 1875, he was buying up other shops, cutting prices, and selling a vast range of goods: 'Everything from a pin to an Elephant.' By 1885, he had a staff of six thousand and, in 1896, earned a Royal Warrant from Queen Victoria. In Shaw's *Pygmalion*, Eliza Dolittle is sent to this store to be attired. In 1907, William Whiteley was murdered here by a man claiming to be his illegitimate son, demanding his inheritance. Apparently, Hitler adored Whiteley's and—planning to make it his headquarters had he seized Britain— ordered the Luftwaffe not to bomb the store. Whiteleys pioneered mail order and had a theatre and a golf course on the roof. After its closure in 1981, the store was renovated. The majestic, curved building on a corner site is crowned by a tower and dome. Metal was used for the intermediate-floor facings, allowing vast expanses of shop windows. Now its Edwardian interior has become a shopping mall, but the great marble staircase still dominates the main atrium. Diana, Princess of Wales, used to shop here and insisted that her two boys queue along with the commoners for the cinema.

1976 CAMPBELL, ZOGOLOVITCH, WILKINSON AND GOUGH

This is a fascinating warehouse conversion in an extravagant Art Nouveau style, with painted brickwork and sweeping, curved lines created by external staircases and metalwork balconies. The bay windows have glass panel roofs, and tiles create interesting textures everywhere. An arcade, supported on slender uprights set into rectangular 'boxes,' has a superb, pantiled roof and surrounds a central court. A strip of glass panels and fanlights caps the roof. Within this exhilarating setting, Phillips Auctioneers deal with mechanical music, radio, and television, and arrange regular sales.

107

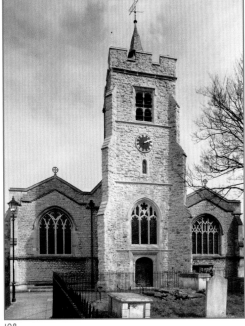

108

RIVERSIDE MANSIONS

CHISWICK MALL

107 W4

CHURCH STREET

ST NICHOLAS

108 W4

c. 1730

This stately mall has many riverside mansions from the 1700s and 1800s, mainly built in brown brick with red brick dressings. All along Chiswick Mall are grand façades and fine, sweeping gardens. Its eighteenth-century houses include Walpole House—named after the Walpole family. This house may have been the home of Barbara, Duchess of Cleveland, favourite of Charles II, and was probably the school at which Thackeray boarded; it may have inspired Miss Pinkerton's Academy in *Vanity Fair* but some believe that was Boston House (see page 68). Strawberry House (with its delightful, late-1700s cast-iron porch) and Morton House were built about 1700 and refronted some thirty years later. Some houses here are considerably older. Bedford and Eynham Houses, near the corner of Church Street, were once one building, built (or rebuilt) in the mid-1600s by Edward Russell, son of the Fourth Earl of Bedford. The corner of Chiswick Lane was the site of College House (demolished 1875), leased by Westminster School in 1570 as a retreat from London during plague, and later home to the Chiswick Press (1810–52). Politician Daniel O'Connell (1775–1847) lodged here as a law student, and the actor-manager Herbert Beerbohm Tree lived in Chiswick Mall in 1904–5.

1400s; 1882 NAVE REBUILT BY PEARSON

This has been a site of worship for over a thousand years. The church is a focal point of Chiswick village, which was once a fishing village. It has an ancient, Kentish ragstone fifteenth-century tower that stands where, long ago, a ford crossed the river; Saint Nicholas was the patron saint of sailors and fishermen. The body of the church was entirely rebuilt some four centuries later by a renowned Victorian architect, John Loughborough Pearson, in Perpendicular style with a nave of almost equal length and breadth. The chapel contains glass (probably eighteenth-century) from the old church's east window; this may have come from the Cologne cathedral. There is a monument to painter William Hogarth in the churchyard on the banks of the Thames. Lord Burlington's protégé William Kent (and his bricklayer) are also buried here, as are daughters of Oliver Cromwell (Mary and Frances); Charles II's mistress, Barbara Villiers (Duchess of Cleveland); the painter James Whistler; and Private Hitch, of Rorke's Drift fame in the Zulu Wars.

1680 AND 1740 BUILT BY HENRY D'AUVERQUERQUE

Boston House is the largest in this group of houses and cottages called Chiswick Square. Boston House is set between the two- and three-storey cottages to create an elegant little group—said to have been built by Henry D'Auverquerque (Viscount Boston and Earl of Grantham). There are legends—fascinating but unfounded—about the murder here by her husband of one Lady Boston, who is now said to haunt the site. During the 1800s, this was a boarding school for girls, and some claim that it may have inspired Miss Pinkerton's Academy in Thackeray's *Vanity Fair*, but Walpole House in Chiswick Mall is also a contender for this claim to fame.

109

HOGARTH LANE, GREAT WEST ROAD, CHISWICK

HOGARTH'S HOUSE

110   W4

c. EARLY 1700s

Hidden behind a high redbrick wall beside the very busy A4, is the former rural retreat of the great painter, engraver, and satirist William Hogarth (1697–1764). His main house and studio was in Leicester Fields (later Leicester Square) so this country abode allowed him to escape the bustle of the city, upriver at Chiswick, from 1749 until his death. The three-storey house, with attic dormer windows in the roof above, is in a lovely medley of mottled pink and red-brown brick, and was restored for the Hogarth Tercentenary in 1997. Its interior has been completely renovated, as has the beautiful white casement window, damaged by bombing during World War II. Here, today, an exhibition documents Hogarth's life and work, with copies of many of his engravings such as *The Harlot's Progress, A Rake's Progress, Marriage à la Mode, Gin Lane,* and *Beer Street*. The garden boasts a mulberry tree that is at least three hundred years old, introduced in the vain hope of breeding silk worms in England. Hogarth is buried in the graveyard of St Nicholas (see page 67).

110

III

HOGARTH LANE AND BURLINGTON LANE

CHISWICK HOUSE

III   W4

1725–29 LORD BURLINGTON

This was the architect's own sumptuous classical country villa—a showpiece of British architecture in the 1700s, albeit inspired by Italian glories (especially Palladio's villa at Vicenza). Lord Burlington used the new, elegant villa to display his works of art and entertain friends, including Pope, Swift, and Handel. Steps lead up to the portico, with statues of Palladio and Inigo Jones by Rysbrack. An art gallery faces the garden, its circular and octagonal rooms lit with single Venetian windows. The library was a long room facing the garden. On the stuccoed first floor, a suite of state rooms are set around a domed saloon. The villa's wonderful, detailed, plaster ceilings and the Inigo Jones–inspired chimney-pieces and fireplaces are by Burlington's protégé, William Kent. He also (with Bridgman) landscaped the natural-style gardens—now a public park—which have statues of Caesar, Pompey, and Cicero from Hadrian's villa at Tivoli, and an Inigo Jones gateway brought from Beaufort House in Chelsea. Strangely, both Charles James Fox (politician and antislavery campaigner) and prime minister and statesman George Canning died in the same room here, in 1806 and 1827, respectively. In the 1950s, the villa was restored, with many original pieces finding their proper home again.

112

113

114

BEDFORD PARK

**STARTED 1875–81 E. W. GODWIN, R. NORMAN SHAW, MAURICE B. ADAMS,
E. J. MAY, AND OTHERS**

In 1875, cloth merchant and property speculator
Jonathan Carr bought 24 acres that would become
London's first garden suburb, built on the grounds of
a Georgian Bedford House, whose owner in the 1860s,
Dr John Lindley, had been curator of the Royal
Horticultural Society gardens. The preservation of his
arboretum's trees led to interesting, curved streets and
many T-junctions in a semi-rural setting. Bedford Park,
with its leafy avenues and relatively cheap but handsome
Queen Anne–style houses, would create a model for later
low-density development. It became identified with
bohemianism, attracting artists and idealists. It was
Godwin who created the first models, but Shaw who set
the style. The houses had rubbed-brick arches, balconies,
bay-windows, terracotta decoration, Dutch gables, tile-
hung gabled walls, huge chimneys, white painted
balustrades, and wooden garden fences instead of
iron railings. Bedford Park, an important landmark of
suburban planning, was declared a conservation area
in 1969–70. It was portrayed it as Saffron Hill in G. K.
Chesterton's *The Man Who Was Thursday*, and famous
residents include playwright, Arthur Wing Pinero
(1855–1934); painter and father of W. B. Yeats,
J. B. Yeats (1865–1939); and painter Lucien Pissarro
(1863–1944).

VOYSEY HOUSE

1902–03 C. F. A. VOYSEY

Voysey designed wallpapers for Sandersons and this is
one of the few instances when he took on the design
for a nondomestic building, but Voysey often designed
many interior elements, such as furniture, fabrics, and
decorative tiles. He received the RIBA Gold Medal in
1940. In white- and black- (formerly blue-) glazed
Staffordshire brick, this building has large-scale windows
set in bays between projecting piers, and a lovely
curving, high, pristine-blank parapet. Today, a new roof
follows the undulating curve of the parapet, concealed
behind it. Voysey House (known then as the White
Building) served as a wallpaper printing works; the main
factory was opposite in Barley Mow Passage, and, at one
time, an iron bridge connected the two buildings. The
entrance doors were oak. On the corners of the piers,
cast-iron quadrants at low level were there to stop
inebriated patrons of the Barley Mow next door using
the piers as urinals. Voysey's works are now considered
to be formative in the Modern Movement and this is a
Grade II–listed building. Sandersons vacated in 1928, and
subsequent owners have included the Alliance Insurance
Company, the National Transit Insurance Company,
National Transit, and the A. L. Group.

STUDIO HOUSE

1889–94 C. F. A. VOYSEY

This Arts and Crafts tower house stands tall in its
suburban setting, a strong contrast to its neighbours,
both in stature and style. It has white, rough-cast walls,
dressings around metal-framed, banded windows, and
an interesting diamond-surrounded porthole feature
just above its small gabled bay. The projecting eaves
are supported on very slim, smart iron brackets. One
of Voysey's early works, it was built for an artist and
included a studio on the top floor, and so is still referred
to as 'the artist's house.'

115

116

CHISWICK PARK

1999–2003 RICHARD ROGERS PARTNERSHIP

This major business park development offers
140,500 square metres of office space for
some ten thousand employees. Locating the
parking areas below the buildings has made
cars less intrusive but, in any case, 75 percent
of those working here arrive either on foot,
bicycle, bus or train. The façades of the twelve
concrete-framed buildings incorporate sun
screening as part of a low-energy agenda,
with blinds activated by light sensors—
while steel columns support louvred screens,
walkways, and escape stairs. The complex
incorporates a restaurant, bar, swimming
pool, and fitness centre, while the lush green
parkland at the heart of the site includes an
open-air performance area, lake, and
nature reserve.

RIVERSIDE HOUSES

1700s

Strand-on-the Green was described in the
1930s as London's last remaining village.
Strande is an old term for a riverside walk,
and these modest but quaint houses are set
by a riverside path that stretches eastward
from Kew Bridge. This is a most attractive
setting with boats on the little stretch of
beach below. The opening of the first Kew
Bridge in 1759 made this a more popular
residential area but it remained a small narrow
strip, mainly associated with fishing and river
traffic. Most of the houses are brown brick
but some several have been painted or
stuccoed. Numbers 45, 56, 60, 61, 63–66,
and 71–72 are especially pleasing. John
(or Johann) Zoffany lived at number 65
(1790–1810) and this is probably the finest
in the row. Numbers 52–55 form a well-
conserved terrace of houses, faced with white
brick and built 1793–96. Writer Nancy Mitford
resided at Rose Cottage, Lord Cudlipp at 14
Magnolia Wharf, Air-Marshall Sir John Slessor
at Carlton House, and Dylan Thomas at Ship
House Cottage.

117

THE CITY BARGE

117   W4

FROM 1484; REBUILT 1940

The famous City Barge public house was so-named because the Lord Mayor's State City Barge had its winter moorings at this point on the river, from 1775—stationed here for the collection of tolls—until 1816. The pub is mainly brick built with some white ground floor areas and a wooden white-painted balcony running along at first-floor level. Its lower half is at the level of the Thames path and has a watertight steel door to keep out the river when high tides threaten. Inside is a tiny, cosy bar with a flagstone floor; the upstairs bar is rather more modern. This pub featured in the Beatles's film *Help* and today is a favourite haunt of TV presenters Ant and Dec.

118

15 STRAND ON THE GREEN, CHISWICK

THE BULL'S HEAD

118   W4

FROM 1600s

Beyond the tracery of a railway bridge over the Thames, built in 1869, this pretty white pub, with small-paned sash windows, has steps up to an arched entrance and a hotchpotch of buildings with overflowing window boxes and hanging baskets. The pub has ancient origins and has ever been a popular spot for artists. Opposite is Oliver's Island, a Civil War refuge of Cromwell. It is said that this pub served as his headquarters when his army was on the run at one point during the English Civil War—and that he used a tunnel under the river from the pub to the island. This tunnel was originally created for Catholic priests to escape Protestant persecutors but remains a legend, as it has yet to be rediscovered.

PITSHANGER MANOR MUSEUM

119   W5

1801–03 SIR JOHN SOANE;
1986 RESTORED JOHN WIBBERLY AND IAN BRISTOW

Pitshanger means 'a wooded slope frequented by kites.' An earlier house had been raised here by George Dance the Younger on the site of Pitshanger Farm. His pupil, John Soane, rebuilt this for himself, leaving just the south wing. A central block joined a detached north wing with a colonnade and a low wall, beyond which he built mock Roman ruins. The frontage is small and simple but grand — in Portland stone, with a triumphal classical arch of Ionic columns and four free-standing classical female statues. There are also eagles in wreaths, roundels with lions, and a fat cherub. At the back, horizontal bands of brick and stucco plus vertical ashlar strips create nine sections, each with a window. Inside are ornate ceilings, a fireplace designed by Dancea, and a lovely breakfast room with dark-red porphyry and grey marbling; Egyptian caryatids support a shallow domed ceiling, painted as a sky with clouds. The small library room also has rich decoration. After 1811, when Soane sold up, the house saw a succession of owners — including Spencer Walpole, the cabinet minister, who lived next door — until it was bought by the council in 1900 and became a public library until 1980. Then the building's interiors were restored. Today, it is a Grade I–listed building and houses the PM Gallery, West London's largest contemporary art gallery, and a museum.

119

120

HOOVER BUILDING

120   W5

1932-35 WALLIS GILBERT AND PARTNERS

Lord Rochdale officially opened the Hoover
Building on 2 May 1933. In the 1930s, this
moderne vacuum cleaner factory plus offices
was built as a veritable palace of industry. The
magnificent Western Avenue elevation has
towers at both ends, with spiral staircases and
corner windows. White pilasters frame long
windows. The white stuccoed Art Deco
exterior has decorative bands of dark blue
and red faience tiles. The building was floodlit.
Parts for aircraft were made at the factory
during the war. In 1992, the supermarket
company Tesco was allowed to buy the
premises on the condition that Wallis and
Gilbert's façade was conserved.

121

STAMFORD HOSPITAL

121   W6

1930–34 SIR JOHN BURNET, TAIT AND LORNE

This was Sir John Burnet's last commission before his retirement from this famous London practice and was opened by King George V in 1933. It was then one of the country's largest Modern International design buildings, where this style penetrated right through to the tiniest detail. It has a steel frame and is laid out symmetrically, with a modish, high entrance hall that looks rather like a cinema foyer: two vast pylons flank the door, with figures of Healing and Charity above, and a window etched with Zodiac signs set between. Four main buildings are linked by glass bridges. Despite its functionalism, the building is beautifully decorated and clad with superb handmade, dark red bricks, with deeply raked pointing. The cost on completion was £335,000, and there were beds for 270 patients.

122

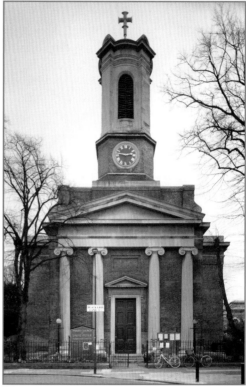

123

ST PETER'S SQUARE AND BLACK LION LANE

122   W6

1825–30 ANONYMOUS BUT POSSIBLY J. C. LOUDON

Set on the east and west sides of this rather pretty square, these large, three-storey houses appear to be semi-detached villas, but closer inspection reveals three dwellings. They are faced with sandy stucco, and have pediments, Ionic porches, and central balconies. Single-storey walls link the houses to garages and garden studios. They are decorated with large scrolls, with pineapples on the gateposts, and eagles and sleeping lions on the doors. The north side of the square has similar properties, but in a two-storey format. A bronze, The Greek Runner by Sir William Richardson, was erected in the centre garden in 1926. There are a few interwar mansion blocks in the square, too. Famous residents include actress Vanessa Redgrave and film director Tony Richardson.

ST PETER'S

123   W6

1827–29 EDWARD LAPIDGE

This is Hammersmith's oldest church, built in Grecian style at a cost of £14,000 and Grade II listed. It has a beautiful Ionic portico with a pediment and an octagonal west tower. A stoneware statue of a reclining woman (created by Karel Vogel) has faced the Great West Road here since 1959. The church's very simple but pleasing interior includes a gallery set above Tuscan columns and fine original pews. The churchyard was laid out as a garden of rest in 1958. The church is presently facing the challenge of trying to raise £500,000 for a new roof.

124

125

I HAMMERSMITH ROAD	19 UPPER MALL, HAMMERSMITH
HAMMERSMITH SURGERY	**THE DOVE**
124 W6	125 W6

1996-2000 GUY GREENFIELD ARCHITECTS

The white sweeping curves of this dramatic building are set close to the church, built on a disused car park near a busy traffic roundabout—almost below a concrete flyover. Because of this proximity to noisy traffic, there are no windows on the street side, while its interesting sculptural shape, curved in two dimensions, also helps to baffle road noise. Upstairs, roof glazing and narrow windows in the 'steps' of the outer wall create a lovely light corridor. There are black slate floors, and bright white walls with turquoise and orange areas. The waiting and consulting rooms all overlook an internal courtyard, where a calm, secluded Japanese-style garden offers an escape from the frantic world outside.

1600s

The riverside terrace here is a good spot from which to watch the University Boat race. At just 2.39 by 1.27 metres (about 7 feet by 4 feet) the tiny, cosy bar features in the *Guinness Book of Records* as Britain's smallest. The bigger saloon bar has a low ceiling with dark oak beams. Double doors lead out into a conservatory which houses an old vine. This pretty little redbrick and white pub, with its lanterns and a swinging sign, has served many famous customers, such as Graham Greene, Ernest Hemingway, and A. P. Herbert, whose novel *The Water Gypsies* features the pub (renamed the Pigeon). James Thomson, who wrote *Rule Britannia*, lodged and died here. William Morris lived next door. It is also claimed that Charles II and Nell Gwynn used this as a secret rendezvous.

126

127

RIVERSIDE: OFFICES, RESTAURANT AND FLATS

126   W6

1984–87 RICHARD ROGERS PARTNERSHIP

Sir Richard Rogers's highly flexible works reject the classical past and embrace all that new technology can offer. At Rainville Road, a splendid development has seen the conversion of an old factory into his elegant new offices with a grand barrel-vaulted steel roof—plus a great restaurant. The River Café on Rainville Road is owned by the architect's wife, Ruth Rogers, with Rose Gray (they wrote the *River Café* cookbooks), and specializes in first-class rural Italian food. Jamie Oliver worked regularly in the kitchen here before he became a full-bloodied celebrity. Meanwhile, three inspiring blocks of apartments were also designed by the Richard Rogers Partnership with large, wrought-steel balconies to create a link between the gleaming glass blocks of flats, overlooking the Thames that is just feet away. Other works by the renowned architect include the Pompidou Centre, Paris (1972–78), the Lloyds Building, London (1979–84), the European Court of Human Rights, Strasbourg (1984), the Millennium Dome, London (1999), a new terminal at Madrid's Barajas Airport (2006), and the Welsh Assembly building, Cardiff (2006).

STUDIO HOUSE

127   W6

1891 C. F. A. VOYSEY

Although the Arts and Crafts Movement idealised the rural life, it thrived in large cities. Here, architect Voysey, who often exhibited a William Morris influence, has shown his enthusiasm for creating an exciting, asymmetrical composition—with his favourite sweeping, slate roof surfaces, projecting eaves, a tall chimney, and horizontal bands of windows. The house is set back behind a low, curving, brick wall, topped by Arts and Crafts iron railings.

128

HAMMERSMITH FLYOVER

THE ARK

128   W6

1988–92 RALPH ERSKINE

This stunning building, a truly imaginative piece of Post-Modern architecture, stands proudly beside the A4 western approach to London and Heathrow. Here, the busy Hammersmith Flyover is elevated, as if to provide a better view of the Ark—and several other glass towers nearby. The Ark's floors of offices (nine floors on one side and five on the other) sweep around a curved, gleaming shape with 4,500 brown-tinted glass panels. The Ark does indeed resemble the swelling hull of an ocean liner, steering forward to the metropolis. It is 76 metres (250 feet) tall. Inside, white walls and a floor-to-roof atrium provide a light, sky-bright setting for open-plan office space—linked by scenic elevators in multilevel decks that continue the ship theme. Hidden below the 'waves' of the overpass, columns, faced in decorative brick, act as buttresses to support the concrete floors.

129

130

131

132

133

134

EDWARDES SQUARE

KENSINGTON

129   W8

1811–20

This is one of London's loveliest late Georgian garden squares, named after William Edwardes, the second Lord Kensington. Here are immaculate, tall town houses, neat gated gardens and the Temple—a Grecian-style lodge with Doric columns that still serves as home to the square's gardener. Paths thread through shrubs, lawns, and flowerbeds in a garden designed by Italian artist Signor Agostino Aglio. The Scarsdale pub at 23a was reputedly built as living quarters for French army officers in anticipation of the invasion of England by Napoleon that, in the event, never occurred (see page 87).

PEMBROKE STUDIOS

PEMBROKE GARDENS

130   W8

1890

In this south west corner of W8, many places are named either Edwardes or Pembroke. Here a very elegant, single-arched entrance with a small central lantern leads through to two rows of glazed studios with a long rectangular garden. This modest mews conversion was inspired by (and given financial support from) the Great Exhibition of 1851. There are neat lawns and many pretty features such as the tiny-paned bow windows.

KENSINGTON SQUARE

ORIGINALLY CALLED KING'S SQUARE

131   W8

1681 THOMAS YOUNG

This is one of the oldest garden squares, and still has several 1700s houses. The area became highly fashionable when William III converted nearby Nottingham House into Kensington Palace. This gathering place for artists attracted Pre-Raphaelite painter and illustrator Edward Burne-Jones (number 41), Sir John Simon, a pioneer of public health (number 40), and renowned philosopher John Stuart Mill (number 18); this was the scene of the infamous burning of Carlyle's manuscript of *The French Revolution*, when Mill's maidservant used it to light a fire. Composer Ralph Vaughan Williams came to this square for music lessons.

THE BRITANNIA

1 ALLEN STREET

132   W8

1834; REMODELLED AND EXTENDED 1960

This charming little pub was built in 1834, as the local market gardens became the site for working men's cottages raised by a Bond Street tailor—one Thomas Allen, who had found his fortune through making uniforms for the Duke of Wellington's army. Its associated brewery went bust twice—in 1902 and 1924—and was eventually demolished but the old brewery stable yard remains as the pub's conservatory. Refurbished, this is an inviting pub with a wooden bar, real fires, and traditional ales but it now has a stylish dining room at the rear.

BENETTON

KENSINGTON HIGH STREET,
FORMERLY BARKERS DEPARTMENT STORE

133   W8

1933–35 P. E. CULVERHOUSE

This towering store is in a mixture of a French Art Deco style and rather more traditional department store architecture. Both Barkers (now Benetton and Jigsaw) and next-door Derry & Toms rise high over their neighbours. This exuberant building, steel-framed and faced with Portland stone, reflects the era's fascination with technical progress. There are magnificent bronze and glass towers and stone reliefs of cars and aeroplanes. In 1998, some restoration work was carried out. Original staircases can be seen in the eastern tower.

BHS DEPARTMENT STORE

KENSINGTON HIGH STREET; FORMERLY DERRY AND TOMS, AND BIBA

134   W8

1933 BERNARD GEORGE

In 1854, Joseph Toms opened his 'Toy and Fancy Repository,' joined in 1862 by Charles Derry. By 1870, they had seven shops—one a Mourning Department—and some two hundred employees. By 1920, the firm, which serviced rich South Kensington clients, was owned by John Barker and Co. Ltd. After 1930, the store acquired its present façade, the Rainbow Room restaurant, plus its famous roof garden with five hundred shrubs and trees, gushing stream, ducks, and flamingos. Spanish, Tudor, and English Woodland gardens cover one and a half acres. In 1973, the store was taken over by Biba and later by Marks and Spencers Limited and British Home Stores.

135

136

10 PALACE GATE	J KENSINGTON SQUARE
1930s FLATS	**THE GREYHOUND**
135　　　　　　　　　　W8	136　　　　　　　　　　W8

1938 WELLS COATES

While Kensington takes its name from Saxon nobleman Cynesige, the Palace Gate complex is so titled for its proximity to the entrance gate into the grounds of Kensington Palace. This was originally a street of large, grand houses occupied by people of professional and social eminence. In these flats, Wells Coates has introduced Le Corbusier style, using an ambitious, complex section to fit into the awkward, narrow site, with small panels of reconstituted stone creating an interesting texture over the reinforced concrete frame.

1890s; 1979

Situated on one of the oldest squares in London that dates from 1685; philosopher John Stuart Mill, actress Mrs Patrick Campbell, and Pre-Raphaelite painter Edward Burne-Jones all used to live here. In the 1800s, the Greyhound publican would grill pork chops or steaks presented to him by local labourers at lunchtime—provided that they bought a pot of beer to wash it down with. This facility vanished when the new Greyhound opened in 1899. Its lovely glasswork was destroyed by a gas explosion in 1979 and the façade was rebuilt as before, but the interior has been turned into an enormous single room, with a low ceiling.

137

138

18 STAFFORD TERRACE

LINLEY SAMBOURNE HOUSE

137   W8

23a EDWARDES SQUARE

THE SCARSDALE

138   W8

LATE 1800s

This was the home of illustrator, *Punch* cartoonist, and photographer Linley Sambourne (1844–1910.) Today, the house (bought by the Greater London Council in 1979) is managed by the Victorian Society and is open to the public. Behind the panelled front door, balustrades, and bay windows, everything has been kept much as it was when Sambourne lived here, and the interior provides a rare glimpse of a late-Victorian household. Here there are cluttered interiors, heavy Victorian furnishings and decoration, velvet drapes, original William Morris wallpaper, china ornaments and other objects d'art—there is even a Victorian lavatory. A collection of books includes many illustrated by Linley Sambourne, and work by other artists, such as Kate Greenaway, George Du Maurier, and John Tenniel.

1811–20 LOUIS CHANGEUR

Tranquil Edwardes Square was named after the second Lord Kensington, and laid out by a French builder between 1811 and 1820. Houses here today cost £2–3 million; one famous recent resident was comedian, Frankie Howerd. The pub has a lovely creeper-clad Georgian exterior and was reputedly built, speculatively, as living quarters for the officers of Napoleon's conquering army. Today, the interior has been 'done up' with a square island bar that projects into a single large room and there is a beautifully flower-filled garden with trees that provide shade.

139

140

KENSINGTON HIGH STREET; KENSINGTON CHURCH STREET
ST MARY ABBOTS

| 139 | W8 |

ALLEN STREET
KENSINGTON UNITED REFORM CHURCH

| 140 | W8 |

1869–72 SIR GEORGE GILBERT SCOTT

This is the parish church of Kensington. The present building is nineteenth century but people have been worshipping here through most of the millennium. The abbot of Abingdon founded the first church here in the 1100s. It was rebuilt in 1370, and again in about 1696 — except for its tower, rebuilt 1772. Monarchs William and Mary worshipped here, and the king helped to finance the new building and contributed a pulpit and reading desk. Today's church has the tallest spire in London at 85 metres (278 feet), and its fine stained-glass windows include the Healing window, funded by the Royal College of Surgeons. Its renowned past worshippers include Sir Isaac Newton, William Wilberforce, George Canning, Beatrix Potter, and Joseph Addison. In 1997, some thousand people gathered in the church to mourn the death of parishioner Diana, Princess of Wales.

1854 A. TRIMEN

In 1974, the Congregational Kensington Chapel and St John's Presbyterian Church, Scarsdale Villas, united to form Kensington United Reformed Church. Partly rebuilt after war damage, this is a very gracious, honey-coloured building with a central portico and pediment before a raised entrance and decorative pilasters to the sides of this with lovely detailing.

141

142

77-79 BEDFORD GARDENS
ARTISTS' STUDIOS

141   W8

119 KENSINGTON CHURCH STREET
THE CHURCHILL ARMS

142   W8

1882 R. STARK WILKINSON

A surprising discovery in the middle of
surburbia, this tall, redbrick, five-storey
group of artists' studios is also deep (at 39
metres/128 feet) and wide (11 metres/34
feet) with generous windows between sturdy
piers to create plentiful light inside the eleven
studios. The well of its central staircase also
enjoys lots of daylight, pouring in through
a large, glass lantern above. It still serves as
working studios today and is home, for
example, to Pontine Paus Designs, who
create collections of luxury handbags.

c. 1870

Originally called the Marlborough after John
Churchill, Duke of Marlborough, this pleasant
mid-Victorian pub was renamed after his
equally celebrated prime minister descendant.
It has a vast, wood-panelled, horseshoe-
shaped lounge full of Churchill bric-a-brac,
and a picture gallery featuring countless other
prime ministers and American presidents.
There are also copper vessels, hat boxes,
numerous chamber pots—and a collection of
butterflies mounted on the walls of the back
bar. The conservatory has a glass roof and a
jungle-like canopy of foliage; this doubles as
a restaurant with Thai food a speciality.

143

114 CAMPDEN HILL ROAD

WINDSOR CASTLE PUB

143   W8

1840s

Once, this pub was frequented by farmers taking livestock to Hyde Park on market days. The name may have derived from its proximity to the castle or through the renaming of the royal dynasty as the Windsors. The small bars have wooden floors, panels that may have come from a ship, dark timbers, and oak furniture. Each 'snug' had its own low street door for different clientele, and the stone-floored courtyard has a shady plane tree. A legend tells how William Cobbett had the skeleton of Thomas Paine (author of *The Rights of Man*) shipped here, to raise a memorial over them. Cobett's son settled his bar tab by selling Paine's bones to the landlord — and the bones may be buried in the cellar.

THE BROAD WALK, KENSINGTON GARDENS

KENSINGTON PALACE ORANGERY

144   W8

1695–1704 NICHOLAS HAWKSMOOR, SIR CHRISTOPHER WREN AND JOHN VANBURGH

Designed for Queen Anne as a greenhouse, dining room, and a place for elaborate court entertainment during the summer months (together with the Sunken Garden), the Orangery is a magnificent building with a splendid brick exterior and fine woodcarvings by Grinling Gibbons. Corinthian columns separate tall windows where sunlight flows into the stunning, long white interior—this now serves as a restaurant.

144

145

24 HILLGATE STREET
THE HILLGATE

145   W8

1854

Here were once humble houses and cottages and later a notorious slum—until the area was developed by a family of builders and local landowners called Johnson, one of whom was the Lord Mayor of London in 1846. Several small, unassuming squares were laid out in the 1840s and 1850s when Hillgate Street was called Johnson Street and the pub was called the Johnson Arms. It opened in 1854 and occupies a curved corner site. There are neat brickwork upper storeys and pretty window boxes full of flowers.

146

KENSINGTON PALACE

146   W8

1661–1702 SIR CHRISTOPHER WREN, NICHOLAS HAWKSMOOR,
WILLIAM KENT, AND (POSSIBLY) THOMAS RIPLEY

Originally called Nottingham House, and then
Kensington House, the palace stands at the western end
of Kensington Gardens. Sir Christopher Wren designed
many improvements and added the Clock Court and
South Front, including the Long Gallery. It remains,
however, a functional domestic building rather than a
place of splendour, with the structure grouped around
three courtyards and with relatively simple interiors. The
palace has been a royal residence since it was bought by
William and Mary in 1689. Originally a private country
house, it was adapted so that, in winter, the asthmatic
sovereign could escape the damp and smoke of
Whitehall. In 1702 it became home to Queen Anne.
George I and George II added rich, ornate furnishings and
elaborate ceiling decorations by William Kent. George II
was the last monarch to live at the palace during his
reign, until 1760. It was the birthplace and childhood
home of Queen Victoria; here, in June 1837, she learned
of her accession to the throne. More recently, it was the
home of Princess Diana and is still the residence of
several members of the Royal Family. Its State
Apartments include the Kings Apartments and a
magnificent collection of paintings. The Court Dress
Collection here has everything from elaborate
eighteenth-century costumes to underwear.

147

148

171–201 LANARK ROAD

INTERESTING HOUSING

147   W9

1979–82 JEREMY AND FENELLA DIXON

At first sight there is nothing very special about the eight houses that occupy this stretch of Lanark Road. They are obviously modern, but match the gables and arched windows of the surrounding Victorian structures. In fact, these are a small masterpiece by the Dixons, who would go on to design extensions to both the Tate Gallery and the Royal Opera House. What appear to be traditional houses are actually blocks of flats with functional modern features.

BLOMFIELD ROAD AND MAIDA AVENUE

TWO STREETS

148   W9

---

c. 1840

This delightful pair of streets line the north and south (respectively) of the Grand Union Canal to the west of the Edgware Road. Of the two, Maida Avenue was developed first, in the years after 1809, when it was known as Maida Hill West. Blomfield Road followed in the 1840s, when builders copied the mix of smart detached houses and semi-detached villas that were to be found in its southern neighbour. The pair of roads has always been prestigious, with trees lining the canal, and the proliferation of flats that have replaced houses elsewhere nearby being kept at bay. Number 30 Maida Avenue was home to the writer John Masefield for two years from 1907; another writer, Thomas Mayne Reid, died at number 12 Blomfield Road in 1883.

149

5a FORMOSA STREET

THE PRINCE ALFRED

149   W9

1863

The Prince Alfred public house is a rare survivor of the grander type of Victorian hostelry that was once common in London. The ground floor is of double height, allowing for plenty of air in the bars and dining areas, but the true glory of this pub is its etched glass. At the time the pub was built, plate glass was a relatively new invention that allowed large expanses of window at affordable cost. The bowed façade of the building is a wall of etched glass, while the interior is a riot of carved mahogany and more etched glass. The pub is named after a popular son of Queen Victoria.

150

1936 ROBERT ATKINSON, MAXWELL FRY, C. H. JAMES, GREY WORNUM

This modernist mini-utopia of sixty-eight flats was built by the Gas, Light and Coke Company on a disused gas works that it owned. The aim was to create a workers' paradise, and this was largely achieved. Each flat was larger than the norm for working-class families in the area and was provided with both balconies and large windows. The two six-storey blocks ran parallel and incorporated not only the school, which still stands, but also a communal laundry centre and several other facilities that have since vanished. The concrete buildings are well maintained and are still most attractive.

151

GOLBORNE ROAD
TRELLICK TOWER
151   W10

1973 ERNÖ GOLDFINGER

Trellick Tower was built at the height of the boom in tower blocks of flats—and before the drawbacks of poorly designed blocks became evident. In building what were, at the time, the tallest flats in England, Goldfinger managed to avoid the pitfalls that beset many other such blocks—although the eye-catching cantilevered boiler room that projects from the lift shaft is now redundant, as each flat has its own heating system. The 317 flats are arranged over thirty-one floors and form part of the Cheltenham Estate of council housing. New security systems installed during the 1990s have made this a much-sought-after place to live.

152

KENSINGTON HOUSE TRUST, 103–123 ST MARKS ROAD
HOUSES AND FLATS
152   W10

1975-80 JEREMY DIXON

The architect Jeremy Dixon was only three years into his fruitful professional partnership with his wife, Fenella, when he undertook this commission. As with his later work in Lanark Road in W9 (see page 94), Dixon masked the modern nature of this complex of forty-four flats and houses behind a traditional façade that resembles those of the surrounding older buildings. The development included back gardens and novel access arrangements—which Dixon hoped would reinterpret the tradition of the London house and its relationship to the street.

65 LADBROKE GROVE
MODERNIST FLATS
153   WII

1933 E. MAXWELL FRY

This was one of the first buildings in London to be clearly influenced by the theories of Swiss architect Charles Jeaneret, better known as Le Corbusier. In his book *Vers une Architecture*, Le Corbusier had suggested that people should be housed in blocks of apartments designed as machines for living. This block of flats with a semi-underground area for the cars—then coming into widespread ownership—reflected these ideas, while its use of steel tube and mesh balustrading lifts another idea from the Le Corbusier repertoire. Most of the building is completed in the yellow stock brick so prevalent in this area of London, although details are picked out in blue glazed tiles.

153

LANSDOWNE ROAD
LANSDOWNE HOUSE
154   WII

1904 H. FLOCKHART

Some fifty years after the Ladbroke Estate was laid out, this seven-storey block of studios was erected to cater for artists, and quickly attracted the likes of Charles Ricketts, Charles Shannon, and Glyn Philpot. The airy rooms and north-facing windows proved to be ideal for artists, but the rental prices soon forced out all but the most successful. Since 1958, the elegant brick-and-stone building has been home to Lansdowne Recording Studios, which boasts one of the city's finest suite of electronics and prides itself on discretion when dealing with famous clients.

154

BOUNDED BY KENSINGTON PARK ROAD, CLARENDON ROAD, CORNWALL CRESCENT, AND HOLLAND PARK AVENUE
LADBROKE ESTATE
155   WII

1850 THOMAS ALLOM

The Ladbroke Estate was laid out by Thomas Allom on the site of the old Hippodrome racecourse as a revolutionary experiment in suburban planning. The houses are arranged so that each has a small private back garden that gives access to a larger communal garden, which is private to the residents. It was the landowner, James Weller Ladbroke, who insisted on the large houses and informal road layout that came to be the hallmark of the area. The layout of the streets, and the Italianate style of the houses, were both hugely influential—copied with varying degrees of success in other suburban developments around London.

155

156

157

80 HOLLAND PARK AVENUE, EX PETER EATON BOOKSHOP

CARD BUREAU

156   WII

ST JAMES'S GARDENS, ADDISON AVENUE, QUEENS DALE ROAD

NORLAND SQUARE AND ROYAL CRESCENT

157   WII

1973 RICK MATHER

Once upon a time, this busy gift and card shop was the first modern antiquarian bookshop to be built specifically for this purpose in London, occupying a site that had once been a front garden. The sheer, plate-glass frontage extends out onto the pavement and there are some seven levels inside, descending down into excavated lower floors, the clever utilitarian construction using the shop shelving as walls and balustrades.

1837–46 ROBERT CANTWELL

These streets form part of the Norlands Estate, which takes its name from the fact that it occupied the 'north lands' of Kensington. Robert Cantwell was hired as architect by the owner of the land, a solicitor named Charles Richardson, to produce a genteel estate of fine houses that would command high rents. The result was the sweeping façade of the Royal Crescent, the verdant charm of St James's Gardens, and the tree-lined Addison Avenue. The area remains popular and exclusive to the present day. The later houses in the area were built in mock-Jacobean style.

158

1606–07 JOHN THORPE (PROBABLY); STONE GATEWAY INIGO JONES

This elegant Jacobean mansion took its name from its previous owners, the Earls of Holland, and later the Barons Holland. It had passed to the Earl of Ilchester by the time it was destroyed by World War II bombs. In 1952, the ruins were bought by the London County Council, which opened the grounds to the public and restored the East Wing as headquarters for the King George VI Memorial Youth Hostel Association. The grounds include woods and formal gardens, such as the tranquil Kyoto Japanese Garden.

159

8 MELBURY ROAD

STUDIO HOUSE

159   W14

1875–76 R NORMAN SHAW

This elegant house was built for the artist Marcus Stone, who had made his fortune illustrating works by Charles Dickens. At this time, Shaw was working in a variety of styles—including the Queen Anne style used here. The ground floor is deliberately asymmetrical, with tall windows, while the upper floor is dominated by three oriel windows. The house opposite, 31 Melbury Road, was also designed by Shaw. Within a decade of his work here, he moved away from his eclectic historic styles to concentrate on the more formal English Domestic Revival movement, which he came to lead.

160

8 ADDISON ROAD

DEBENHAM HOUSE

160   W14

1905–07 HALSEY RICARDO

When Ricardo was commissioned to build a house for Sir Ernest Debenham of department store fame, he took advantage of the fact that the de Morgan tile company had recently closed down. He bought up the entire stock of plain and decorative tiles, then designed the house to act as a showcase for them. In a riot of ceramic colour, bold panels of green- and blue-glazed bricks break up the white tile façade. Even the chimneys are tiled. More were used inside, combined with fine timber. Debenham must have been fond of glazed tiles; he had already covered the façade of his main store with them.

161

OLYMPIA EXHIBITION HALL

161   W14

1930 FAÇADE JOSEPH EMBERTON

The imposing façade of the Olympia Exhibition Hall was erected in brick and steel to give a united appearance to the collection of buildings that lie behind it. The Grand Hall was built in 1884 and extended in 1895; the National Hall was added in 1923, and the Empire Hall in 1929. The rather untidy appearance of these buildings was thought to be one reason why some businesses preferred to use the newer Earls Court Exhibition Building, so the new façade was put up to try and overcome this image problem. Emberton also designed the four-storey car park just around the corner in Maclise Road.

12 HOLLAND PARK ROAD

LEIGHTON HOUSE MUSEUM

162   W14

1865-79 GEORGE AITCHISON AND LORD LEIGHTON

This magnificent riot of Victorian extravagance was built for Lord Leighton, a noted Royal Academy artist of his day. The relatively restrained, brick exterior (in Italianate style) was designed by Leighton himself, but he hired his friend George Aitchison to design the interior. The result established Aitchison as a master of interior design. Some rooms aped Venetian style with red walls and black woodwork; others had classical columns and mosaics, but the highlight is undoubtedly the astonishingly ornate Arab Hall, based on sketches made by Aitchison as he visited Moorish palaces in Spain and Sicily.

162

29 MELBURY ROAD

TOWER HOUSE

163   W14

1876-81 WILLIAM BURGES

When William Burges designed this house to be his home, he set out to recreate 'a model residence of the fifteenth century,' equipped with all the modern conveniences of the Victorian age. The house takes its name from the circular tower, topped by a conical roof, which dominates the façade and houses the main staircase. The Gothic style is continued within, where the library has a stone fireplace complete with battlements, and the dining room is based on the House of Fame described by Geoffrey Chaucer. Burges had earlier worked on Cardiff Castle and Cork Cathedral as an architect, but he also designed wallpapers, furniture, and jewellery.

163

135-149 TALGARTH ROAD

ST PAUL'S STUDIOS

164   W14

c. 1870

The great arched glass façades of these houses dominate the south side of the road. When the houses were built, this was a recently developed and fairly quiet residential road, but is now a dual carriageway and part of the A4 through road that carries heavy loads of thundering traffic. The houses were designed as artist studios and all face north so that no direct sunlight falls through the large expanses of glass to trouble the painters within. Each house features a tall narrow window (through which even the largest canvasses could be removed) as well as seats in the porch, where customers or models could sit in comfort while waiting for the artist.

164

WEST CENTRAL LONDON (WC)

Here are long straight roads, dotted with many neat green squares and tangled alleys and lanes that weave an intricate pattern of contrasts on the map.

This section travels from the fringes of Tottenham Court Road south to Trafalgar Square, with its pigeons and Nelson's Column, and continues to the Victoria Embankment— built for 'trains and drains' but which created new land and gardens beside the Thames when London's sewage systems arrived in 1870.

Beginning immediately south of St Pancras and Kings Cross stations, one threads through Bloomsbury, rich with literary associations, including the Bloomsbury Group—writers, philosophers, and artists who gathered here in the early 1900s.

The university quarter includes University College in Gower Street, where dead philosopher Jeremy Bentham still sits in the college lobby: his clothed skeleton is on display here, as requested in his will.

Next comes the massive grandeur of the British Museum, the Elgin Marbles and Egyptian mummies among its many treasures.

In Lincoln's Inn Fields, lawyers learn their skills, while the Inns of Court at Gray's Inn bustle with barristers. Meanwhile, the curving sweep of High Holborn, once a publishing domain, runs close to the division of WC1 and WC2.

Drury Lane leads off from here, its historic eponymous theatre the place where pretty Nell Gwynn caught the eye of Charles II and, in St Martin's Theatre, Agatha Christie's *The Mousetrap* is still being performed in a run of over fifty years. A little further west is Covent Garden—with its famous market and opera house.

WC1

179
180
169
170
178
171
172
176
177
165
166
181
182
167
168
175
173 174
186
183
184
185
189
188
206
187
207
190
199
198
205
208
Holborn Rd.
191
197
203
204
266
196
202
265 267
192
195
269
264
193 194
201
268
263 262
210
200
271
261
211
214
270 272
259 260
209
212
257 258
213
256
215
237
243
255
236
242
248
254
233 234
247
249
253 252
219
235 238
245
250
251
217
239
246
216
218
244
241
222
225 232
240
220-221 223
226 231
224
230
227
228 229

WC2

WC1 Bloomsbury
WC2 Covent Garden

165

SQUARES AND AFFAIRS

165   WC1

1820s THOMAS CUBITT

Developed by Thomas Cubitt in the 1820s, as a pair with Tavistock Square, this was the last of the Bloomsbury squares to be finished and is a prime example of the transition into Victorian style. As with most London squares, the central garden was originally for private use. The University of London now owns it, together with many of the other buildings surrounding the square. Writer Virginia Woolf, a famous member of the Bloomsbury group of authors and painters who met in London during the 1920s, lived in 46 Gordon Square before her marriage to Leonard Woolf. Dorothy Parker wrote that the Bloomsbury Group, 'comprises pairs who had affairs in squares.' Their promiscuous and complicated relationships were frequently described in diaries, correspondence, and later memoirs. Bertrand Russell lived at number 57 from 1918–19.

166

GORDON SQUARE

UNIVERSITY CHURCH OF
CHRIST THE KING

166   WC1

1853 RAPHAEL BRANDON

This university church boasts the steeple that never was!
It was planned that the building would be surmounted by
a pinnacle some 90 metres (295 feet) high—which would
have made it even higher than Senate House (still the
highest London building at the start of the 1950s).
The large Victorian church, which was raised in traditional
Gothic style, was originally built for the Catholic
Apostolic Church—a fraction that split from the
Catholic Church in 1870.

SCHOOL OF ORIENTAL AND AFRICAN STUDIES

1973 SIR DENYS LASDUN AND PARTNERS

Founded in 1916 as the School of Oriental Studies, an African element was added in 1938. The school's mission was to train British administrators for overseas postings across the empire. This concrete building is clad in white pre-cast panels, with vast areas of windows. Its clean lines and uncompromising 1970s design are highlighted by its Georgian surroundings. The double-height, roof-lit library is the United Kingdom's national resource for materials on Asia and Africa—the largest of its kind in Europe. In 2004, SOAS was voted the eleventh-best university in Europe. Alumni include Jemima Khan, Sultan Salahuddin (sultan of Selangor and king of Malaysia), and Mette-Marit (crown Princess of Norway).

BLOOMSBURY'S SMALLEST SQUARE

1828 JAMES SIM; 1969 MUCH DEMOLISHED

This, the smallest of all the Bloomsbury squares, is named for Woburn Abbey, the main country seat of the Dukes of Bedford, who developed much of the Bloomsbury area. The terraces on the northeast and southwest sides are original. Today, the square is owned by the University of London and houses the famous Slade School of Art, which traces its roots back to 1868. Well-known members of the teaching staff have included Lucian Freud, Reg Butler, and Roger Fry. Here also is the Warburg Institute—a University of London research institution that includes resources for the study of Renaissance and early modern culture, with a library of more than 350,000 volumes.

BOW-FRONTED SHOPS

1822 THOMAS CUBITT

Here there are some lovely well-preserved, bow-fronted shops in a short but pretty pedestrian street. This was designed as a whole to serve as a small shopping centre by Thomas Cubitt—who designed much of the area to the north and east of Russell Square. It was restored in the 1960s and today its façade would serve well on nostalgic Christmas cards. W. B. Yeats lodged here from 1865–1919. Now it is the home of many art galleries, newsagents, bookshops, museums, and places to eat.

BRITISH MEDICAL ASSOCIATION

1911-13 AND 1922-29 SIR EDWIN LUTYENS AND C. WONTNER SMITH

BMA House is a Grade II–listed building—initially built for the Theosophical Society before World War I but then sold to the BMA. It finally opened in 1925. The building is neo-classical Palladian with Portland stone and red brick façades and dressings, with green Westmorland slate roofs. The long Great Hall that formed the centrepiece of Lutyen's scheme was originally intended as a Theosophists' temple. Now it has been converted into a library, with committee rooms occupying the roof space. The BMA, established in 1832, represents over 137,000 British doctors, including some 3,000 overseas members and 19,000 students.

167

168

169

170

MARY WARD HOUSE

171   WC1

1895-98 SMITH AND BREWER

This free-style building with a Charles Rennie
Mackintosh flavour explores a variety of arches and
canopies, with interesting patterns created by the
windows and their positions and lovely entrances. Areas
of white on parts of the upper stories and around the
windows act as a contrast to the immaculate brickwork.
Mary Ward was a late Victorian who acquired fame and
riches through her best-selling novels, writing as Mrs
Humphrey Ward. She founded the settlement to provide
cultural and educational opportunities to those denied
these through circumstances of birth. She was also
instrumental in setting up Somerville College, the first
women's college at Oxford, and introduced to England
the first school for physically handicapped children and
the play centre movement. This settlement offers
facilities to enjoy music, debating, and chess; mother
and toddler groups; a 'poor man's' legal service; and
retraining facilities for the unemployed.

171

172

173

TAVISTOCK SQUARE

A GEORGIAN SQUARE

172   WC1

UNIVERSITY OF LONDON, BEDFORD WAY

INSTITUTE OF EDUCATION

173   WC1

1806–26 THOMAS CUBITT

Developed in the 1820s by architect Thomas Cubitt, only the west side of the square remains as it was then. The square is part of the estate owned by the Dukes of Bedford, and takes its name from the title always given to the eldest son, the Marquess of Tavistock. The terrace shows the early nineteenth-century trend towards creating individual houses, and has many fine Georgian façades. In the middle is a peace garden, with a statue of Mahatma Gandhi as its centrepiece (installed 1968). There is also a memorial to conscientious objectors, and a cherry tree planted in 1967 in memory of the victims of the nuclear bombing of Hiroshima. The square houses the British Medical Association (the professional association for doctors in the United Kingdom), which has one of the city's blue plaques stating that Charles Dickens once lived here (and built a little theatre in the garden). The square was in the news more recently during the July 2005 London bombings, when a double-decker bus exploded in its northeast end, killing thirteen people.

1975–79 SIR DENYS LASDUN AND PARTNERS

Founded by the former London County Council in 1902 as a teacher-training school, this became part of the University of London in 1932, when it received its present name. The school has since diversified into educational research. The institute's main building on Bedford Way was designed by Sir Denys Lasdun. The face of the building that looks out over Bedford Way is an impressive 236-metre (774-foot) sweeping curtain wall, broken only by powerful buttress-like, triangular-edged concrete and the multiple windows that stripe its dark blue-grey façade.

174

175

LONDON'S LARGEST SQUARE

174   WCI

1800 JAMES BURTON, HUMPHREY REPTON

At 210 by 205 metres (690 by 673 feet), the centrepiece of this huge square is a fountain with jets coming straight from the pavement. Some of the large terraced houses have survived on the southern and western sides. The nearby street lamps carry the Bedford Arms, after the Duke of Bedford, who originally set out the square and surrounding streets. Author T. S. Eliot worked here for many years, and self-exiled Oscar Wilde spent his last evening in London at 21 Russell Square on May 19, 1897, before leaving for Victoria Station to catch the boat for Dieppe. On the eastern side of the square is the rather formidable Russell Hotel, built in 1898.

THE RUSSELL HOTEL

175   WCI

1898 C. FITZROY DOLL

The first large Victorian-style building to rise in these Georgian Bloomsbury surroundings was twice as high as the tallest of the surrounding 'domestic' buildings. It is an imposing nine storeys of terracotta with many arches, tall chimneys, and motifs in beige faience. Fitzroy Doll also worked on the grand facilities of the *Titanic*, and the hotel restaurant that carries his name is almost identical to the one on the ill-fated ship. It has over 370 guestrooms, and interior features include Sicilian marble columns, large chandeliers, high vaulted ceilings, oak panelling, a grand marble staircase, and two ballrooms. The building underwent a £12 million refurbishment in 2004–5.

176

177

HERBRAND STREET, OFFICES
McCANN-ERICKSON

176   WC1

1931 WALLIS GILBERT AND PARTNERS

After the Paris Exhibition of 1925, Art Deco flourished through the twenties and thirties, exploring not only cubism, ancient Egyptian, Aztec, and Mayan art, but also the advantages of the machine age. Plastics, chrome, and aluminium were used. Speed and streamlining became synonymous with the first commercial flights, such celebrated trains as the Orient Express, vast ocean-going liners — and elegant cars. These offices began as the Daimler Car Hire Garage and later served as a taxi garage. The building is in baroque 1930s style and has car ramps worked into its styling; it celebrates all the finesse and flair associated with these prestigious vehicles.

CORAM'S FIELDS
FOUNDLING HOSPITAL

177   WC1

1790-1812

On the south side of Coram's Fields is the grounds of the former Foundling Hospital, founded by Captain Thomas Coram in 1742 — a place where unwanted children and orphans could be housed. Boys and girls were kept apart, except on Christmas Day, and, even after death were laid to rest in separate mortuaries. Only the entrance gates of the hospital still stand (it was demolished in 1928) but there is a large playground in the fields; unaccompanied adults may be refused permission to enter. The hospital was one of several in operation in London in the first half of the eighteenth century, and Dickens wrote about it in *Little Dorritt*.

178

179

180

181

MECKLENBURGH SQUARE
GARDEN AND SQUARE
178   WCI

1790-1812 S. P. COCKERELL AND JOSEPH KAY

The square was developed by the governors
of the Foundling Hospital, in nearby Coram's
Fields. Brick and stucco with Greek detailing,
it was named after Queen Charlotte, formerly
Princess of Mecklenburg-Strelitz. The Grade
II–listed, two-acre garden, first laid out in
1810–12, remains close to the original design,
with ornamental trees, formal lawns, and gravel
paths. This is one of the squares around the
area in which Virginia Woolf lived—namely at
number 37, which was bombed in 1940 and
replaced by William Goodenough House in 1957.
Number 21 (pictured here) was home to
historian and author R. H. Tawney and Sir Syed
Ahmed Khan, reformer and scholar.

BRITANNIA STREET
DERBY LODGE
179   WCI

LATE 1800s

The design of the flats in this six-storey
tenement building, with its sturdy iron arched
staircase landings and railings, was based on
a small two-storey set of 'model cottages'
commissioned in 1851 by Prince Albert,
who wanted to encourage better designs
for homes for the industrial classes. Britannia
Street is also the site of the Gagosian Gallery.

LLOYD SQUARE
1800s HOUSES
180   WCI

1819 JOHN AND WILLIAM BOOTH

This tranquil and secluded square is surrounded
by houses with very pleasing, well-proportioned
façades that were designed by father-and-son
team, John and William Booth, for the Lloyd
Baker family who owned the estate until the
mid-twentieth century. The traditional garden
layout has trees around the perimeter and a
central flowerbed with gravel paths leading to a
pergola. At the northwest corner is Cumberland
Gardens, a rather unusual, single-sided paved
alley with back gardens on one side. The lawned
children's play area was once a tennis court.

48 DOUGHTY STREET
DICKENS MUSEUM
181   WCI

EARLY 1800s

Charles Dickens and his family lived here from
1837–39. At that time it was a private street,
sealed off at both ends with gates and porters.
The move to this address from previous cramped
chambers in Furnival's Inn, Holborn, was made
possible by the success of The Pickwick Papers.
Here, Dickens completed some of his most
important works, including Oliver Twist and
Nicholas Nickleby. Doughty Street was saved
from demolition in 1923 by the Dickens
Fellowship, and the society has since lovingly
restored the building. Inside, a fascinating
collection of memorabilia includes the author's
letters, furniture, portraits, and even the quills
with which he penned his masterpieces.

182

183

200 GRAY'S INN ROAD

ITN OFFICES

182   WCI

JOHN STREET

CENTURIES TICK BY

183   WCI

1987-90 FOSTER ASSOCIATES

This building has now been fully taken over by news broadcasters Independent Television News, although it was originally built as a property investment. Outside, all is glass and blue-green reflection, with slender pillars supporting the upper-storey levels. Inside, the offices surround a large, ceiling-height atrium. ITN was founded in 1955 and has presented the main national news bulletins for the ITV network ever since (now branded ITV News); it now also manages a television news archive. Gray's Inn Road was the ancient route from the north to the city markets, described by Stow as a 'lane furnished with fair buildings,' and was the route taken by Fielding's antihero Tom Jones.

1760

Boasting several great examples of eighteenth-century architecture, the houses in John Street are very well preserved—often with intact mews. This wide street, named after John Blagrave, a carpenter, was the site of the Shaftesbury School and, from 1914, the Ragged School Union headquarters at number 32. Today, it is home to an extension of the Architectural Association and AA School of Architecture.

184

185

GREAT JAMES STREET

184   WC1

1720-30

This is one of the best and most complete examples of an elegant early seventeenth–century London street, and is named after James Burgess who helped to develop the area. The buildings sport the typical redbrick, bracketed door-hood style of the time, some with arched windows and balconies, and all set behind railings. Dorothy L. Sayers, writer of detective stories, lived at number 24 between 1921 and 1929. Other famous occupants have included novelist Virginia Woolf, and poet T. S. Eliot.

LAMB'S CONDUIT STREET

THE LAMB PUB

185   WC1

1720s

Both pub and street were named after philanthropist William Lamb who, in 1577, improved the conduit that brought fresh water to the area. When this eighteenth-century pub was 'improved' in Victorian times, much of the original structure was lost. Its interior was restored in 1961 and contains original woodwork and glass. The exterior has striking green-tiled walls. Inside, above the U-shaped bar, they still keep snob screens—small pivoting panels of etched glass, positioned at head height to conceal a drinker's identity. One corner of the bar houses a Polyphon, a Victorian-style jukebox. The pub was a meeting place of the Bloomsbury group of writers and painters in the 1920s.

186

187

188

189

A GARDEN SQUARE

1716

This relatively small square was originally named Queen Anne's Square, after the misidentification of its statue—now believed to portray Queen Charlotte, wife of King George III. Many of the buildings are health-care orientated—such as the National Hospital of Neurology and Neurosurgery, and the Royal London Homeopathic Hospital The former institute for public health covers most of the north side. At the southern end is the church of St George the Martyr, the Mary Ward Centre, and the former Italian Hospital—now part of Great Ormond Street Hospital. George III was treated in a house on the square when he was thought to have gone mad—as portrayed in the 1995 film *The Madness of King George*. The public house on the southwest corner is called the Queen's Larder because, some claim, the building was used by Queen Charlotte to store food for the king during his treatment.

EDWARD VII GALLERIES

1904-II SIR JOHN BURNET

Part of the British Museum, this lovely sweep of galleries, with tall windows set behind a façade of fine columns, was a north-wing extension to the earlier museum building. Helped by a legacy from Vincent Stuckley Lean, work began on the galleries and the foundation stone was laid by King Edward VII in 1907. The building cost £200,000 and was opened by the king in May 1914. Then the outbreak of World War I delayed the transfer of many of the collections until the early 1920s. The British Museum was also bombed in air raids of 1941, but was not seriously damaged. This extension was the first of a planned series of three galleries for which the land was bought back in 1894.

SENATE HOUSE

1932-37 CHARLES HOLDEN

Although completed by 1937, a lack of funding and the imminence of World War II meant that some elements of the initial plan had been abandoned. When war broke out, the building's library was moved out and some of the offices of the Ministry of Information moved in. The author George Orwell worked for the ministry, so this building is thought to be the inspiration for the Ministry of Truth buildings in his book *1984*—written in 1951, when the Senate House was the tallest building in London at 64 metres (210 feet) high. The building is also thought to have a mention in John Wyndham's *Day of the Triffids*, and legend claims that Hitler intended the building to be his headquarters after the invasion of Britain. It houses the chancellor's offices, one of central London's largest restaurants, and the vast Senate House Library that flows from the fourth to the nineteenth floor.

SCHOOL OF HYGIENE AND TROPICAL MEDICINE

1926-28 MORELY HORDER AND VERNON REES

Founded in 1899 by Sir Patrick Manson, this was first located in the London Docks. A physician who had worked in the Far East and who famously discovered that mosquitoes transmit malaria, Manson believed that British doctors should have the opportunity to study tropical medicine. The school was granted its Royal Charter in 1924 and opened in 1929. The raising of a new building was made possible through a generous gift of $2 million from the Rockefeller Foundation. With its 'stripped classical' façade in Portland stone, this building is not dissimilar to the nearby Senate House. An unusual feature is the golden insect decoration on the balconies. A frieze of twenty-three illustrious names honours Jenner, Pasteur, Koch, and others who studied infectious diseases. Today, the school undertakes research, and trains more than eight hundred students from 120 countries each year.

COVENT GARDEN
AND DRURY LANE

The original Covent Garden (then Convent Garden) was where medieval Benedictine monks buried their dead. Eventually they developed a garden, and the sale of their surplus produce mutated into a marketplace. Inigo Jones designed a piazza here and then, over the years, its houses were replaced by shops and stalls—selling flowers, roots and herbs, exotic fruits, and vegetables from all over the world. In the 1970s, the market was relocated, and now Covent Garden is a bustling shopping precinct with many fascinating small shops and several museums, as well as piazza-based market stalls offering everything from antiques to CDs.

Covent Garden is famous for its music, too. It is home to the Royal Ballet, the Royal Opera, and the Orchestra of the Royal Opera House. In the 1600s, Charles II gave Covent Garden (and Drury Lane) playhouses almost sole rights to present spoken drama in London. The royal box here today has its own private entrance and dining room. Queen Victoria's gold chairs remain—as well as a settee for her ladies-in-waiting, facing away from the stage. A mirror was set on the opposite wall, so that her attendants could see the reflected performance.

At the Theatre Royal in Drury Lane, fifteen-year-old Nell Gwynn, an orange seller, made her stage debut. Charles II was enamoured immediately he saw her and she soon became his mistress. The current Theatre Royal opened in 1812 and has since hosted many memorable performances, not least by the Man in Grey—the ghost of a handsome young fellow in a white wig, long riding cloak, riding boots, tricorn hat, and a sword at his waist. He is said to haunt the upper circle, often sitting in the fourth row, then walking along at the back to disappear into the wall by the royal box. His appearance in the early days of a new show usually heralds a success. During the 1800s, workmen discovered the skeleton of a man—with a dagger lodged between his ribs—in a small room, bricked up at the exact spot where the ghost disappears.

Other ghosts here include Dan Leno, a popular comedian who reappears in his favourite dressing room, actor-manager Charles Kean (who died in 1868), and King Charles II and his retinue. Other friendly ghosts help actors to find the right spot to perform on the stage.

ALFRED STREET AND STORE STREET
IMAGINATION OFFICES AND GALLERY

190   WCI

1990 RON HERRON AND ASSOCIATES

This building was transformed in just twelve months from the ruins of an Edwardian school. The building is a mixture of heavy masonry walls, light steel, and bridges that span each of the floors. Behind the original curved, six-storey redbrick façade, the building stretches back and encompasses another five-storey building behind, with the gap between enclosed by a unique fabric roof that creates an atrium—bridged on every floor by steel and aluminium walkways. From the gallery at the top of the building, there is a splendid view over Bloomsbury—or down into the impressive atrium below.

190

BEDFORD SQUARE
A 'CIRCULAR SQUARE'

191   WCI

1775-83

Named after the Dukes of Bedford, once a major landlord in Bloomsbury, this 'circular square' is the only complete Georgian square in the area. The central garden has remained private, its keys held by the owners of surrounding buildings. Many of the Grade I–listed buildings have four-storeys, and are brick-built with Coade stone ornaments. Most have been converted into offices—many focused on the publishing industry. Residents have included Lord Eldon (a long-serving Lord Chancellor), scientist Henry Cavendish, and architect William Butterfield. Led by Dante Gabriel Rossetti, the Pre-Raphaelite Brotherhood was founded in 1848 in a house here.

191

112 GREAT RUSSELL STREET
CENTRAL YMCA

192   WCI

1976 ELLESWORTH SYKES PARTNERSHIP

Central YMCA was established in 1844 and was the world's first YMCA. One of the founders, George Williams, lived nearby in Russell Square. The new YMCA was raised on the site of an older 1911–12 building—designed by architect R. Plumbe. The tall concrete towers of today's Central YMCA have strips of windows set into the building's interestingly angled narrow facets, stepped one behind another. As well as accommodation, the current building offers an excellent range of facilities and fitness programmes, and has a superb gymnasium and swimming pool.

192

193

194

GREAT RUSSELL STREET

CONGRESS HOUSE

193   WC1

STREATHAM STREET

MODEL DWELLINGS
FOR FAMILIES

194   WC1

1953–60 DAVID DU ROI ABERDEEN

This Grade II–listed building is home to
Britain's Trade Union Congress (TUC), which
campaigns for workers and for social justice at
home and abroad (member unions represent
over 6.5 million working people). The building
sprang from an architectural competition to
design a new headquarters in 1948 and was
officially opened in March 1958. Within the
courtyard, a sculpture by American-born
Jacob Epstein remembers the trade unionists
lost during the two world wars. There are
splendid bronze window frames and
impressive areas of plate glass, marble, and
mosaic—in a style that both fits and sets the
building apart from the rest of the street.

1849 HENRY ROBERTS

Henry Roberts was an architect renowned for
the design of model dwellings for the working
classes. Close to both city and countryside,
Bloomsbury had become a fashionable place
to live by the eighteenth century. Many
imposing townhouses were raised for families
who spent weeks in town and weekends in
the country. By the mid-1800s, the area was
densely populated. The Society for Improving
the Condition of the Labouring Classes was
one of many such groups set up in the 1840s;
this was their first attempt to provide homes
within an urban area. The courtyard contains
open galleries, supported by brick piers, which
lead into the flats. A top floor was added later.
Prince Albert, Queen Victoria's consort, was
fascinated by the problem of finding housing
for lower-income groups and he paid for
prototype model housing, also designed by
Henry Roberts, for the 1851 Great Exhibition
at Crystal Palace.

195

196

BLOOMSBURY WAY

ST GEORGE

195   WCI

49 GREAT RUSSELL STREET, FORMERLY THE DOG & DUCK

MUSEUM TAVERN

196   WCI

1716-31 NICHOLAS HAWKSMOOR

In October 2001, St George's became a World
Monuments Fund heritage site, and generous
donations have allowed the church to begin a
£6.7 million restoration, including work on the
crypt, churchyard, and ancillary buildings. The
Commissioners for the Fifty New Churches Act
of 1711 appointed Nicholas Hawksmoor (a
pupil and former assistant of Sir Christopher
Wren) to design the church that has a stepped
tower topped by a statue of George I. None
of Hawksmoor's other churches use the grand
Corinthian portico—probably based on the
Temple of Baalbek, in the Lebanon.
St George's is depicted in William Hogarth's
well-known engraving, *Gin Lane* (1751), and
Charles Dickens used it as the setting for 'The
Bloomsbury Christening' in *Sketches by Boz*.
The funeral of Emily Davidson, the suffragette
who threw herself in front of the King George
V's horse, took place here in 1937.

1723; 1798 REBUILT; WILLIAM FINCH HILL

The Museum Tavern, one of the oldest in
Bloomsbury, was first recorded as the Dog
& Duck in 1723, when the district was an odd
mixture of grand mansions, market gardens,
and marshy fields where duck hunting with
dogs was a common sport. This small tavern,
patronised by servants from the surrounding
mansions, came into its own once the British
Museum was built—it became the British
Museum Tavern in 1762. It may have been
visited by Karl Marx and was certainly the
model for Sir Arthur Conan Doyle's Alpha
Inn in *The Case of the Blue Carbuncle*.
J. B. Priestley imbibed here, too. It still
has lovely 1889 stained-glass panels and
etched windows.

197

BRITISH MUSEUM

197   WC1

1823-47 SIR ROBERT SMIRKE

One of the largest collections of human history and culture—and the oldest museum in the world—this is home to the Elgin Marbles, Rosetta Stone, Egyptian mummies, and some 7 million other objects. Founded 1753, the British Museum opened (as Montague House) in 1759 and sprang from the collections of physician and scientist, Sir Hans Sloane. The current neo-classical building appeared almost a century later, taking some twenty-four years to complete. Smirke was asked to create a building for the King's Library. The original museum had four wings arranged around a vast, open courtyard. No sooner had it been completed than storage demands meant that a new, round, copper-domed reading room was raised in the middle of the courtyard and opened in 1857—with a dome the same size as Saint Peter's in Rome. Its famous visitors have included Lenin, Marx, Oscar Wilde, and George Bernard Shaw. A rebellion against classical Italian styling, the wonderful Greek Revival façade of the museum follows the form of ancient Greek temples, and the 1852 pediment over the main entrance is decorated with sculptures depicting *The Rise of Civilisation*.

GREAT COURT

198   WC1

1994-2003 FOSTER AND PARTNERS

The magnificent new Queen Elizabeth II Great Court at the centre of the British Museum has turned an open courtyard into a glazed, covered space. It is the largest covered square in Europe, with 3,312 triangular, double glazed panes in a lightweight roof that spans 6,100 square metres (65,662 square feet). This is enough glass to glaze five hundred domestic greenhouses. Each pane is slightly different in size and shape because of the roof's complex geometric form. The Great Court has created a new focal point for the museum, one of the most famous cultural institutions in the world. It stays open late into the evening, and has become a space to linger as well as a useful through-route from the University of London precinct to Great Russell Street. The huge mass of the museum has become permeable, part of the fabric of the city. It throngs with museum visitors as well as those dropping into its shops and café.

199

c. 1820 JAMES BURTON

These parallel streets lead into the south side of Russell Square. Bedford Place has retained most of its original features, but the southwest corner of Montague Street was lost when the British Museum was built. Edward Jenner, who pioneered smallpox vaccination, lived in Bedford Place, and number 38 is the office of the Clockmakers' Company. Pretty Montague Street Garden stands behind two huge wrought-iron gates. The Montague Hotel (at number 15) is one of the new places to be registered for civil weddings and civil partnerships—as of January 2006.

200

22 HIGH HOLBORN

CITTIE OF YORK

200 WC1

1695; 1890s

This Victorian gothic, Grade II–listed frontage has stone mullions and Early English-style archways. Inside, a high vaulted ceiling, clerestory windows, and carved woodwork suggest a medieval great hall. The pub replaced the Gray's Inn Coffee House, built in 1695 on a site of a 1450s inn. Part of the ancient cellar is now a bar. There are portraits of Holborn residents such as William Morris, Charles Dickens, Dr Johnson, Sir Thomas More, and Sir Francis Bacon. Great thousand-gallon wine butts are mounted over the bar and a triangular stove, taken from Gray's Inn, dates from 1815. Along the walls are private wooden booths where lawyers could have intimate conversations with their clients.

201

HAZELWOOD HOUSE, 53 NEW OXFORD STREET

JAMES SMITH AND SONS

201 WC1

1880

James Smith and Sons, founded in 1830 to sell and repair umbrellas, moved here in the 1850s. The shop is a perfect example of a Victorian shopfront with original typography. It has remained virtually unaltered for almost 150 years, and is still run by direct descendants of the original Mr Smith. Row upon row of umbrellas and walking sticks line the walls in racks, glass-fronted cases, and baskets. Customers have included prime ministers Gladstone and Bonar Law. Custom-made umbrellas and walking sticks cost from £130 and many are sold to the USA. One client asked for sticks to be made in every English wood possible—over seventy in total.

AN ITALIAN FLAVOUR

202 WC1

1905 W. S. WORTHY

A hidden gem between Bloomsbury Way and Southampton Row, this charming avenue reflects its name, with many Italianate pillars, turrets with curved windows, and other decorative features. This is a wide, pedestrian passage, flanked on both sides by bookshops and spaghetti restaurants, and shielded from the busy roads on either side by Ionic screens (pillared-style gateways) with large inscriptions. The edges of the walkway are lined with flowers and bushes. The four storeys that rise above the ground-level shops were once public flats but are now offices, decorated in brick and terracotta—a sharp, peppery red with white edges and stripes.

202

CENTRAL SCHOOL OF ARTS AND CRAFTS

203 WC1

1906 L. C. ARCHITECTS DEPARTMENT

This was established in 1896—spearheaded by the Arts and Crafts leaders William Morris and John Ruskin—to provide specialist art teaching for the craft industries and art scholars. This sturdy but elegant building has many arches, reliefs, and fine details. The first principal, architect William Lethaby, was involved in its design. Central Saint Martins arose from the merger of the Central School of Arts and Design (formerly Arts and Crafts) with St Martins College of Art in 1989. Famous alumni include designer Terence Conran, painter Lucien Freud, and fashion designer Stella McCartney.

203

FORMER OFFICES OF W. S. CRAWFORD LTD

204 WC1

c. 1930s FREDERICK ETCHELLS AND WELCH

High Holborn was once the main road from the old city to the west and, until the fifteenth century, it remained open country. It was named after the high ground above Hole Bourne stream. This building was commissioned by W. S. Crawford Limited, a reputable advertising agency of the 1920s. Set on a corner site, it has a fine, polished, black marble ground floor, with white stucco and multiple mullion windows above. Architect Frederick Etchells had a reputation of being at the forefront of the modernist movement, but this is his only real contribution to the London scene.

204

1680 NICHOLAS BARBON

The west side of the street has many examples of the original building work in brown brick, with multiple sash windows sporting a red trim. Numbers 36 to 43 are perhaps the best examples. Sadly, many of the other buildings had to be rebuilt after World War II bombing. The concept of terraced housing had taken off in the 1670s as a solution to a preference for ground-level living with a garden. Between 1670 and 1700, entrepreneur Nicholas Barbon purchased huge areas of building land across London, on which he raised a standardised design of terraced house. He was also the founder of house insurance; following the Great Fire of London, he thought the idea might take off!

1678-88

Once, this square was in two halves, with a hall and chapel on the south side. The Inns of Court, dating back to the 1300s, were originally eating and lodging places for law students. Of some thirty inns, only four survive—including Gray's Inn. During the 1500s, these were supported by various statesmen and judges, including Thomas Cromwell, and hosted colourful celebrations and street processions. William Shakespeare may have performed here. In the 1680s, there were several disastrous fires, and, in 1684, the library on Gray's Inn Square burnt down—lots of ancient records were lost and 30,000 books destroyed. At this time, being called to the Bar often depended on gaining the favour of a judge or bencher, or consuming a certain number of dinners in the hammer-beam main hall of Gray's Inn, but from about the 1850s, legal examinations were imposed. Gray's Inn Hall has been its present size since it was 're-edified' in 1556–58. Despite heavy war damage in 1941, some sixteenth-century walls and stained glass have survived. Tradition claims that the screen at the west end is made from the wood of a captured Spanish Armada galleon—a gift from Queen Elizabeth I.

VARIOUS, FROM 1780s

Field Court, in the southwest corner of Gray's Inn Square, is a private court, although the public can enter. Number 2 dates as far back as 1780 but the next house was built in 1936; some of the surrounding area was razed to the ground by World War II bombs. The gardens, accessed from Field Court, were laid out by one of the inn's most celebrated members, Francis Bacon. Here, two rare catalpa trees are reputed to have been brought from America as seedlings by Sir Walter Raleigh. Bacon's bronze statue occupies a prominent position in the square, surrounded by three rows of seventeenth-century houses and, on the north side, the hall and chapel—the oldest surviving part of the inn, dating from the early 1500s. The hall, completed in 1560, is beautifully panelled and hung with rich paintings, its roof supported by impressive hammer beaming. An oak screen was reputedly donated by Queen Elizabeth (see number 206). An impressive gate leads from the square onto Gray's Inn Road.

1685; MID-1700s RAYMOND ERITH AND OTHERS

Number 1 South Square is the only building to survive World War II destruction here, in the south-east corner of Gray's Inn Square, but many buildings have been rebuilt to the original specifications. Number 1 is the banqueting hall for Gray's Inn, the Inn of Court nicknamed the 'Northern Inn.' Gray's Inn of Court, often said to have a left-wing political slant, is home to many top barristers' chambers, including Matrix Chambers, the human rights set of which Cherie Booth (Mrs Tony Blair) is a member. The banqueting hall is a Grade I–listed building. Outside, a fine statue of Sir Francis Bacon marks the fact that he wrote several masques and plays during his tenure at Gray's Inn. Shakespeare's *Comedy of Errors* was first performed in 1594 at Gray's Inn Hall.

205

206

207

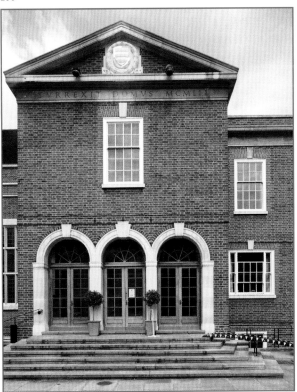

208

209

CENTRAL ST MARTINS

209   WC2

1937–38 E. P. WHEELER

St Martin's School of Art began in 1854, when the Rev. M. McKenzie of St Martin-in-the-Fields felt that industrial art and design should be taught to apprenticed boys. By 1937, over seven hundred students were enrolled and this new building was raised. A major fine art and commercial art school by1986, it became part of the London Institute and merged with the Central School of Art and Design in 1989 to form Central Saint Martins College of Art & Design, today part of the University of Arts London. Immortalised in the Pulp song, *Common People*, it was also the site of the first-ever Sex Pistols gig. Alumni include artist Peter Blake, fashion designer John Galliano, and actor John Hurt.

210

CENTRE POINT

210   WC2

1963–67 RICHARD SEIFERT AND PARTNERS

One of the first London skyscrapers and the world's tallest pre-cast concrete office building then, Centre Point's thirty-five floors reach 117 metres (384 feet)—permitted in return for the provision of a new road junction at St Giles Circus. This controversial building , unoccupied for twelve years, was described as coarse but, with the passage of time, gained credential stature and, by 1995, had been Grade II listed. It cost £5.5 million. Since 1980, it has been the headquarters of the Confederation of British Industry. Now there are plans to create a restaurant at the top. This area was once notorious for its slums, and in earlier times had been occupied by a gallows.

211

ST GILES-IN-THE-FIELDS

211   WC2

1731–33 HENRY FLITCROFT

The church was built on the site of an 1100s leper hospital and chapel, when leprosy was a most serious health risk—more feared than the plague—and it is named after the patron saint of outcasts. In later centuries, prisoners passing by on the way from Newgate prison to Tyburn gallows were given 'cups of charity' by the church wardens—in the form of a drink at the next-door pub, the Angel. The Great Plague of London started in this parish, and the churchyard is full of its victims. The galleried, Palladian design of the present church was based on sixteenth-century Italian and early Christian basilicas. Architect John Soane was buried in the churchyard here in 1818.

79 ENDELL STREET
SWISS PROTESTANT CHURCH
212   WC2

1853 GEORGES VULLIAMY

The Swiss Church was raised to offer a spiritual home to the Swiss community in London, welcoming a Christian congregation into a Protestant Reformed church. It aimed to complement the nation's mix of culture and languages, and to help members keep in touch with their roots while mixing with people from other cultures and traditions. The building, set tightly between its neighbours, is not in the Gothic style generally used for Protestant churches at that time but is in late Palladian, with tall columns astride the entrance, and generously sized blockwork making interesting patterns.

212

NEAL STREET, EARLHAM STREET, SHELTON STREET
WAREHOUSES
213   WC2

C. 1850

Earlham Street warehouse has impressive mid-Victorian brickwork and simple arched windows. It has been used by a brewer, a paper manufacturer, one of the first 1920s film companies to use colour, and as a place to ripen bananas. From the 1970s, many warehouses here have provided space for local community groups, shops, studios, and galleries—helping the area's regeneration. In 1960, Donald Albery bought and converted 41 Earlham Street into a rehearsal studio for the London Festival Ballet, naming it the Donmar (after himself and Dame Margot Fonteyn). After a 1977 renovation, the theatre was leased to the Royal Shakespeare Company.

213

31 ENDELL STREET
CROSS KEYS
214   WC2

1848

The Cross Keys arrived when Endell Street was created as a relief road to carry traffic to and from Westminster Bridge. Masses of foliage hide a rather grand Grade II–listed façade with three arches in green marble, columns supporting gilded capitals, and pretty, arched upper windows. A stone bas-relief plaque shows two cherubs holding the crossed keys of Saint Peter, keeper of the gates to Heaven. Inside is a long, cosy, wood-panelled bar. Musical instruments, copper and brass pots, kettles, and scuttles hang from low beams, while the walls are covered with old prints, stuffed fish, and cigarette cards. A fine long-case clock ticks away the drinking time in one corner.

214

215

1957-59 SIR BASIL SPENCE AND PARTNERS;
1990 RHWL PARTNERSHIP ARCHITECTS

Built by a pivotal 1900s architect, this tall, white tower rises above many of the older buildings and was one of the first in London to be set on a podium, albeit a low, two-storey one. Renamed Orion House, it was redesigned in 1990. Its many offices include those of publishers Orion that, by pure coincidence, share the building's name. Another tenant is the Now and Zen restaurant. A long, spiky sculpture on the north face is by Geoffrey Clarke. From the 1700s until 1926, this site was occupied by Aldridge's Horse and Carriage Repository—providing horses for the middle classes and tradesmen.

216

TRAFALGAR SQUARE

CANADA HOUSE

216   WC2

1824-27 SIR ROBERT SMIRKE

This building was originally used by the Union Club and the Royal College of Physicians but the Canadian government took it over in 1923. Home to the High Commission of Canada to the United Kingdom, it hosts conferences, receptions, lectures, and vernissages (where Canadians and Britons meet). It also houses the Canada House Gallery. It was originally built in Bath stone, with a recessed portico to the square and additional porticoes set either side of the building but only the Royal College of Physicians portion remains unchanged. The building, restored in 1993 and reopened by Queen Elizabeth II in 1996, has an impressive staircase and library.

217

LEICESTER SQUARE

THE ODEON

217   WC2

1937 HARRY WHEEDON AND ANDREW MATHER

With its huge, black, polished granite façade and high tower, outlined by blue neon in the evening, this is the largest cinema in England, seating some 1,700 people, and a royal premiere venue, with a 'royal retiring room' for visiting monarchs. It stands on the site of the Alhambra, a large music hall that lost its licence in 1870 after presenting 'an indecent dance' called the can-can. The Art Deco interior had a ribbed ceiling, sculptured nymphs on the walls, and faux leopard skin seats. A 1967 modernisation stripped away some this grandeur. The cinema still has an operating Compton Organ, and a safety curtain detailed with 1930s Art Deco motifs.

218

ST MARTIN'S LANE;
PREVIOUSLY THE COACH AND HORSES AND BEN CAUNT'S HEAD
THE SALISBURY

218   WC1

1840s; 1892

Long ago, there was a tavern here called the Coach and Horses. Its landlord was the great prize-fighter Ben Caunt (whose father had been a servant to Lord Byron), who won the national title in 1841. Prize fights were held here. In 1892, the tavern was replaced by the ornate, magnificent, Salisbury Stores—restaurant and wine merchant's. It was named after then current prime minister, the third Marquis of Salisbury. Rich, glittering mirrors, bronze, nymphs, Art Nouveau lamps and gleaming mahogany arrived in an 1898 refurbishing. In time, the Salisbury became a theatre pub with a gay clientele and had a starring role in the film *Victim*, with Dirk Bogarde.

219

33 ROSE LANE
LAMB AND FLAG

219   WC2

1500s; 1623

This is one of the oldest pubs in London and claims a Tudor past. Over 380 years old, it is one of the few wooden-framed buildings left, in what was once a rough area with gambling houses, overcrowded tenements, and riotous inns. It was nicknamed the Bucket of Blood, after the prize bare-fist fights held here. In 1679, poet John Dryden was set upon in an alley outside and nearly killed by thugs after being accused of penning verses about a mistress of Charles II; today, the upstairs bar is called the Dryden Room in his honour. Now a more respectable entity, the pub has a Georgian exterior, a dark pressed-paper ceiling, a parlour fireplace, and decorated glass screens.

220

NATIONAL GALLERY, TRAFALGAR SQUARE
SAINSBURY WING

220   WC2

1990 VENTURI, RAUCH, SCOTT BROWN;
EXECUTIVE ARCHITECTS SHEPHERD ROBSON AND PARTNERS

This new post-modern gallery in its prestigious site has invited some controversy but, in fact, it fits comfortably into the square, with only the vast expanse of roof lights compromising its elevations. The lofty galleries within provide a permanent home for a magnificent collection of early Renaissance works, Italian and Northern European masterpieces from 1260–1510, and host many exhibitions. It was financed by the grocery family after whom it was named and includes an interactive computer information centre; visitors can discover any painting in the collection, print out reproductions, or customise a tour.

221

NATIONAL GALLERY

221   WC2

1832–38 WILLIAM WILKINS; 1867–76 INTERIORS, EDWARD MIDDLETON
BARRY; 1885 CENTRAL HALL, SIR JOHN TAYLOR

This grand, neo-classical Grade I–listed building forms
a splendid theatrical backdrop to Trafalgar Square. It has
thirteen sections, six set each side of a central portico,
and holds one of the world's greatest collections of
paintings. Forty-six rooms show the development of
European painting from the 1200s by artists such as
Leonardo da Vinci, Raphael, Rembrandt, Van Dyck,
Rubens, Hogarth, Constable, Stubbs, and Gainsborough.
The galleries' first director, Sir Charles Eastlake, travelled
through Italy every year from 1854–65, buying many
Italian Renaissance works. As war loomed, in 1939,
the National Gallery closed for the duration, having
evacuated its collection to secret destinations in Wales
and Gloucestershire—the removal completed just the
day before war was declared.

NATIONAL PORTRAIT GALLERY

222   WC2

1890–95 EWAN CHRISTIAN

The National Portrait Gallery was opened in 1856,
and moved to its present building in 1896. It has been
extended twice, with the wing along Orange Street,
funded by Lord Duveen, opening in 1933. Ondaatje Wing,
funded in 2000 by Christopher Ondaatje, occupies a slither
of land between the National Gallery and the National
Portrait Gallery. Its two-storey escalator takes visitors to
the early part of the collection at the top of the building.
Above the entrance to the gallery are busts of the three
men responsible for the its existence—Philip Henry
Stanhope, Thomas Babington Macauley, and Thomas
Carlyle. The gallery was established with the criteria that
it was to be about history (the status of the sitter), not
art. The site was previously occupied by St Martin's
Workhouse. There are three distinct components: the
east block, the entrance block, and the north block,
the entrance block acting as a pivot between the others.
Each was faced with Portland stone and realised in
Florentine Renaissance style, while respecting the
architecture of the National Gallery in the east block. The
entrance block was recessed to fit into the angled corner
of the site with its design based on the façade of Santo
Spinto oratory in Bologna. The north block is modelled
on Florentine Renaissance palazzi. The exteriors of the
entrance block and north block are decorated with
Portland stone and images of eminent portrait artists.

222

223

ST MARTIN-IN-THE-FIELDS

223 WC2

1721-26 JAMES GIBBS

In 1222, monks used a church here. It was rebuilt by Henry VIII in the middle of fields—an isolation that helped it to survive the Great Fire. The building has a classical-style pediment, huge Corinthian columns, and a high steeple with a gilt crown. Traditionally the bells are rung to proclaim a victory in naval warfare. Among the sixty thousand buried here are Robert Boyle, Nell Gwynn, William Hogarth, and Thomas Chippendale. Charles II was christened here and, allegedly, George I was a churchwarden. The church hosts the Pearly Kings and Queens Costermonger's Harvest Festival. During World War I, the chaplain set up a refuge for the homeless— still in operation today.

224

SOUTH AFRICA HOUSE

224 WC2

1933-35 SIR HERBERT BAKER

This sturdy, white building houses the offices of the High Commissioner of South Africa, and the South African Consulate. Built on the site of a derelict hotel, African animals feature on its stone arches, and it has sweeping porticoes. During World War II, Jan Smuts (South Africa's Prime Minister) lived, and conducted his war plans, here. During the 1980s, the building was the focal point for anti-apartheid protestors and, in the 1990s, poll tax rioters set it alight. Today, it is a focal point for South African culture and, in 2001, Nelson Mandela appeared on the balcony to mark the tenth anniversary of Freedom Day, when the system of apartheid ended.

225

AGAR STREET, WILLIAM IV STREET; FORMERLY CHARING CROSS HOSPITAL

CHARING CROSS POLICE STATION

225 WC2

1831-34 DECIMUS BURTON, ALTERED BY J. THOMPSON

The original hospital was founded in 1818—one of several built and rebuilt in this decade—and formed one element of Nash's plan for the west Strand. Stuccoed Corinthian was used for the rounded corner, and Doric styling for the entrance. The new Charing Cross Hospital opened in 1834 with sixty beds, plus a medical school. One famous student was Dr David Livingston, who studied here before he set off on his missionary work and exploration of Africa. In 1973, the Charing Cross Hospital moved to larger premises in Fulham, and the old hospital building was adapted to accommodate a police station in 1994.

WEST STRAND IMPROVEMENTS

226   WC2

1830 JOHN NASH

The Strand was originally a riverside bridle path. Large mansions and palaces arrived from the 1100s onwards but, by 1532, the Strand was 'full of pits and sloughs, very perilous and noisome' and had to be paved. In the 1700s, its coffee shops became the hub of news and gossip. Thomas Twining, supplier of tea to Queen Anne, established his business at number 216 in 1706. Still here, the firm claims to be the oldest property-taxpayer in Westminster. In the late 1700s, the area was full of pickpockets and prostitutes but, after 1830s improvements, Disraeli considered it 'perhaps the finest street in Europe.' Now it is a mix of theatres, hotels, restaurants, offices, and shops.

226

THE STRAND

CHARING CROSS STATION HOTEL

227   WC2

1863-64 EDWARD MIDDLETON BARRY

As the railways boomed, hotels sprang up to serve travellers. Here, as in many other places, a hotel façade created a decorative front to disguise the practical necessity (but less attractive view) of train sheds. Built on the site of the Hungerford Market in a French Renaissance style—with appropriately styled motifs—this hotel boasts one of the first English frontages to use reconstituted stone. It opened on May 15, 1865, and was extended in 1878 and again in 1952, when its two top floors were added. This Grade I–listed building has 239 bedrooms.

227

NORTHUMBERLAND AVENUE

THE METROPOLE

228   WC2

1885

The crumbling Metropole hotel—with its regal, curved, Bath stone façade—was once the place for 'ladies and families visiting the West End during the Season ... to Officers and others attending the levees at St James; to Ladies going to the Drawing Rooms, State Balls, and Concerts at Buckingham Palace; and to colonial and American visitors unused to the great world of London.' A popular venue for banquets and balls, it is said that the Prince of Wales (later Edward VII) entertained guests here. It became a Ministry of Defence office in 1936 and continued to house government staff, many from the Air Ministry. The building was vacated in 2004 and is now in the hands of the Crown Estate.

228

229

CHARING CROSS STATION

229   WC2

1863–64 JOHN HAWKSHORE; 1990 TERRY FARRELL AND PARTNERS

This used to be two separate stations: the Bakerloo Line's Trafalgar Square station from 1906 and the Northern Line's Strand Station from 1907. The concourses were linked by underpasses and merged as Charing Cross in 1979, when the station became the southern terminus for the new Jubilee Line. The platforms once used as the Jubilee Line terminus are now disused but featured in the 2005 film *Creep*. Situated on the forecourt is the Eleanor Cross: Edward I of England erected these lavishly decorated stone monuments in memory of his beloved wife, Eleanor of Castile. The name Charing Cross comes from this, plus the original hamlet of Charing (the old English word *charing* means a bend in the river). Often regarded as the very centre of London, it was one of twelve places where Eleanor's coffin rested overnight during her funeral procession from Lincoln to Westminster. The long mural along the Northern Line platforms measures 100 metres (328 feet). It was designed by David Gentleman and shows a scene from her funeral journey. The Eleanor Cross here is a larger and more ornate Victorian copy of the original. Over 37 million people pass through Charing Cross every year and some visit the famous gay Heaven Nightclub located below the station. Samuel Johnson once said, very appropriately, 'I think the full tide of human existence is at Charing-Cross.'

230

1-3 ROBERT STREET

230   WC2

1768-74 THE ADAM BROTHERS; POST 1938 COLCUTT & HEMP

The original Adelphi Terrace was an ambitious riverside development, by the Adam brothers (John, Robert, James, and William) with the stately Royal Terrace of eleven houses its centrepiece. It rose to the sound of bagpipes as Scottish labourers worked here. Its magnificence faded, the vaults became grim haunts, and much of the terrace was demolished in 1936–38. The current buildings have decorative metalwork and interesting stone zodiacal symbols. Remnants at numbers 1-3 Robert Street show pretty honeysuckle decoration on sunken panels. Famous residents included John Galsworthy, and Sir James Barrie, famous for *Peter Pan*.

231

4-6 JOHN ADAM STREET

231   WC2

1768-74 JOHN ADAM

Adelphi Terrace was originally set beside the busy Thames until the 1771 Victoria Embankment created a new frontage and, in 1772, eleven new houses were built. Two years later, a lottery was held to raise funds for the scheme; considering money values then, an astounding 4,370 tickets were sold at a cost of £50 each. At numbers 4–6 John Adam Street (named for the Adelphi designer) is a stone façade with Ionic features; and a fine library is found within that building. The architect of Westminster Cathedral, John Francis Bentley, had offices in John Adam Street from 1868–1902, and the London School of Economics was launched here in three rooms in 1910.

232

429 THE STRAND; FORMERLY WESTERN INSURANCE OFFICE, BRITISH MEDICAL ASSOCIATION AND RHODESIA HOUSE

ZIMBABWE HOUSE

232   WC2

1907-08 CHARLES HOLDEN

This building became Zimbabwe House in 1980. It has a complex system of narrow bays in free-style classicism, a Cornish granite ground floor and beautiful, arched window features. The entrance from Agar Street is restrained but impressive. Set between the second-floor windows are naked figures depicting the *Ages of Man*, by Jacob Epstein. These caused quite a stir and some claim that the windows of a building opposite were replaced with frosted glass to limit the view. It is rumoured that an embarrassing part of one statue dropped off — possibly because of frost — narrowly missing a passer-by. All the offending projections were then cut away.

233

COVENT GARDEN PIAZZA

233   WC2

COVENT GARDEN

THE MARKET

234   WC2

1631 INIGO JONES AND 1830 CHARLES FOWLER

A settlement has existed here, in London's first square, since Roman times. The name Convent Garden (later changed to Covent Garden) was given to a forty-acre (16-hectare) patch during the reign of King John (1199–1256). The monks of St Peter maintained a large kitchen garden during the Middle Ages, and their surplus became a major source of fruit and vegetables for the city. In 1540, Henry VIII dissolved the monasteries but seized their land. In the 1600s, Inigo Jones designed the new market piazza with Italian styling, fine arches, and elegant façades. The first Punch and Judy show in Britain was said by diarist Samuel Pepys to have taken place here in May 1662. Hitchcock's 1972 film, *Frenzy*, was shot around the markets and pubs of the area. The wholesale market relocated to New Covent Garden Market in Nine Elms in 1974 and, today, Covent Garden is home to many small shops and is the only part of London licensed for street entertainment.

1828–31 CHARLES FOWLER

This was built on the site of the famous flower, fruit, and vegetable market that developed from the sale of surplus produce grown by monks prior to Henry VIII's Dissolution. In the early 1600s, Francis Russell, the fourth Earl of Bedford, commissioned Inigo Jones to design houses here. It wraps around three sides of a piazza (market square), inspired by bastide market towns and Roman colonial styles. By 1678, there were over twenty shops with cellars, but the residential buildings were not a success and many were demolished to make way for more stalls and shops. The daily fruit and vegetable market continued and, in 1830, the current piazza building was raised to create permanent trading premises. In time, Covent Garden attracted wholesalers in foreign and domestic flowers, plus exotic fruits and vegetables from many countries across the world. The market prospered but by 1750, the area was renowned for immorality and rowdiness. In 1829–30 a central market building, designed by Charles Fowler, was built at a cost of £70,000—but trade grew so much that yet further halls were required. The Floral Hall was opened in 1860, the Flower Market in 1871, and the Jubilee Market in 1904. In 1974, the market was relocated south of the river at New Covent Garden Market in Nine Elms, and today a variety of specialist shops, cafés, boutiques, and antique stalls occupy the area.

235

1631-38 INIGO JONES

In 1631, William Russell, first Duke of Bedford, commissioned Inigo Jones to design this church; it cost £4,000. In 1645, Covent Garden was made a separate parish and the church was dedicated to St Paul. Its main entrance is through Inigo Place off Bedford Street; George Bernard Shaw based the opening scene of *Pygmalion* under the monumental portico that graces the Covent Garden side. The church became known as the Actors' Church because of its long association with the theatre community from 1663, when the Theatre Royal was established in Drury Lane, a link further strengthened in 1723 through its proximity to Covent Garden Theatre (now the Royal Opera House). The first known victim of the plague in England, Margaret Ponteous, was buried in the churchyard in April 1665. Artist J. M. W. Turner was baptised at St Paul's, and Thomas Arne, composer of *Rule Britannia*, is buried in the grounds. Memorials within the church remember Charlie Chaplin, Noel Coward, Ivor Novello, Gracie Fields, and Vivien Leigh. Since 2005, the area in front has been home to the Avenue of Stars (London's answer to Hollywood's Walk of Fame).

1857-58 EDWARD MIDDLETON BARRY
1982 GOLLINS MELVIN WARD PARTNERSHIP
2000 SIR JEREMY DIXON

This building is home to the Royal Ballet and Royal Opera (and its orchestra), granted Royal Charters in 1956 and 1968 respectively. The site was originally a nunnery attached to the Abbey of Westminster. Actor/manager John Rich helped raise funds to build the first Theatre Royal at Covent Garden and, on its opening night, in 1732, was carried there in triumph for a performance of Congreve's *The Way of the World*. Admission to one of the fifty-five boxes was then five shillings; a seat in the pit cost half a crown and, in the gallery, one shilling. A seat on the stage cost ten shillings (servants could arrive at 3.00 p.m. to save places for their masters). In 1743, a royal performance of Handel's *The Messiah* set in motion the custom of holding oratorio performances here every Lent. Handel bequeathed his organ to John Rich; sadly, it was lost in a fire that destroyed the theatre in 1808. The second theatre was one of the largest in Europe; during its reign a price rise caused riots! The current building is the third theatre on this site, following yet another fire in 1856. During World War I, it was used as a furniture repository and, during World War II, became a dance hall—but after the war it reopened in 1946 with a performance of *The Sleeping Beauty* by Sadler's Wells Ballet. The royal box has its own private entrance and gold chairs made for Queen Victoria and Prince Albert remain. A settee for her ladies-in-waiting faces away from the stage so that they could remain in constant attendance to her but Victoria had a mirror set on the opposite wall, so that they could still watch the performance reflected there. The frontage, foyer, and auditorium date from 1856 (the main auditorium is a Grade I–listed building) but other parts underwent major reconstruction from 1996 to 2000, costing £216 million. It now seats 2,174 people and has four tiers of boxes and balconies, plus the 400-seat Linbury theatre and the Clore, which is a Royal Ballet studio. The building was used for shots in the 1990s film *The Fifth Element*.

236

237

21 CATHERINE STREET
THE OPERA TAVERN

237   WC2

1879 GEORGE TREACHER

With an unusual, stucco, classic façade in
dark green marble, with two very pretty, tiny,
gilded bay windows, this Victorian tavern's
elaborate design was by a popular pub
architect of the time. Inside, it has a theatrical
flavour, with photographs of stars and opera
posters; the ghost of actor Robert Baddely,
who died in 1794, is reputed to still haunt
the Opera Tavern.

238

2–10 TAVISTOCK STREET; FORMERLY COUNTRY LIFE OFFICES
PALLADIA HUDSON HOUSE

238   WC2

1904 SIR EDWIN LUTYENS

The magazine *Country Life* was first published
by Edward Hudson in 1897 in this grand
company headquarters. It has a magnificent
stonework façade and rich traditional rooms,
where high ceilings and tall windows create
light and space. The new building was
commissioned as Lutyen's first building in
London and was meant to symbolise refined
country life set in the centre of town. It is a
palatial building in a transitional style —
exhibiting 'Wrenaissance' and Edwardian
baroque. Today, this unique Grade II–listed
building houses a modern business centre,
with offices, suites, and meeting rooms on
seven floors. The interiors have been
completely refurbished.

239

440 THE STRAND
COUTTS BANK

239   WC2

1973-79 SIR FREDERICK GIBBERD

Coutts Bank is one of London's oldest surviving banks—
formed in 1692 by a young Scot, John Campbell. He was
a goldsmith-banker, and set up the business in the Strand
under the sign of Three Crowns, the national emblem of
Sweden. The crowns still form part of the Coutts logo
but, today, Coutts is part of the Royal Bank of Scotland.
In 1904, the bank moved to its newly built premises at
440 The Strand, on the site of John Nash's West Strand
Improvements of 1830-32. More recently, the entire
block was threatened with demolition—but, instead,
the interior was replaced by enlarged bank premises.
The frontage, a four-storey glazed entrance, is a marked
variation on The Strand's design. The tall, triangular
central hall is visible from the street. Coutts is a private
bank: its clients are by invitation only and must have
liquid assets in excess of £500,000 or an investment
portfolio of over £1 million. It is most famously known
in the United Kingdom as being the banker of Queen
Elizabeth II, and has, in fact, held an account for every
British sovereign since George III.

240

241

ADELPHI TERRACE
7 ADAM STREET
240   WC2

STRAND AND VICTORIA EMBANKMENT
SHELL-MEX HOUSE
241   WC2

1768-74 JOHN ADAM

Famous residents in the Adelphi Terrace included Richard D'Oyly Carte (1844–1901), of light opera fame; author Thomas Hardy (1840–1928), and author, playwright, and wit George Bernard Shaw (1856–1950). The London School of Economics and the Savage Club also had their premises here. The terrace was much altered in the 1870s, when, unfortunately, the unique decoration by Adam was destroyed. Here at Adam Street, however, a few buildings remain. At number 7, on the offices of the Lancet building, light stucco work and neo-classic features can be seen with honeysuckle pilasters and delicate lacy ironwork.

1931 ERNEST JOSEPH

Ernest Joseph was a Jewish architect who was a leading designer of synagogues. This secular building is, in broad terms, Art Deco, and stands on the site of the Cecil Hotel (the largest hotel in Europe with 800 bedrooms when it opened in 1886). The Strand façade of the hotel remains. Shell-Mex House is 58 metres (190 feet) tall and has twelve floors plus basement and sub-basement. It takes up a full block between the Embankment and the Strand, and can be recognised easily from the Thames by its clock tower. The building was constructed as the London headquarters of Shell-Mex and BP Ltd—a joint venture company created in 1932. Today, the building is occupied by the companies of Pearson Plc, which include Penguin Books. Back in World War II, Shell-Mex House was home to the Ministry of Supply, which dealt with the flow of equipment to the national armed forces. The building was badly damaged by a bomb in 1940, and did not revert to Shell-Mex and BP Ltd use until July 1948.

242

243

DRURY LANE	HIGH-RISE OFFICES
THEATRE ROYAL	**1 KEMBLE STREET**
242 WC2	243 WC2

1810–12 BENJAMIN WYATT

This is one of the West End's largest theatres and is a Grade I–listed building. In the 1500s, cockfighting was a popular pastime here, but the building was converted from a cockpit into a theatre during the reign of James I, to the design of Christopher Wren. Charles II's famous mistress, Nell Gwynn, made her debut here in 1665. The theatre has an unfortunate history of conflagration. It was razed to the ground by fire in January 1672, succeeded by a larger and more elaborate theatre—again designed by Wren—that was demolished and updated in 1791. The third theatre, designed by Henry Holland, opened in March 1794. This building survived a mere fifteen years before burning down in 1809. The present Theatre Royal opened in October 1812 with a production of *Hamlet*. Since then, the interior has been redesigned many times but the shell of the building and foyer still date from the early 1800s. The impressive side colonnade was added in 1831 and the present auditorium dates from 1922. Legendary actor David Garrick made his debut here and managed the theatre during the mid-1700s. In 1716, there was an attempted assassination of the future George II here and, in 1800, one on George III. The theatre has a ghost, of course, which appears in the Circle, usually during matinee performances.

1966: R. SEIFERT & PARTNERS

With sixteen floors, this high-rise building is one of many built under the direction of Richard Seifert, whose company has been responsible for some five hundred office blocks throughout Europe, including London's Centre Point and Tower 42. Some claim that Richard Seifert has done more to change the skyline of London than any other architect since Sir Christopher Wren. Notwithstanding such criticism, he became Britain's first architect millionaire. Here the simple but delicious honeycomb patterning creates a stunning impact.

1889 AND 1903–04 ARTHUR MACKMURDO, THOMAS COLLCUTT

This five-star hotel, with some 230 rooms, takes its name from the Savoy Palace, commissioned by Count Peter of Savoy (the uncle of Henry III) in the 1240s. A century later, it became the home of John of Gaunt, Earl of Lancaster, and grew into a centre culture—one of its residents was Geoffrey Chaucer. Gaunt's unpopularity as the king's chief minister led to the palace being burned in the Peasant's Revolt. The fame of the palace lasted, and the current hotel on the site was commissioned in the late nineteenth century by Richard D'Oyly Carte (owner of the nearby Savoy Theatre). There are two buildings—the one visible from the Strand was designed by Thomas Collcutt (who also designed Wigmore Hall), whereas the bedroom wing overlooking the Thames is by Mackmurdo. In 1929, the entrance court was restyled by Easton and Robertson, introducing a steel Art Deco look. The first manager was Cesar Ritz, who later founded the Ritz Hotel. The Savoy has boasted several resident artists: Claude Monet and James Whistler both painted river views from here. Famous chefs include Auguste Escoffier and Gordon Ramsey, and Pêche Melba and Melba toast were supposedly invented in these kitchens. Its forecourt is the only street in the United Kingdom where vehicles have to drive on the right-hand side.

1890 THOMAS COLLCUTT

This imposing red building dominates the west side of Cambridge Circus. The grand exterior is striped with red brick and cream faience. This was commissioned by Richard D'Oyly Carte in the late 1880s as the home of English grand opera, much as his Savoy Theatre on the Strand had become the home of light opera in the days of Gilbert and Sullivan. The foundation stone, laid by D'Oyly Carte's wife in 1888, can still be seen at the right of the entrance (almost at ground level). The Royal English Opera opened in January 1891 but proved unsuccessful, and D'Oyly Carte sold the theatre within a year. It was renamed the Palace Theatre of Varieties, and then, in 1911, the Palace Theatre. This was the venue for Fred Astaire's final stage musical, *Gay Divorce*, which opened in November 1933. Since 2004, the theatre has been refurbished, its fine marble walls uncovered and restored, and new chandeliers hung.

244

245

1776–86, 1830–35, AND 1856 SIR WILLIAM CHAMBERS,
SIR ROBERT SMIRKE, SIR JAMES PENNETHORNE

The first Somerset House was built in 1547–50 as a riverside mansion—one of a row of noblemen's houses—for the Lord Protector and Duke of Somerset. He was executed for treason in 1551 and the house was presented to Princess Elizabeth (queen by 1558). The bodies of Anne of Denmark, James I, and Cromwell all lay in state here. By 1775, the tired old building was demolished and a new non-royal Somerset House rose on the site. The present neo-classical building dates from 1776 and was later extended by Victorian wings to the north and south. Until Victoria Embankment was built, the building stood on large arches rising directly out of the Thames. It has been used by the Inland Revenue (now HM Revenue and Customs) since 1849, and, during the 1900s, was home to the General Register Office, where the records of births, deaths, and marriages were kept. In the late 1900s, the building became a centre for visual arts. Its Courtauld Gallery, whose holdings are old masters and impressionist paintings, is also home to the Gilbert Collection of decorative arts and the Hermitage Rooms (offering exhibitions on loan from St Petersburg's Hermitage Museum.) The courtyard—which sometimes features outdoor large-screen film events—has become the building's centrepiece, accessed via an impressive triple-arched gateway.

247

ONE ALDWYCH

247   WC2

1906–07 MEWÈS AND DAVIS

This grand Edwardian building was one of London's earliest steel-frame structures and is one of several creations by architects who brought their French styling to Edwardian London with the Ritz Hotel (they also built the Paris Ritz). One Aldwych has sturdy Norwegian granite facings, a Parisian-style façade and is crowned by a copper dome that makes a pleasing focal point. Like New York's Flatiron Building, it is designed to fit into a wedge-shaped footprint between the angle of the streets. Built initially for the *Morning Post* newspaper, it later housed a Lloyds Bank but, in 1998, was converted into an luxury hotel, restaurant and bar. This is still 'putting on the ritz' with hundreds of expensive original artworks in both public areas and guest rooms, and with a health club pool that boasts underwater music.

248

BUSH HOUSE

248   WC2

1923–35 HARVEY W. CORBETT

Bush House was in 1929 declared as the 'most expensive building in the world,' having cost around £2 million. This is home to the BBC's World Service department, which occupies four out of five wings of the building (the fifth wing housing HM Revenue and Customs). The BBC's lease on the building runs out in 2010, when the departments may move to Broadcasting House in Portland Place, W1. Although the design of the building is very British, it was commissioned, designed, and originally owned by Americans. In 1919, Irving T. Bush gained approval for his plans to construct a major new trade centre. The opening ceremony (performed by Lord Balfour in 1925) even took place on American Independence Day. Two statues by American artist, Malvina Hoffman, set at the building's entrance, symbolise Anglo-American friendship.

249

250

ST MARY-LE-STRAND

249   WC2

KING'S COLLEGE

250   WC2

1714-17 JAMES GIBBS

This parish is an ancient one. The earliest church stood on the site now occupied by Somerset House and, from Norman times to the Reformation, the Strand was home to many bishops and princes. The site of the present church was occupied in medieval times by Strand Cross—thought to date back to Norman times, perhaps as a market cross. Thomas à Becket is said to have been a rector here in the 1100s. The building of the present church was funded by the Commission for Building Fifty New Churches. Gibbs's architectural training had been in Rome—the church's Mannerist design reflects this, and its walls show a Michelangelo influence. The tower is not part of the original design. The present position of the church was, in 1634, the site of the first hackney carriage stand in England. A famous maypole was erected here in 1661—parts of which were sold to Sir Isaac Newton as the base for a telescope; the parents of Charles Dickens married here in 1809. During Edwardian times, the building became surrounded by roads. Today this is the official church of the Women's Royal Naval Service.

1829-35 SIR ROBERT SMIRKE

This formed part of an overall river frontage plan with Somerset House. The largest and second-longest-serving college in the University of London with over 21,000 registered students, it was founded in 1829 and named for King George IV. It had Church of England and political support as part of popular opposition to the humanist and egalitarian University College London (UCL). There is still a strong rivalry between King's and UCL, although they are now both part of the University of London. The former claims it is more famous, the latter that it is academically superior. The college's Students' Union is the oldest in London. King's is consistently rated in the top twenty universities in Europe. Its medical school is the largest in the United Kingdom. Perhaps the most famous research performed here was carried out by Rosalind Franklin and Maurice Wilkins; this led to the discovery of the structure of DNA by James D. Watson and Francis Crick. Famous alumni include Florence Nightingale, Sir Arthur C. Clarke, and Nobel Prize–winner Archbishop Desmond Tutu.

251

5 LITTLE ESSEX STREET
CHESHIRE CHEESE

251 · WC2

1500s (POSSIBLY EARLIER)

This is a small, intimate, back-street pub, a handsome, brick-built mid-Victorian hostelry with dark wood settles, panelled walls, and black beams overhead. The Jacobean-style leaded windows have frosted glass. Inside there are flagons, plates, a collection of American, Canadian, and English police shoulder-epaulettes and badges, and several butter dishes.

252

40 ESSEX STREET; FORMERLY THE ESSEX HEAD
THE EDGAR WALLACE

252 · WC2

FROM 1777

This black-painted pub has cream-coloured windows, solid square pilasters, and one main square room. The first pub was built on the site of Essex House. It was well-known to Dr Johnson —a member of Sam's Club, which first met on the premises in 1783. He noted, 'We meet thrice a week, and he who misses forfeits twopence.' In 1975, the pub was renamed to mark the centenary of the birth of mystery writer Edgar Wallace, and has lots of memorabilia donated by his daughter. The Edgar Wallace Society holds its annual lunch here.

253

20 DEVEREUX COURT
THE DEVEREUX

253 · WC2

1844

This handsome, pink stucco, neo-classical pub, with square sash windows, stands on the site of Essex House—until 1646 home to the Earls of Essex, including Robert Dudley, executed by Elizabeth I. The third earl led the Parliamentary army in the Civil War. As Essex House vanished, Devereux Court arrived, with taverns and coffeehouses, including the Grecian, haunt of Sir Isaac Newton, Edmund Halley, and Oliver Goldsmith. In the 1840s, it was replaced by Eldon Chambers and this tavern.

254

255

THE STRAND
ST CLEMENT DANES

254   WC2

1680 SIR CHRISTOPHER WREN

The first church here was probably built in
the 800s by Danes—many then lived between
Westminster and the City. A seafaring race,
they named the church for the patron saint of
mariners. This may be the church featured in
the nursery rhyme *Oranges and Lemons* but
St Clement Eastcheap also makes this claim.
It was rebuilt by William the Conqueror, and
then again in the Middle Ages, before being
demolished and rebuilt by Wren in a two-
storey design. The steeple was added in the
1700s by James Gibbs. In May 1941, German
bombing virtually destroyed the church; only
the tower, steeple, and outer walls survived.
It was restored and re-consecrated in October
1958, and became the Central Church of the
Royal Air Force—with statues outside of
RAF wartime leaders Arthur Harris and
Hugh Dowding.

213 STRAND
THE GEORGE

255   WC2

1723; 1890s

The George developed from a coffeehouse,
founded in 1723, but today this is a late-
Victorian-style inn with mock medieval half-
timber inside and out, leaded lights, wooden
barrels, black oak, and carving that includes
monks—one with a blue cat and one with a
blue dog. The sign outside depicts King
George III, but the pub was actually named
after its first owner, George Simpkins. Locals
here have included Oliver Goldsmith, Horace
Walpole, Samuel Johnson, and notorious
conman Henry Perfect, whose aliases included
the Rev. Mr Paul and the Rev. Mr Bennett.
Today, the legal profession from the nearby
Temple and Law Courts seek refreshment here
in between court proceedings.

256

ROYAL COURTS OF JUSTICE

1874–82 GEORGE EDMOND STREET

This is a grey stone edifice in Victorian Gothic style. It was the last Gothic revival building to be built in London. It houses the Court of Appeal and the High Court of Justice of England and Wales. The courts are open to the public in most cases. This complex of courtrooms, halls, and offices deals mainly with civil litigation through the sessions of the Court of Appeal, the High Court of Justice, and the Crown Court. It was completed in 1882 but its design emulates thirteenth-century building styles. Here are the courts of admiralty, divorce, probate, chancery, appeals, and the Queen's Bench. George Edmond Street was a solicitor turned architect; it is thought that the strain of the construction of the Royal Courts led to his untimely death. The building is surrounded by the four Inns of Court and has almost five kilometres (over three miles) of corridors, more than a thousand rooms (including eighty-eight courtrooms) and 35 million bricks on its 2-hectare (5-acre) site.

257

258

53A CAREY STREET

THE SEVEN STARS

257   WC2

CHANCERY LANE AND CAREY STREET

THE LAW SOCIETY LIBRARY

258   WC2

1602

This was once the location of the bankruptcy courts, and the term 'being in Carey Street' used to mean being broke. The ancient, long low pub was first known as the League of Seven Stars, after the seven provinces of Holland—its first customers being Dutch sailors who settled hereabouts in the 1600s. Set opposite to the rear entrance of the Law Courts, it attracts many drinkers from the legal profession and the walls are decorated with cartoons of eminent lawyers. The simple bar has bare floorboards, oak beams, and scrubbed tables with checked tablecloths. It was one the few buildings in the area to survive the Great Fire, and in 2002 celebrated its 400th anniversary with a street party.

1902 H. PERCY ADAMS AND CHARLES HOLDEN

The Law Society (formerly the Law Institute) dates from 1825, and its extensive library holds some 80,000 books. This building is in stripped classical style, featuring horizontal lines on the cornice and window heads, and Venetian windows arranged symmetrically across the corner. The lovely stained-glass windows of the Law Society's Hall show the arms of the former Serjeants (that were once part of the Serjeants Inn). One of the architects, Holden, also designed the Senate House and two Piccadilly Line underground stations. The Law Society Library may be seen as the first step in this journey towards English modernism.

259

260

LINCOLN'S INN	
NEW SQUARE	
259	SW2

c. 1690 HENRY SERLE

Although home to many legal chambers in suitable collegiate-style buildings, New Square is not part of the Lincoln's Inn complex and is a U-shape rather than a full square. Its sheltered position has allowed a vine and a fig tree to thrive. It is connected to Carey Street by a quaint arched passageway and thence to Lincoln's Inn itself. The saying 'We shall be in Carey Street soon' referred to the many insolvency lawyers who used to practise here.

LINCOLN'S INN	
OLD BUILDINGS	
260	SW2

1524–1613

Lincoln's Inn was founded in the 1300s, but what is today called the Old Buildings was completed later, in the 1500s. Of the fourteenth-century structures, only number 1 remains, its entrance place in the northern segment of the Gate House. The very attractive turreted brick houses shown here underwent extensive reconstruction work in the 1960s, especially numbers 22 to 24. Today, the numbers run from 16 to 24, with mixed ordering.

261

GATEHOUSE

261   WC2

1517-21

The main entrance into the inn used to be from Chancery Lane through this gatehouse—until the Great Hall was built in the 1840s and the present entrance from Lincoln's Inn Fields was constructed. The heavy oak doors date from 1564, and the bricks were made on site. Nearly a third of the total cost of £345 for building the gatehouse was contributed by Sir Thomas Lovell, who had been a member of the inn for over twenty years. (He helped to bring the Tudors to the throne at the Battle of Bosworth in 1485.) Much of the brickwork is original but the windows were added in the 1600s. Above the gateway are three fine coats of arms.

262

CHAPEL

262   WC2

1619-23 PROBABLY INIGO JONES

This mixture of Gothic, Perpendicular, and Tuscan styles, stands on pillars over an undercroft where anguished mothers left their babies, trusting the inn to bring them up well; they were often named Lincoln. Distinguished Inn members were interred here. Until 1839, burials of women were not allowed but Lord Brougham fought to change this on behalf of his daughter. Most of the pews were made in 1623 by 'Price the joiner.' The chapel bells toll a 9.00 p.m. curfew. They also ring if a bencher dies—possibly since Dr John Donne (a preacher here) wrote 'No man is an island…any man's death diminishes me…never send to know for whom the bell tolls; it tolls for thee.'

236

LINCOLN'S INN NEW HALL

236   WC2

1845 PHILIP HARDWICK

By the beginning of the 1800s, as its membership grew, Lincoln Inn's Old Hall was beginning to prove too small, and the foundation stone for a new building was laid on April 20, 1843. Ultimately, the new hall was opened by Queen Victoria in October 1845 (an event depicted in an artist's impression at the south end of the hall) and, at twice the size of the Old Hall, was now the largest of any inn. During the four twenty-three-day dining terms, the hall is used for dining. It also provides lunches for members all year. The Great Hall hosts the formal ceremony that calls students of the inn to the Bar—to become barristers.

LINCOLN'S INN
OLD HALL

264   WC2

1490s; 1624 POSSIBLY INIGO JONES; 1924-27 REBUILT SIR JOHN SIMPSON

A tablet on the outside states that the hall was built in the fifth year of King Henry VII—Henry having come to the throne in 1485. Sir Thomas More joined the inn in 1496. In 1624, the hall was enlarged by a southern bay; from 1924–27, Sir John Simpson dismantled the hall stone by stone and brick by brick, and straightened the timbers. You can still see location numbers on the bricks. From 1717, this was a court of justice, and from 1737 served as the High Court of Chancery at certain times of the year. Today, it is used for examinations, lectures, and social functions. The opening scene of Dickens's *Bleak House* is set here.

264

LINCOLN'S INN
OLD SQUARE

265   WC2

1872-87

Lincoln's Inn is London's largest square. However, just opposite, lies the smaller but equally historic Old Square, much of which (numbers 8–15) stands on a site that used to be known as the 'Old Buildings.' Old Square certainly appears to match its name, featuring fine historic buildings that would be perfectly at home next to an Oxford University quadrangle and that have an ambience reeking of antiquity. This is still the place to find barristers, clerks of the court, and other legal services.

265

LINCOLN'S INN
STONE BUILDINGS

266   WC2

1775-80 AND 1845 PHILIP AND PHILIP CHARLES HARDWICK

Apart from number 7 (built in 1845), this stone block was raised between 1775 and 1780. Despite World War II damage, the exterior has remained largely unchanged. Number 10 was formerly the Six Clerks' office, linked to the old Court of Chancery, but today is the Regimental Headquarters of the Inns of Court and City Yeomanry of the Territorial Army. High on the wall of number 4 is a sundial erected when William Pitt was Treasurer in 1794; his chambers were here. Back in 1585, ninety-five members of the inn pledged to defend Queen Elizabeth against Spain and, since then, in times of national peril, volunteers have been recruited from among the lawyers.

266

267

FORMER PUBLIC RECORD OFFICE

267   WC2

1851–96 JAMES PENNETHORNE, SIR JOHN TAYLOR

At the beginning of the 1800s, public records were scattered among fifty or so buildings, including the Tower of London, the treasuries at Westminster, the State Paper Office, and casual wards, prisons, and castles. In 1807, a commission reported that this was a 'growing national scandal' that encouraged falsification and embezzlement. A central organisation was at last established by Act of Parliament in 1838, and this massive mock-Tudor building in Chancery Lane received its first deposits in the late 1860s. Pennethorne, architect and surveyor to the Office of Works, had studied under Augustus Pugin and John Nash, as well as in Italy. His functional Gothic design faces Fetter Lane; Taylor's later extension and museum (holding such treasures as the *Domesday Book* and Shakespeare's will) was completed in 1903 and faces Chancery Lane. Selecting, storing, preserving, and making available to the public ever-increasing numbers of documents and housing ancient records (some medieval) had its problems; finally a new office opened at Kew in 1977. This was expanded in the 1990s and, in due course, all records were transferred there or to the Family Records Centre in Islington. The Chancery Lane building was taken over by King's College, London, which uses it as a library.

HOLY TRINITY

1910–12 BELCHER AND JOASS

This church was originally built on Little Queen Street (which became part of Kingsway) in 1829–31, on the site of the house where Mary Lamb had stabbed her mother in a fit of madness in 1796. Galleries on either side of the organ were erected for the use of Holborn Charity Children until they moved to a new church adjoining the workhouse. This church was demolished in 1909, after having been undermined by the excavations for the Piccadilly Line—and a new church rose on the site. It has a lovely stone façade in Roman baroque style, with some English baroque influences evident. It is modelled on Pietro da Cortona's church of St Maria Della Pace, in Rome. Its simple interior has white plastered walls with exposed brick above.

68

SIR JOHN SOANE'S MUSEUM

1792–94, 1808–12 AND 1823–24 SIR JOHN SOANE

Today, this former house and studio of neo-classical architect Sir John Soane (number 13) is—with its neighbour—a museum of architecture, whose best parts are at the rear of the museum. These top-lit rooms provide a miniature version of the ingenious lighting contrived by Soane for the top-lit banking halls at the Bank of England. The picture gallery has walls of folding panels, to house multiple items. The domed ceiling of the breakfast room has influenced architects all over the world. Two courtyards outside contain collections of artefacts and medieval stonework from the Palace of Westminster. Soane demolished and rebuilt all three houses from numbers 12 to 14. Number 12 was externally a brick house, typical of the period, while number 13 was rebuilt in two phases between 1808–9 and 1812. Number 14 was bought in 1823 and turned into a picture gallery. The museum was established by a private Act of Parliament in 1833, taking effect later— on Soane's death in 1837. The trustees bought the main house at number 14 with the help of the Heritage Lottery Fund, and this is being restored to expand the museum's educational activities.

269

270

271

272

1911 SIR JOHN BURNET

On the corner of Wild Court, this freestanding, six-storey commercial office building has fine Portland stone and decorated bronze. It is both elegant and traditional with an austere, stripped classicism that would be greatly imitated throughout Britain in the 1920s and '30s. Scotland's foremost interwar architect, Sir John James Burnet, formed a practice with his father. He studied at the École des Beaux-Arts in Paris in 1878 and was responsible for many greatly admired buildings in both Scotland and London. He was knighted to honour his achievements after designing the British Museum's King Edward VII Gallery.

GREAT QUEEN STREET

FREEMASON'S HALL

270   WC2

1927-33 ASHLEY AND NEWMAN

Roughly half of the south side of Great Queen Street is taken up by the United Grand Lodge of England, the headquarters of the English Freemasons. It boasts a magnificent tower and door on the corner of Wild Street, but when it was built, its Edwardian style was already twenty years out of fashion. The Grand Lodge has the date 1717 near the top of the building in deference to the first English Lodge formed then. It is Grade II listed—and the only Art Deco building in London that remains unchanged and still used for its original purpose. This is the third Freemason's Hall on the site. In 1775, the Freemason's Tavern stood where the New Connaught Rooms (at numbers 61–65) now stand. It was replaced in the nineteenth century. Number 23 Great Queen Street houses the Central Regalia, where Masonic aprons are sold. The current building was a memorial to 3,224 freemasons who died in active service in the World War I. It was initially known as the Masonic Peace Memorial, but was changed to Freemason's Hall at the outbreak of the World War II.

59-60 LINCOLN'S INN FIELDS

LINDSEY HOUSE

272   WC2

1640 PROBABLY INIGO JONES

When its houses were originally built, Lincoln's Inn Fields was a very fashionable part of London and this was the city's first garden square—laid out by William Newton in 1640—with houses on three sides. The only building still surviving from this time is Lindsey House, so-named because it was, for a period in the 1700s, owned by the Earls of Lindsey. Its design is attributed to Inigo Jones but this is uncertain. It was built in brick but later stuccoed, and has a very pleasing, almost theatrical symmetry, with double doors and lovely, slender first-floor windows set between tall pillars.

EAST CENTRAL LONDON (EC)

East Central London spreads out from around the City of London—often referred to as the Square Mile, as it is about one square mile (2.6 square kilometres) in area. In the medieval period this was the full extent of London, as distinct from the separate village of Westminster.

The city is where London began. Roman walls still run alongside London Wall, and the remains of a temple to Mithras were found on what was once the bank of the Walbrook stream. The ancient city was surrounded by a fortress wall with seven gates: Aldgate, Bishopsgate, Moorgate, Cripplegate, Aldersgate, Newgate, and Ludgate. These have long since vanished, but their names live on in streets and buildings. Just as in Cheapside, the names give clues as to what was once sold here—Milk Street, Bread Street, and Poultry.

There have been over six hundred Lord Mayors of London—the first being Henry FitzAilwyn in 1189, with the citizens' right to elect a mayor formalised by King John in 1215. Sir Francis Child, Lord Mayor in 1698, is credited with having founded the banking profession when he left his goldsmith business for the world of finance.

The major occupations here are still banking and finance, with more foreign banks in London (well over five hundred) than any other centre worldwide. The Bank of England, the 'Old Lady of Threadneedle Street,' was founded in 1694, and has issued banknotes ever since. Author of *The Wind in the Willows* Kenneth Grahame was a secretary here. In 1836, a man working on sewers discovered a tunnel leading into the bullion vaults of the bank. He sent a note arranging to meet the directors there at midnight and duly emerged from below a flagstone. He was rewarded for his honesty—and the tunnel was blocked in.

The origins of the London Stock Exchange go back to the coffeehouses of 1600s. Lloyds insurance also began here, initially insuring ships and cargoes, but its undertakings since have covered everything from a two-thousand-year-old wine jar to crocodile attacks and spider bites in Australia. They have protected the taste buds of food critic and gourmet Egon Ronay, Betty Grable's 'million-dollar' legs, and a merchant navy officer who sailed from Dover to France in a bathtub; he was insured provided the plug stayed in place!

The first printing press was set up in about 1500 in Fleet Street (named after the River Fleet, which runs close by) and, in time, this area would become the hub of the newspaper industry, just as most of the livery companies and guilds gathered around medieval Guildhall.

A hundred thousand Londoners died in the Great Plague, which struck London in 1664–65, and then the following year, four-fifths of the city burnt down in the Great Fire—but the city survived. Now, thousands of people commute into its offices, banks, and shops each day to work.

Here are some incredible buildings, from St Paul's Cathedral to the new Lloyds of London and the Gherkin, but this is also a place that thronged with people—from the illustrious names like Samuel Pepys, Doctor Johnson, and Sir Christopher Wren to the unnamed builders who raised these great edifices. One such unfortunate workman is remembered by a little sculpture of carved mice on a building in Philpot Lane. This commemorates the fact that, during its construction, he had been accused of stealing another labourer's sandwiches and was somehow pushed to his death. The real culprits were the mice—now sculpted here. It is in such details that the city's story is encapsulated.

EC1   EC1

275
274
273
276
Spencer St.
North ampton
Rosebery Avenue
Moreland St.
City Road
Longmore Row
EC1
277
279
280
281
282
284
285
287
286
288
290
291
292
293
289
Holborn
Clerkenwell Road
St. John Sq.
Farringdon Road
Charterhouse St.
Clerkenwell Green
Percival St.
Level St.
308
307
309
310
311
312
313
314
315
316
317
318
319
320
321
322
Old Street
Roscoe
Chequer St.
Dufferin St.
Whitecross St.
Bunhill Row
Worship St.
Leonard St.
Great Eastern St.
Finsbury Square
Finsbury Pavement
Wilson St.
294
295
296
297
298
299
300
301
306
303
304
305
302
331
332
333
334
335
336
337
Beech St.
Silk St.
325
326
327
328
329
330
323
324
EC2
358
357
359
360
361
362
363
364
365
366
Moorgate
Finsbury Circus
Bishopsgate
London Wall
356
352
339
340
342
343
344
345
346
348
347
349
350
351
352
353
354
355
Guildhall
Gresham St.
Cheapside
Poultry
Threadneedle St.
Princes St.
Cornhill
367
368
369
370
371
372
373
374
375
376
377
378
379
380
381
382
383
384
385
386
387
388
389
390
391
392
393
394
395
396
397
398
399
400
401
402
403
404
405
406
407
408
409
410
411
412
413
414
415
416
417
418
419
420
421
422
423
424
425
426
427
428
429
430
431
432
433
434
435
436
437
438
439
440
441
442
443
444
445
446
447
448
449
450
451
452
453
454
455
456
457
458
459
460
461
462
463
464
465
466
467
468
469
474
037
Fleet Street
Ludgate Hill
St. Bride
New Fetter Lane
Holborn Viaduct
Newgate St.
New Change
Amen
Churchyard
Carter Lane
Queen Victoria St.
Upper Thames St.
Victoria Embankment
Tudor St.
Watling
Cannon St.
Eastcheap
Great Tower St.
Fenchurch St.
Mark Lane
Leadenhall St.
Aldgate
Mino
Tower Hill
Trinity Square
St. Mary Axe
Lothbury
EC4
EC3
RIVER THAMES
St. Andrews St.

EC1 Clerkenwell
EC2 Moorgate
EC3 Monument
EC4 Fleet Street

273

FINSBURY TOWN HALL

273   EC1

1895-99 G. EVANS VAUGHAN

Finsbury Town Hall was built in 1895 to serve the Metropolitan Borough of Finsbury. With revived Tudor style and rosy coloured brick, it is a flamboyant building, heavily decorated with pillars and piers, arches, and tall chimneys—not to mention an ornate wrought-iron canopy over the entrance, and a very pretty clock. In 1939–40, its basement housed a civil defence reporting centre to protect key targets in the area, including the Research Building on the opposite side of Rosebery Avenue (see page165). During the threat of nuclear attack in the early 1950s, its basement served for a while as a sub-area control unit.

274

275

276

1938 SIR HOWARD ROBERTSON

Set behind railings, this sweeping building curves around to culminate in an impressive rounded structure with upright lines that may be seen to echo the shape of a water tower. Its award-winning architect also designed the Royal Horticultural Hall in 1928, and the Shell Tower on the South Bank in 1961.

1931 FRANK MATCHAM AND COMPANY;
1998 RENTON HOWARD WOOD LEVIN ARCHITECTS AND NICHOLAS HARE ARCHITECTS

This renovated theatre, the sixth on the site, seats 1,500 plus a further 200 in the Lilian Baylis Theatre. It is the first completed London project funded by the National Lottery. The building includes a vast frontage of glass that reveals the principal staircase and the arriving audience — usually here to enjoy ballet, contemporary dance, or opera. Richard Sadler launched his Musick House in 1683, the name Sadler's Wells a combination of his name and the medicinal wells discovered on his property — effective against 'dropsy, jaundice, scurvy, green sickness . . . ulcers, fits of the mother, virgin's fever.' During the 1800s, performers here included actor Edmund Kean, comedian Joe Grimaldi, music-hall star Marie Lloyd, and founder of the theatrical dynasty Roy Redgrave.

1896 EDWARD MOUNTFORD

This powerful building was part of the Edwardian baroque revival. A Grade II–listed college building, its grand entrance with ornate detailing boasts a tower topped by a shallow dome. Behind this, the triangular section of building is set neatly into the taller structures behind. Sadly, in May 2001, a major fire damaged the building and some parts have had to undergo major repairs. City University sprang from the Northampton Institute, founded in 1894 and named after the Marquess of Northampton — on whose lands it was built. The university has close links with the city and the professions. A new building for the School of Social Sciences opened in Northampton Square in 2004.

277

278

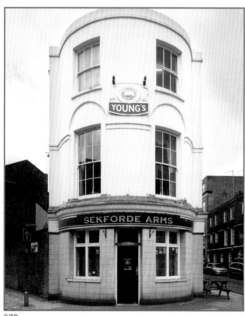

279

280

281

282

FINSBURY HEALTH CENTRE

277   EC1

1935–72 BERTHOLD LUBETKIN

This Grade I-listed building has been in continual use since it arrived as a startling new building, epitomising the exciting changes in Modern Movement architecture. Berthold Lubetkin, born in 1901 in Georgia, Russia, was one of the great modernist architects, and founder of the radical Tecton group. He was responsible for the excellent penguin pool at the London Zoo. The health centre, a truly revolutionary project, was part of a slum clearance in Finsbury and reflected the style of Le Corbusier's public buildings.

ROSEBERY SQUARE

278   EC1

1889–92

In Victorian times, the creation of Rosebery Avenue and Rosebery Square was a somewhat vain attempt to improve the slum areas by creating wider streets and more space between the buildings. This resulted in the demolition of the western side of Coldbath Square—thus named because one Mr Baynes, hoping to make his fortune, had raised a bath-house over a spring he had discovered here in 1697.

SEKFORDE ARMS

279   EC1

1830s

In a quiet area of Georgian and Victorian terraces, this handsome, yellow-tiled corner pub has an inviting interior with a large saloon and small snug. Thomas Seckford came to London in the 1500s to make his fortune and became a judge and MP. Elizabeth I granted him three acres in Clerkenwell, where he built a grand house. When he died in 1587, the rents from his London estate helped to fund good works. Part of the estate became a house of detention—developed in the 1830s into homes, school, chapel, distillery—and the Sekforde Arms.

ST JAMES

280   EC1

1788–92 JAMES CARR

Georgian St James is brick-built with a tall, white Palladian stone tower in Portland stone, topped by an ornate spire. The interior still retains some remains of the twelfth-century church, plus two fine staircases and a gallery. There are memorials to the Smithfield martyrs, a pleasing window, and an organ.

MARX MEMORIAL LIBRARY

281   EC1

1738 (SURVEYOR) JAMES STEERE

This neat Georgian house is Grade II-listed and cost £332 to build for the housing of a Welsh charity school by the Honourable and Loyal Society of Ancient Britons. It is as immaculate as a new doll's house. Here in 1902, in a tiny office, Vladimir Lenin edited and printed issues 22 to 38 of *Iskra* (*The Spark*). Since 1933, the building has housed the Marx Memorial Library, with over 100,000 books, periodicals, and manuscripts on all aspects of Marxism, socialism, and the working-class movement, plus a Workers' School.

OLD SESSIONS HOUSE

282   EC1

1779–82 (ALTERED 1850s AND 1878) THOMAS ROGERS

This was once the largest busiest courthouse in England, replacing the original Sessions House near Smithfield market. The Portland stone front has bas-relief panels, carved figures representing Mercy and Justice, plus a portrait medallion of George III. Here were courtrooms, dungeons, and rather better accommodation for the judges. Its entrance hall and dome were modelled on the Pantheon in Rome, with fine heraldic detail. It ceased to function as a court in 1920 and now serves as a conference and Masonic meeting house.

283

BOURNE ESTATE

283   EC1

1901–07 LCC ARCHITECTS DEPARTMENT; OWEN FLEMING

This five-storey, brick-built mansion block once housed nearly four thousand people, far more than its façade—albeit extensive—would suggest. Arched openings lead to courtyards and buildings beyond. Built in classical Edwardian grand style in a Victorian street on a medieval site, this is a place where history converges. Clerkenwell developed from a tiny hamlet in the 1100s (serving a nunnery and a priory) to crowded slum areas by the 1800s. It wasn't until the 1990s that the neighbourhood became once more fashionable.

284

24 BRITTON STREET

OFFICES AND FLATS

284   EC1

1976–79 YRM PARTNERSHIP WITH FITZROY ROBINSON AND PARTNERS

The name Clerkenwell derives from 'Clerk's well.' Medieval parish clerks met here to play music where healing waters were discovered. This modern structure makes no concession to its historic surroundings: it is an orderly office building, the upper levels raised on a podium that also creates a courtyard at the higher street level. Its frame is covered with gleaming aluminium panels. Once upon a Dickens's story, Fagin in *Oliver Twist* had his pick-pocketing den just off nearby Clerkenwell Green.

285

ST JOHN'S SQUARE

ST JOHN

285   EC1

CRYPT 1140–80; GATE 1504 SIR THOMAS DOCWRA; RESTORED BY JOHN OLDRED SCOTT 1903

St John's Gate was rebuilt as Priory Gate, still standing here. This square was the birthplace of *Gentleman's Magazine* in 1731—to which Dr Johnson contributed. The gatehouse became the headquarters of the St John Ambulance Association in the 1900s. An Early English crypt lies beneath the church where, in the 1100s, stood the priory church—damaged during the Peasant's Revolt in 1381 and dissolved under Henry VIII. The circular site of the original church is marked out in cobbles.

THE JERUSALEM TAVERN

286   EC1

1723

This was once a merchant's house and then a clock and watchmaker's workshop; it has been a pub since 1996—named after another famous hostelry visited by Dr Johnson, Goldsmith, Garrick, and Handel. The front room has bay windows and a tiny main bar. Britton Street (originally Red Lion Street) took its name from Thomas Britton, a coal man. He lived in the loft over his coal shed in Jerusalem Passage. Leading musicians would join Britton in his loft as he played his viola; even the young Handel played a miniature organ here.

286

A HOUSE OF TRIANGLES

287   EC1

1987 CZWG ARCHITECTS (CAMPBELL, ZOGOLOVITCH, WILKINSON AND GOUGH)

This unusual property in Clerkenwell focuses on diamond patterns and triangular shapes—from the pitched roof that houses a studio to the latticework on the windows and the diagonals of the exterior screens and balconies. It has concrete log lintels, and the brickwork has been used to create interesting patterns as it mutates from dark tones at the base of the building to lighter tones above.

287

WREN HOUSE

288   EC1

POSSIBLY SIR CHRISTOPHER WREN

Built by Lord Hatton to serve the needs of the neighbourhood after St Andrew's Holborn had been destroyed in the Great Fire, this church was adapted for use as a charity school in about 1696. Severely damaged by incendiary bombs during World War II, it has been reconstructed to include offices inside—the restored facade includes the fascinating figures of scholars in eighteenth-century costume that, during the war, had been sent for safekeeping to Berkshire.

288

289

290

PRUDENTIAL INSURANCE

289   EC1

1879, 1899-1906 ALFRED AND PAUL WATERHOUSE

This piece of Gothic splendour in bright pink-red terracotta reflects the status of insurance companies in the 1800s. The building was extended between 1899 and 1906 to achieve its grandiose effect. The main façade is symmetrical, with tall lancet windows, multiple gables and spires, and a central tower with a fine pyramid-shaped roof (like those of several skyscrapers in New York). Set in a corner of the piazza behind the great building is a little shrine housing a bust of Charles Dickens, who began his writing career in rooms near here, penning *Pickwick Papers* while sitting in Furnival's Inn.

BLEEDING HEART TAVERN

290   EC1

1746

This tavern was first recorded in a register of licensed victuallers of 1746. In 1785, the Bleeding Heart and its yard were part of lot 71 when the Hatton family sold the whole area in an auction. The name may derive from the arms of the Douglas family (which include a red heart); or from the Church of the Bleeding Heart on or near the site; or from the 1626 murder in the crypt of Sir Christopher Hatton's widow, Lady Elizabeth, during a ball at Hatton House. She was killed by her jilted lover, the Spanish ambassador Gondemar. Dickens chose it for a location in *Little Dorrit* and *Oliver Twist*, and Fagin's den was set close by. The whole area was cleared and rebuilt in 1845-46. Inside are panelled walls and a collection of Dickens's books and prints.

291

292

ELY PLACE
ST ETHELREDA
291   ECI

HOLBORN
ELY PLACE
292   ECI

1291 JOHN DE KIRKEBY; 1874 RESTORED BY FATHER LOCKHART

St Ethelreda was an abbess who founded Ely Abbey in the seventh century and an Anglo-Saxon saint; part of one of her hands is an ancient relic that has been preserved in a jewelled casket here. Despite being hemmed in on both sides, the church has a pleasing façade with the sweeping curves of its stained-glass windows singularly beautiful. This church served as the private chapel for the bishops of Ely. It also has a crypt and undercroft in what may be the oldest pre-Reformation Catholic church in England. The best strawberries in the city were said to be grown in the gardens here, and a strawberry fayre—mentioned in Shakespeare's *Richard III*—is still held here every June. The building was used as a prison and hospital during the Civil War.

1773 CHARLES COLE AND JOHN GORHAM

Neat rows of houses and clipped bay trees stand on the site of a palace, built as the Bishop of Ely's London base. Here, powerful men of the Church played host to Henry VIII and Elizabeth I—the Queen made the bishop rent some of the land to her courtier, Sir Christopher Hatton—hence the name Hatton Garden—and she was said to have danced around its maypole. The palace was demolished in 1772 but eighteenth-century Ely Place is still a sanctuary, its entrance watched by a beadle from a tiny lodge with wrought-iron gates. Once in the street, you are in sanctuary and cannot be arrested. A passageway leads to Ye Olde Mitre tavern, dating from 1546 (see page173).

293

294

YE OLDE MITRE

293   EC1

CHARTERHOUSE STREET, SMITHFIELD

SMITHFIELD MARKET

294   EC1

1546; REBUILT AFTER 1772

This ancient tavern is hidden down an alleyway with an old crooked street lamp. First built for the servants of the palace of the Bishops of Ely, the tiny tavern is, technically, still part of Cambridgeshire, and the pub license was issued there for centuries. Its small sign is in the shape of a bishop's mitre, and a stone mitre from the bishops' palace gatehouse is built into a wall, nearly hidden under the ivy. There are two cosy, wood-panelled bars. The preserved trunk of a cherry tree, which marked the boundary of the diocese, is in the corner of the front bar. Queen Elizabeth I is said to have done a maypole dance around this.

1961–63 T. P. BENNETT AND SON

Reconstruction and modernisation of this ancient market has cost over £70 million. A new poultry house and forty-four temperature-controlled stalls have been installed, and now there are proposals for further development by architects KPF. Here, neat roof triangles are echoed by hexagonal features on the walls below. The market began with 'Smoothfield' horse market and fair some eight hundred years ago, and it was long a place for jousting and execution. In 1357, the kings of England and France attended a royal tournament here. It was converted into a proper meat market in 1615. Two centuries later, Horace Jones, the great Victorian architect, was commissioned to build the 'new' Smithfield—a wrought-iron and glass edifice completed in 1868.

295

THE BISHOPS FINGER

295   EC1

1890s

The modern name of the pub derived from a strong ale brand; this in turn was named after a road sign from the brewery's home county of Kent. The signs were meant to represent a bishop's finger beckoning pilgrims, showing them the way along the holy route to Canterbury. The signs (and the ale) were also sometimes called the Nun's Delight! The pub's exterior is neat and plain, and the interior, with bare, polished floorboards, has a small single bar downstairs and a second one upstairs.

296

WEST SMITHFIELD

ST BARTHOLOMEW'S HOSPITAL

296   EC1

1729-70, 1834 JAMES GIBBS AND PHILIP HARDWICK

St Bartholomew's (St Bart's) is London's oldest hospital, having provided medical care on the same site for longer than any other hospital in England. It began in 1123 as an Augustinian priory and hospice. Here, after the Peasants Revolt in 1381, Wat Tyler took refuge, only to be dragged out and beheaded at the hospital entrance. The great hall and main staircase are English baroque with murals painted free of charge by Hogarth in 1734. The church was added in 1823. A Venetian gateway leads into a courtyard surrounded by the Palladian Gibbs Court, raised in fine Bath stone. In 1850, Elizabeth Blackwell, a pioneer of medicine as a career for women, was allowed to study here.

297

HOLBORN VIADUCT

HOLY SEPULCHRE
WITHOUT NEWGATE

297   EC1

MID-1400s; 1666-70 REBUILT; 1878 RESTORED

Built on the site of a Saxon church, with its west tower still dating from the 1400s, this is the largest parish church in the city. Named in Oranges and Lemons as the bells of Old Bailey, the church bells used to toll for executions in Newgate prison while the church clerk rang the execution handbell (now in a glass case in the nave) outside the condemned person's cell. Conductor Sir Henry Wood, a former organist at the church, is buried here—as are composer John Ireland, singer Dame Nellie Melba, and John Smith, governor of Virginia and friend of Pocahontas.

126 NEWGATE STREET
VIADUCT TAVERN
298   EC1

1869

The tavern cellars were once part of Newgate prison. Today, this Victorian pub has a large, curved frontage facing the Old Bailey; an ornate, red-painted, plaster ceiling over beaten, patterned copper; and a horseshoe bar with mahogany barley-sugar-twist pillars. Three paintings of maidens represent agriculture, banking, and the arts. The 'arts' painting was either shot or bayoneted by a drunken World War I soldier and still bears the scar. Small busts depict fifteen former hanging judges from the courts opposite. Ghosts 'seen' here include a prostitute murdered in the ladies' toilet, and Fred—who likes to move objects about and turn off lights.

298

NEWGATE STREET
CHRISTCHURCH
299   EC1

1677-87 SIR CHRISTOPHER WREN

In 1224, an order of the Franciscans was given a poor piece of land around which such streets as Stinking Lane and the Shambles sprang up. In 1306, they raised a magnificent church, possibly the largest in England at the time. After the Dissolution, it became a parish church and, following the Great Fire, was rebuilt by Wren on a smaller scale. In ever smaller stages, triple-tiered squares of columns form the steeple. The bell stage has segmental pediments, and the tiny spire is crowned with a vase. The church was gutted during the 1942 Blitz and only the tower remains as a memorial, now standing in a garden.

299

ALDERSGATE STREET
ST BOTOLPH
300   EC1

1788-91 NATHANIEL WRIGHT

Completed in 1791, this church has a late-Georgian stuccoed exterior. Its fine interior has a decorated plaster ceiling; original woodwork, including rich wooden galleries and box pews; an elegant organ case; and an oak pulpit set above a carved palm tree. Some of the memorials date from the original fourteenth-century church. Today, the churchyard is known as ' Postman's Park' because so many workers from the nearby Post Office headquarters come to relax here. Victorian artist George Frederick Watts dedicated one wall to a set of plaques marking acts of bravery and self-sacrifice, and 1973 saw the arrival of a bronze Minotaur by sculptor Michael Ayrton.

300

301

302

WAREHOUSE

301   EC1

1858 T. YOUNG AND SON

Little Britain is a small cluster of narrow streets and courts near St Bartholomew's Hospital and Smithfield. In ancient times it was the residence of the Dukes of Brittany—hence the name—and at one time it was home to numerous booksellers behind low arched doorways. As warehouses go, this one is a gem, with its multiple arched windows, tiers of arcades, columns, cornice—and detailing that gives the whole façade a richness generally reserved for less functional buildings.

ST BARTHOLOMEW THE GREAT

302   EC1

1123; RESTORED 1880–90 SIR ASTON WEBB

This is a piece of medieval London and one of the city's oldest churches. It began in 1123 as an Augustinian priory and hospital, raised under Henry I (who had some twenty-five illegitimate children, more than any other English king, and was the fourth son of William the Conqueror). The church survived the Great Fire of 1666 and the bombs of both world wars, and has appeared in *Four Weddings and a Funeral, Shakespeare in Love, The End of the Affair*, and in BBC television's *Madame Bovary*. Today's church has grown around the old priory building with its apsidal east end—rebuilt in the 1800s when the Lady Chapel (built c. 1330) was restored. Part of the chancel and crossing are original.

303

38 CLOTH FAIR

RISING SUN

303   EC1

c. 1800s

Set in an alley, this old pub spent some time as an office but has now been rescued and restored. It has brown marble at ground level and brown London brick above. There is an attractive court with hanging baskets and window boxes while, inside, two rooms are divided by wooden partitions with a pressed paper ceiling and bare floorboards. In the early nineteenth century, the upstairs room was reputedly the haunt of body-snatchers who would steal corpses from the nearby graveyard of St Bartholomew's church and sell them to St Bartholomew's hospital.

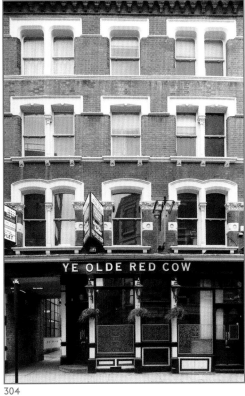

304

71 LONG LANE

YE OLDE RED COW

304   EC1

1854

One of the earliest ancient taverns of Smithfield, named after an old rhyme:

The Olde Red Cow gives good milk now,
'tis such good liquor 'twould puzzle a vicar.

Today the very small, ground-floor bar is smartly refitted but a painting in the Guildhall depicts the tavern as it appeared in 1854. The pub's show-business landlord of the 1970s and '80s, Dick O'Shea, used to welcome friends here that included actor and principal instigator of the Mermaid theatre, Bernard Miles, and actor-writer Peter Ustinov.

305

41–42 CLOTH FAIR

TIMBER HOUSES

305   EC1

c. 1640

Cloth Fair has long been associated with the drapery and tailoring trade. Near here, in the Middle Ages, was held the largest cloth and clothing fair in the country that, by the 1500s, lasted for a fortnight every August. Sadly, most of the city's timber houses burned to the ground in the Great Fire and brick buildings sprang up in their place. These fine specimens were among those few houses that escaped the flames. Owned by the Landmark Trust, they are set on the corner of narrow Rising Sun Court and Cloth Court. Tall timber windows, capped by pediments, are set above arches at street level. They provide a tantalising glimpse of pre-Wren London.

4–5 CHARTERHOUSE SQUARE

CHARTERHOUSE SQUARE

306   EC1

1727–33

Charterhouse Square dates from about 1700. It developed as a residential quarter in the 1600s, on the site of earlier plague pits. One of the city's few remaining gated squares, it was enclosed by 1717 and improved in 1741; the wrought-iron gates were added in the early 1800s. Its fine diagonal walks are lined with lime trees and fine mansions set upon three sides. Old monastic buildings from the 1300s line the northern side. These four-storey houses seem rather stern, despite their many windows and lovely surroundings. Florin Court, on the eastern side, featured in the 1990s Hercule Poirot television series.

306

307

GOSWELL ROAD, GOLDEN LANE ESTATE

GREAT ARTHUR HOUSE

307   EC1

MID-1960s CHAMBERLIN, POWELL AND BON (CP&B)

Great Arthur House was, for a brief time, the tallest residential building in London. It has a distinctive 'space shuttle' feature on top which some have compared to Corbusier's Unité d'Habitation at Marseilles and Berlin. The Golden Lane Estate, completed in the mid-1960s with some 557 flats and maisonettes, is now listed Grade II. The estate office is set within Great Arthur House.

SLIM HOUSE

1999-2000 JO HAGAN

This narrow house, only 3.5 metres (11 feet) wide, was built on the site of a shed used by a mini-cab firm, and is squeezed between a brick Victorian commercial block and a bright yellow pub. With space for just one room on each of the five floors—plus a basement and a small set-back behind a roof terrace—the various stages are reached by a lift set into a concrete shaft in a steel-framed structure, or a stairway with a huge light-well. This unusual building's frontage is all gleaming steel and glass.

308

PEABODY TRUST HOMES

FROM 1860s ARCHITECTS INCLUDE H. A. DARBYSHIRE

Built to house the working poor, these are some of London's oldest residential towers. George Peabody (1795–1869)—banker, dry goods merchant, and father of modern philanthropy—moved from America to London in the 1830s. To combat insanitary slums and chronic disease, he set up a fund (now the Peabody Trust) to provide cheap housing for 'artisans and labouring poor.' Donations of over $8 million included $2.5 million to the London fund; by 1867, he was made a Freeman of the City. The first homes opened in Spitalfields in 1864. Tenants worked to pay rent, which was used to build more flats, including accommodation after World War II bomb damage.

309

WHITBREAD'S BREWERY

FROM 1749; RESTORED BY WOLF OLINS, RODERICK GRADIDGE, AND JULIAN HARROP

This is a famous English brewery in fine Georgian style. By the late 1700s, it was the largest in England, and in 1787 was visited by King George and Queen Charlotte. Here stands the original early eighteenth-century house, in carved brick 'artisan' style, plus the brewing buildings set around a courtyard with a canopied door and arched window above. A ramped colonnaded exit provided a route for barrels into the cobbled courtyard. There is a wonderful king post timber truss roof, a barrel vaulted ceiling, exposed brickwork, and eighteenth-century lanterns. In 1976, brewing ceased here and the buildings were restored.

310

311

312

313

314

315

316

103–105 BUNHILL ROW
FINSBURY TOWER
311   EC1

1967

This tall building provides office space for numerous businesses, from technology experts to health-care commissions and actuaries. It is 56 metres (184 feet) tall with 16 floors. The simple design of both the tower and its broad adjoining block allows for a pleasing rhythm of neat window verticals with large, light rectangular horizontals set between. It also has an interesting curved crown with projecting struts set above its entrance.

CITY ROAD AND BUNHILL ROW, GOLDEN LANE ESTATE
ARMOURY HOUSE
312   EC1

1735; 1828; 1857 JENNINGS

This is the headquarters of the Honourable Artillery Company that moved here in 1641—to defend the realm and maintain the shooting of longbows, crossbows, and handguns. It has an apt fortress style and cannon-balled parapet—built in 1735—with wings added in 1828. The former artillery grounds are now vast gardens. The armoury houses a museum of uniforms, armour, silver, medals, weapons, and early printed books. Today the HAC provides intelligence for the deep-strike systems of the British Army and NATO, and supplies the saluting battery at the Tower of London and guards of honour for state occasions.

23 BUNHILL ROW
BUNHILL ROW
313   EC1

Bunhill Row is situated adjacent to the Barbican, between Old Street to the north and Chiswell Street to the south, close to Moorgate tube and railway stations. The area was long associated with burials and its name derives from the earlier 'Bone Hill.' Here were a series of burial grounds from an ancient Saxon one; a Quaker place of burial from 1661 to 1855; and a burial ground for Dissenters, where authors William Blake and John Bunyan were laid to rest.

BUNHILL ROW
BRAITHWAITE HOUSE
314   EC1

1960S, TMO, LONDON AND DIAMOND ??CONFIRM

World War II bombing cleared this area and soon new buildings filled the space, including the tower block Braithwaite House. This 55-metre (181-foot) tower with 19 floors was first approved in 1963. A local-authority-built development with landscaped communal gardens, it is set to the east of the Quaker Bunhill Fields burial ground— bought by them in 1661 and used until 1855 for 12,000 burials, including George Fox and many plague victims. The building is named after a young Quaker, J. B. Braithwaite Jr., who helped set up an adult school, medical mission, and the first meeting house here in the 1880s. In May 1968, the notorious Kray twins were arrested in Braithwaite House.

47 CITY ROAD
WESLEY'S CHAPEL (AND HOUSE)
315   EC1

1777 GEORGE DANCE THE YOUNGER; 1972–78 RESTORED (1779 HOUSE)

The foundation stone for the chapel was laid by John Wesley himself in 1777 when the founder of Methodism was seventy-four years old. The site had been too swampy to build upon—until excavations for the new St Paul's Cathedral led to massive dumping of soil here. This brick chapel, a late Georgian design, was altered in the 1890s, when its elegant porch and columns were added. By 1972, £1 million was raised from all over the world to restore the chapel, which reopened in 1978. The crypt is now a Museum of Methodism. In between his mission travels, Wesley lived in the small Georgian town house and is buried in the churchyard behind the chapel.

OLD STREET
ST LUKE
316   EC1

1727–33 NICHOLAS HAWKSMOOR AND JOHN JAMES

Nicholas Hawksmoor worked with Christopher Wren and Sir John Vanbrugh (helping him build Blenheim Palace for John Churchill). He designed six new churches in London plus the west front of Westminster Abbey. The fluted obelisk spire was much admired, but sadly, after decades of settlement, St Luke's was declared unsafe and its roof was removed. Today, this Grade II–listed building is home to the London Symphony Orchestra music education centre and performing arts venue, taking great music into the local community. It has retained the original walls and window alcoves, the church clock has been renovated, and the golden dragon restored at the top of the spire.

317

SHOREDITCH COUNTY COURT

317   EC2

This building houses an active county court to deal with civil cases, such as divorce and bankruptcy. Its imposing, raised classical entrance is framed by Doric-style columns and a decorated triangular pediment—all features befitting an imposing public building. The Romans set up the first formal system of justice in Britain two thousand years ago. In 1066, William the Conqueror introduced common law and, in 1155, riots led King Richard I to appoint knights to judge breaches of the King's Peace. A 1360 statute by Edward III established justices of the peace to administer the King's law; by the 1700s they had become persons of great prestige.

318

91–101 WORSHIP STREET; FORMERLY KNOWN AS HOGG LANE

SHOPS AND HOUSES

318   EC2

1863 PHILIP SPEAKMAN WEBB

The street name was probably changed when a former Civil War cannon foundry here was leased by John Wesley as a place of worship, ultimately leading to the building of a chapel in City Road. Numbers 91–101 were designed as workshops and shops. Webb had worked with William Morris and set up the Society for the Protection of Ancient Buildings in 1861. Here, a buttressed façade divides the terrace into six bays with arched entrances. The ground floor shops are set under a continuous shallow pitched roof, and have multi-paned windows. There are generous dormer windows in the roof and tall chimney pieces.

319

10 FINSBURY SQUARE

SPACIOUS OFFICES

319   EC2

This prominent building is situated on the west side of Finsbury Square, with its large number 10 set in white figures on the glass of the door. It is in a lovely cream stone, with almost with a tinge of pink—all very neat and ordered, with vast sweeps of office space inside. It is close to Bunhill Fields Burial Ground, which covers four acres and was founded as a cemetery for non-conformists in the early 1700s.

ISLINGTON
FINSBURY SQUARE

320   EC2

320

Sadly, all the original houses raised around the 1770s by George Dance the Younger have vanished, but this southeast corner of Islington, set just a few a blocks north of the city, was once the place of residence for many Georgian merchants. The rectangular square was constructed 1777–92. Here one James Lackington, bookseller, ran the Temple of the Muses—a famous shop with a vast circular counter large enough, it was claimed, for a coach and six to be driven around. Albeit the old houses have vanished but there are still impressive buildings here.

52a WILSON STREET
CHAPEL OF THE OPEN BOOK

321   EC2

MID TO LATE 1800s

Set in a conservation area, this non-denominational chapel is picturesque Gothic style and is situated near to the Grade II–listed Flying Horse public house and a terrace of six rather dilapidated Georgian houses. The building is all points and triangles, bar for the window tracery and trefoils.

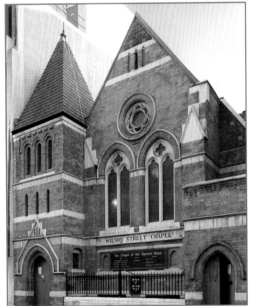

321

01 ADDRESS
OFFICES, SHOPS AND SKATING RINK

322   EC2

1984–86 ARUP ASSOCIATIONS

Here 150,000 square metres (1,615,000 square feet) of office buildings are arranged informally to compose two new linked squares, one left empty, the other filled with an terraced elaborate circular feature under glazed roofing that contains shops and a skating rink. The entrance to the offices is through semi-public atriums with glass roofing. The decorative treatment of the Broadgate exteriors uses 'curtains' of fretted granite. The gently curved frontage shown here has multiple windows, square and rectangular, while other complex structures rise beside and behind it.

322

323

324

I MOOR LANE	I ROPEMAKER STREET; FORMERLY BRITTANIC HOUSE
GREEN REFLECTIONS	**CITY POINT**
323 EC2	324 EC2

1987–90 DENIS LASDUN, PETER SOFTLEY AND ASSOCIATES

This is a vast office building with a double layer of glass. The exterior surface is sheer green glass, and lots of fascinating reflections are created in this surface by daylight and, at night, it looks especially impressive when the framed glass of its interior becomes visible behind. The green façade rises to tall corner towers.

2001 SHEPPARD ROBSON

First called Brittanic House in its 1967 guise, this was sold as the headquarters for British Petroleum. Wates City bought the building for £143 million, making it the most expensive real estate in the world (per acre) in 1999. At over 122 metres (400 feet) tall, it remains the largest single available-for-let building in the whole of the city and it has been valued at about £500 million. The award-winning architects of this exciting, vibrant building (for a short while the second tallest in the city) are part of the Sheppard Robson architectural practice, the fifth largest in the United Kingdom, with many highly experienced architects and cutting-edge young designers.

325

CROMWELL TOWER

325 EC2

1973 CHAMBERLIN, POWELL & BON

Part of the Barbican complex in the City of London, the imposing Cromwell Tower rises to 404 feet (123 metres) with forty-two floors. This impressive tower was given Grade II–listing in 2001. Its style is denoted as brutalist with an exterior that has a bush-hammered finish on a sharply ridged pattern of horizontals and verticals—its severity of line undoubtedly reflecting the harsh attitude of its 1600s Puritanical namesake. It is a residential skyscraper, offering one of the few places to make a home in an area dominated by offices and banks. This is the fourteenth-tallest building in London—together with its partners in height, the almost identical Shakespeare Tower and Lauderdale Tower (also part of the Barbican Estate). The tower is named for Oliver Cromwell (1599–1658), the only non-royal ruler of Britain to be crowned as Lord Protector and who ruled England, Scotland, and Ireland from 1653. He played a major part in bringing King Charles I to his trial and subsequent execution in the wake of the English Civil War—in which Cromwell led the New Model Army, often called Roundheads after the shape of their helmets.

326

FROBISHER CRESCENT

326 EC2

1959–79 CHAMBERLIN, POWELL & BON

This sweeping crescent links north and south Barbican and looks down on the Sculpture Court behind the arts centre. It houses arts centre offices and the City of London Business School—and serves as an entrance to the library. It is named after Sir Martin Frobisher (1535–94), the explorer of Canada's Frobisher Bay, who is buried in nearby St Giles (although St Andrew's in Plymouth claimed his heart and entrails).

327

SHAKESPEARE TOWER

327   EC2

1976 CHAMBERLIN POWELL AND BONN

This is part of the Barbican Estate raised on a World War II bomb site. The complex is considered a major London landmark, and a principal example of concrete brutalist architecture. Shakespeare Tower is forty-two storeys high, its neat slim outline rising 123 metres (403 feet). Overall, the estate is home to around four thousand people in over two thousand flats and was officially opened in 1969. The flats reflect the widespread use in the 1960s and 1970s in Britain of concrete as the visible face of a building—in this case, treated with a bush-hammered finish. Shakespeare Tower is named for William Shakespeare (1564–1616)—and is a Grade II–listed building.

328

SILK STREET

THE BARBICAN CENTRE

328   EC2

1959–79 SIXTY ARCHITECTS, INCLUDING CHAMBERLIN, POWELL AND BON

Tall residential towers surround the arts centre, with an ornamental lake, fountains, and lawns. This is Europe's largest multi-arts and conference ensemble, offering theatre, music, dance, art, film, facilities for education, and a conference venue. It has a concert hall, theatre, library, and gallery. It is home to the Guildhall School of Music and Drama as well as the renowned London Symphony Orchestra.

THE CONSERVATORY

329   EC2

The Barbican's Conservatory is a high area surrounded by glass panels — hence the name — set on the top floor of the arts complex. Here tropical and semi-tropical flora and many other exotic plants flourish beside the pools, walkways, and fountains. This well-stocked conservatory is one of the largest greenhouses in London. In 1986, an Arid House was added to house cacti plus the largest *Carnegiea gigantea* in Europe — kindly donated by the mayor of Salt Lake City.

329

330

331

332

WILLOUGHBY HOUSE

330   EC2

1971 CHAMBERLIN, POWELL & BON

This building is another exploration of 'brutal' architecture in the Barbican complex. The blocks have a north-to-south axis, with apartments on either side of a central corridor—so fewer lifts are needed. The living rooms in Willoughby House face west—over the gardens and lake. The building is named for Catherine Willoughby, lady-in-waiting to Henry VIII's last wife, Katherine Parr. A prominent Protestant, she fled into exile during Mary I's reign. Catherine married the lord of the Barbican manor and inherited this estate. One of her descendants was a train-bearer at Elizabeth II's 1953 coronation.

150 LONDON WALL

MUSEUM OF LONDON

331   EC2

1975-76 POWELL AND MOYA

Raised above street level by the Barbican, where busy Aldersgate meets London Wall, the museum's concrete 'drawbridge' offers a safe route over the traffic. Set on the site of a Roman fort, this is one of the largest, most comprehensive city museums in the world, with exhibits that trace London's story from 400,000 years ago through Roman settlement in AD 50 to today. Reconstructed street scenes and interiors discover a Roman room with mosaic pavement, the 'Great Fire Experience,' a Stuart interior, Newgate prison cells, Victorian and Edwardian restaurants and shops, and even a Selfridges Art Deco elevator.

ONE LONDON WALL

OFFICES AND 'PLAISTERERS'

332   EC2

2003 FOSTER AND PARTNERS

This vast glass expanses in this thirteen-storey curved 'ship-prow' office offer magnificent views over the city. The site includes the original wall that protected a Roman garrison nearly two thousand years ago, while its basement floor preserves the old Plaisterers Hall of the Worshipful Company of Plaisterers, whose first charter was granted by King Henry VII in 1501. Long before that, in 1189, the first Lord Mayor of London, Henry FitzAlwyn, made an order that all houses should be plastered and lime-washed—endorsed by King John in 1212, who commanded that all shops on the Thames and London Bridge should be plastered—inside and out.

333

334

I0 NOBLE STREET	OAT LANE
ALDER CASTLE	**PEWTERERS' HALL**
333 EC2	334 EC2

1999 DEGI INTERNATIONAL

Close to St Paul's Cathedral and in the most historic surroundings, this fine modern office building comprises 10,202 square yards (8,530 square metres), with seven floors and an underground car park set below. This example of new city architecture cost Degi International in the region of $97 million (£55 million). The offices were initially let to long-term tenants Ernst & Young and also to Hale & Dorr. The sweeping glass curved façade at the front of the building creates a focal point, with the change from glass to a conventional structure beyond emphasizing the lovely rounded corner most effectively.

1496; 1961

The Pewterers (the sixteenth London guild) joined the London guilds in 1384 and gained their charter in 1473. Their first Lime Street hall, built in 1496, burned in the Great Fire of 1666. The second, raised 1670, burned in 1840. The third opened in 1961 in Oat Lane— with panelling and chandeliers from the Lime Street building. An apprentice had to serve seven years before presenting his work to the court of the Pewterers' Company and being allowed to strike his mark on the touchplate.

335

336

88 WOOD STREET

AWARD-WINNING OFFICES

335   EC2

WOOD STREET

THE POLICE STATION

336   EC2

1990–98 RICHARD ROGERS PARTNERSHIP

This remarkable office complex is near to both contemporary skyscrapers and much older sites—such as the tower of Wren's St Alban's Church and the two ancient churchyards of St Mary's and St Olaves. There are three blocks. The numbers of storeys in these stepped blocks rise from ten, to fourteen, to eighteen—to remain in keeping with the height of the surrounding buildings. The gaps between the blocks are used for stairs, lifts, and services, thus keeping the main buildings free for occupation and retaining the maximum number of corner offices. Wide, triple-glazed, ultra-clear windows mean that the external walls almost disappear; the stairs and the panoramic lifts have frameless glazing, too, making the most of the stunning views in all directions. Integrated, internal blinds are controlled by photo-cells and automatically adjust to suit the sunshine levels.

1962–66 MCMORRAN AND WHITBY

The Romans originally created Wood Street as a parade ground for a fort that was set just outside the city wall. Today, the street showcases the contrasting styles of many modern architects, and here amongst them is a remarkable and rather dignified police station built in the early sixties by McMorran and Whitby, in a 1930s stripped-back classical style.

337

338

GRESHAM STREET, ALSO KNOWN AS ST ANNE IN THE WILLOWS AND ST ANNE NEAR ALDERGATE

ST ANNE AND ST AGNES

337   EC2

1677–80 SIR CHRISTOPHER WREN; 1966 RESTORED BY BRADDOCK AND MARTIN SMITH

First described in 1137, this small church was named after St Anne, the mother of the Virgin Mary, and St Agnes, a thirteen-year-old virgin martyred about AD 304. It burned down in 1548, after which (in 1649), its vicar was beheaded for protesting against the execution of Charles I. Rebuilt again by Wren in pink brick, after the Great Fire, the work—done by one John Fitch of the Grocers' Company— cost £2,448. Anne and St Agnes has one of Wren's purest centralised plans. It has a central Dutch-style pediment, three bays, arched windows, and a short spire—added in 1714. It is in early Christian, Greek-cross plan, with a large dome set above four columns, four smaller domes gracing the corners, and a beautiful carved ceiling. The church has been very well restored after the Blitz. Today, dwarfed by city office blocks, it serves as a guild church for Lutheran worship.

25 GRESHAM STREET

BUILT ON A ROMAN FORT

338   EC2

2002 NICHOLAS GRIMSHAW AND PARTNERS

This stunning new building catches the eye because of its unusual shape, its various sections curving in at the top. It presents a pattern of stripes and textures, topped by an interesting overhanging roof format in a gentle rise with protruding edges. Ten floors of column-free office space occupy 10,193 square metres (109,717 square feet) and it stands 41 metres (135 feet) high on an island site in the city. It straddles the remains of a Roman fort and is set next to St John Zachary churchyard. This imaginative multi-storey steel framework embraces both the sunken garden and Roman archaeology. The accommodation is set around an open-sided, south-facing atrium to overlook the garden— extended with terraced planting beds that rise up the external face of the atrium.

GOLDSMITH'S HALL

339   EC2

1835 PHILIP HARDWICK

The Goldsmiths' Company has been located here for over six hundred years. The first hall was raised in 1339; a second 1634–36 hall was restored after the Great Fire and ultimately demolished in the late 1820s. A World War II bomb exploded inside the southwest corner in 1941 but this damage was later repaired—and a major refurbishment was completed by 1990. The Goldsmiths' Company is one of the Twelve Great Livery Companies of the City of London and has been responsible for hallmarking since 1300. Over the ensuing seven hundred years it has supported both goldsmiths and silversmiths. Its collection of antique plate includes Queen Elizabeth I's coronation cup.

339

31 GRESHAM STREET,

SCHRODERS INVESTMENT BUILDING

340   EC2

04 ARCHITECT DETAILS

This building was designed to serve as the new prestigious headquarters of Schroders Investment Management Limited. The building totals 20,438 square metres (220,000 square feet) and took less than nineteen months to complete. It uses few columns so as to maximise both daylight and space—and aims to provide a strong corporate image for the company as well as creating an attractive and functional working environment for the staff employed there.

340

341

ST VEDAST-ALIAS-FOSTER

341   EC2

CHURCH 1670–73; 1697 TOWER SIR CHRISTOPHER WREN;
1941 RESTORED STEPHEN DYKES-BOWER

First mentioned in 1170 (some sources claim 1280), this church was rebuilt in 1519, repaired in 1614, and then destroyed in the Great Fire. The church was again rebuilt in the 1670s—its subtle but elegant Italian baroque tower added two decades later. Inside, there is some excellent plaster work and woodwork, a magnificent organ, and a 1600s font. Only two churches in England are dedicated to the fifth-century Saint Vedast, bishop of Arras—the other one being Tathwell in Lincolnshire.

342

6 GRESHAM STREET

THE WAX CHANDLERS

342   EC2

1670; 1793; 1853; REBUILT 1956–58 SEELY AND PAGET

The xvij day of August was the Waxchandler fest, for ther was good chere.—Henry Machin, 1562

This building has elegant styling, with granite lower walls and the company crest set over the main entrance. The Wax Chandlers were first noted in 1330 and received a Royal Charter in 1484. Their first hall was destroyed in 1666, rebuilt successively, and then destroyed again in 1940. At last the present structure took its place as home to the Worshipful Company of Wax Chandlers, one of the City's famous livery companies—twentieth in order of precedence. Their motto is 'Truth Is the Light.'

343

GRESHAM STREET

ST LAWRENCE JEWRY

343   EC2

1670–87 SIR CHRISTOPHER WREN

This church, by the medieval Jewish area, was founded in 1136—over the tiered section of a Roman amphitheatre—and dedicated to Saint Lawrence, who was roasted alive on a gridiron. The sumptuous building is one of Wren's most expensive and was gutted in both the Great Fire and 1940s Blitz. Remarkably, a 1500s painting (showing St Lawrence's martyrdom) has survived. The decorated east front is based on St Paul's Cathedral, with rounded arches, and swags of flowers and fruit. Inside, goldleaf and chandeliers gleam in a vast white interior. Windows commemorate Sir Thomas More (who preached here) and Wren with his master-mason and master-carver.

GUILDHALL YARD
GUILDHALL
344   EC2

1411-40, 1788-89 JOHN CROXTON AND GEORGE DANCE THE YOUNGER

Despite alterations over the centuries, the Guildhall retains its glorious medieval outlines. The first mayor was installed here in 1192. It was rebuilt in 1411 when Henry V granted the free passage of stone by boat and cart. The executors of mayor, Richard Whittington (of Dick Whittington folk tale fame), helped to pay for the paving and window glazing. The 1430 Gothic porch is still the entrance from Guildhall Yard. Here, in 1554, was held the trial of Lady Jane Grey. The large medieval crypt is the most extensive in London. Windows in the east crypt depict the Great Fire, Chaucer, Caxton, More, Wren, and Pepys. The west crypt has a superb vaulted ceiling.

344

20 KING STREET; FORMERLY BANCA COMMERCIALE ITALIANA
OFFICES
345   EC2

1850 SANCTON WOOD

This elegant corner building in a classic 1800s commercial style—with all its arches, Tuscan columns, and pediments—was raised originally for an insurance company. The architect is well known for his railway stations (such as the original Shoreditch and Dublin's Heuston Station). Here, he uses a palazzo theme, with long runs of majestic arches and multiple upper-floor windows placed almost as close together as those on Venetian palaces. An Italianate cornice links the two sweeping façades and the imposing, nicely rounded corner has sturdy pillars flanking the door and rather more slender ones on the curved windows above.

345

9 KING STREET
GLASS ENTRANCE
346   EC2

1997 NEW ENTRANCE

Here the tall slender glass panels of the entrance shimmer darkly. The main floors of this building, initially GRE's new banking and office building at 9-12 King Street, was later let to the International Energy Bank for £475,000 per annum (£296 per square metre)—a very high rent considering that the site is outside the main banking area of the city. New entrance doors were created on the front elevation in 1997 for Zambia National Commercial Bank. Other occupants here include CMT (Capital Markets Trading).

346

ST MARY-LE-BOW

1091; 1521; 1670–83 SIR CHRISTOPHER WREN; 1956–62 REBUILT
BY LAURENCE KING AND RECONSECRATED 1964

The church was called le Bow because of the
bowed arches of stone in the eleventh-century
crypt—where Norman columns can still be
seen today. The glorious tower and spire soar
to over 66 metres (217 feet)—set forward
from the church and topped by a huge,
golden, flying-dragon weather vane. The
famous bells were first mentioned in 1091
when the roof blew off in a storm and later, as
legend has it, for summoning Dick Whittington
back to London town. The curfew was rung on
Bow Bells during the Middle Ages, probably
leading to the idea a true cockney must be
born within hearing distance of these. The
church had to be reconsecrated in the late
1200s after a series of incidents: one William
Fitz Osbert escaped up the tower, after killing
an archbishop's guard—he was smoked out,
and hanged in chains at Smithfield. In 1271,
the tower collapsed, killing twenty people. In
1284, after a goldsmith was murdered here,
sixteen men were hanged and one woman
burned. In 1331, a wooden balcony collapsed
during a joust to celebrate the birth of the
Black Prince, hurling the Queen and her ladies,
to the ground—an event marked, after Wren
rebuilt the church, by a memorial balcony,
from which Queen Anne watched the Lord
Mayor's pageant in 1702. The church burned
down in the Great Fire and was rebuilt by
Wren, who remodelled it on Rome's basilica of
Maxentius. In 1818–20, the upper spire was
rebuilt by George Gwilt. An elaborate doorway
in a rusticated opening leads into the neat,
white-and-gold interior, restored by Sir Arthur
Blomfield in 1878–89. The church was severely
damaged by 1941 bombs, and the beautiful
steeple was taken down and stored away for
almost twenty years. A plaque on the exterior
wall remembers John Milton, born in nearby
Bread Street, while a statue outside celebrates
locally born Captain John Smith (1580–1631),
who became governor of Virginia.

347

1776 ADAM BROTHERS

The 1900s writer of architectural guides Nikolaus Pevsner described Frederick's Place as an 'oasis of domesticity.' This speculative venture by the Adam brothers still has some relatively-intact, terraced Georgian houses—built on the site of a house which had belonged to Sir John Frederick, Lord Mayor of London in 1661. Benjamin Disraeli worked with a firm of solicitors here at number 6 in 1821. 'You have too much genius for Frederick's Place,' a woman friend once said to him. 'It will never do.'

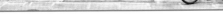

1924–39 SIR EDWIN LUTYENS; EXECUTIVE ARCHITECTS GOTCH AND SAUNDERS

This vast, former bank headquarters building has façades on both Poultry and Princes Street. This was Lutyens's largest English structure and is a magnificent and elegant classical building. Despite its great size, it remains comfortable in its setting, with delicate detailing and a shallow dome. Inside, the grand pubic ground floor rooms are clad in black and white marble, and there is an elegant banking hall.

1930–32 SIR EDWIN COOPER

The Westminster Bank first opened as the London and Westminster Bank in Throgmorton Street in 1834 and soon became a leading professional bank. Today, it has become a vast concern—an amalgam now of many clearing banks, including the National Provincial Bank of England, which was founded in 1833 by banking pioneer Thomas Japlin. The shorter name of Westminster Bank was adopted in 1923. Set on a challenging busy corner site, this very gracious building has numerous tall columns and fine sculpture work but is not overworked. Its arched entrance is set on the relatively broad corner façade.

351

NUMBER ONE POULTRY

1994–98 JAMES STIRLING AND MICHAEL WILFORD

This leading post-modern building was constructed where the offices of J & J Belcher once stood. The exciting new structure uses bold forms and strong colours, and is lavishly decorated with many forms and motifs. An office and retail development, it was designed to stand on a site owned by Peter Palumbo, a controversial property developer who had inherited part of the site from his father. The project had to overcome many obstacles and some thirty-five years would pass before the concept came to fruition. During its construction, a major archaeological dig by the Museum of London Archaeological Service excavated several significant finds. These included a wooden drain along the main Roman road that dates back to AD 47 — at the time of the very foundation of Roman London (a town the Romans then called Londinium). It is interesting that such a striking new building stands where Roman London 'launched' the city. Set at a road junction, it maximizes this triangular position to dramatic effect with a tall 'prow' that revels in both cylindrical and angular shapes. A deep open courtyard below allows pedestrian access and also provides a way through to Bank Underground station. The final flourish at the top, above all the offices, is a roof-garden with surreal landscaping created by Arabella Lennox Boyd. There is also a fine restaurant here, Le Coq d'Argent, which is run by Terence Conran.

352

352

THREADNEEDLE STREET

BANK OF ENGLAND

352   EC2

FROM 1732, SIR JOHN SOANE

The Bank of England is the central bank of the United
Kingdom. Often called 'The Old Lady of Threadneedle
Street,' it has changed many times over its three hundred
years of development to become an imposing edifice that
spreads across four acres. The first bank opened in 1694
in the Mercers' Hall above the site of the ancient Roman
temple of Mithras, appropriately the god of contracts.
Later on it moved to the Grocers' Hall and finally, in
1732–34, into its present site. The stately colonnade on
the northwest 'Tivoli' corner was based on the Temple
of Vesta at Tivoli which Sir John Soane had sketched in
1779. The bank was founded by a Scotsman, William
Paterson, in 1694 to act as the English government's
banker. Its Royal Charter was granted in 1694. The first
governor was one Sir John Houblon—who is depicted
in the 1990 issue of the £50 note.

51 THREADNEEDLE STREET
NATIONAL WESTMINSTER BANK
353   EC2

1922–33 EXTENDED 1936 MEWÈS AND DAVIS

Arthur Davis went to Paris at the tender age of sixteen to study architecture, and, in 1898, worked for Charles Mewès—famous for the creation of the Ritz hotel in Paris and then, with Davis, for London's Ritz. In 1910, Mewès and Davis designed the first overseas branch of the Westminster Bank in Brussels, which led to commissions for banks in Antwerp, Nantes, and Valencia. Here, Mewès and Davis followed Italian palazzo style—rather than French styling—with the very gentle curve of this bank's façade. They went on to be the architects of many renowned hotels and offices, and Davis also designed the interiors of several luxurious Cunard liners.

353

38 THREADNEEDLE STREET
ROYAL BANK OF SCOTLAND
354   EC2

Founded in 1727, with its headquarters in Edinburgh, the Royal Bank of Scotland acquired the English NatWest bank in 2000—in the biggest takeover in British banking history. This is now one of the largest banks in the world. This robust building is absolutely fitting for such a prestigious concern, with its sturdy columns, arched canopy over a rather daunting entrance, with numbers firmly placed each side of the door. The windows are set within brick arches, above intricate wrought-iron decoration. A lively imagination could perhaps relate the walls' decorative theme of circular motifs to counters or coins!

354

LOTHBURY
ST MARGARET LOTHBURY
355   EC2

1197; REBUILT 1440; 1686–90 SIR CHRISTOPHER WREN

This is the parish church of the Bank of England. Rebuilt in the Great Fire, it has a rectangular plan, with a square, white-stone tower, and a tall lead spire and obelisk rising up high from a domed base. Its robust entrance has delicate twisted pillars that support a cornice. Inside are wonderful examples of seventeenth-century woodwork. The elaborate pulpit and the great rood screen with its spread eagle came from All Hallows the Great; the reredos, communion rails, and Grinling Gibbons font (its cover has a sweet dove and bough) were rescued from St Olave Old Jewry.

355

356

INSTITUTE OF CHARTERED ACCOUNTANTS HALL

356   EC2

1889–93 JOHN BELCHER

Moorgate was one of the minor gates of the old London Wall and today the area is a financial centre with many investment and commercial banks. This sturdy building is an excellent example of Victorian neo-Baroque inspired by Italian Renaissance buildings. This style gave Belcher (a founder of the Art Workers' Guild) the freedom to incorporate the sculpture he so enjoyed and here there are works by Thorneycroft and Stevenson that sometimes almost become Art Nouveau (with sweet examples of women turning into leaves). Belcher's partner, J. J. Joass, built an extension in 1930–31, continuing the earlier design, with the 1959 William Whitfield design adding yet another extension, including a Great Hall. Sir Nikolaus Pevsner described the building as 'eminently original and delightfully picturesque.'

357

BRITANNIC HOUSE

357   EC2

1924–27, 1987–89 SIR EDWIN LUTYENS, PETER INSKIP AND PETER JENKINS ARCHITECTS

Finsbury Circus was originally laid out in 1815–17 with handsome houses by William Montague, raised to the designs of George Dance the Younger, but long since demolished. In this setting with such an inspiring past, Britannic House was Lutyens's first large London building and is today an historic building with a Grade II–listing. Its seven-storey, classical façade makes a stately curve, with Corinthian attached columns and lovely arched windows. Its exciting renovation introduced a contemporary—and very impressive—semicircular atrium, allowing natural light to pour into the office areas.

THE PAVILION

This curves of this superb cylinder of gleaming glass are all the more dramatic because of its proximity to the straight high slabs of building all around it. The reflections make a pleasing play of light and shade. This building is rendered stunning by its very simplicity and sheer surface.

358

NEO-CLASSICAL OFFICES

1991 GMW ARCHITECTS

In a prime location, this impressive eight-storey office building has a confident neo-classical façade in natural stone with neat details. Crowned by an arch and pediment, it stands adjacent to Finsbury Circus and blends in perfectly with the other historic buildings in the vicinity. The total floor space is 11,508 square metres (123,826 square feet).

357

360

361

BISHOPSGATE

BISHOPSGATE INSTITUTE

360   EC2

1894 C. H. TOWNSEND

The institute opened in 1894 to provide
educational courses, the use of Bishopsgate
Library—with its historical collections of
London prints and drawings, and early labour
movement documents—plus meeting rooms,
and halls for examinations, conferences, and
exhibitions. Designed by Charles Harrison
Townsend, the institute is a most unusual
building with its beige faience façade and
lovely mix of Victorian Romanesque styling
and Art Nouveau decoration. A generous
round entrance arch is set between tall, narrow
angular towers that rise to pinnacles—with a
pretty, overhanging, steep roof squeezed in
between them.

BISHOPSGATE AND LIVERPOOL STREET

LIVERPOOL STREET STATION AND HOTEL

361   EC2

STATION 1874 E. WILSON; 1891–94 EXTENSION W. N. ASBEE;
1980s RENOVATED

HOTEL 1884 CHARLES BARRY; 1901 ALTERED BY R. EDDIS;
1997–99 REFURBISHED

On the site of the old Bethlem Hospital
(1200s–1600s) and countless streets, courts,
and alleys, this was one of the last major
stations to be built in London. It would serve
as the metropolitan terminus for what would
become the Great Eastern Railway, plus the
place to catch local trains to the northeastern
suburbs. It soon became one of the busiest
stations, with more daily passengers than any
other London terminus and some 123 million
visitors each year. A daily express train
connects with the ferry from Harwich to
Hoek van Holland. Built in restrained Gothic
redbrick, with its platforms well below ground
level, it was named after the street on which
it stands, in turn named to honour prime
minister Lord Liverpool. In 1922, a large World
War I memorial in the main booking hall was
unveiled by Field Marshall Sir Henry Wilson—
assassinated by the IRA on his return home
that day. In May 1917, the station was the
first London site hit by German Gotha bomber
aircraft; 162 people died.

362

363

OFFICES IN EAST INDIA COMPANY WAREHOUSES

362   EC2

1798–1820 RICHARD JUPP AND HENRY HOLLAND

Elizabeth I granted Britain's Honourable East India Company its Royal Charter in 1600, and, from then on, it held a monopoly on trade in the East Indies—eventually, in practical terms, almost ruling India until the company's dissolution in 1858. These grand warehouses, today owned by the Port of London Authority, are six storeys high and cover about five acres. With the present buildings restructured internally as offices, only the façade remains to tell of former glories. The Bengal warehouses on the south side of the street are earlier, and date from 1764.

MANSION, MEETING HOUSE, AND HOMES

363   EC2

c. 1500s, 1678, 1708, 1740

Jasper Fisher, goldsmith and clerk to the Court of Chancery, built an Elizabethan mansion here in the 1500s. Ever in debt, he was derided by his neighbours, who called the house Fisher's Folly. Eventually, he sold it to William Cavendish, the second Earl of Devonshire, who renamed it Devonshire House. What was once its large forecourt now forms Devonshire Square. Part of it was leased in 1666 to Quakers for a meeting-house. The minister, George Whitehead, used to take his night-cap to meetings in anticipation of raids and his being dragged off to prison. In 1675, Nicholas Barbon bought the house. It was demolished two years later; a new Quaker meeting-house was built and the square developed. A few 1600s houses still stand here, and there are lovely Georgian houses with multi-paned sash windows and steps leading up to elegant entrances.

364

365

366

367

STONE HOUSE

364   EC2

1927 RICHARDSON AND GILL

This is a very handsome 1920s addition to Bishopsgate. It stands on the site of a thirteenth-century stone building owned by Augustinian friars, and known in the locality as 'the stone house'—most buildings then were made of timber. The office block here today has inherited this title. It has a very generous, curved corner, ornate Art Nouveau–style metalwork above the double-storey plinth, and multiple rows of windows and sweeping cornices that serve to emphasise the building's flowing lines.

83 LONDON WALL

ALL HALLOWS

365   EC2

1765-67 GEORGE DANCE THE YOUNGER; 1891 REPAIRED; 1960-62 RESTORED DAVID NYE

The old Roman city wall (of which there are still traces in the churchyard) formed the foundations of the first church here, raised by Queen Matilda in 1108. In 1474, a hermit's cell was built next to the chancel wall—occupied for twenty years by recluse Simon the Anker, whose work, *The Fruyte of Redemcyon,* was printed by Wynkyn de Worde in 1514. The church escaped the Great Fire but was rebuilt in the 1700s. Dance would later call this masterpiece 'my first child.' The simple, dark-brown brick exterior (now exposed by bomb damage and road widening) encloses a light, airy, white-and-gold interior with no aisles, semicircular windows, a delightful frieze, and decoration inspired by ancient temples in Rome. The barrel-vaulted nave is supported by lovely, fluted Ionic columns. Dance was heavily influenced by Italian classical design in his work. In 1954 this became a guild church.

BISHOPSGATE

ST BOTOLPH WITHOUT BISHOPSGATE

366   EC2

1725-29 JAMES GOULD, GEORGE DANCE THE ELDER

Saint Botolph, a Benedictine monk who preached far and wide, was adopted as the patron saint of travellers. All four churches by the old city gates bore his name. Knights Templar were examined here over charges of corruption in about 1307. Described by Stow as overlooking the city ditch, the church was rebuilt 1571–72, in what was then a silk-weaving area, where Shakespeare lodged. It escaped the Great Fire but was rebuilt in the 1700s (cost—£10,400), and restored another seven times; alterations included a glass dome and new windows. John Keats was christened at the marble fluted font in 1795. In 1413, a female hermit, surviving on an annual pension of 40 shillings a year, lived in the churchyard. Here, several smallpox victims are buried, Ben Jonson would later mourn the loss of his young son to the plague, and there is a memorial to Sir Paul Pindar (a wealthy 1500s merchant and ambassador.)

15 BISHOPSGATE, FORMERLY NATIONAL WESTMINSTER BANK AND NATIONAL PROVINCIAL BANK

GIBSON HALL

367   EC2

1865 JOHN GIBSON

This is a really gorgeous Victorian bank. The lavishly decorated, single-storey Corinthian pavilion revels in pretentious flourishes—with a grand entrance; panels exploring themes such as industry, agriculture, and education; and statues perched high on its parapet. Gibson designed many banks and this one, refurbished in 1981, is as splendid inside as it is out—with its Gibson Hall (named for the architect), Garden Room, and marble Corinthian columns and crystal chandeliers in evidence everywhere.

25 OLD BROAD STREET, FORMERLY NATIONAL
WESTMINSTER TOWER

TOWER 42

368   EC2

1980 RICHARD SEIFERT AND PARTNERS

Tower 42 was originally built by National
Westminster and its unofficial title, the
NatWest Tower, remains in most common use.
This, Britain's second tallest building, is also
Europe's third tallest—and the world's tallest
cantilevered building. It rises to 183 metres
(600 feet) high. Building began in 1971 but,
in the meantime, the listing in 1974 of the City
of London Club on the site as a building of
historical or architectural interest meant that
the ground-floor area of Tower 42 had to be
redesigned. The building cost £72 million and
was valued at £226 million in 1998. Britain's
highest bar, Vertigo 42, has spectacular views
of the Thames, St Paul's, and Tower Bridge—
and equally spectacular prices for its cocktails,
champagne, and oysters.

52–68 BISHOPSGATE AND ST HELEN'S PLACE; FORMERLY HUDSON BAY HOUSE
HASILWOOD HOUSE
369   EC2

1926–28 MEWÈS AND DAVIS

Once there were several Hudson Bay Offices in London. This last one at Bishopsgate is a huge seven-storey building with a confident stone façade and lines of rectangular and square windows. At the centre is a double-height gateway with sturdy Tuscan columns. Appropriately for its first owners, the building has Canadian-inspired carvings and a gold, beaver-shaped weathervane on top of its cupola. It was built by the Dove Brothers, renowned for their high standard of craftsmanship. Today, the building has been completely rebuilt behind this robust frontage, and has changed its name to Hasilwood House, offering premium office space.

369

19 OLD BROAD STREET
CITY OF LONDON CLUB
370   EC2

1833–34 PHILIP HARDWICK, INTERIORS RESTORED 1980

Once upon a medieval time, this was a very fashionable place to live. A well-known glasshouse made Venetian-style glass from the early 1600s until the Great Fire. Today, the City of London is a traditional gentlemen's club, established for over 170 years in this Italianate building where the balustrades on the wall are echoed by those on its balcony fronts. The high-ceilinged ground- and first-floor period rooms were restored in 1980, when a proposed development of a neighbouring National Westminster Bank threatened to absorb the club. This was thwarted and so gentlemen still meet here, maintaining this unique London practice in apt surroundings.

370

1 BISHOPSGATE
PACIFIC ORIENTAL
371   EC2

This bar and restaurant occupies a very elegant building, with slender columns, ornate capitals, and tall windows—set behind arches on the ground floor and balustrades above—with delicate but rich decoration on every surface. Bishopsgate was one of the Roman gates in the walls around the city through which Roman soldiers would have marched and Anglo Saxons bustled about. Today it is a busy thoroughfare that runs north through the city—with many banks, institutions, and offices lining the route, plus restaurants—like this popular place; its stylish interior includes a six-metre (19-foot)-high waterfall and a copper-clad micro brewery.

371

ROYAL EXCHANGE

372   EC3

1841–44 SIR WILLIAM TITE

The original Exchange was founded in 1565 by Sir Thomas Gresham, a rich merchant and advisor to Queen Elizabeth I. A meeting place for merchants and brokers, it became a focal point for merchants and financiers who made London the commercial centre of Europe. Samuel Pepys took refreshment in the courtyard here. This building was destroyed in the Great Fire; a second 1669 Exchange burned down in 1838. Today's building was opened by Queen Victoria in 1844, and faces Threadneedle Street (famous for opticians and makers of microscopes and telescopes). Roman lettering and sculpture decorate the large Corinthian portico; stout columns hide statues of Queen Elizabeth, Queen Victoria, and Charles II; a fine baroque spire graces the eastern end; and an immense glass ceiling covers the interior courtyard. The Exchange ceased to act as a centre of commerce in 1939, and now houses a luxurious shopping centre.

372

ST MICHAEL CORNHILL

373   EC3

1421, REBUILT 1670–72, 1715–22, 1856–60
SIR CHRISTOPHER WREN, NICHOLAS HAWKSMOOR,
SIR GEORGE GILBERT SCOTT

This church was first mentioned in 1055 and its tower was rebuilt in 1421. Set as it was among medieval alleys, it is not surprising that only its tower survived the Great Fire. Wren rebuilt the nave, and then the fifteenth-century tower was renovated and raised by Nicholas Hawksmoor to his own Gothic design in 1715–22. The tall, gleaming white tower once served as a direction point for travellers but is now dwarfed by modern buildings. In the nineteenth century, Scott restored the building yet further and added the north entrance porch and Venetian tracery to the windows. Seventeenth-century survivors include a wrought-iron sword rest, a wooden pelican, and the splendid Renatus Harris organ, upon which Henry Purcell once played a recital.

373

68 CORNHILL
NEW OFFICES AMONGST THE OLD
374   EC3

1983 ROLFE JUDD; DESIGN BY RICHARD DICKINSON

Here is a large and very fine façade in Portland stone, set on a granite base. This architectural practice has undertaken many redevelopment and refurbishment projects, including both commercial and residential buildings, and here has achieved a a very pleasing modern frontage that fits in well with the much older buildings surrounding it.

374

CORNHILL, VIA ST PETER'S ALLEY AND GRACECHURCH STREET
ST PETER UPON CORNHILL
375   EC3

1680–87 SIR CHRISTOPHER WREN

This church was founded on the site of a very early site of worship—a Roman basilica raised in AD 179. By the Middle Ages, now set in a busy network of medieval alleys and courtyards, the church had a large library and a grammar school attached to it. Its post-Fire stuccoed exterior has a simple brick tower capped by a dome and obelisk. The façade is Palladian, with arched windows separated by pilasters, and two circular windows. Mendelssohn played the Father Smith organ here in 1840 and 1842. To the south is a raised graveyard described by Dickens in *Our Mutual Friend*. The adjacent terracotta building reveals a piece of architectural revenge. Because a Victorian rector at St Peter's had complained about a new office site encroaching onto church land by a few inches, the architects had to redesign the entire building. They added three angry devils—one spitting, one sticking up its fingers rudely, and one that resembles the protesting rector.

375

376

377

LEADENHALL MARKET

376   EC3

ST MICHAEL'S ALLEY, CORNHILL

JAMAICA WINE HOUSE

377   EC3

1881 SIR HORACE JONES

Here, on the site of a large Roman Basilica, there has been a poultry market since the 1300s when Leadenhall's mansion had a lead roof—hence the name. In the 1600s, Spanish ambassador Don Pedro de Ronquillo remarked to Charles II, 'There is more meat sold in your market than in all the Kingdom of Spain.' Both market and mansion burned down in the Great Fire and the market was rebuilt with three large courtyards—one primarily for beef, leather, and wool; the second for veal, mutton, lamb, poultry, and fish; and the third for herbs, fruit, and vegetables. Now, most wholesale trade operates from Smithfield, and Leadenhall has become a retail market with shops and stalls. The grandiose design is restored Victorian splendour—an ornate, iron roof structure with glazed arcades painted green, maroon, and cream, and cobbles everywhere. It was used as a backdrop for the Leaky Cauldron and Diagon Alley in the film *Harry Potter and the Philosopher's Stone*.

1652

This pub was the Turks Head tavern, until its merchant owner returned from overseas, loaded with coffee beans and with a Greek servant who knew how to prepare the brew. This Pasqua Rosée helped to found London's first coffeehouse—re-launched in the 1670s after Wren's post–Great Fire rebuild. Coffeehouses became a key element of Restoration London. The numerous ones in the Cornhill area catered for financiers, stockbrokers, and bankers. Because Rosée's was a centre for merchants in the West Indies trade, dealing with Jamaican rum and sugar, it was soon known as the Jamaica. Underwriters wrote their policies here but, as the century wore on, the focus shifted to entertainment and more alcoholic refreshment. In 1869, it was renamed the Jamaica Wine House and by 1892 had been bought by Shoreditch wine merchants E. J. Rose. Today the redbrick Jamaica Wine House still emanates its history: the bar is divided into little compartments by polished mahogany partitions. There is an oak bar with pine planking behind, superb oak-panelled walls, dark linoleum on the floor, and stout beams above. Fine coffee is still served, as well as beer and wine. A plaque in the wall outside records its status as London's first coffeehouse.

378

LOMBARD STREET

ST EDMUND THE KING

378   EC3

1100s FOUNDED; 1670–79 SIR CHRISTOPHER WREN, ROBERT HOOKE

The first church here in the twelfth century was dedicated to the East Anglian king and martyr who, despite being tied to a tree by Danes and shot with arrows, refused to renounce his Christianity. After the Great Fire, it was rebuilt by Wren and Robert Hooke with a three-bay street façade, arched windows, and a short spire that was completed in 1708. Inside is some handsome seventeenth-century woodwork and panelling, reorganised by Butterfield in 1846, and a fine font cover and pulpit.

379

SHIP TAVERN PASSAGE, 77–80 GRACECHURCH STREET

THE SWAN

379   EC3

1867 ARCHITECT UNKNOWN

This tiny, narrow, but very popular pub is reached by a rather forbidding alleyway off Gracechurch Street. The place is so small that, once you step inside, you are up against the ground floor bar, which serves ale only. Dickens may well have drunk here, as he did in many a city tavern. There are bare stone flag floors, and behind the bar, the wall is of rough brick. Upstairs, the lounge spans the alleyway and is a little wider than the minute saloon.

380

381

10-12 LEADNEHALL MARKET
LAMB TAVERN

380   EC3

140-144 LEADENHALL STREET
A LUTYENS BANK

381   EC3

1780 PARDY

On the site of a Roman basilica, this pub
served Leadenhall Market and was once
packed with market porters and traders. Today,
most of the drinkers work in the surrounding
financial sector. The first Lamb was an inn with
rooms to let, built in 1780 by a wine and spirits
merchant named Pardy. It mutated over the
years to become the ornate Victorian pub here
today, its windows decorated with sprays of
corn, birds, and foliage, a ceramic depiction
of Wren showing his plans for the Monument,
and a spiral iron staircase leading to an upper-
balcony mezzanine area. The City's first
smoke-free bar was here, in the upstairs
lounge. The Lamb has featured in the films
Brannigan (with John Wayne) and *Winds of
War* (with Robert Mitchum).

1929 SIR EDWIN LUTYENS, WHINNEY AND A. HALL

While Lutyens was creating this bank branch,
he was also working on the vast Midland Bank
headquarters which faces two streets (see
page 197). This bank, by contrast, was an infill,
squeezed in between its neighbours—one of
which has now been removed. Rather pretty
towers rise above a tidy seven-bay façade with
pleasing rows of windows, supported on lofty
arches that front the street.

382

LEADENHALL STREET AND ST MARY AXE,
FORMERLY P & O GROUP BUILDING

COMMERCIAL UNION INSURANCE

382   EC3

1968–69 GOLLINS MELVIN WARD PARTNERSHIP

Leadenhall Street, once part of the A11, is a major street running from Cornhill to Aldgate. Here are many company headquarters, banks, and financial institutions such as Lloyd's of London. One of the first-ever telephone exchanges was installed at 101 Leadenhall Street in 1879. At number 122, the P & O building is a complex glass-fronted structure with horizontal banding, and is relatively low by comparison with its neighbours. In its day, it was considered to be a highly sophisticated example of a glass-walled office but now it is to be replaced by a Richard Rogers skyscraper, tapering as it rises to protect views of St Paul's Cathedral from Fleet Street—to be built by 2010. Meanwhile, also fronting this large piazza, the tall Commercial Union Tower is a confident and technically sound building, set back from the street with its floors suspended on cantilevers around a central core.

LEADENHALL AND LIME STREETS

LLOYD'S OF LONDON

383   EC3

1978–86 RICHARD ROGERS PARTNERSHIP

This fascinating building (home to Lloyd's of London, the insurance institution) is based around a simple rectangle but reverses the conventions and—not unlike a medieval castle with its six vertical towers, albeit clad in stainless steel—keeps the lifts, staircases, electrical power conduits, and water pipes clinging to its exterior and so retains a dramatic twelve-storey atrium in the centre. The steel frame has a glass curtain wall and is 95 metres (312 feet) tall and looks especially dramatic when floodlit. This is one of the city's most celebrated and controversial modern buildings—set in the heart of the ancient quarter where Lloyd's began a coffeehouse in the 1600s.

383

384

1970s OFFICES

384   EC3

1973 Y. R. M. ARCHITECTS AND PLANNERS

This nicely proportioned commercial building has a simple frame, covered with travertine (a porous, light yellow rock). Home to companies such as the Bank Bumiputra Malaysia Merhad, its neat styling reflects the Chicago School. This group of Chicago architects influenced European Modernism, promoting the new steel-frame construction with masonry cladding and simple unornamented exteriors.

385

1980s OFFICES

385   EC3

1987 TERRY FARRELL AND CO

These modern but very elegant offices maximise their prominent, triangular, corner site beautifully, highlighted in particular by the rounded main entrance and the tower that rises above and just beyond the interesting 'balustrade' elements. Clad in granite, stainless steel, and painted aluminium, the building has other interesting entrances and many fine details that serve to emphasise its neat structure.

CUNARD HOUSE

386   EC3

1930 MEWÈS AND DAVIS

The London headquarters of Cunard was designed by Davis (Mewès had died in 1914). Arthur Joseph Davis had also designed the interiors of two Cunard liners, *Franconia* (1922) and *Laconia* (1923). The Cunard line—founded in 1840 by Samuel Cunard, of Nova Scotia, to carry the Royal Mail from Britain to North America—built the doomed *Lusitania, Queen Elizabeth* (1939), *QE2* (1969) and *Queen Mary 2* (2004). This large building arrived at a time when Edwardian baroque was being replaced by modernism and many major companies and financial institutions rebuilt or raised new headquarters in the city as architecture sought up-to-date ways to express their power. Today, this grand façade fronts many offices with several eateries at street level (including Caraveggio for Italian cuisine and a Caffè Nero coffee shop).

386

LEADENHALL STREET AND ST MARY AXE

ST ANDREW UNDERSHAFT

387   EC3

1147 ST ANDREW CORNHILL; 1520–32 RESTORED 1684

The church gained its new name in the 1400s, *undershaft* meaning 'under the maypole.' The maypole shaft used here for the spring festival was taller than the highest pinnacle on the tower. However, on Evil May Day, in 1517, a riot of apprentices led to three hundred arrests and one hanging. The shaft was stored under house eaves in Shaft Alley (also allied to the church's name) until, seen as a pagan symbol, it was chopped up and burnt. In 1520–32 the church was rebuilt in Gothic style and then restored in 1627. This was one of the rare medieval churches to survive the Great Fire (in part due to a vacant plot beside it) and the Blitz. It has stained glass and a font from the 1600s. Historian John Stow was buried here in 1605: every year, the Lord Mayor attends Stow's memorial service, placing a new quill pen into the hand of Stow's monument.
He gives the old quill and a copy of Stow's book to the child who has penned the best essay in London.

387

388

388

SWISS RE BUILDING

388   EC3

2004 LORD NORMAN FOSTER AND KEN SHUTTLEWORTH

The building's official name derives from its primary occupants, the Swiss Re re-insurers, but its rocket shape has lead to its more popular name, the Gherkin, and has also inspired the nickname of the 'Towering Innuendo.' With forty-one storeys that rise 180 meters (590 feet) high, this new landmark has some 745 dazzling glass panes clad over many thousands of tons of structural steel. Despite its overall curve, there is only one piece of actual curved glass on the building—the cap at the summit. Its restaurant at 165 metres (541 feet) is one of the highest in London. The design won the 2003 Emporis Skyscraper Award and the prestigious RIBA Stirling Prize for the best new building by a RIBA architect in 2004. It was voted as both the most admired new building in the world, in a 2005 survey of the world's largest firms of architects and, that same year, the Best New Building on the Planet in *Building Design Magazine*. The Gherkin has recently featured in television's *Doctor Who* and Woody Allen's film *Match Point*.

389

390

GREAT ST HELEN'S

389 EC3

NATIONAL EMPLOYERS HOUSE

390 EC3

300s; 1200s; 1400s; 1800s; J. L. PEARSON

On the site of a pagan temple, the first church here may have been built in the 300s by Emperor Constantine, when he was converted to Christianity, and was named for his mother, Helena. Today, St Helen's is the largest medieval London church to have survived both the Great Fire and World War II (but was subjected to IRA bomb damage in the 1990s). In the 1200s, a convent church arrived and now two naves stand side by side, the northern one then for nuns and the southern one for laity—separated by a screen. In 1385, the prioress was scolded (for keeping too many small dogs) and the nuns for kissing 'secular persons' and wearing showy veils. In 1538, the nunnery was surrendered to King Henry VIII. The interior remains largely 1400s. There are many monumental brasses from 1470 onwards, and Elizabethan and Jacobean tombs, including one for the Spencers. A memorial window marks Shakespeare's residence in the parish.

1914 H. P. BERLAGE

Commissioned by a Dutch shipping company, this rather splendid office building by the eminent Dutch architect is constructed on a steel frame and covered in green, glazed tiles. The main entrance doorways are set in the black, polished granite plinth which rises the full height of the building at each end. A grand, nautical sculpture on the corner is by Joseph Mendes da Costa.

391

SPANISH AND PORTUGUESE SYNAGOGUE

391   EC3

1700–01 JOSEPH AVIS

This is London's oldest synagogue, built by Sephardic Jews in 1701. Its congregation have included members of the Disraeli family, and the birth of Benjamin Disraeli in 1804 is recorded in the register. Built by a Quaker master-builder, the synagogue was the first to be opened after Jews were allowed to return to England in 165. Queen Anne donated one of the main beams. The design is a plain rectangle with two tiers of windows, a flat ceiling, and three galleries. There are original Jewish furnishings and seven chandelier candlesticks from Amsterdam.

392

LEADENHALL STREET

ST KATHERINE CREE

392   EC3

1280; TOWER 1504; CHURCH REBUILT 1504 AND 1628–31; 1700s CUPOLA ADDED; RESTORED BY MARSHALL SISSON 1962

This was built in 1280 for the parishioners so that the 'canons be not disturbed by the presence of laity' at the priory. Its vaulted ceiling, decorated with city livery company arms, rises above Tuscan columns. The east rose window symbolises the toothed wheel on which St Katharine was martyred by Emperor Maximilius in 307. The chapel contains the tomb of Sir Nicholas Throckmorton, advisor to Elizabeth I. In the 1600s, Lord Mayor John Gayer endowed the Lion Sermon to be preached annually after his survival of a face-to-face confrontation with a lion. Purcell, Wesley, and Handel have played the 1686 organ here.

393

ALDGATE

ST BOTOLPH

393   EC3

1741–44 GEORGE DANCE THE ELDER; 1880S JOHN FRANCIS BENTLEY

In the reign of King Edgar, this belonged to the Knighten Guild, thirteen knights granted land here. The Priory of Holy Trinity, Aldgate, rebuilt the original church just before the Reformation. During another 1740 rebuilding, the well-preserved body of a boy was found standing in the vaults; folk paid twopence to peep at him. Today this unassuming, brick building has a fine coved ceiling and bold balustrade. A monument remembers Lord Darcy and Sir Nicholas Carew, beheaded on Tower Hill in the 1500s for their Catholic faith. Daniel Defoe (married here in 1683) described two pits in the churchyard being filled with 5,136 plague victims in just four months.

42-47 MINORIES
IBEX HOUSE
394   EC3

1937 FULLER, HALL AND FOULSHAM

This large, nine-storey block features curved walls that
sweep around the corners very pleasingly. It is clad in
beige faience with very long 'stripes' of windows—
these were the longest in London when created in 1937,
measuring some 21 metres (70 feet). Refurbished
1997–98, today the building has 17,650 square metres
(190,000 square feet) of air-conditioned office and
leisure space plus ancillary accommodation with a rental
income of £3.1 million. Tenants have included a secretary
of state for the environment.

394

THE CRESCENT AND AMERICA SQUARE
DANCE'S DREAM
395   EC3

1760-74 GEORGE DANCE THE YOUNGER

This crescent was the earliest in London but only a
small group of five-storey houses remain of the original
scheme. Numbers 7 and 8 are in stock brick, and number
9 is brick with red dressings. Dance planned a square, a
crescent, and a circus. Built 1768–74, at the same time
as the Crescent, America Square was planned to provide
homes for middle-class merchants and sea captains and
was probably so-named to attract those with American
dealings; Baron Meyer de Rothschild lived at number 14.
The London and Blackwall Railway had encroached here
by 1836 and then it was bombed in 1941. None of the
original houses remain in America Square.

395

48 CRUTCHED FRIARS
CHESHIRE CHEESE
396   EC3

Housed under the railway lines, this is an atmospheric
two-bar pub with high arches enclosing doors, windows,
and signage—set between brick columns and gas lights.
The street is named after an order of friars who arrived
in England in the thirteenth century from Italy, so-called
because its members bore the sign of the cross on their
staves and a red cloth cross on their habits; they were
sometimes called the crossed, or crouched, friars.

396

397

398

2000 RICHARD ROGERS PARTNERSHIP

Here are two stunning, glazed slabs. Rising up twelve and fourteen storeys respectively, they are connected to another six storeys of space set behind the original façades of Lloyd's listed headquarters building on Lloyds Avenue. A long-lost churchyard, buried within the city block, has been freed up again—as public space—and so now an ancient part of London makes a marked contrast with the transparent gleam of the service towers. Although this is a confined site, the mass of glass channels all the natural light into the area most effectively.

1853–54; 1881–83 GEORGE BERKELEY; REBUILT 1935

Opened in 1841, this was the first railway station in the city. Until 1849, when steam locomotives were used, trains had to be dragged from Blackwall to Minories by cables and then reach Fenchurch Street under their own momentum—leaving by gravity, encouraged by a little push from the platform staff. In 1854, this new station opened. The completion of a line to Willesden Junction brought the Victorian suburbs of Hackney, Highgate, and Kilburn within commuting distance of the city. Now a minor terminus of the Eastern Region, its four platforms serve over 28,000 passengers in the rush hour. The grey stock-brick façade has eleven, round-arched windows, a classic station clock, and a rounded gable roof. The arched bow of the train-shed roof continues over the brick offices at the front to form a pediment. Novelist Douglas Adams named his character Fenchurch (in *The Hitchhikers Guide to the Galaxy*) after the station—where she was conceived.

HART STREET AND SEETHING LANE
ST OLAVE

399   EC3

c. 1025, 1200s, 1450; 1732 TOWER; 1954 REBUILT E. B. GLANFIELD

The first wooden church here honoured King Olaf, who had helped Ethelred the Unready fight the Danes; it may mark the battle site. A grisly gateway is decorated with horrid spikes and grinning skulls but inside are cool, whitewashed walls, Purbeck marble columns and an ancient crypt. Samuel Pepys worshipped here and, with his wife, Elizabeth, is buried in the nave. King Haakon VII of Norway (who had worshipped here during war exile) laid the foundation stone for the 1954 restoration. Plague victim burials here have a *p* after their name and include Mary Ramsay—said to have introduced this disaster to London.

399

400

TRINITY SQUARE
TRINITY HOUSE

400   EC3

1796 SAMUEL WYATT; 1953 REBUILT RICHARDSON AND HOUFE; 1990 REFURBISHED

This is the headquarters of the corporation that, since the first lighthouse was built in 1609, organises the nation's harbour pilots, buoys, and lighthouses. Its foundation stone was laid by William Pitt, then master of the corporation. The elegant rooms have a maritime flavour—with royal paintings, shipwrights' models, and the ship's bell from the Royal Yacht *Britannia*. Its Ionic façade survived World War II bombing. Trinity House reports directly to the sovereign.

10 TRINITY SQUARE, FORMERLY PORT OF LONDON AUTHORITY
WILLIS FABER

401   EC3

1912 SIR EDWIN COOPER

Once the headquarters of the Port of London Authority, this dominant feature of the square was built in extravagant Edwardian style, as befitted the status of the London Docks—then the centre of the mercantile world. With its high, ornate tower, huge columns, domes, and sculpture, the enormous building occupies an entire block. Inside is a vast, circular hall with a diameter of 34 metres (110 feet). Today this palatial building is occupied by Willis Faber, a prestigious insurance company. Nearby are gardens with Lutyens Mercantile Marine Memorial, and a stone in the pavement notes that this was the site of the scaffold where some 125 people were executed outside the Tower of London walls.

401

-02

WHITE TOWER, TOWER OF LONDON

402   EC3

1078-97

The White Tower was begun by William the Conqueror, as a strong defence keep in Caen stone and Kentish ragstone. The walls are up to 4 metres (15 feet) thick. The lower floors now contain an incredible armour collection. The curtain walls, enclosing some 18 acres, were started under Henry III and completed under Edward I. The Tower guards the Crown Jewels and has been a palace, a royal menagerie (from 1235, when the Holy Roman Emperor gave Henry II three leopards), a prison, a mint, an observatory, and a place of execution. Its dungeons included the Little Ease, a dark cell too small for a prisoner to stand or lie down in. Soldiers' and servants' quarters were on the first floor, the banqueting hall, St John's Chapel, and nobles' bedrooms on the second, and royal bedrooms and the council chamber on the third. After the killing of the two young princes (Edward V and the Duke of York), the Garden Tower became known as the Bloody Tower. Tradition states that the State will fall should the resident ravens—which have nested here since the 1600s—ever leave. In 1554, the future Elizabeth I was brought through Traitor's Gate to be imprisoned in the Bell Tower. Executions here have included Anne Boleyn and Lady Jane Grey—both said to haunt the tower. In 1972, a nine-year-old tourist saw an execution scene re-enacted before her and correctly told her family that Anne Boleyn had been beheaded by sword, not an axe. But this is probably the most haunted building in London. Spectres include headless women, a giant bear, a man on a stretcher with his head tucked in his arm, two boys in white nightgowns who may be the murdered princes, Saint Thomas à Becket (his ghost was the first one reported here in 1241) and a lady being chased around the scaffold by the axeman. Countless screams and moans haunt the torture chambers. Henry Percy, Earl of Northumberland (probably murdered in the Bloody Tower) walks the ramparts, as does another famous prisoner, Sir Walter Raleigh.

403

404

26 GREAT TOWER STREET
CHRIST'S HOSPITAL OFFICES

403   EC3

ST DUNSTUN'S HILL AND IDOL LANE
ST DUNSTAN IN THE EAST

404   EC3

1915 SIR REGINALD BLOMFIELD

This is a very pretty building with beautifully crafted brickwork and fine Dutch styling. From its regal door with the cross above to the dormer windows peeping out at the top, all is elegance and neat detail. Architect Reginald Blomfield was also a garden designer and author. He designed the Menin Gate Memorial in Ypres, Flanders, and the Carlton Club in Pall Mall (destroyed in World War II), and remodelled Regent Street in the 1920s.

1697 SIR CHRISTOPHER WREN; REBUILT 1817

Named for a St Dunstan, a great Saxon Archbishop of Canterbury, the first and very prosperous parish church was raised here during the late 1200s. The main body of the church survived the Great Fire but Wren rebuilt the damaged tower and steeple, in seventeenth-century Gothic style. The tower is surmounted by tall pinnacles, behind which flying buttresses support the lantern and spire, topped by a ball and vane. The effect is strikingly delicate but it resisted a fierce hurricane in 1703 that damaged many another city steeple. Today, only the four-stage tower remains after World War II bombing. The shell of the church still stands, trees and foliage growing out of its windows, and the Worshipful Company of Gardeners have now transformed the area into a garden.

405

18 ST MARY AT HILL

WATERMEN'S HALL

405   EC3

1778–80 WILLIAM BLACKBURN; 1951
AND 1961 HENRY V. GORDON

The Watermen's Company was established by
an Act of Parliament in 1555 and by 1585
Queen Elizabeth I had granted them a coat of
arms. These oarsmen enabled Londoners to
travel along the Thames but mainly served to
help them to cross from one side to another—
at a time when bridges were relatively few.
They had to serve a seven-year apprenticeship
to learn how to navigate the complex tides
and water currents. The company's first hall
(in Upper Thames Street, in the 1600s) was
destroyed in the Great Fire and twice rebuilt
before they moved their headquarters to St
Mary-at-Hill in 1780. After World War II
damage, this hall with its sturdy, stone Ionic
front was repaired and improved in 1951 and
1961. All is curves and arches, with some
decorative detailing and a central pediment.

406

ST MARY AT HILL AND LOVAT LANE

ST MARY-AT-HILL

406   EC3

1100S FOUNDED; 1400S REBUILT; 1670–76 SIR CHRISTOPHER
WREN; 1848–49 RESTORED JAMES SAVAGE

Damaged in the Great Fire, this church was
rebuilt by Wren, who incorporated the old
tower into a square, Dutch-like church,
entered via a garden courtyard. The interior
has a fine central dome and vaulted ceiling,
supported by corner Corinthian columns. The
nave was partly rebuilt by James Savage who
restored the church again in 1848–49 after
a fire. Much of the woodwork is original but
some was expertly replaced by Williams Gibbs
Rogers in the late 1800s. Close to Billingsgate
fish market, this is an old fisherman's church
and, each October, the Billingsgate fish
merchants hold their harvest festival here.

407

PEEK HOUSE

1873 SIR ERNEST GEORGE AND THOMAS VAUGHAN

This High Victorian façade incorporates very neatly positioned, decorated openings in a solid wall and delicate arches above the second-storey windows. An entrance to the church is through an open arch and small courtyard beyond. Sir Ernest George was one of the most successful later Victorian architects. He went into partnership with Thomas Vaughan in 1861, and later (with Harold Peto) formed one of the most successful practices of his day. He built many houses, including one for W. S. Gilbert in 1881–65, was responsible for the Royal College of Music in 1910, president of RIBA 1908 to 1910, made a knight in 1911, and elected to the Royal Academy in 1917.

408

ST MARGARET PATTENS

1530 REBUILT; 1684–89 SIR CHRISTOPHER WREN

The church entrance is flanked by an early 1800s house and shop but a 1067 inscription on the old stone porch indicates the church's longer history. It drew its name from a local industry: pattens (wooden soles worn to protect shoes from mud) were made here and sold in Rood Lane. Glass cabinets by the entry hold a few examples. After the Great Fire took its toll, Wren's rebuild included a 61-metre (200-foot) spiky spire. Inside are canopied pews from 1686—one carved with with 'CW 1686' may have been Wren's—plus a beadle's pew, and a punishments bench with a devil's head where naughty folk had to sit during the service. An hourglass is set beside the pulpit for timing sermons. Relics include a baptismal register some 450 years old, and a 1543 silver communion cup.

409

SHOPS AND OFFICES

409   EC3

1868 R. L. ROUMIEU

Eastcheap is on the site of a medieval meat market and, in 1831, a Roman road was discovered here. The stretch that used to run north past Gracechurch Street was demolished in 1829–31 when King William Street was built. The south side of the street was set back when the Metropolitan Railway was built in about 1875. This rather fine block has quite dramatic Gothic elements—more usually associated with churches. There are high gables, arches, and columns everywhere. Numbers 33–35 were described by Sir Nikolaus Pevsner as, 'one of the maddest displays in London of gabled Gothic brick.'

THE GREAT FIRE OF LONDON

This conflagration began on Sunday, September 2, 1666, in Pudding Lane in the king's bakery. Fires were fairly common in this town of close-knit timber buildings but soon, fanned by a stiff wind, it spread rapidly. There was no fire brigade, water sources and wells were low after a hot, dry summer—and the fire was further fuelled by highly flammable pitch, tar, timber, and brandy in the Thames-side warehouses.

Local people, armed with leather buckets, tried to douse the flames or to beat them out with staves, but soon melted lead from St Paul's ran down into the streets, burning pigeons fell from the sky, stones flew like hot grenades, and the pavements glowed red. The eastward-spreading fire lasted for almost five days until checked by gunpowder explosions that cleared a vast area and so saved the Tower of London. The westward flames were not finally doused until the Thursday night.

The city was virtually destroyed at a cost of some £11 million. Almost all the remains of medieval London had burned. Within the city walls, five-sixths of London had vanished. In total, 1.8 square kilometres (436 acres) lay in ruins, and the losses included palaces and mansions, markets, and prisons, the Guildhall, the Royal Exchange, Bridewell Palace, St Paul's Cathedral, plus eighty-seven churches, six chapels, fifty-two company halls, 13,200 houses, three city gates, and four stone bridges.

Only a few people died but about 100,000 people were left homeless.

London's regrowth

In just five years, 75 percent of the houses lost had been replaced in new, wider—and far more elegant—streets. From 1666–1711, Sir Christopher Wren helped to rebuild the city and designed over fifty-one churches, including the new St Paul's Cathedral—completed by 1710 and then the largest cathedral in Europe. With Robert Hooke, he designed the monument that marked where the fire began.

The new buildings were no longer timber but made of solid stone or brick. The areas of London became more distinct in style. In the West End, shops and wealthy homes arose, the City was the centre for business and banking, and the East End was where labourers, immigrants, and dockworkers lodged. Insurance companies sprang up in the wake of the financial crisis that the fire had caused—and many set up fire brigades. Each company had its own 'fire mark' on a lead plaque placed high on the front of a building—many still visible today.

THE MONUMENT

410   EC3

1671–77 SIR CHRISTOPHER WREN, ROBERT HOOKE

The site of the outbreak of the Great Fire of 1666 is marked by a Doric column in fine white Portland stone. It stands 62 metres (202 feet) high on a square pedestal, decorated with griffin wings—and cost £13,450. The Act of Parliament initiating the rebuilding of the city also covered the raising of this commemorative edifice—still the tallest, isolated, stone Doric column in the world. Three panels on the pedestal bear Latin inscriptions. One, translated, tells how: in the year of Christ 1666, on September 2, at a distance eastward from this place of 202 feet, which is the height of this column, a fire broke out in the dead of night which, the wind blowing, devoured even distant buildings, and rushed devastatingly through every quarter with astonishing swiftness and noise. The balcony at the top is approached by a spiral staircase of 311 steps. In 1788, a baker threw himself from here, the first of six people to commit suicide before the gallery was enclosed in an iron cage. The column was completely renovated in 1834; the gilt-bronze 'flaming' urn was regilded, as it was again in 1954, when the stone was steam-cleaned and World War II bomb scars removed.

410

411

412

OFFICES IN FORMER BILLINGSGATE MARKET

411   EC3

ST MAGNUS THE MARTYR

412   EC3

1875 SIR HORACE JONES;
1990 RICHARD ROGERS AND PARTNERS

Billingsgate fish market had occupied this site since Roman times, but the city markets received their royal charters from Edward III in 1327. Behind the arcades were two large halls, busy with the sale of two hundred tons of fish daily—while porters rushed everywhere with fish on bobbing basket hats. The exterior is reminiscent of French Renaissance style, with mansard roofs, pavilions at each end, a magnificent statue of Britannia, and golden dolphins on the weathervanes. The fish market moved to new premises on the Isle of Dogs in 1982, and Sir Richard Rogers was responsible for a sympathetic conversion to offices.

FOUNDED PRE-1067; REBUILT 1234;
1671–76 SIR CHRISTOPHER WREN; 1705 TOWER

Set almost underneath London Bridge, St Magnus was an important meeting point in medieval London where notices were read and punishments meted out: three of Wyatt's rebels were hanged here in 1544. Demolished by the Great Fire, the church was rebuilt by Wren—its high steeple added in 1705. The roof was replaced after a fire in 1760 and in 1762, the aisles were shortened by George Dance to allow the pavement to pass under the tower when the road was widened. The nave has Ionic colonnades, tunnel vaulting, and oval windows. To reduce the noise of the iron-rimmed carts working in nearby Billingsgate market, the windows in the north wall were altered to their present round form in 1782. In the churchyard are the remains of a Roman wharf and some ancient stones from old London Bridge.

413

75 KING WILLIAM STREET

ADELAIDE HOUSE

413   EC4

1924–25 SIR JOHN BURNET TAIT AND PARTNERS

This city office building adopted an exotic Egyptian style—so fashionable in the 1920s, following the discovery of Tutankhamun's tomb by Howard Carter in 1922. The building has huge curved cornices, striking vertical bays and four black marble Doric columns astride its wonderful, glittering entrance. Today, the building is the headquarters of solicitors Berwin Leighton Paisner.

KING WILLIAM STREET, NEAR LONDON BRIDGE

FISHMONGERS HALL

414   EC4

1310; 1434; 1671 EDWARD JARMAN; 1831–34 HENRY ROBERTS;
1951 RESTORED AUSTEN HALL

The Fishmongers' Company, is one of the oldest livery companies, established in 1272. Their first company hall was raised in 1310; the next one burnt down in the Great Fire; and this replacement, designed by Edward Jarman, opened in 1671—but was demolished to make way for the new London Bridge in 1827. Inside are an embroidered fifteenth-century funeral pall, the dagger with which Lord Mayor Walworth (a fishmonger) killed Wat Tyler (leader of the Peasants' Revolt) at Smithfield in 1381, and a life-size wooden statue of the Lord Mayor, dagger in hand.

414

415

416

ST CLEMENT EASTCHEAP

415   EC4

LONDON LIFE ASSOCIATION

416   EC4

1000S; 1632; 1683–87 SIR CHRISTOPHER WREN

The first little church here was dedicated to the martyred bishop of Rome, who was thrown into the sea with an anchor round his neck—and so became the patron saint of seamen. It has a stuccoed exterior, and exposed brickwork in the tower. The interior is plain, greatly altered by Butterfield in 1870–89. It is probably the church featured in the nursery rhyme 'Oranges and Lemons, say the bells of St Clements.' Sadly, its stained-glass windows were destroyed in the Blitz.

1925–27 W. CURTIS GREEN

This rather grand building has a sturdy palazzo frontage with a central screen of recessed stone columns set above its fine entrance and many immaculate decorative motifs. A short flight of steps lead up to a neat door in a rectangular entrance. An oval decorative feature poses grandly above the door—and four cheery cherubs are perched here, too.

417

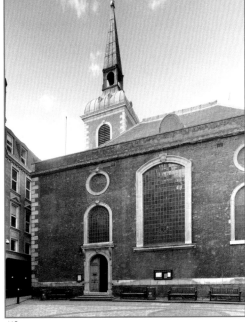

418

LOMBARD STREET AND KING WILLIAM STREET
ST MARY WOOLNOTH

417   EC4

ABCHURCH LANE
ST MARY ABCHURCH

418   EC4

1273 KNOWN; 1442 REBUILT;, 1670–77 REPAIRED SIR CHRISTOPHER WREN; 1716–27 NICHOLAS HAWKSMOOR

This church stands on the site of a Roman temple to Concord and a Saxon church founded by Wulfnoth, a prince. This 1700s building was one of Queen Anne's fifty new churches and was designed by Wren's extraordinary pupil, Hawksmoor. The broad tower almost fills the west frontage. Gorgeous clusters of Corinthian columns are inset from the corners and support a clerestory with large windows. The regal interior is based on the Egyptian Hall of Vitruvius, with a dramatic inner space created as a square within a square, and black columns sporting sinuous gold decoration. In 1897–1900, Bank tube station was built below the church; this involved the grisly task of removing all the bodies from the vaults. Edward Lloyd, owner of Lloyds Coffee House (where the insurance company, Lloyds of London, began) was buried here in 1712.

1100s; 1681–86 SIR CHRISTOPHER WREN; 1953 RESTORATION

The first church here may have been named 'Up Church' because it was upstream from its owner, the Priory of St Mary Overie (now Southwark Cathedral). Surrounded by a tangle of alleys and set before a tiny cobbled square (once its graveyard), this is one of the prettiest of Wren's churches. Built in dark redbrick with stone dressings, its style Dutch influenced, it has a lovely shallow dome within—supported by eight arches, pierced by round stained-glass windows, and painted by William Snow in 1708–14. There is some glorious seventeenth-century woodwork with the original dark, oxblood stain. The splendid altarpiece, dripping with carvings of fruit and garlands, is by Grinling Gibbons; 1940 bombs broke this into two thousand pieces that took five years to restore. Some of the carved pews incorporated dog kennels and sword rests.

419

MANSION HOUSE

419 EC4

1739-52 GEORGE DANCE THE ELDER

Built in Palladian style, this is the official residence of the
Lord Mayor of London. It has three main storeys, a fine
entrance façade with a six-column Corinthian portico,
and many state rooms, including the long Egyptian Hall
where the Lord Mayor holds banquets. The Lord Mayor's
Police Court is the only Court of Justice in a private
residence in England. Eleven holding cells include one
for women (called the birdcage) where the women's
suffrage campaigner, Emmeline Pankhurst, was once
imprisoned. Mark Twain wrote about the building in
A Connecticut Yankee in King Arthur's Court. Here, the
Chancellor of the Exchequer makes an annual speech
about the British economy.

20

ST STEPHEN WALBROOK

600s; REBUILT 1429–39 AND 1672–79;
1717 SPIRE SIR CHRISTOPHER WREN

Once upon a seventh century, a Saxon
church stood here on the banks of the River
Walbrook (a Thames tributary that now flows
underground). Wren's majestic church has
a centralised plan—just as at St Paul's
Cathedral—with its beautiful, central dome
set above glorious arches and columns.
Despite bomb damage in 1940, the rich
seventeenth-century fittings, gifted by the
Grocer's Company, survived. Here, in the Lord
Mayor's parish church, dramatist and architect
John Vanbrugh (most famous for Blenheim
Palace) was buried in 1726. The huge, white,
polished stone altar is by Henry Moore. The
Samaritans charity was founded here in 1953
at a time when there were some three suicides
a day in London. A telephone in a glass box
marks the establishment of this important
hotline for people in distress.

421

103 CANNON STREET

ALL BAR ONE

1866 FREDERICK JAMESON

This was known as Candelwrithe Street, back
in the 1100s, and then later as Candlewick
Street—because of the candle makers who
once lived and worked here. Today, this mid-
Victorian, four-bay building makes a sharp
contrast to the more recent buildings in its
vicinity. The façade has many pretty features
including arches, columns, and Venetian
windows that change in scale with each
storey. This is now a pub and restaurant.

422

INNHOLDERS HALL

422   EC4

c. 1521, 1670; FAÇADE 1886 J. DOUGLASS MATHEWS;
1947–52 RESTORED E. D. JEFFERIS MATHEWS

College Street is sometimes called Great Elbow Lane because of the way it bends. This hall has an early-1700s doorway, with a decorated scroll pediment and coat of arms. The building was badly damaged in World War II, but the Old Court Room—with its seventeenth-century panelling, plaster ceiling, and fireplace—and the magnificent dining hall survived. In May, 1941, a bomb fell nearby and set the hall alight. The Hall Keeper asked the Enfield Fire Brigade to help, promising, in exchange, something that would help to put them out, too! He duly reported that a quantity of wine had also been 'blitzed.' A new entrance hall and reception room were created here in 1990.

423

BUSH LANE HOUSE

423   EC4

1976 ARUP ASSOCIATES

Here, in a delightful mix of practicality and design excellence, the tubular stainless steel on the building's exterior is filled with water as fire-protection, but also creates a most unusual diamond pattern. In 1995, a glazed atrium was added to the entrance lobby, by Malcolm Payne Design Group Limited. Roman remains have been found close by and it is believed that Roman pavements once extended to Cannon Street and Bush Lane. Set behind an iron grille in the wall of offices near here is the London Stone—possibly over three thousand years old, and of Druid or Roman origin, that may indicate the mystical centre of London or Ancient Britain.

CANNON STREET

CANNON STREET STATION

424   EC4

1865–66 J. HAWKSHAW AND J. W. BARRY, ENGINEERS

This is where, from the 900s, the Hanseatic merchants had their mediaeval steelyards until 1598. Today, all that remains of the original station—built for the South Eastern Railway's City terminus—are the huge brick walls (that once carried an almost semicircular, single-span arch of glass and iron) and two magnificent redbrick towers at the mouth of the train shed. Prior to 1926, when electrification arrived here, most trains had to reverse in and out of Cannon Street to reach Charing Cross. During the 1960s, the station was revamped to include shops, office blocks, and a pedestrian walkway.

425

426

MASTER-BUILT HOUSES

425   EC4

1703 MASTER-BUILDERS; REBUILT 1976

Here, in a small city street, these beautifully decorated houses are the work of master-builders. Numbers 1 and 2 are immaculate, possibly the finest early eighteenth-century houses still to be seen in the city. Laurence Pountney Hill is named after a church here that burned down in the Great Fire and one Sir John de Poultenay, who lived nearby and was lord mayor four times in the 1300s. The Black Prince lived in a house here in 1359 and, in 1646, William Harvey (Charles I's physician and the discoverer of the circulation of the blood) also lived in this street.

VINTNERS HALL

426   EC4

1446, 1671, 1870,
1909–10 A. H. KERSEY, EDWARD JARMAN AND OTHERS

The site for Vintners Hall was bequeathed to the company in 1446. The hall was rebuilt in 1671 after the Great Fire broke out in Pudding Lane, only a few hundred metres away. Its thirteen almshouses were also lost. During the 1700s, the windows were sashed and new iron gates with two lamps were installed. Later, in 1822, some of the rooms were sacrificed when Upper Thames Street was widened. However, today's Court Room retains some lovely old carvings and several paintings. In the entrance are a pair of Coade Stone swans (1800) and a figure of a charity boy (1840). A stained-glass window depicts the meeting of five kings.

427

428

QUEEN'S STREET AND UPPER THAMES STREET
THAMES HOUSE

427   EC4

1911 COLLCUTT AND HAMP

This rather splendid Edwardian baroque office block with its imposing entrance, sturdy wrought-iron balcony, and a mix of long, narrow, and round windows plus one bay window, have survived the post-war reconstruction of Upper Thames Street all around them. Now the building presents a stern frontage that challenges anyone threatening this stalwart survivor.

COLLEGE HILL
ST MICHAEL PATERNOSTER ROYAL

428   EC4

1219; 1400s EXPANDED RICHARD WHITTINGTON;
1686–94 SIR CHRISTOPHER WREN; 1713 STEEPLE;
1967 RESTORED E. DAVIES

The name Royal has nothing to do with kings but is a corruption of Reole, a nearby street, where local merchants imported wine from La Reole, in France. Here, Richard (Dick) Whittington established a college for priests and expanded the church (that duly burned down in the Great Fire), and also lived next door. He was buried here in 1423; a memorial tablet marks the site of his tomb, and the Dick Whittington window, by John Hayward, has beautiful stained glass. The stone-faced front is the work of Wren's master mason, Edward Strong, and the elegant spire was completed in 1713. The pulpit is attributed to Grinling Gibbons. This is now the chapel and headquarters of the Missions to Seamen.

429

10 DOWGATE HILL
DYER'S HALL

429   EC4

1482, 1545, 1681, 1731, 1760S; 1839–40 CHARLES DYER;
1948 REPAIRED

The dyers' first Royal Charter was issued by Henry IV in 1471. Through the succeeding centuries, from 1482, several of their buildings have succumbed to fire and collapse, but throughout, the dyers have continued overseeing and developing their craft of dyeing. The current hall opened in 1842 and is one of the smaller and more intimate city livery halls. The entrance, set in a classical brick and stucco façade, leads to a beautiful, glass-vaulted corridor and, thence, to an interior with decoration in hues that reflect the role of dyers. The superb Millennium window, in particular, shows the various dying processes in magnificent colours. Along with the vintners, the dyers are charged with the care of the swans on the River Thames.

430

21–22a COLLEGE HILL
WHITTINGTON COLLEGE GATEWAYS

430   EC4

c. 1680 RICHARD WHITTINGTON EXECUTORS

Named after the famous mayor of old London town, this college for priests shared its name with its associated almshouses and came under the jurisdiction of St Michael Paternoster Royal on College Street. After Richard Whittington's death in 1423, his executors received a charter from King Henry VI to establish the two entities but the college would later be suppressed—during King Henry VIII's Reformation—and new almshouses would be raised elsewhere. Today, truly sumptuous doorways and pediments, with wreaths of decoration and a canopy above, mark the site.

DOWGATE HILL
SKINNERS' HALL

431   EC4

1666; 1770–90 W. JUPP; REBUILT 1850 AND 1984–86 J. SAMPSON LLOYD

Skinners' Hall is one of the three livery company halls still in Dowgate Hill. The guild has owned this site since the 1200s. Today's building, a scheduled Ancient Monument, has a five-bay façade, set back from the street, and an elegant, Coade stone pediment, modelled by John Bacon in 1770. An arched passage leads through a charming, small court and the livery hall beyond. Rebuilt in 1850, this is decorated with paintings of the fur trade and skinners—from the Middle Ages to the late 1600s—and has carved cedar panels, and a staircase from 1670. There is a sweet roof garden with a fountain. The Skinners' Company has a history of some seven hundred years, during which it has overseen the production and sale of furs for trimming garments, and apprenticeships in the trade.

431

36 QUEEN'S STREET
SEVEN-STOREY OFFICES

432   EC4

1985 TERRY FARRELL AND CO.

Here, in miniature palazzo style, seven storeys incorporate set-backs, with keystones and curved shapes giving the top levels extra interest. Queen Street was once home to the church of St Thomas the Apostle, first mentioned in 1170, which was rebuilt by the Lord Mayor in 1371 but destroyed in the 1666 Great Fire. Rather more recently, the street has become the focus of Light up Queen Street, a campaign by the Corporation of London to energise the mid-winter cityscape and draw attention to the streets, buildings, and history, with imaginative illuminations created by selected artists.

432

433

433

GARLICK HILL AND SKINNERS LANE

ST JAMES GARLICKHITHE

433   EC4

1100S; 1326 RICHARD DE ROTHING; 1676–83 STEEPLE
1714–17 SIR CHRISTOPHER WREN; 1954–63 RESTORED
LOCKHART SMITH AND ALEXANDER GALE

The first known record of the church was in
a will dated around 1100; and Stow's *Survey
of London*, in 1598, mentions garlic being
landed and sold near here (*hythe* means
'jetty'). The church was rebuilt in 1326 and
again after the Great Fire. Its delicate baroque
spire, with ascending tiers, was added some
thirty years later. Here, once again, Wren
explores a central theme with an open central
nave and the highest church roof in the city,
second only to St Paul's Cathedral. Flooded
with natural light, the church became known
as 'Wren's Lantern.' There are sword rests with
lions and unicorns, a pulpit with a wig stand, a
magnificent organ, and a mummified body in
the vestry. Several medieval Lord Mayors were
buried here.

30 CANNON STREET

DISTINCTIVE OFFICES

434   EC4

1978

This vast office building, set on an island site,
looks like a great liner with its high curved
'prow,' raised 'forecastle,' and multiple
windows. Glass canopies on both facades
mark the entrances while glazed revolving
doors lead to the reception area. There are
granite floors and tall double-glazed windows
around the entire perimeter, providing
excellent natural light and the bonus of
superb views over the city. The 6,898 metres
(74,255 square feet) of offices have been
refurbished several times and occupiers have
included IASB (International Accounting
Standards Board), Asahi Bank, Credit
Lyonnais, Bank of New York. Goldman Sachs,
the London Stock Exchange, the Royal Bank
of Canada, and BT.

434

435

436

QUEEN VICTORIA STREET
ALBERT BUILDINGS

435   EC4

QUEEN VICTORIA STREET
ALBERT BUILDINGS

435   EC4

1872 FREDERICK J. WARD

Queen Victoria Street cut through from the Victoria Embankment to the Bank of England in 1867–71, at the same time as, down below, the District Line was being burrowed underneath. Many of the Victorian offices have now been replaced by modern blocks but this rather fine, French Gothic edifice still stands, its elegant splendour raised to glorify commerce and filling its triangular, corner wedge with arcades, arched windows, and pretty cornice decoration. The offices on page 247 seem, in some respects, like a modern and more angular variation on the theme.

QUEEN VICTORIA STREET
NUMBER 60

436   EC4

1999 FOGGO ASSOCIATES

In 2002, this building was given the City Heritage New City Architecture Award. The façade is of patinated bronze by Capisco and is, in fact, the largest patinated exterior in Britain. Its brise-soleil grilles are supported by bronze columns. A relatively low-rise building, it has nine floors and an atrium at the rear. Both the interior and lift lobbies have fine granite paving.

437

438

ST MARY ALDERMARY

1510–18 REBUILT; 1626–29 TOWER REBUILT;
1682 POSSIBLY SIR CHRISTOPHER WREN;
1702–04 TOWER;
1867–68 RESTORED RICHARD TRESS AND CHARLES;
POST-1945 RESTORED ARTHUR NISBET

The name means 'older Mary,' so the original church was probably older than eleventh-century St Mary-le-Bow and was certainly raised over nine hundred years ago. Queen Victoria Street was cut through the City in 1867–71, and so this church was not raised on the original site. Moreover, it is a Gothic copy, complete with a fan-vaulted ceiling and pinnacled spire. The sword-rest for the lord mayor's ceremonial sword is one of only two wooden sword rests to survive in a city church; the others are metal, usually wrought iron. Early benefactors here included Richard Chaucer, vintner, a relative of poet Geoffrey Chaucer. In 1510, Sir Henry Keeble, grocer and Lord Mayor, financed the building of the new church. Henry Gold (rector here 1526–34), opposed Henry VIII's first divorce, and so was hanged and beheaded at Tyburn. Parish registers, dating from 1558, note the 1663 marriage here of poet John Milton to his third wife.

25 CANNON STREET

2003

This fine building explores various orientations of neat windows and has a splendid sense of symmetry—with even the street number set to each side of its fine arched entrance. Here, today, King and Spalding International LLP's team of lawyers specialise in commercial and financial transactions . . . but this has been a busily occupied site from earliest times. Excavations have uncovered Middle Bronze Age pottery, early Roman quarries and timber buildings, and a Roman road set just to the north.

I GROVELANDS COURT, BOW LANE

WILLIAMSON'S TAVERN

439   EC4

1700s; REBUILT 1930s

This tiny alley of Groveland's Court was the site of a new Lord Mayor's house, built over Roman ruins after the Great Fire. In 1739, the tavern was sold and converted into a hotel, but the mayors stayed here until 1753; one of the rooms in the pub is still called Mansion House lounge today. Originally at the mouth of the court, the wrought-iron gates include the initials of their donors, the royals William and Mary. Rebuilt in the 1930s, the tavern is believed to hold the oldest excise licence in the city, with a stone in the main bar, marking the centre point of the old City of London.

439

I8-20 CANNON STREET

PARALLEL LINES

440   EC4

Greycoat took over the lease to this building in Cannon Street, from a subsidiary of Reit Asset Management for some £17.5 million. They had already very recently secured number 30 Cannon Street (see page 246) so this completed the unification of an important island site—bounded by Cannon Street, Queen Victoria Street, and Friday Street. The property was let until 2008 at a gross rent of £1,956,000 per year. Cannon Street was once called Candlewick Street, named after the candle makers who lived and worked here long ago.

440

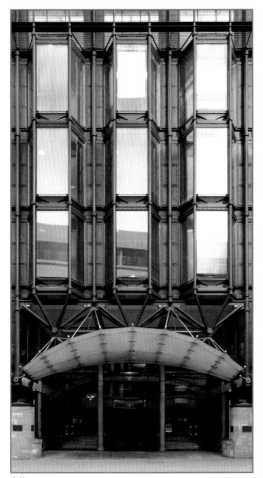

441

442

CANNON STREET, FRIDAY STREET AND DISTAFF LANE, FORMERLY FINANCIAL TIMES BUILDING

BRACKEN HOUSE

441   EC4

1988–90 SIR ALBERT RICHARDSON; MICHAEL HOPKINS AND PARTNERS

This was once the main office of the *Financial Times*, busy with furnaces, plate casting, and the setting of metal type. It was the first post-war London building to be listed and is now regarded as a classic twentieth-century milestone. Albert Richardson was awarded the Royal Gold Medal for Architecture in 1947, made president of the Royal Academy in 1954, and knighted in 1956. Now, renovations have seen the central hall replaced by a seven-storey circular atrium, offering lots more office space. All is steel and glittering glass, to maximise the effect of transparency. Four-storey, dark-red brick piers stand on a plinth of red sandstone, while a high, copper cornice is set back on tiny, glass-brick piers. An interesting feature is the gleaming, Zodiac sundial calendar, which some claim features the face of Winston Churchill.

UPPER THAMES STREET

ST MARY SOMERSET

442   EC4

1686–95 SIR CHRISTOPHER WREN

Only the 36-metre (120-foot) tower remains of this seventeenth-century church, the main part of which was demolished in 1871. Another church (St Mary, Hoxton) was built with the proceeds of the sale, and the single 1678 bell was transferred there. The tower has arched and round windows and is surmounted by pinnacles that look rather like tall, narrow chess pieces. Upper Thames Street is largely occupied by paper makers and dealers. Just south lies Queenhithe Dock, the site of the earliest fish-market in London.

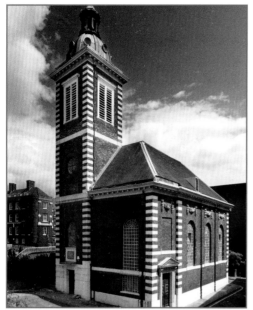

443

ST BENET PAUL'S WHARF

443   EC4

1100s, 1677–83 SIR CHRISTOPHER WREN AND MASTER MASON THOMAS STRONG

Shakespeare lived nearby and, in *Twelfth Night*, a clown mentions this church. After the Great Fire, it was replaced by a Dutch country-style building in red and blue bricks, with a hipped roof and curved stone garlands above large windows. Its short tower has a small dome, lantern, and simple spire. Its square inside has a monument to Inigo Jones—buried in the old chancel. St Benet was the Parish church for the Doctor's Commons—a legal institution that could arrange hasty marriages—some 13,423 were solemnized from 1708 to 1731; Henry Fielding (author of *Tom Jones*) married his first wife's maid here in 1747. Parish records refer to a Welsh presence here, from about 1320. Queen Elizabeth I despatched the Welsh to the area and this is now a Welsh church, with services conducted in that language.

444

QUEEN VICTORIA STREET

ST NICHOLAS COLE ABBEY

444   EC4

1144, 1671–77 SIR CHRISTOPHER WREN; 1962 RESTORATION ARTHUR BAILEY

Wren's first post-Fire church, it cost £5,042, including a charge for 'Dinner for Dr Wren and other Company—£2 14s 0d' and 'Half a pint of canary for Dr Wren's coachmen—6d.' It was partly demolished in 1868 but the unusual tower was spared—with its elaborate balcony, railings, pinnacles, obelisks, and vases. After World War II damage, the church was restored to Wren's original design. Numerous fishmongers were buried here during the 1500s. The first celebration of mass after Queen Mary I's accession took place here, but the priest, accused of selling his wife to a butcher, was soon pelted with rotten eggs. A later patron was Puritan Colonel Hacker, who commanded the guard at the execution of Charles I. In the film *The Lavender Hill Mob*, the gold bullion robbery takes place just outside Cole Abbey.

445

QUEEN VICTORIA STREET

COLLEGE OF ARMS

445   EC4

1671–77 MAURICE EMMETT (MASTER BRICKLAYER)

This is the home of the royal heralds, granted their first charter by Richard III in 1484. In medieval times, the heralds organised tournaments as well as the knights' arms on their shields and crests. Built by master bricklayers in artisan style, the building has a simple brick façade that surrounds three sides of a shallow open court, with two wings linked by magnificent black and gilded wrought-iron gates (from Goodrich Court in Hertfordshire). The College still examines and records pedigrees and grants family coats of arms, while the Earl Marshall (always the Duke of Norfolk) arranges state occasions such as coronations, funerals, and state openings of Parliament. Inside is a splendid wood-panelled entrance room with portraits.

WATLING STREET
ST AUGUSTINE WITH ST FAITH
446   EC4

1148; 1630-31 ENLARGED AND REPAIRED;1680s SIR CHRISTOPHER WREN; 1695 SPIRE
(PROBABLY HAWKSMOOR); 1829, 1866 AND 1954 RESTORED; 1965-67 SPIRE LEO DE SYLLAS

The rebuilding of this small church in the 1680s incorporated
St Faith-under-St-Paul's, formerly in St Paul's Cathedral crypt and
used by the Company of Stationers. The tower and graceful steeple
survived the Blitz and are now part of the Choir School of St Paul's
Cathedral. Faith, the church cat, was awarded a silver PDSA Dickin
Medal, 'For steadfast courage in the Battle of London,' at a
ceremony attended by the Archbishop of Canterbury. The first cat
to receive a medal for courage, she had her portrait painted and
featured in a book, *They Also Serve*. She and her kitten survived
the church collapse moving into basement just before the bombing.
The rector rescued them from the rubble.

446

ST PAUL'S CHURCHYARD
TEMPLE BAR
447   EC4

1293; 1533 RESTORED FOR ANNE BOLEYN'S CORONATION; 1672 SIR CHRISTOPHER WREN

The first Temple Bar was a turnpike. By 1293, a chain and wooden
posts marked the boundary of Westminster; in time there was a wooden
archway here, and a prison above. Elizabeth I passed through it en route
to St Paul's to give thanks for the 1588 Armada defeat; since then, a
ceremony has been performed here when the sovereign enters the
city on state occasions. A new stone Temple Bar in 1672 had figures of
Charles I, Charles II, James I, and Anne of Denmark, and a central arch
for carriages. The boiled heads (or other remains) of traitors were
displayed here. In 1806, the gate was covered in black velvet to mark
Lord Nelson's funeral. The only main city gateway to survive, it was
moved from the Fleet Street/Strand junction in 1878 to Paternoster
Square in 2004—and is now crowned by a dragon.

447

ST PAUL'S CATHEDRAL, ST PAUL'S CHURCHYARD
CHAPTER HOUSE
448   EC4

1712-14 SIR CHRISTOPHER WREN

The Chapter House was gutted in World War II and has since been
restored. Today, it is a modest but neat seven-bay building, with
brick quoins creating interesting patterning at the corners and on
each side of the central three-bay section. Brass plates denote the
occupants: St Paul's Cathedral Retail Ltd, St Paul's Cathedral
Enterprises Ltd, and Friends of St Paul's Enterprises Ltd. This is
where the secular aspects of St Paul's are controlled today. Remnants
of the earlier, medieval chapter house cloister can be glimpsed in
the gardens to the south side of the nave. This chapter house was
octagonal, with an open, stone-flagged area, eight buttresses, and
four central columns. Wren's site office was probably located in the
partially rebuilt chapter house.

448

449

604; 675–686, 962, 1087; 1675–1711 SIR CHRISTOPHER WREN

On the site of a Roman temple, five cathedrals have risen here—one built by Saint Ethelbert, the first Christian king in England), one destroyed by Vikings in 961, and one burnt (1087.) In the 1560s, the nave bustled with trade, debate, and fierce fights—while services were held in the choir. Later, Cromwell's army used the nave as a cavalry barracks. After the Great Fire, Wren's new cathedral had a spire over a domed crossing. The vast exterior dome is set above a cone of brick and an inner dome where frescoes depict St Paul's life. At one point during their creation, artist Sir James Thornhill stepped back to inspect his work—right to the edge of the platform. His assistant, afraid that a warning shout might make him fall, began to smear the painting. Thornhill leapt angrily towards him and so away from danger. Rising some 360 feet (110 metres), the elaborate dome is one of the highest in the world, supported by eight huge piers, above which is the galleried Whispering Gallery—famous for its acoustics; a whisper against the wall on one side can be heard on the opposite side. Higher still, are the Stone and Golden Galleries, from which there are superb views of the city. Wren checked the work every week, hoisted up to the lantern in a basket. It took thirty-five years, by which time he was seventy-nine years old. Every year, until his death (at ninety-one), he returned to sit under the dome. He was one of the first to be buried in the crypt (the largest in Europe); his inscription translates as, 'Reader, if you seek his monument, look about you.' Here, too, rest Wellington, next to his magnificent funeral carriage; Horatio Nelson; and artists Reynolds, Lawrence, and Turner. Holman Hunt's *Light of the World* in the south aisle is the artist's own copy. The flower-carved choir stalls are the work of Grinling Gibbons, as is the organ—played by Handel and Mendelssohn. The exquisite wrought-iron sanctuary gates of 1700 are by Jean Tijou. The west front of the cathedral, with its portico of twelve columns, is approached by a wide sweeping flight of steps. The huge bell, Great Tom, tolls the deaths and funerals of members of the royal family, bishops of London, St Paul's deans, and lord mayors of London still in office. Great Paul, the largest bell in England, weighs seventeen tonnes and is tolled each day at one p.m. St Paul's has been the setting for many ceremonial occasions including the 1965 funeral of Sir Winston Churchill and the wedding of Prince Charles and Lady Diana Spencer in 1981. The cathedral survived the fierce bombardment of World War II that totally devastated buildings all around. Vigilant volunteers bravely removed incendiary bombs and land mines but one bomb did explode inside, making some walls bulge outwards. Ringed by raging fires and falling masonry, lit red by the glow of fierce flames, the dome remained a symbol of British tenacity. A recent survey has shown St Paul's to be the best-loved building in England, a symbol of the city and the nation.

450

1875, F. C. PENROSE

This famous school (now a youth hostel) was almost certainly founded in the 600s; Gregorian chant or plainsong was being sung in the first St Paul's from about 604. Nothing is known about the school until 1127, when it was refounded and provision was made for eight youngsters 'in need of alms' to serve as 'almonry' boys to the cathedral. The building was a home and school for the choristers, so the boys did not have to be boarded out with various canons. In 1989 non-chorister dayboys were enrolled for the first time, and in 1998, the school admitted girls. Set very close to Saint Paul's Cathedral, the present building has a richly decorated façade, fine Venetian windows and flowing panels of Renaissance sgraffito decoration.

451

ST MARTIN WITHIN LUDGATE

451   EC4

FOUNDED CADWALLER 600S;1677-84 CHRISTOPHER WREN

According to Geoffrey of Monmouth (not always a reliable source), the church was founded by the Welsh hero, Cadwaller, in the seventh century. In the wake of the Great Fire, this building provided another opportunity for Wren to explore his centralised plans—as a cross within a square, with columns supporting barrel vaulting. A delicate slender lead steeple is set on a dome and octagonal stone tower. Some fine seventeenth-century woodwork survives inside, including the altarpiece, pulpit, and organ case.

CENTRAL CRIMINAL COURT

452   EC4

1539; 1774; 1900-07 E. W. MOUNTFORD; 1972 SOUTH EXTENSION DONALD MCMORRAN

The first Old Bailey Sessions House was erected in 1539 beside Newgate Prison and was named after the street. The area has been the scene of many public floggings, pressings, burnings at the stake, and hangings. In 1868, mass public hangings outside the prison were stopped but prior to that, 'execution breakfasts' were served across the road at the Magpie and Stumps inn—and rooms could be hired out to view the scene. Built on the site of Newgate Prison, this grand Edwardian building, with oak-panelled courtrooms, is crowned by a dome above the entrance hall, and the famous statue of Justice—featured in many movies. By tradition, judges still sometimes carry posies of scented flowers, originally used to dispel the rank smells and gaol fever associated with the prisoners. Judge Jeffreys served here in the 1670s. Famous trials include those of Daniel Defoe (1703), Oscar Wilde (1895), Dr Crippen (1910), 'Brides-in-the-bath' murderer George Joseph Smith (1915), 'Lord Haw-Haw' William Joyce, (1945), J. R. Christie (1953), the Kray Twins (1969), 'Yorkshire Ripper' Peter Sutcliffe (1981), politician Jeffrey Archer (2001), and Ian Huntley (2003). A black-cloaked figure of a highwayman—hanged and buried in lime where the court now stands—haunts the site.

DEFEND·THE·CHILDREN·OF·THE·
POOR·&·PVNISH·THE·WRONGDOER·

453

454

WARDROBE PLACE

453   EC4

c. 1710

In medieval days, there were many small courts, alleys, and yards here. This tranquil close with neat, ordered buildings is named after Great Wardrobe, the royal storehouse that was moved here from the Tower of London in the 1300s, during Edward III's reign. In 1720, over fifty years after the Great Fire had taken its toll, Strype described how: 'The Garden of the King's Wardrobe is converted into a large and square court, with good houses.' Numbers 3–5 date from about 1710 but, sadly, part of the east and north sides were demolished in 1982 during a rush of redevelopment.

THE BLACK FRIAR

454   EC4

1875, 1904–05 H. FULLER CLARK

On the site of a 1200s Blackfriars Dominican monastery—and the only Art Nouveau public house to survive in London—this wedge-shaped building is set close to the railway line at Blackfriars. It has an extravagant brick-and-tile exterior by Henry Poole, wrought-iron signs, and the statue of a laughing friar set above the main door. There are mosaics and carved figures can be seen everywhere, inside and out; the fun, ornate interior is busy with bright-coloured marble, bronze figures of jovial monks, mirrors, and brass glimmering all around, carved friezes, and wise sayings. Scenes in the 1987 movie, *Maurice*, were filmed here.

455

456

19 NEW BRIDGE STREET

BLACKFRIARS HOUSE

455   EC4

1913 F. W. TROUP

Set just back just from the north bank of the River Thames on a historical site dating back to the time of Henry VIII, this finely proportioned steel-frame building has neat runs of windows, delicate cornices, and a simple, unassuming—but very pleasing—white faience frontage. It has now been converted into the Crowne Plaza hotel, with 203 bedrooms, an executive boardroom, three function conference suites, and with restaurants and bars as part of the complex.

14 NEW BRIDGE STREET

PALACE, PRISON, AND OFFICES

456   EC4

1515–20 PALACE; C. 1805 JAMES LEWIS; 1860 REFURBISHED

Bridewell served as a palace for Henry VIII, built in 1515–20 on the banks of the Fleet River. It was named after a nearby holy well dedicated to St Bridget. In November 1529, this was probably the place where Catherine of Aragon and Henry VIII last met, when they dined together here. Young Edward VI gave the palace to the city a few days before his death in 1553 and, from the late 1500s, it served as a prison and workhouse for vagrants, beggars, and immoral women. During the Civil War, Cromwell's troops were billeted here. The prison was demolished in the 1800s (except for the gateway), and replaced by these chaste, immaculate offices.

457

PUNCH TAVERN

457   EC4

This opulently glazed pub has a tiled lobby, a large front bar with an ornate skylight, painted panels, huge mirrors, and glass panels etched with birds. In the 1880s, this was the recreational headquarters of *Punch* magazine staff and was renamed it its honour. At some time, the building was split between two owners, and a shop behind the pub has now been turned into a separate bar. A Punch theme dominates its décor—both the puppets and the famous magazine.

458

95 FLEET STREET, FORMERLY THE SWAN

THE OLD BELL

458   EC4

1678 SIR CHRISTOPHER WREN

This is said to stand on the site where Caxton's assistant, one Wynkyn de Worde from Alsace, set up the press he had inherited from his master: De Worde's official printing licence read: 'Emprynted at the sign of the Swan in Fletestrete.' This place has also been called Ten Bells, the Twelve Bells, the Golden Bell, and the Great Tom of Oxford. After the Great Fire, it was rebuilt to feed and house the reconstruction workers. In the Blitz, landlady Nellie Bear kept the Old Bell open, even when a German bomb half-demolished St Bride's. The ancient wooden floor undulates and customers might think they are drunk ahead of time.

459

47 FLEET STREET

EL VINO'S

459   EC4

1879 FOUNDED BY ARTHUR BOWES

Founded by a wine shipper, El Vino claims to be London's oldest wine bar, where the very first customers were invited to free samplings. Soon, drinks had to be paid for, and the place prospered. Author of the Father Brown detective stories, G. K. Chesterton, did some 'hard drinking and hard thinking' here. Women are now allowed to buy drinks at the bar, but must wear a skirt while doing so.

460

120 FLEET STREET; FORMERLY DAILY EXPRESS BUILDING

GOLDMAN SACHS OFFICES

460   EC4

1932 ELLIS CLARKE, ROBERT ATKINSON AND SIR OWEN WILLIAMS

Here, Sir Owen Williams proves his reputation as an original and exciting architect. The exterior is a stunning sweep of shiny black Vitrolite and clear glass with curved corners. The top three floors are set back behind a cornice gantry so that daylight can penetrate through to the street below. The magnificent entrance hall has elaborate metal decoration and sculptures, and is an Art Deco extravaganza. Even the handrails are twisted chromium snakes. In 1989, the *Daily Express* moved to new offices across the Thames near Blackfriar's Bridge.

461

461

135 FLEET STREET; FORMERLY THE DAILY TELEGRAPH BUILDING

MORE GOLDMAN SACHS OFFICES

461   EC4

1928 ELCOCK AND SUTCLIFFE WITH TAIT 1990s EXTENSION BY KOHN PEDERSEN FOX

This huge building is an Art Deco delight from the jazz age. It has a splendid façade with lovely detailing, interesting patterns created by the recessed areas set between fine pillars and uprights, a delightful ornate clock with a bright blue face, and, originally, a grand entrance hall. In 1989, the *Daily Telegraph* moved the printing works and offices housed here to the Isle of Dogs, so this fine Fleet Street headquarters building became available for development. A huge extension designed by Kohn Pedersen Fox was built on the north side. The rear of the building has been rebuilt and the lovely front façade restored.

17 GOUGH SQUARE
DR JOHNSON'S HOUSE
462   EC4

Doctor Johnson lived here from 1748–59, paying a rent of £30 a year as, with six copyists, he slaved for years to create his famous dictionary. He also published a twice-weekly periodical, *The Rambler*. His wife, Tetty, died here in 1752, after taking an overdose of opium. After great efforts to restore the building, much has been preserved, including a fine staircase and American pine panelling— brought back as ballast in ships trading with the colonies. Visitors today can see the dictionary itself, many portraits of Johnson and his friends, an alleged piece of the great Wall of China collected by Johnson, a chair from the Old Cock Tavern, and Johnson's silver teaspoons and sugar tongs. The curator's house next door is the smallest in the city.

462

WINE OFFICE COURT, 145 FLEET STREET
YE OLDE CHESHIRE CHEESE
463   EC4

1538; 1667

When the Whitefriars convent was sold in the 1500s, its guesthouse became an inn; the medieval vaulted cellars remain. A pub from 1538, it was rebuilt after the Great Fire as a tavern and chop-house. There is a small, dark panelled bar, black oak panelling, low oak-beamed ceilings, and the stuffed body of pub parrot, Polly, whose death in 1926 was noted in a BBC obituary. Each year a vast pudding (full of steak, kidneys, oysters, and mushrooms) is cut by celebrities that have included prime minister Stanley Baldwin, prize-fighter Jack Dempsey, and writer Sir Arthur Conan Doyle. Charles Dickens and Samuel Johnson drank here, and Johnson's table and a copy of his dictionary are on display. In the 1890s, the upstairs room hosted the Rhymers Club, which included W. B. Yeats and Oscar Wilde.

463

22 FLEET STREET
YE OLDE COCK TAVERN
464   EC4

1549; 1660s; 1887

The original Old Cock was opposite, at 190 Fleet Street; here, many famous Elizabethan and Jacobean literati gathered. A fireplace and over-mantel (said to be by Grinling Gibbons) survived the Great Fire, but the inn had to be rebuilt. It was a favourite haunt of Samuel Pepys—the landlady, one Mrs Knipps, was one of his mistresses. In 1887, this old building was demolished to make way for a bank but the pub licence was transferred across the road to this tavern. Writers Sheridan, Tennyson, Dickens, and Goldsmith came here. Sadly, some of its old mementos were lost in a 1990 fire but, today, the pub still has a great feeling of history as well as a new mezzanine and an upstairs room with a stained-glass ceiling.

464

465

466

THE TEMPLE, FLEET STREET, AND VICTORIA EMBANKMENT

MITRE COURT

465   EC4

THE TEMPLE, FLEET STREET, AND VICTORIA EMBANKMENT

TEMPLE CHURCH

466   EC4

1830 UNKNOWN

Mitre Court is named after the court, which in turn had been named after the old Mitre Tavern that once stood here, built before 1475, but burnt in the Great Fire. In the early 1700s, Strype described the area as being much taken up by coffeehouses and leading down into the Temple by steps. This 1830 building was raised on the site of the old Mitre Court and Ram Alley—now number one, but once a narrow passage running into Fleet Street past Serjeants' Inn. Above the archway that leads from Mitre Court into King's Bench Walk, the name of Sir Alexander Croke is recorded (he was treasurer here in 1830). Number two is a replica of the old Mitre Court building destroyed in 1941.

C. 1160–85; 1220–40; RENOVATED 1800s SIR ROBERT SMIRKE AND E. LORE; 1948–58 WALTER GODFREY

This temple (so called because it was a Knights Templar church) encompasses eight hundred years of history. It is the only circular Norman church in London and is one of the earliest in true Gothic style. Its round nave was inspired by the church of the Holy Sepulchre or the Dome of the Rock in Jerusalem. Here are life-size stone effigies of nine knights (including William Marshal, Earl of Pembroke, who mediated between King John and the Barons in 1215), Purbeck marble, high lancet windows, and grotesque carved stone heads. In one gruesome cell, Walter-le-Bacheler, Grand Perceptor of Ireland, was left to starve to death after disobeying the Master of the Order. Later the Temple was leased to the Temple lawyers. In the mid-1600s, Samuel Pepys bought copies of the latest songs from a music shop in the west porch. The building was renovated in the 1800s, but still resonates with the events of centuries past. Temple ghosts include Sir Henry Hawkins, a distinguished barrister. Dressed in wig and gown, he glides silently through the Temple's cloisters with a bulging file of paperwork tucked under his arm.

467

468

INNER TEMPLE LIBRARY

467   EC4

1506, 1800s, 1958 SIR HUBERT WORTHINGTON

This is one of the oldest law libraries in the country—in continuous use since the early 1500s. Bombing in 1941 destroyed the building but, although about 45,000 volumes were lost, the most valuable manuscripts and early printed books that already been removed to a safer place. The library had already been destroyed in the Great Fire of 1666; and was blown up again in 1679. Its treasures include fifteenth-century illuminated manuscripts; the Petyt Manuscripts, bequeathed in 1707 by William Petyt, Keeper of the Records in the Tower of London and Treasurer of the Inner Temple; Edward VI's Devise for the Succession (written in his own handwriting when he was just sixteen, in an attempt to exclude his half-sisters Mary and Elizabeth from the succession in favour of his cousin, Lady Jane Grey); and a letter signed by Lady Jane Grey as Queen. Today, the library is used by barristers, judges, and students, and has over 70,000 volumes of English law.

INNER TEMPLE HALL

468   EC4

1100s; RENOVATED 1609 AND 1629; REBUILT 1870; 1955 SIR HUBERT WORTHINGTON

This is the site of one of the ancient halls of the Knights of the Temple. Part of the medieval hall—an old buttery and undercroft with a fifteenth-century fireplace—survives here, at the western end. In 1868, the medieval hall was replaced by a larger, Gothic Hall, but ultimately this was destroyed, too—by 1941 bombs. The present neo-Georgian hall has grand arched windows showing the arms of former lord chancellors, and a marble floor.

KING'S BENCH WALK

469   EC4

I670s POSSIBLY SIR CHRISTOPHER WREN

Some seventeenth-century chambers remain here—some still with the iron rings to which barristers once tied their horses. The King's Bench Office (where the chief clerk or master of the Court of King's Bench worked) has been sited in the Inner Temple since 1621. The original buildings burned down in the Great Fire, and so King's Bench Walk was rebuilt—only to be destroyed again in another fire just eleven years later. Numbers 1–11 on the east side are particularly fine. Several buildings were destroyed in the Blitz and had to be reconstructed, but the doorway of number 1 was rescued intact. There are three lovely brick doorways at numbers 3, 4, and 5.

469

470

471

1562–74 MIDDLE TEMPLE HALL; 1680 FOUNTAIN

As Boswell put it in 1763, this is 'a pleasant academical retreat.' It remains peaceful in this L-shaped court, whose original fountain (built in 1680, restored in 1919) still splashes merrily. The fountain appears in Dickens's *Martin Chuzzlewit* as a meeting place for Ruth Pinch and John Westlock; and Godfrey Turner wrote:

*And—when others fled from town to lake and
    moor and mountain—
I have laid my troubles beside the Temple
    Fountain*

Charles Lamb described sitting by the fountain with his friends during the late 1700s; poet William Blake lived at number 3 from 1821 until his death 1827.

1320, 1562–73/74

Lying on the south side of Fountain Court is Middle Temple Hall, opened in 1570 by Elizabeth I. The original, brilliant redbrick was encased in stone in 1757 but the interior remains much as it was when the Virgin Queen danced here. There are suits of armour and coats of arms on the walls that date from 1597. A large open fireplace stood in the centre of the hall, which would once have been covered with rushes. Here were staged lavish banquets, masques, and plays—including the first known performance of Shakespeare's *Twelfth Night*, performed for the Queen in 1602. It has a superb oak double hammer-beam roof, a rich, wooden screen, and tables made from a tree felled in Windsor Great Park (presented by Elizabeth I) and from the timbers of Drake's *Golden Hind*. The hall escaped the Great Fire— partly because other buildings were demolished in its path and partly because the wind changed course while twentieth-century wartime bombing destroyed just a small part of the eastern end. In 1894, workmen discovered a box, hidden in a wall recess, containing a man's skeleton, perhaps some two hundred years old.

472

473

474

ESSEX COURT

472   EC4

REBUILT 1883 AND 1910

John Evelyn, diarist, architect, and gardener, lived at number 1 in 1641 and described his new abode as, 'a very handsome apartment. The site was cleared in 1656 and replaced by a larger block. The rest of the buildings here arrived in 1677, when part of the grounds of Essex House were sold to the Middle Temple. Certain parts of the south and west sides were replaced in 1910. The north side had already been rebuilt in 1883 and, until a few years ago, was home to the fascinating little shop of J. F. Albin, wigmakers.

2 GREYSTOKE PLACE, HOLBORN
MODERNIST OFFICES

474   EC4

1960 YRM

This striking Grade II–listed building, located close to Fleet Street and the Law Courts, was originally raised to house the offices for the architects responsible (YRM). This team of architects, planners, and designers was founded in 1944 as a partnership by three leading Modernist architects, Yorke, Rosenberg, and Mardall—known for their post-war housing, airports, schools, hospitals, and universities. Here, the style is somewhere between European modern and Chicago style, and the building has a pleasing flow of white tiles and long, wide runs of windows.

BRICK COURT

473   EC4

LATE 1500s (FIRST MENTIONED 1674)

This was the first of the Temple courts to be built in brick. Here, in the late 1700s, one Mr Eddington was murdered by his jealous lover, Miss Broderick. One of the most famous residents of Brick Court was Oliver Goldsmith, at number 2—he purchased it for £400 and wrote *She Stoops to Conquer* here. To the annoyance of his neighbours, he also often held noisy all-night parties. He died here in 1774 and is buried in the churchyard. Novelist, William Makepeace Thackeray (1811–63), also lived at Brick Court—in 1855. Today, Brick Court appears larger after the World War II demolition of a block of chambers that had separated it from Essex Court on the western side.

EAST LONDON (E)

Down by the Docks, they consume the slimiest of shell-fish, which seem to have been scraped off the copper bottoms of ships. . . the seamen roam in mid-street and mid-day, their pockets inside out, and their heads no better. . . Down by the Docks, scraping fiddles go in the public-houses all day long, and, shrill above their din and all the din, rises the screeching of innumerable parrots brought from foreign parts, who appear to be very much astonished by what they find on these native shores of ours.

—Charles Dickens, 'The Uncommercial Traveller' 1820

London spread eastward at this, the working end of the metropolis, following the Thames as it looped around the Isle of Dogs, bound for wider waters. Woods, meadows, farmland, and marshland surrendered to the march of industry; hamlets turned into suburbs, while urbanisation pointed a sharp greedy finger northward, too.

Meanwhile, the traffic flowed through—at first cows and pigs being driven to markets, then horses and carts laden with produce and, ultimately, trains and trucks. And all the while, ships plied up and down, to and from the bustling docks—and many a merry inn sprang up at the seafaring end of town where carousers could forget the threat of gallows, pirates, and press-gangs.

In recent years, much has changed. The greatest docks in the world shrank and closed. London paused and did a rethink but then attacked with renewed vigour. Now its eastern edge is an area of massive regeneration, with exciting new architecture to express this energy.

E1   Whitechapel
E2   Bethnal Green
E3   Bow
E4   Chingford
E5   Clapton
E6   East Ham
E7   Forest Gate
E8   Hackney
E9   Homerton
E10 Leyton
E11 Leytonstone
E12 Manor Park
E13 Plaistow
E14 Poplar
E15 Stratford
E16 Canning Town
E17 Walthamstow
E18 South Woodford

475

TOWER BRIDGE

475   EI

1886–94 J. WOLFE BARRY, ENGINEER SIR HORACE JONES; 1982 RESTORED

This stunning Victorian Gothic-style bridge with its pinnacles and decorative wrought iron is a world-famous London icon. An upper level originally allowed pedestrians to cross the river but closed to the public in 1910 because of the large number of suicides. The massive steel-framed towers house stairs and the lifting machinery (originally steam driven, now electric) that raises the two halves of the lower level to allow for the passage of tall ships. There was a near catastrophe in 1951 when a bus found itself at the point of no return as the bridge opened. The driver accelerated and cleared the gap safely. After a major renovation of Tower Bridge in 1982, the walkways were glassed in and opened as a tourist attraction. Two years later, a museum opened on the south side of the bridge. The old steam engines can still be seen in the pump rooms.

ALMS HOUSES, TRINITY HOSPITAL

476   E1

1695 CORPORATION OF TRINITY HOUSE (POSSIBLY CHRISTOPHER WREN AND JOHN EVELYN)

These pretty little houses are laid out in two rows that face each other with trees and grass between them and a neat little chapel at the end of the avenue. They were originally built for '28 decayed masters and Commanders of Ships or ye widows of such.' They have survived the threat of demolition in 1896, 1941 bombing, and more recent modernisation by the London County Council.

SILKWEAVING HOUSES

477   E1

1721

This part of Stepney has houses from the 1700s where weavers created damask and silk brocade, and needed good light in which to work at the looms—so there are generous high windows. The street would have been busy with merchants, dyers, retailers and master weavers—as well as those beavering away inside—with twelve to fifteen thousand looms in action when the industry was at its peak, and a workforce of thirty thousand. Huguenot weavers liked singing birds, and ornamental cages hung at the windows. It is hard to envisage such heavy industry today among these houses with tall chimneys and sash windows, behind scant pavements.

FOURNIER STREET

478   E1

1722-28

Originally called Church Street, the houses sprang up here while work was in progress on the nearby Christ Church. This is a delightful slice of the early 1700s, lined with tall houses—including a four-bay rectory on the south side by Hawksmoor. Set in the midst of the silk-weaving district, many houses here have wide attic windows, designed to give plenty of light to the weavers as they worked away inside. Others have elegant porches and shutters. Remnants of the textile industry still continue here today.

ST LEONARD

479   E1

1100s; 1736-40 GEORGE DANCE THE ELDER

This junction of two important Roman roads has been the site of a church since the 1100s. This one's predecessor collapsed in 1713. The bells of Shoreditch are mentioned in the nursery rhyme 'Oranges and Lemons'—and the name of Shoreditch is thought to suggest that the nearby ditch was, in fact, a sewer. The pretty steeple and obelisk, a copy of St Mary-le-Bow's spire, rise about 60 metres (200 feet). A whipping post and village stocks lurk in the churchyard where those buried include Will Sommers, Henry VIII's jester—and Richard Burbage, Shakespeare's friend, the first actor to play Hamlet, and the builder of the Curtain Theatre. His epitaph read: 'Exit Burbage.'

ALBERT GARDENS

480   E1

c. 1810; LATE 1970s RESTORED ANTHONY RICHARDSON AND PARTNERS

This is a well preserved and very attractive small square that linked the docks to the city. Here neat four-storey Victorian terraced houses occupy what is now a relatively quiet and exclusive area. It is set quite close to the docks where all was hustle and bustle a few years back; Commercial Road, originally built to service the East and West India Docks, is still a busy thoroughfare.

ST GEORGE IN THE EAST

481   E1

1714-29, NICHOLAS HAWKSMOOR; 1964 RECONSTRUCTED

This is one of the fifty churches of Queen Anne in an area once inhabited by wealthy merchants, until the arrival of the docks and the railway—when it became a slum. During the 1860 'anti-Popery' riots, disorderly congregations shouted, lit matches and firecrackers, threw orange peel and nut shells, and shot peas at the rector—until the police arrived to restore order. The church was bombed in the Blitz, but the 'pepper-pot' towers survived and a new interior was constructed within the Romanesque walls. The original cemetery, St George's Gardens, has been maintained as a public park since mid-Victorian times.

476

477

478

479

480

481

482

483

WHITECHAPEL ART GALLERY

482   E1

THE ROYAL MINT

483   E1

1897–99 CHARLES HARRISON TOWNSEND
1985 REFURBISHED BY COLQUHOUN AND MILLER

This gallery, established by the local vicar of St Jude's and his wife to bring art to the people of the East End, opened to the public in 1901. The building has a distinctive façade, with galleries over two floors. In 1985's, major rebuilding, the gallery re-opened with an upper gallery, a restaurant, and extra exhibition space. Its impressive massive doorway has a fine semicircular arch (in its sturdiness rather like a Norman arch), Arts and Crafts foliage decoration, square corner towers and a high row of simple windows. Its first exhibition attracted 206,000 local people. Important artists whose works have been shown here include Picasso (1938), Jackson Pollock (1950s), David Hockney (with his first-ever show, in 1970), and Lucian Freud (1993).

1807–09 JAMES JOHNSON AND SIR ROBERT SMIRKE;
1989 RENOVATED BY SHEPHARD ROBSON

In 1798, a man named Turnbull managed to rob the Royal Mint of the princely sum of 2,804 guineas by holding the staff at gunpoint. Whether or not this promoted a rethink is uncertain but the mint moved to Mansell Street from the Tower of London in the following decade—in 1809. The stone building has a long neo-classical façade and portico, a scallop-edged pediment, and two lodges. In 1986–89, the manufacture of coins was transferred to South Wales, and the buildings were renovated as offices.

484

485

---

84 COMMERCIAL STREET

THE TEN BELLS

484   E1

---

48 COMMERCIAL ROAD

THE PROOF HOUSE

485   E1

1752

This old pub has ornate Victorian tile work on the walls—depicting the days when this area was countryside—and is full of old battered sofas, low tables, and candles. It is infamous for its connections with Jack the Ripper. Two of his victims were seen here close to the times of their murders, and all five lived close by. Mary Kelly was said to have plied her trade outside the pub; her body was discovered in Millers Court off Dorset Street, on the opposite side of the road from the Ten Bells. The pub also has several hauntings to add to its allure, including an old man dressed in Victorian clothes, possibly a former landlord named George Roberts who was murdered with an axe in a cinema.

Here the Worshipful Company of Gunmakers tests shotguns and other small arms to ensure their safe use. This custom dates back to 1637, when the Gunmakers Company of London was granted its Royal Charter and set about protecting the public against unsound arms, and gun makers from discredit. Charles I selected sixty-two gun makers, freemen of the City, to form the company. They had the rights to search, view, gauge, proof, trial-fire, and make all handguns and pistols in London or the suburbs, or within a ten-mile radius. The company secured its ordinances in 1670 and their original proof marks are still in use today.

486

COMMERCIAL STREET
CHRIST CHURCH

486   EI

1714–29 NICHOLAS HAWKSMOOR; 1850 ALTERED EWAN CHRISTIAN; RESTORED 1964–87

This is a marvellous example of Nicholas Hawksmoor's inspiring work. This church originally welcomed the Huguenot refugees who had fled Europe and were working with the silk weavers living hereabouts—over half of the eighteenth-century gravestones remember French 'occupants.' The sumptuous interior has a high, coffered ceiling and a gallery. Struck by lightning in 1841, the building suffered drastic changes, but remains a masterpiece, with a strong portico of four Tuscan columns and a lovely tower with an octagonal spire that dominates the surrounding area. This looks particularly splendid when floodlit at night, piercing the dark sky above the Commercial Street warehouses. The crypt has been used as a refuge and home for recovering alcoholics since 1965.

487

WAPPING HIGH STREET
WAPPING TUBE STATION

487   EI

1869; 1995–98 RENOVATED

Wapping has been colonised since Anglo-Saxon times, named after a tribesman called Waeppa. Gradually, a few fishermen's cottages became a medieval hamlet and eventually, a busy, thriving dock. Wapping underground station occupies the north end of the former Thames foot tunnel built by Marc Isambard Brunel between 1825 and 1843. Murals on the platforms show this original Thames Tunnel. It was later adapted for railway traffic. The station stands on the site of Execution Dock, where pirates were hanged, including Captain Kidd in 1701, and where their rotting corpses were strung up as a warning to any passing seafarers (see also the Town of Ramsgate pub, page 279).

488

57 WAPPING WALL, FORMERLY THE DEVIL'S TAVERN
PROSPECT OF WHITBY

488   EI

1520

This timber-framed inn, associated with pirates and smugglers, may be London's oldest, with beams and pillars made from a ship's mast. There are bare stone flags, a long pewter counter on barrels, and riverside bars. In the early 1700s, a sailor drinking here sold a new plant he had discovered on his travels to a local market gardener—the first fuchsia to reach Europe. In 1777, the inn's name changed when the ship *Prospect* (registered at Whitby) moored here. Customers have included Judge Jeffreys; Dickens; artists Doré, Whistler, and Turner; Pepys, and actors Paul Newman, Glenn Ford, and Rod Steiger. Sir Hugh Willoughby sailed from near here in 1553 on his attempt to find the northeast passage to China. A replica hangman's noose swings over the river, as a reminder of former gruesome hangings hereabouts.

62 WAPPING HIGH STREET, FORMERLY THE RED COW
TOWN OF RAMSGATE

489   E1

1758

This long, narrow, Grade II–listed pub is next to an alleyway called Wapping Old Stairs that leads down to the riverside where fishermen from Ramsgate once sold their catch. Next to an old warehouse and a merchant's house, this pub was where men were often press-ganged into serving on ships, while convicts awaiting transportation to the Colonies were held in its cellars. Execution Dock was situated nearby, where the condemned were first hanged and then chained to posts in the river. Here, in 1688, Judge Jeffreys was captured whilst trying to flee the country dressed as a sailor. Captain William Bligh and Fletcher Christian both drank here before their ill-fated voyage in the *Bounty*.

489

ARNOLD CIRCUS
BOUNDARY STREET ESTATE

490   E2

LATE 1800s EARLY 1900s LONDON COUNTY COUNCIL

One of the first large housing schemes, this late Victorian and early Edwardian estate forms a complex of streets around Arnold Circus and replaced an infamous slum near Shoreditch Parish Church. The redbrick five-storey tenements have high gables with bands of yellow brick highlighting the façades. Interesting building details include projecting bays that are almost like turrets. Over five and a half thousand people (some two hundred per acre) were given new homes with shops, a surgery and a school provided as part of the estate scheme.

490

CLAREDALE STREET, BETHNAL GREENN
KEELING HOUSE

491   E2

1957–60 SIR DENYS LASDUN AND PARTNERS

A Modernist architect, Lasdun was influenced by Le Corbusier's concept of 'streets in the air' as well as Cubist painting; classical influences are also evident—such as the work of Hawksmoor. He worked for a while with Lubetkin before setting up his own practice, and ultimately was responsible for the South Bank's National Theatre. These blocks of stacked maisonettes are separated by wide bands of concrete and arranged around a central staircase and lift shaft. Lubetkin hoped that the shared landing would encourage sociability. Two six-storey blocks of maisonettes in dark brick are part of the same scheme. Now a Grade II–listed building, Keeling House has been saved from the threat of demolition and transformed into luxury loft-style apartments.

491

MODEL DWELLINGS

492   E2

1860–62 H. A. DARBISHIRE

Until 1840, this area was the site of a large farm and watercress beds. Baroness Burdett-Coutts, granddaughter of banker Thomas Coutts, donated millions to charities and was the first woman to become a baroness through her own achievements. She spearheaded the Metropolitan Association for Improving the Dwellings of the Industrial Classes, set up in 1852. Her favourite architect was Darbishire (see also Holly Village, page 315). These flats are set in a flow of four- and five-storey blocks with open staircases. Access is via short galleries. They were part of an ambitious plan that included Columbia Market, an imposing Gothic building, sadly demolished in 1958. By the 1980s, the flats still had no heating and cold water only; some retained gas lighting. Many houses here were boarded up and the entire area was due to be cleared, but a local association prevented this and now most of the properties have been restored.

SULKIN HOUSE

493   E2

1952 SIR DENYS LASDUN

A Tudor ballad describes the Blind Beggar of Bethnal Green—a man the locals believed to be very poor but who provided a vast dowry for his daughter's wedding. This lead to the supposition that he was, in fact, the son of Simon de Montfort—the Earl of Leicester, who had been married to Henry III's sister, but led a rebellion against the king and fell at the Battle of Evesham in 1265. Today, the parish coat of arms is based on the tale. Here, some four hundred years later, modernist cluster blocks by eminent architect Sir Denys Lasdun aimed to create an interesting and very practical formation of homes that would help to reshape and define the modern city. This scheme was a precursor for his ambitious fifteen-storey cluster, Keeling House, in 1957 (see page 279.)

GARNER STREET HOUSE

494   E2

2000–02 SEAN GRIFFITHS (FAT)

FAT stands for 'Fashion, Architecture and Taste'—a design group that revels in breaking the rules. This unconventional building incorporates a cut-out shape like a child's drawing of a house with its little chimney and wavy garden hedge. This is set in front of another cut-out—an office-block façade like a miniature skyscraper that bends around the side where the cut-outs turn into high Dutch gables—all in sky blue clapboard. Inside, an office, apartment, and family house wrap around each other and are just as full of surprises.

MUSEUM OF CHILDHOOD

495   E2

1855–56 AND 1875 J. W. WILD, C. D. YOUNG AND COMPANY, SIR WILLIAM CUBITT

Profits from the Great Exhibition of 1851 were used to buy land in South Kensington, where Prince Albert hoped to create museums, societies and educational institutions. This highly decorative redbrick building has a frieze of terracotta and inlaid panels, semi-circular windows, mosaic and cast-iron galleries. Inside (where the marble mosaic tiles were made by women prisoners in Woking jail) are over six thousand exhibits—toys, books, games, costumes, nursery items, art, furniture, and doll's houses, many items dating from the 1500s.

492

493

494

495

496

497

498

GEFFRYE MUSEUM ALMSHOUSES

496   E2

1715

Named after its benefactor, Sir Robert Geffrye, this museum explores the changing styles of English domestic interiors through a series of middle-class living rooms—from 1600 to the present day. Here, 1600s oak furniture and panelling, refined Georgian splendour, a Victorian parlour, a 1930s flat, a contemporary 1950s room, and a late-1900s converted warehouse can be compared. The museum is housed in fourteen two-storey Ironmongers Company almshouses set on three sides of a huge courtyard. From the gated entrance a formal avenue of lime trees leads to a chapel in the centre. The almshouses were converted into a museum in 1910–14, when floors, stairs, and many party walls were removed to create galleries that display collections of furniture, textiles, and paintings. Outside, a series of period gardens includes an award-winning walled herb garden.

CAMBRIDGE HEATH ROAD

ST JOHN ON BETHNAL GREEN

497   E2

1825-28 SIR JOHN SOANE; 1871 REPAIRED

This church has a rather short stocky tower with a circular cupola, and lovely tall windows with simple but elegant tracery. It has a new roof and was extensively repaired in 1871 after a fire. In 2003, St John's held a memorial service and hosted an exhibition in the crypt to remember those lost on March 3, 1943, at Bethnal Green station. This had been converted into an air-raid shelter with five-thousand bunks. When the siren sounded that night, a woman rushing to carry her baby to safely inside tripped and fell on the steep steps. As many more people crowded into the dim-lit area with no handrails, many more tumbled down. In all, 173 people died, either crushed or suffocated.

THREE MILL LANE

TIDE MILL DISTILLERY

498   E4

1776, 1813

The Domesday Book refers to eight mills here, and there were still three in medieval times. Set in a complex pattern of water channels, possibly created by order of King Alfred the Great, the mills have ground gunpowder, as well as flour for the city's bread, and distilled gin. The House Mill of 1776 and the Clock Mill of 1817 are the only surviving tide mills in the Greater London area and the largest in England. Tide mills are far rarer than wind or water mills. The House Mill has a Grade I listing and stretches across four internal mill races and two waterways. The Tide Mill Distillery has a lovely cupola. Here, grain was brought by barge or cart, lifted by the sack hoist, and stored on the top floor. Today, the mills have been restored as a working museum. Nearby, on an island in the river, are Three Mills Studios with sixteen film stages. This is where *Lock, Stock and Two Smoking Barrels* was filmed, as well as scenes for television's *London's Burning* and *Bad Girls*.

499

500

501

502

503

504

DOWN ROAD AND DOWNS PARK

MOSSBOURNE COMMUNITY ACADEMY

499 E5

2004 RICHARD ROGERS PARTNERSHIP

Built as a school for some nine hundred students (aged eleven to sixteen), this £23 million building has risen on the rubble of a 1960s school and is set in a triangular site, edged by railways. It is timber-framed with rooftop wind towers that draw in fresh air and built in a series of vertical units. Classrooms are reached by staircases and galleries like cloisters. All is in bright, stimulating primary colours and is a bold, courageous, and completeley new approach to an educational building.

FOREST STREET

FOREST GATE SCHOOL

500 E7

1963 COLQUHOUN AND MILLER

The name 'Forest Gate' derives from a southern gate of Epping Forest, which once stretched down here. One of the schools in this residential area is a fine early example of the architects' move from English Brutalism towards a softer approach with Dutch influences. Two classroom wings extend out from a square, double-height assembly hall. The aim was to create a flexible multi-purpose space suitable for a variety of activities. Nine tubular steel columns on a square grid support the steel roof and the building is clad in pre-formed concrete. Doors have been painted in bright colours—in lively reds, greens, and yellows.

BROWNLOW ROAD

1980s HOUSING

501 E8

1982–84 LONDON BOROUGH OF HACKNEY; COLQUHOUN AND MILLER

Set in a Victorian street, these are very generous semi-detached villas that would work well in their own right as individual dwellings aside from creating an interesting little terrace, as they do here. Steps with railings lead up to tall, slender central columns set before the deep front recess that tends to dwarf the front doors. Focus is drawn to the windows by their lighter surrounds and to the entrance area by its white lintel. Just a few streets north is 1860s Fassett Square, the inspiration for Albert Square in BBC1's *East Enders*.

HACKNEY

ALBION SQUARE

502 E8

c. 1840s ARCHITECTS INCLUDE J. C. LOUDON AND ISLIP ODELL

With railway expansion and improved roads in the latter half of the 1800s, there was a rush to raise new properties in many of the outer boroughs, including Hackney. Especially popular was the urban villa. The larger of these versatile and often rather grand houses were often occupied by more than one family. This early Victorian railed square surrounds a garden with a lovely (now restored) water fountain. Designated a conservation area in 1975, the square includes elegant Italianate villas and a number of Grade II–listed buildings. The house shown here has neat brickwork, and lovely arched first-floor windows and entrance porch.

HOMERTON

24 CHURCH CRESCENT

503 E9

1984 LONDON BOROUGH OF HACKNEY; COLQUHOUN AND MILLER

This interesting house, one of four, has an overhanging hipped roof—not unlike many Alpine buildings. There are extensive expanses of white rendering and its many unusual features include the second-floor loggia, a high circular window, and glass and timber panel strips. Creating a sharp contrast to these modern examples of public housing, is nearby St John of Jerusalem Church (1845–48) and a plaque marking the fact that, in 1669, Henry Monger left money for almshouses here and annuities for six poor men over sixty.

ROBIN HOOD GARDENS, COTTON STREET, AND ROBIN HOOD LANE

STREETS IN THE SKY

504 E14

1968–72 ALISON AND PETE SMITHSON

This building scheme was featured in an exhibition at the Design Museum. An estate of over two hundred homes, built near to the docks and motorways, it was conceived as a 'streets in the sky' complex. It comprised both single-storey flats and two-storey maisonettes, with wide balconies on every third floor. Unfortunately, a combination of the high crime rate here and structural flaws led to the estate being regarded as a modernist folly.

505

506

240 EAST INDIA DOCK ROAD,
BLACKWELL TUNNEL APPROACH

FINANCIAL TIMES
PRINTING WORKS

505   E14

1987-88 NICHOLAS GRIMSHAW AND PARTNERS

This long block was built to house the new
Financial Times presses when these were
moved from their old home in Fleet Street.
It incorporates office and services at its
two aluminium-clad extremes with staircase
towers. The enormous printing presses and
plate-making machines are housed in the
centre section. Fin-like steel columns and
braces support the roof and glazing—a
veritable wall of frameless toughened glass.

STEWART STREET

PUMPING STATION

506   E14

1985-88 JOHN OUTRAM ASSOCIATES

This monumental building presents a mix of
ancient historical inspirations with its Greek-
style pediment and stout Egyptian-style
columns. The building has no windows and
strict security boudaries for its interior is full
of machinery and computers; if these were
vandalised, parts of London could be flooded.
The control room is surrounded by concrete
that could withstand the collapse of the
structure during an earthquake or explosion.
The lowest walls are built in hard engineering
bricks—in red, yellow, and dark blue.

WATERGARDEN HOUSING
507   E14

1987–89 IAN RITCHIE ARCHITECTS

This architect won a RIBA award for London Regatta
Centre in Dockside (see page 295). Here the aim was
to create a pleasing urban landscape, a contemporary
interpretation of Georgian homes. The site had to include
a public pedestrian route from Limehouse Basin to the
Thames at Blyth's Jetty. The seventy-seven flats are set
around a shared landscaped courtyard garden with a
miniature canal, and are raised above a garage area. There
are neat metal casements and metal basket-like balconies
are set in front of French doors.

BARCLAYS PREMIER
508   E14

2004 HOK INTERNATIONAL

The headquarters of the high street bank, Barclays Bank
PLC occupies about two-thirds of this building. With 32
floors and at 156 metres (512 feet) high, it is London's
seventh (and Canary Wharf's fourth) tallest building.
Raised in the wake of the 9/11 tragedy, the building is
designed to be especially resistant to terrorist attacks.
Built around four secure staircase columns, its large, central
thrust carries the lifts and toilets. London was a busy port
from Roman times and, from the 1800s until1960, the area
now known as Docklands was home to the biggest port in
the world, with 100,000 men handling 35 million tons of
cargo in the 1930s.

CASCADES
509   E14

1987–88 CZWG ARCHITECTS
(CAMPBELL, ZOGOLOVICH, WILKINSON AND GOUGH)

CZWG was launched by four young architects who
began working together in the 1960s while still at the
Architectural Association School. In particular, Piers
Gough became well known for his post-modern buildings.
Here the Cascades Apartment Tower (the first private
high-rise housing development in Docklands) on the
Isle of Dogs riverbank includes 171 apartments with
cantilevered balconies on twenty floors, a suspended
swimming pool, fitness centre, sauna, and floodlit tennis
courts. Designed to look like a berthed ocean liner, it
has spectacular views over the river.

ST ANNE'S
510   E14

1714–30 NICHOLAS HAWKSMOOR;
1851–57 RESTORED JOHN MORRIS AND PHILIP HARDWICK;
1891 RESTORED SIR ARTHUR BLOMFIELD; 2006 WILLIAM DRAKE

This Baroque church has a broad-based Gothic-style tower,
the second highest in Britain, topped only by Big Ben
(raised by the same builders). Its tower was a landmark
for ships using the East End docks and boasts the highest
church clock in London. When it was consecrated, then set
in open fields, the bishop partook of 'a little hot wine and
took a bit of ye sweetmeats and then ye clergy and ye laity
scrambled for ye rest for they left not a bitt.' Shaped like
a Greek cross, the church has Corinthian columns and an
elongated nave. The ceiling forms a great flat circle, edged
by Corinthian moulding.

25 CANADA SQUARE
511   E14

2001 CESAR PELLI

25 Canada Square, along with 33 Canada Square, make
up the Citigroup Centre—a forty-five-floor office
complex. This gleaming skyscraper is 200 metres (656
feet) high, occupies 170,000 square metres (1.8 million
square feet), and is home to the Citigroup companies, as
their European headquarters. This impressive building has
entrances on two streets and underground floors that lead
to the Canada Place shops plus the underground station.
The two Citigroup buildings seized their rank as the
second tallest buildings in the United Kingdom as they
rose above Docklands—nicknamed Oliver 1 and Oliver 2
by local employees.

HOUSING 'COMPASS POINT'
512   E14

1987 JEREMY DIXON BDP

Viewed from the river, the terraces of Mariners' Mews—
town houses with sharply pointed 'serrated' or curved
gables—have an Old Amsterdam flavour. There are long
windows, curved bays, and no chimneys. The compex also
includes landscaped terraces of three- and four-bedroom
villas, four-storey apartment towers, and a riverside walk.
Some French film makers who rented a property here
aroused some local curiosity by leaving a coffin (just
a prop) in their garden while filming *Cement Garden*.

507

508

509

510

511

512

513

514

ASPEN WAY		CANARY WHARF	
REUTERS		**ONE CANADA SQUARE**	
513	E14	514	E14

1987–88 RICHARD ROGERS PARTNERSHIP

Reuters is a news agency and financial service founded in London in 1851 by German immigrant Paul Julius Reuter. He began by using carrier pigeons but then cables and telegraph transmission made sending stock market quotations far more efficient. Today, Reuters employs some 15,300 staff in nearly ninety countries. This very large building is set beside the Thames, with services and computers occupying its lower levels, and offices rising above—faced with interchangeable glass and opaque panels. From here news—as text, graphics, images, or video—can be sent to media oranisations all around the world.

1991 CESAR PELLI AND ASSOCIATES WITH ADAMSON ASSOCIATES (TORONTO) AND FREDERICK GIBBERD, COOMBES AND PARTNERS

At 244 metres (88 feet) high, One Canada Square is Britain's tallest building and Europe's second tallest—visible as far away as the hopfields of Kent and Hampstead Heath. A giant obelisk, with a pyramidal top, and stainless steel cladding, it make an impressive sight as it rises above docklands and the flat, marshy landscape, its bright, red warning light flashing at its pinnacle. The building is designed to sway as much as 35 centimetres (14 inches) in strong wind, and its fifty floors are served by a lift that can rise to the top in forty seconds. Seven thousand people work here, including employees of the *Independent, Daily Telegraph,* and *Daily Mirror* newspapers.

SAXONS, PIRATES, AND PUBS

Set on the north bank of the River Thames between the city and Shadwell, Wapping lies between the river and an ancient thoroughfare called the Highway. This area was settled first by Saxons, and its name means 'the place of Wæppa's people.' In the 1500s, historian John Stow described it as, 'a filthy strait passage, with alleys of small tenements. . . inhabited by sailors' victuallers.' Here, as well as 'victuallers.' lived sailors, boat-builders and mastmakers, carpenters, ropemakers, smiths, instrument-makers, and gunpowder manufacturers.

At the notorious 'Execution Dock', pirates were hanged on a gibbet by the low-water mark. Their corpses were left to dangle there until they had been washed over by three tides. Captain Kidd was one such victim—a Scottish privateer and pirate who was hanged on the Wapping foreshore in 1701. The pub named after him has been busy telling the tales for a century or more.

Another seafarer here, Captain Cook, perhaps one of the world's greatest explorers, promised to marry one little Wappinger, Elizabeth Batts—if she grew up and waited for him. At the time she was but a sickly child helping her parents in the Bell Inn but indeed, she survived—and Captain Cook kept his word. They made a home together in a redbrick terraced house on the Highway and later in a bigger Mile End house.

Wapping was also home to Zachariah Hicks, the second lieutenant who first sighted Australia, and Captain Bligh of 'Mutiny on the Bounty' fame.

As the docks spread, giant warehouses arrived along the riverfront and Wapping became rather isolated until Brunel's tunnel to Rotherhithe arrived and a tube station opened in 1869. The area was devastated by German bombing in World War II and then by the post-war closure of the docks, but now the Docklands regeneration has given the area a new lease of life —as has the arrival of printing and publishing works that moved here from Fleet Street.

A number of quaint old passages and steps lead down to the foreshore, such as Wapping Old Stairs—and Pelican Stairs by the popular Prospect of Whitby pub that claims to be the oldest riverside inn—here in one form or another since the reign of Henry VIII.

515

STRATFORD REGIONAL STATION

515   E15

1994–99 WILKINSON EYRE AND TROUGHTON MCASLAN

Since the first trains chugged into the station here in
1839, Stratford, has been an important railway centre:
The Docklands Light Railway opened a century later
in August 1987. This new regional station is a great
steel and glass building with sweeping lines, a glazed
concourse, and a roof with curved, cantilevered girder
ribs covered by a double skin—to draw warm air out of
the building. There is a magnificent lofty hall (with a vast
clock), a sheer glass façade, and an upper-level walkway.
All the staircases are wide and there is a general feeling
of spaciousness.

516

517

ABBEY LANE, STRATFORD

ABBEY MILLS PUMPING STATION

516   E15

DOCKSIDE ROAD

LONDON REGATTA CENTRE

517   E16

1865–68 J. BAZALGETTE AND E. COOPER

At a time when sewage poured into streams and the Thames often overflowed into the streets, London was rife with such diseases as cholera. Joseph Bazalgette came to the rescue. His pioneering sewage system saved the city from any repetitions of the Great Stink of 1858—when a massive overflow caused thousands to flee the city. Some 132 kilometres (82 miles) of new sewers were built, many hidden below new Thames embankments. North London's waste was routed to Abbey Mills Pumping Station. Sometimes referred to as the 'Cathedral of Sewage,' its exterior is a sturdy but splendid mixture of Victorian, Byzantine, and Gothic styles, with a mansard roof and ornate dome. It had two, high ornate chimneys but these were demolished during World War II—to avoid their serving as a landmark for German bombers. Inside, eight huge coal-fired beam engines (replaced by electric motors in 1933) were housed in a grand machine hall.

1999 IAN RITCHIE

The Regatta Centre was one of the first new buildings completed in the long-closed Royal Docks—on Royal Albert Dock, where there is an Olympic-size rowing course. Next to the finishing line of this is a new exciting structure. There are, in fact, two buildings. These incorporate a clubhouse, changing rooms, accommodation for athletes, a practice rowing tank (with flowing water to better simulate real open-water rowing,) workshop, changing rooms, gym, restaurant, and bar. The sharp nose of the clubhouse, the timber 'hull' of the boathouse ceiling, stairways, and decking all have a nautical appeal. Steel columns with brackets support both the stored boats and a stainless-steel roof.

518

519

DOCKLANDS CAMPUS, UNIVERSITY WAY

UNIVERSITY OF EAST LONDON

518   E16

LLOYD PARK, FOREST ROAD, WALTHAMSTOW

WILLIAM MORRIS GALLERY

519   E17

1997–99 EDWARD CULLINAN ARCHITECTS

Set alongside the Royal Albert Dock, and facing London City Airport across the water, this campus was built in just eighteen months. The aim was, ultimately, to provide accommodation for seven thousand students. Built as a group of cylinders with dips and curves and 'pancake' roofs, the surfaces are pierced with windows making neat rows of little squares, and round ventilation 'buttons,' rather like rather like the patterns a child creates with folded paper and scissors—a very satisfying effect. Blue, yellow, and green has been used liberally for the surfaces. The complex includes a Learning Resource Centre, an auditorium, academic departments, shops, and cafés. It was opened by the mayor of London on his first day in office.

1762

From 1847 to 1856, the young William Morris (designer, craftsman, author, and socialist) lived in this large, double-fronted, three-storey Georgian house at a time when this area was a comfortable Victorian suburb. The former Water House, set in its own extensive grounds, has a portico and entrance that is flanked by two circular bays and multiple sash windows. Between the ground floor and the first storey, and below the roof, the building's lovely curves are emphasized by decorative horizontal panels. It is now a gallery (opened by Prime Minister Clement Attlee in 1950), and houses an extensive collection of furniture, fabrics, wallpapers, stained glass, painted tiles, books, drawings, and sketches produced by Morris and Company.

520

521

FOREST ROAD

WALTHAMSTOW CIVIC CENTRE

520   E17

20B BISTERNE AVENUE

WALTHAM FOREST HOUSING

521   E17

1937–42 P. D. HEPWORTH

Bordered by the River Lea, marshes, and Epping Forest, Walthamstow was for centuries a rural village, mentioned in the Domesday Book in 1086 as Wacoumstou or Wilcumestow. The arrival of the railways turned it into a popular suburb. Here, in about 1893, Frederick Bremer built the first British-built petrol-driven motor and Alliot Verdon tried to fly his early aeroplanes. William Morris was born here (his former house is now a museum.) The daily street market may be Europe's longest. This building was created in the progressive style of the day and more closely resembles a classical 'palace' than a utilitarian town hall. Grade II–listed, it was the town's first purpose-built town hall. The neat narrow columns of its elegant sweeping frontage are mirrored by neat narrow windows, and it is crowned by an elegant turquoise steeple.

1990 WICKHAM AND ASSOCIATES
(NOW WICKHAM VAN EYCK)

The dramatic colours of this housing development for the London Borough of Waltham Forest caused quite a stir in the 1990s with their bright blue and burnt sienna. The three floors house six two-bedroom flats set on each side of an external communal staircase enclosed by a glass canopy. There are sweeping curved balconies and interesting changes in roof levels. The ground-floor flats were designed for disabled residents.

NORTH LONDON (N)

Long ago, parts of these northern climes offered an escape from the city for the rich. Highgate, London's highest point, is renowned for its fine Georgian houses and cemetery, the resting place of many, including Karl Marx. Hampstead Heath comprises vast acres of woodland and ponds, and was once part of the bishop of London's hunting estate. He set up a tollhouse on the main northward road out of the city and many inns sprang up along the route—as did highwayman Dick Turpin.

Sovereigns visited these parts when en route to (or returning from) the midlands, the north, or Scotland. Here, Henry VII was received by the corporation and citizens of London, after the battle of Bosworth Field and, in 1589,

Queen Elizabeth I paid a royal visit. Mary, Queen of Scots was detained for a short time at the house of the Earl of Arundel, on Holloway Hill, where in 1626 philosopher Lord Bacon died—having succumbed to a chill while experimenting with the freezing of poultry in snow. The ghost of a featherless squawking chicken is still said to haunt Pond Square.

Here, too, was a leper hospital, marked with a wayside cross and later the site of the Whittington stone where Dick Whittington, future Lord Mayor, heard the sound of Bow Bells summoning his return to the City. As the railways spread in the 1800s, houses were built and these northern surburban areas thrived.

N1   Islington
N2   East Finchley
N3   Finchley Central
N4   Finsbury Park
N5   Highbury
N6   Highgate
N7   Holloway
N8   Hornsey
N9   Lower Edmonton
N10 North Finchley
N11 New Southgate
N12 North Finchley
N13 Palmers Green
N14 Southgate
N15 South Tottenham
N16 Stoke Newington
N17 Tottenham
N18 Upper Edmonton
N19 Upper Holloway
N20 Whetstone
N21 Winchmore Hill
N22 Wood Green

522

523

524

525

526

527

DUNCAN TERRACE
GEORGIAN HOUSES
522   NI

c. 1710 AND 1786

These houses—with beautiful façades, fine brickwork, and pretty balconies—once overlooked the New River created by Sir Hugh Myddleton. This pioneer of London's water supplies brought an artificial stream to Islington from Hertfordshire springs in 1613. A garden now follows the culverted course. This is the setting for the huge church of St John the Evangelist (1843). Douglas Adams, who wrote *The Hitchhiker's Guide to the Galaxy*, lived in the terrace during the 1980s.

DE BEAUVOIR SQUARE
DUTCH-STYLE HOUSES
523   NI

1838 ROUMIEU AND GOUGH

The houses in this gem of a square present a mixture of Tudor, Dutch, and Jacobean styles. The district was developed in the 1830s and '40s, its prized centrepiece the ornate neo-Jacobean villas here. It is Georgian in layout but there are Tudor-style details such as oriel windows and mullions, and high Dutch-style roofs. Here the gable has beautiful curves and swirls, and the bay windows and decorative white window surrounds stand out from the gentle texture of the brickwork.

16 CHARLES SQUARE
FIVE-BAY HOUSE
524   NI

The only original house that exists in this square today, the three storeys of this neatly symmetrical, five-bay frontage are set behind multiple railings. It has painted keystones above the sash windows of the first two storeys and there are five smaller windows above. The manor of Hoxton was recorded in the Domesday Book as being worth 45 shillings and was held by the bishop of London until the 1300s. It became a fashionable 'overspill' area during the 1500s.

KILLICK STREET
STUART MILL HOUSE
525   NI

c. 1937 JOSEPH EMBERTON

Curving brick walls edge the approach to Stuart Mill House (renowned nineteenth-century philosopher John Stuart Mill was born in Pentonville). Tall glass floor-to-ceiling panels set above the entrance on the gallery areas form a focal point on the six-storey building. This low-cost housing shows some Dutch influences. Architect Joseph Emberton was a pioneer of modern building design in England in the 1930s, and many of his works have become icons of design for that period.

COLLIER STREET
PRIORY GREEN ESTATE
526   NI

1938–52 SKINNER, BAILEY AND LUBETKIN

With a mix of horizontals and verticals emphasized by white edging, these apartments are set in two eight-storey and four four-storey blocks. World War II interrupted the development but, by the early 1950s, 269 flats had been built here on 3.5 hectares (8.6 acres)—following the old street pattern. Designer, theorist, and philosopher, Russian-born Berthold Lubetkin was a highly influential architect who came to Britain in the early 1930s, bringing radical ideas of architecture.

CLOUDESLEY SQUARE
CLOUDESLEY SQUARE
527   NI

1800s

Here, the houses have delicate wrought-iron balconies and railings and prettily patterned fanlights over the doors, with neat brickwork on the upper storeys. This Islington square, with its wedge-shaped corners and wide pavements, is named after the local benefactor Richard Cloudesley, who died in 1517 (his tomb can be found near the entrance to the crypt of St Mary's Church). The parish school, completed 1839, is at the top of Cloudesley Street.

CRIME AND PUNISHMENT

In the late 1200s, the mayor of London decided to fight crime by reviving a curfew and building the new Cornhill Tun prison. There are two major prisons in North London—Holloway and Pentonville—but the city has had a plethora of fascinating places of detention. These include Fleet Prison, built in 1197—mainly to incarcerate debtors and bankrupts, who often had to beg for money from their cell windows. Any ecclesiastical inmates could earn extra cash by performing 'Fleet marriages' for eloping couples.

Newgate Prison was first built by Henry II in 1188 but had to be rebuilt several times after fire and riots. This was the place for London's worst criminals in the 1600s, when its gloomy cells were poorly ventilated and the stenches vile. There were frequent outbreaks of gaol fever. Lice crunched underfoot and prisoners became so rank that they had to be doused with vinegar before being taken into court. Prisoners here included Daniel Defoe, William Kidd, and William Penn. Elizabeth Fry (1780–1845) spearheaded prison reform from 1813—specifically focusing on the conditions of women in Newgate.

Meanwhile, in 1805, a horse patrol, sixty men strong, was created to rid the main roads of highwaymen within a twenty-mile radius of the city. London's first 'police,' the Bow Street Runners, arrived in 1750—named after the newly established courthouse in Bow Street. They could serve writs, do detective work, and arrest offenders. Execution Dock, in Wapping, was the riverside setting for pirate hanging, but other kinds of criminals might be taken by cart to such places of execution as Tyburn, Smithfield, or Aldgate. The gallows at Tower Hill saw off some three hundred people, some were hanged on its riverside marshes, and the Tower itself was the place of execution for nobility. King Charles I, however, was executed outside the banqueting hall of Whitehall Palace, claiming that he was a 'martyr of the people.' He wore warm clothing so that he would not shiver and appear afraid—not a problem for those who were burned, usually at Smithfield.

Even into the nineteenth century, over two hundred offences carried the death penalty. The derrick crane is named after the gallows devised by hangman Derrick, who was himself sentenced to death. The Earl of Essex reprieved him but any gratitude Derrick felt must quickly have diminished, for he later beheaded the selfsame earl. The new drop-style gallows was introduced at Newgate, and in 1864 five pirates were hanged here, side by side. Public executions attracted huge crowds. In 1807, a pie seller fell over among forty thousand people and nearly one hundred died in the ensuing chaos. After 1868, executions took place behind prison walls. The death penalty for murder was abolished in 1965, but was still viable for treason and 'piracy with violence' until 1999.

528

ISLINGTON HIGH STREET AND LIVERPOOL ROAD

BUSINESS DESIGN CENTRE

528   N1

1861–62 F. PECK, ENGINEERED BY HEAVISIDE; 1986 CONVERTED

This, the former Royal Agricultural Hall, is a huge,
splendid hall set back from Islington High Street, behind
a giant entrance arch and vast, glass façade that creates
lovely sweeping curves. The column-free venue provides
vast exhibition and product-launch space, flexible
conference facilities, and rooms for banquets for up
to two thousand guests. It has a huge exhibition floor,
a high, barrel-vaulted ceiling, and masses of natural light.
It was converted into the Business Design Centre in 1986.
Once upon a time, in the 1870s, it was used for walking
races on two tracks—one requiring seven laps, and one
needing eight laps to the mile.

HOLY TRINITY

1826–28 SIR CHARLES BARRY

Set in the centre of an Islington square at a time of Gothic revival, this church, like the architect's later Houses of Parliament, explores neo-Gothic forms and was modelled on King's College Chapel, Cambridge. It could hold over 2,009 parishioners. This view shows the east end with its tall window and pinnacles.

THORNHILL SQUARE

c. 1848 THOMAS CUBITT

This, the largest square in Islington, was laid out from 1848. The adjacent streets and St Andrew's church were completed by 1854. It forms an ellipse with Thornhill Crescent. Once available only to residents, the gardens were donated to the public by Captain Thornhill in 1946. With Georgian embellishments, such as lintels over the doors and arches above the windows, the houses face the lovely square—the setting for Hugh Grant's home in the movie *Four Weddings and a Funeral*.

TERRACED HOUSES

c. 1820 THOMAS CUBITT

There were just cottages here until 1810, when the Thornhill family leased the land for development. Richmond Avenue has some of the earliest houses—many graced with the then popular Egyptian details: sphinxes and miniature obelisks flank entrances. The terraced houses have simple façades with brick upper storeys, neat railings, and wrought-iron balconies. Prime Minister Tony Blair lived in adjoining Richmond Crescent, prior to his move into 10 Downing Street.

HOUSES ALL AROUND THE SQUARE

1830–40

The west side of this square was built in 1836, and the rest in 1839. The houses have warm honey-coloured bricks above white ground floors, and those on the corner have giant pilasters. There are sweet little balconies, and the square has an interesting 1970 feature: The construction of the Victoria underground line required a ventilation shaft here. To calm local opposition, the brick and stone shaft was designed to look like a temple.

ST MARY'S CHURCH

1751–54 LAUNCELOT DOWBIGGIN; REBUILT 1956

During the Reformation, statues were taken from the church and smashed on Islington Green. Later, under Queen Mary, forty locals who refused to attend Mass, were burned at the stake. Curates here have included David Sheppard, the cricketer George Carey (later the Archbishop of Canterbury) and John Wesley's brother. Wesley preached here ten times in 1739, before both brothers were thrown out by the churchwardens. The lovely steeple is the sole survivor of the Blitz.

PEABODY TRUST HOUSING

1865 H. A. DARBISHIRE

American philanthropist George Peabody rose from poverty to riches and endowed many building schemes to house the poor—some rather sombre. This block has deeply recessed windows, a sturdy arch and canopy over the front door, and an Italianate style (soon adopted by other local buildings). Four blocks surround an open square. Islington was an overnight stop for cattle on their way to Smithfield market so many pavements are raised high above the cattle run's mire.

529

530

531

532

533

534

535

536

537

MILNER SQUARE
VENETIAN-STYLE HOUSES
535   NI

1841-43 ROUMIEU AND GOUGH

This lovely big square has houses with arched attic windows set above a continuous cornice. The houses are in three tall, four-storey bays separated by slim pilasters with very narrow windows that emphasize the height. Their Venetian style is rather austere but this is now one of London's most prestigious locations. The building of Milner Square was begun in 1827, but those houses on the east side were not leased until 1840, and building on the west side was completed only in the 1850s.

33-35 CROSS STREET
GEORGIAN HOUSES
536   NI

c. 1780

Islington grew from an Anglo-Saxon settlement through Roman and then medieval development. This was an area of good dairy farms, known for its pure water springs. Queen Elizabeth I is said to have visited Sir Walter Raleigh in Upper Street (at the westward end of Cross Street). Charles Wesley and Daniel Defoe were educated here. Authors George Orwell and Joe Orton, artist Walter Sickert, and the notorious gangster Kray twins have all been part of the Islington scene. These neat late-eighteenth-century Georgian houses are set behind railings, close to the slope of the street and with scant frontage between the houses and the pavement.

ESSEX ROAD AND ST PAUL'S ROAD
MARQUESS ROAD ESTATE
537   NI

1970 DARBOURNE AND DARKE

As a reaction to some of the negative aspects of high-rise building in the late sixties, many low-level urban estates were built—sometimes sprawling, dense villages. Here, the horizontal flow of this complex is emphasized by long stripes of brick on the lower floors with light render running along above—all topped by a slate roof. Some of the small, tidy windows have balconies. Close by is the New River, brought to London in 1613 by Sir Hugh Myddleton—goldsmith, Member of Parliament, and associate of Sir Walter Raleigh. A waterside walk has been rebuilt and replanted along the frontage of the estate.

BARNSBURY
THORNHILL CRESCENT

538 N1

c. 1850 THOMAS CUBITT

These immaculate, elegant houses are the work of Thomas Cubitt, who began as a ship's carpenter and went on to create housing at Camden Town and Islington. Queen Victoria, for whom he built Osborne House, said at his death, 'In his sphere of life, with the immense business he had in hand, he is a real national loss. A better, kind-hearted or more simple, unassuming man never breathed.' These unassuming but perfectly balanced houses reflect Cubitt's very character.

LIVERPOOL ROAD
SAMUEL LEWIS BUILDINGS

539 N1

1910 CHARITABLE TRUST

Here were built five blocks of flats offering much-needed housing in tall Dutch-style buildings with high mansard gables, sandstone trim, and other interesting details and brickwork. There are some bay windows, as well as the sash ones shown here.

LONSDALE SQUARE
TUDOR-STYLE HOUSES

540 N1

1838–45 R. C. CARPENTER

Here, the use of Tudor styling breaks away from the Georgian tradition of London's streets, and the houses in this lovely square have fine pointed gables. There are decorative lintels above the tall windows, and the Tudor-shaped doors are set below appropriate quatrefoil decoration. The houses were designed by Richard Cromwell Carpenter (known then as a church architect) in 1835–43 for the Draper's Company—which eventually sold the buildings in 1954.

BARNSBURY SQUARE, BARNSBURY
MOUNTFORT CRESCENT

541 N1

c. 1830 THOMAS CUBITT

These white-stuccoed, semi-detached villas have a refined air, with their neat porches and multi-paned windows. The tiny top windows are delicately glazed. The villas are set back, on the corner of Barnsbury Square—a place that some claim to be the site of the moated Roman fort where Seutonius Paulinus camped before fighting Queen Boudicca. Architect Thomas Cubitt (1788–1855), a leading master builder in London, was responsible for the east front of Buckingham Palace.

538

539

540

541

542

543

BARNSBURY PARK
TWO-STOREY HOUSES

542   N1

COMPTON TERRACE
UNION CHAPEL

543   N1

1830s

Before the railways introduced suburbia, there were just fields and villages here. Then, in the 1800s, the Thornhill family leased pieces for development and Barnsbury Park sprang up. In some of the late Georgian terraces, there were experiments in various styles and constructions. The south side of this street has elegant two-storey terraced houses divided by lovely entrances with pillared porches and delicate wrought-iron gates. Artist Walter Sickert lived in Barnsbury Park in the 1920s.

1888 BONELLA AND PAUL

This is a flamboyant, Gothic Victorian building —with an extravagance not generally associated with a Congregationalist chapel. There are arches, spires, pinnacles, imposing doors, and a large clock set at right angles to the façade. The chapel was built amid neat Georgian terraces at a time when the Congregational (now United Reform) Church had a huge following. Its large octagonal interior has raked seating and galleries. It hosts religious services plus recitals and concerts.

544

WEST LIBRARY, BARNSBURY

544   NI

Traces of a Roman camp have been found in Barnsbury, and Islington was once a place where royalty (especially Elizabeth I) would pause on journeys to and from the city. It became a refuge during the plague and after the Great Fire—and, from Jacobean times, served as the nearest staging post to London. By the late-eighteenth century, it began to grow, and its many squares soon housed city merchants and tradesmen. Today, this fine library is found in an elegant russet-red building with lovely sash windows—those on the ground floor are set below rows of rounded arches and, on the upper storey, below pointed Asian-style lintels, and all have striped brick surounds. The façade has a rich striped texture. As well as providing the usual book services, the library serves as a centre for community activities.

545

546

547

548

549

550

ALMEIDA STREET

ALMEIDA THEATRE

545   N1

1837 ROUMIEU AND GOUGH

This small, handsome neo-classical theatre in the Greek Revival style so popular for public edifices, once housed reading rooms and a lecture hall for Islington's Literary and Scientific Institution. It has since been a Victorian music hall, a Salvation Army citadel, a factory making carnival novelties, and a fringe theatre in the 1970s. Home to a full-time company by 1990, it had a £7.6 million restoration in 2001. Kevin Spacey and Cate Blanchett have performed here.

CANONBURY SQUARE

AROUND THE SQUARE

546   N1

1800 LEROUX

Islington has many elegant squares, with grandly proportioned villas. Here, the houses have tall, rectangular first-floor windows, with arched brickwork and windows below. They surround a finely proportioned, well-preserved square and garden. There are raised pavements on the south side. George Orwell lived at number 27b in 1945, Evelyn Waugh at 17a in 1928 (as did fellow-writer Nancy Mitford), and the Grossmiths (*Diary of a Nobody*) once lived at 5 Canonbury Place.

CANONBURY PLACE

CANONBURY HOUSE

547   N1

c. 1780

The house is an elegant two-storey villa and an interesting early example of stucco. Built for the developer of the Canonbury House Estate, it has a fine entrance with a centre lantern and windows set under arched brickwork, plus high, dormer, attic windows with pagoda-style roofs that are linked by a balustrade. This house should not be confused with a former Canonbury House—now called Canonbury Tower—on the hill.

ALWYNE ROAD AND OTHERS, CANONBURY

CANONBURY HOUSES

548   N1

1835–45

In the 1820s, Canonbury developed as a pretty suburb with fine villas and grandly proportioned houses. Many semi-detached houses appeared, often in Italianate style. A loop in the New River was straightened out to allow for expansion in the 1840s to '50s, that included Canonbury Park—laid out across Canonbury Field by the Marquess of Northampton. The collection of roads called 'Alwyne' were named after a family branch.

ISLINGTON

HIGHBURY TERRACE

549   N5

1700s

Near where once Queen Elizabeth I hunted, this is a handsome eighteenth-century terrace with wide pavements. There are slender windows, delicate curved balconies, and ornate fanlights over the doors—with brick upper storeys. Highbury took its name from a small Roman summer camp for the London garrison. Roman Ermine Street passed near the station. In 1381, the manor was largely demolished by Wat Tyler's mob.

180 HIGHBURY HILL

A MODERN FAMILY HOUSE

550   N5

1999–2000 CHARLES RHOMSON AND RIVINGTON ST STUDIO

This classic modern family house occupies the site of a derelict workshop in an area of modest, Victorian terraced houses. It has two storeys evident from the street but rises to three at the rear, with a zinc roof, and slim, steel-framed, and large bay windows. Indoors, the large spaces and high ceilings reflect the Victorian influence. Its design by architects responsible for a great variety of buildings, was a finalist in the Blueprint 'Residential Building of the Year 2001.'

551

552

HIGHGATE	91–103 SWAINS LANE
THE GROVE	**BRICK TERRACED ROW**
551 N6	552 N6

LATE 1600s

This remarkably well-preserved group of houses are set around a small green that still conveys a village atmosphere. There are broad sash windows, fine Doric porches and, as shown here, ornate iron gates. Poet Samuel Taylor Coleridge lived at number 3 in 1816. Later residents in the Grove have included Sir Yehudi Menuhin, Robert Donat, author J. B. Priestley, plus Sting, and Annie Lennox of the Eurythmics, whose homes here sold for over £5 million and £6 million, respectively.

1970–72 HAXWORTH AND KASABOV

Steep, winding Swains Lane is an ancient road that dates back to 1380. It runs from Highgate village and divides the cemetery into two distinct halves. This is a close-up of one of seven properties that form a rather more modern element—this row of houses, with its wide neat brick frontage on a sloping site, presents a sharp contrast to ancient Highgate. Entrances and garages are at street level. The central section houses kitchen and dining areas that lead onto the gardens at the back, while the top-floor living rooms face old Swains Lane. There is a good view of Highgate cemetery through the railings along the lane.

553

81 SWAINS LANE
STEEL-FRAMED HOUSE

553   N6

1969 JOHN WINTER

This three-storey steel-framed house was designed by the architect and author as his own home. John Winter worked and travelled in the United States during the 1950s and '60s and returned enthused about the new approaches he discovered there, including the use of Corten steel. Structural steelwork was exposed and so able to rust gently and to give the building interest and a feeling of age that contrasts well with its 1960 ultra-modern lines. Its use in this house is the only domestic example in London. Meanwhile, vast sheets of clear glass create a light interior and many interesting reflections.

554

SWAINS LANE, HIGHGATE
HOLLY VILLAGE

554   N6

1865 H. A. DARBISHIRE

Swains Lane separates the two parts of Highgate Cemetery. Here, the campaigner and benefactor of the East End poor, Baroness Burdett-Coutts, was responsible for this group of eight rustic Gothic-style dwellings for her servants. They are set around a village green within a private courtyard behind the highly ornate entrance gate. Everywhere, there is a huge indulgence in flamboyant detail. Highgate still has a nineteenth-century atmosphere and remains much as it was when Dickens first came here in 1832; he returned many times and used it as a setting for David Copperfield's residence. Dickens's wife and one of his daughters, Dora, are buried in Highgate's West Cemetery.

555

HIGHGATE CEMETERY

1839 STEPHEN GEARY, J. B. BUNNING AND J. OLDRED SCOTT

The imposing entrance to this 37-acre cemetery celebrates death as only the Victorians could, a solemn gateway to 51,000 tombs, vaults, graves, mausoleums, and catacombs for 167,000, including Karl Marx, George Eliot, John Galsworthy, Charles Cruft (who founded the famous dog show), and prize fighter Tom Sayers, whose chief mourner was his dog. Egyptian Avenue, the Circle of Lebanon, and winding paths are dug into hillsides. Geary also designed gin palaces.

556

17 OLD HALL

1690s

This elegant house behind high hedges, stout pillars, and a gate with delicate ornamental ironwork, has sash windows each side of its elegant porch, tall chimneys rising at each edge—and an additional structure to the left. Francis Bacon (1561–1626) died in the Earl of Arundel's house that was here formerly. Bacon's Lane, leading off South Grove, is named after him. Rather later, actor, writer, and director Terry Gilliam, of *12 Monkeys* and *Monty Python* fame, lived at the Old Hall.

557

17–21, 23, AND 42 HIGH STREET

1700s

Highgate's hilltop position has been the setting for rich, elegant homes for over four hundred years, and here are many excellent eighteenth-century houses. Typically, these neat brickwork houses are set behind railings, have slim front doors below pediments, and are approached by a short flight of steps. There are sliding sash windows with small panes, and basements provide extra space below the ground floors.

HIGHGATE CEMETERY, SWAINS LANE
CATACOMBS AND VAULTS
558   N6

FROM 1839

The cemetery was launched when space for burials in London became critical in the early 1800s. By 1975, many of the buildings were dilapidated and the gardens had run wild with brambles. In 1981, the freehold of both parts of the cemetery was acquired, and the Friends of Highgate were able to conserve and restore both structures and landscaping. The buildings are both eerie and beautiful, and include tombs, monuments, catacombs, and family vaults. Chemist Michael Faraday and novelist George Eliot are buried here.

558

SOUTH GROVE HIGHGATE
1-6 POND SQUARE
559   N6

LATE 1600s

Here a group of relatively small houses are set between taller buildings. This one has a very slim front door, delicate brickwork, and sash windows with small panes set below arched brickwork. Pond Square is where poultry was for the first time ever frozen in 1626, when Francis Bacon tested whether snow would act as a preservative. Sadly, the scientist collapsed in the cold and died soon afterwards. Ever since, the ghost of a featherless bird has been seen squawking in fear in Pond Square.

559

CHOLMELEY LANE, HIGHGATE HILL
CHOLMELEY LODGE
560   N6

1934 GUY MORGAN

The Highgate hills rise to the height of St Paul's Cathedral. Built on the site of the Mermaid Inn and an earlier Cholmeley Lodge, this sweep of forty-eight flats is near the entrance to Cholmeley Park. On its curving front, redbrick bands alternate with flowing balconies and pretty small-paned windows — the central ones in bays. The nearby free grammar school was founded in 1562 by Sir Roger Cholmeley, a knight who procured its two charters from Queen Elizabeth I.

560

561

562

563

564

565

566

GARTON HOUSE

561   N6

1980 COLQUHOUN AND MILLER

These flats, built for single people, were commissioned by the London Borough of Haringey. The tall, narrow building is simple and modern, with clean lines and very small, neat balconies. It presents a tidy mosaic of windows set within the criss-crossed lines that are made by the bright redbrick walls within their own rectangular frame. The criss-cross pattern of the balcony 'network' echoes this in miniature.

44 NORTH HILL

A GROUP PRACTICE

562   N6

1986 DOUGLAS STEPHENS AND PARTNERS

Here, with trees reflected in its central glass frontage and triangular pediment, is a purpose-built health centre for Highgate Group Practice. Fitted neatly into a deep, slim site, it has a simple gabled façade of glass and brick. Inside are consulting rooms, and a double-height waiting and reception room. Highgate was once part of the bishops of London's hunting estates, marked by a tollhouse, and was later associated with the famous highwayman, Dick Turpin.

DAVY CLOSE, SOUTH OF BRIDGE STREET

ST CLEMENT

563   N7

1863–65 SIR GEORGE GILBERT SCOTT

This fine tall façade has a triple door and arch arrangement echoed by triple bells set in the high bellcote. The church was converted into flats in the early 1990s but, despite being surrounded by a new housing estate, retains its soaring elegance. The architect was prominent in the Gothic renaissance and worked on the restorations of Ely Cathedral and Westminster Abbey. His designs included the Albert Memorial, St Pancras Station, and numerous Victorian workhouses.

NORTH ROAD AND MARKET ROAD

CALEDONIAN MARKET

564   N7

1855 J. B. BUNNING

Farmers used to drive their cattle on foot to this 6-hectare (15-acre) market—that held some 6,000 bullocks and 1,400 calves (plus nearly 35,000 sheep and 900 pigs). When the railways came, the market vanished. All that remains are railings, three tall Italianate public houses, and a solitary white tower that once housed banks and a telegraph office. The Clock Tower is surrounded by a housing estate where some names, such as the Drovers Centre and Ewe Close, recall the area's history.

CHILLINGWORTH ROAD

ST MARKS STUDIOS

565   N7

1837–38 INWOOD AND CLIFTON

The elegant south façade of this once-upon-a-time church has a sweeping portico where four columns are topped by swirling Ionic capitals. Set to the left of this is a tall, square tower decorated with grapes and ears of wheat. The building was converted into rather attractive flats and studios in the 1980s.

DARTMOUTH PARK HILL AND CHESTER ROAD

HIGHGATE NEW TOWN

566   N7

1965–80 PETER TABORI
(LONDON BOROUGH OF CAMDEN ARCHITECTS)

Set close to historic Highgate Cemetery, these buildings are part of the first stage of a public housing scheme that was developed over fifteen years. In a precast construction, the long rows have slightly staggered storeys, and generous balcony space, divided by tall stepped divides.

567

568

166–220 HOLLOWAY ROAD; GRADUATE CENTRE

LONDON METROPOLITAN UNIVERSITY

567   N7

2004 DANIEL LIBESKIND

A small plaza leads to the entrance where three intersecting blocks clad in stainless steel are set at interesting angles to create a dramatic impact as the triangular shapes seem to rise from the ground—the whole effect augmented by the diamond patterns on the surfaces. Even the doorways and windows are irregular and create sharp slashes in the metal façade. Meanwhile, the embossed stainless-steel surface panels reflect the sky and busy world around them to create an ever-changing pattern. The building, built on the north campus on the Holloway Road, cost less than £3 million but is now regarded as one of the most exciting new developments in London. The portfolio of architect Daniel Libeskind includes the Jewish Museum in Berlin and his acclaimed proposal for the redevelopment of the World Trade Center site in New York.

CALEDONIAN ROAD

PENTONVILLE PRISON

568   N7

1840–42 SIR JOSHUA JEBB (FIRST SURVEYOR GENERAL OF PRISON)

This model prison (based on the plan of the Eastern Penitentiary in Philadelphia) has five brick wings with cells in three storeys, radiating out from a central control block—all set behind a massive, forbidding portico and wall. Today, it holds 1,177 convicts. Back in the 1800s, many male convicts were taught a trade here, prior to their being transported. Some worked on the crank, a hard-labour machine, others at picking coir (tarred rope) and weaving. To relieve mental problems, the amount of exercise in the yards was increased and areas of brick walking were introduced. Prison numbers rose as capital punishment for many crimes ended and transportation was reduced. One hundred and twenty men, including Dr Crippen, were hanged at Pentonville between 1902 and 1961, and this is still the place to learn the skills of execution—a one-week course teaches how to calculate and set the drop. Today, there is a pre-release hostel where suitable prisoners are able to live and work outside during the day as their sentence reaches its close. Despite one and a half centuries of history and refurbishment, the prison layout remains little altered.

569

570

571

SCHOOL OF ARCHITECTURE AND INTERIOR DESIGN

569 N7

1995 BRADY MALLALIEU

Brady Mallalieu Architects have worked on a wide and varied range of buildings in fifteen major cities and, in 1997, won a RIAI Design Award for this new school of architecture (a part of London Metropolitan University) that specialises in teaching contemporary architecture, interior design, and the spatial arts. Six sturdy pillars support the upper floors that project over the pavement, creating a five-bay arcade, and there is interesting use of yellow brick.

PARKHURST ROAD

HOLLOWAY PRISON

570 N7

1849-52 J. B. BUNNING; 1903 REFURBISHED; 1971-85 REBUILT

Only a fragment of one gatehouse remains of the old, castellated, Gothic prison—plus two griffins and a glass foundation stone inscribed, 'May God preserve the city of London and make this place a terror to evil doers.' Oscar Wilde was held here but, from 1902, it was used exclusively for women, including Mrs Pankhurst and other suffragettes. Ruth Ellis, the last woman executed in Britain, was hanged here in July 1955. The new prison is built in redbrick with its rear perimeter wall in a sinuous line to make escape by climbing more difficult. It can hold 532 prisoners and has a mother-and-baby unit.

PARKHURST ROAD

HOLLOWAY ESTATE

571 N7

1962-69 MCMORRAN AND WHITBY

Holloway Estate has been in the ownership of the City of London since 1832. This modern building complex with its clean slate roofs and sash windows comprises flats, maisonettes, and houses—many of which have now been adapted for use by people with disabilities. The arrangement of neo-Georgian style buildings is set around three simple courtyards, arranged within eight four-storey buildings with arched entrances in black brickwork—all set in pleasant lawns.

572

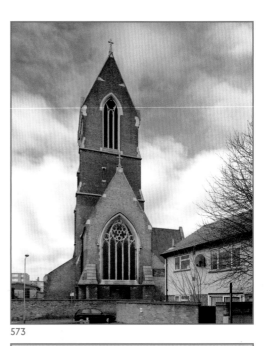

573

THE BROADWAY, CROUCH END

HORNSEY TOWN HALL

572   N8

WORDSWORTH ROAD

ST MATTHIAS

573   N16

1934–35 REGINALD HAROLD UREN

Hornsey first appears in written records in
the 1200s, as part of the bishop of London's
lands, but it was the arrival of the railways in
1850 that brought wealthy professionals into
suburbia here. Set back from the road, behind
a garden square, this Grade II–listed building,
with its tall square tower, is a fine example of
the Modern Movement in Europe and won the
RIBA bronze award for the best public
building in London. A dignified landmark
structure, it fits neatly into the narrow site
and marked a clear departure from elaborately
decorated Victorian civic buildings. Uren
was clearly influenced by Dutch architecture
and by America's Frank Lloyd Wright. A fine
example of Art Deco public building, its interior
owes more to Germany's Bauhaus style.

1851 W. BUTTERFIELD

William Butterfield (1814–1900) was a
pioneer of the High Victorian phase of Gothic
revival and one of the first to experiment
with the use of colour in construction. This
old church, damaged in World War II and
since restored, is a fine early example of
Butterfield's work in elemental Gothic style.
Set in a leafy churchyard, it has tall, steep
gables—and is now a centre for dance and
martial arts. From the time of the Quakers and
Dissenters, Stoke Newington has been home
to radicals and to several who have opposed
authoritarian traditions. Now the area is home
instead to a lively mix of authors, merchant
bankers, actors, academics, and many
immigrant communities.

574

575

574

GREEN LANES

WATERWORKS PUMPING STATION

574   N16

1854–56 CHADWELL MYLNE

It is said that this imposing castle-style edifice—with its turrets, towers, crenellations, chimneys, and buttresses—could pump one million gallons of water a day. The course of the New River now finishes at Stoke Newington. Until the reign of Elizabeth I, most Londoners drew water from open water-courses (often contaminated by sewage) or it was carried up from the river in barrels by water-bearers. In 1608, James I agreed to fund the New River Company (in return for half the profits). In 1709, the Upper Pond was constructed. William Chadwell Mylne, engineer to the 1811 New River Company, was involved in many water-supply and canal projects—and is buried in St Paul's Cathedral.

STOKE NEWINGTON CHURCH STREET

ST MARY

575   N16

1858 SIR GEORGE GILBERT SCOTT

The growing population of the parish in the nineteenth century led to the building of a new Gothic Revival church in the 1850s on the site of the old rectory. Its architect was also the designer of the Albert Memorial, the Foreign Office in Whitehall, and St Pancras Station frontage. A tall spire was added to this church in 1890. Fifty years later, the building suffered extensive World War II damage in 1940 when the roof was bombed and much had to be repaired. By 1998, this was the first London church to be fully floodlit.

576

OLD ST MARY

1563; 1824–29 SIR CHARLES BARRY

The history of Old St Mary goes back nearly one thousand years, for a chapel existed on this site at the time of the Norman Conquest. Unfortunately, the church records were held in St Paul's, and so were destroyed in the Great Fire in 1666, but the church definitely had a rector by 1313. The nave is late medieval; the vestry, west tower, and south aisle date from 1560. Sir Charles Barry added the north aisle in 1824, and the timber spire dates from 1829—when he also installed gas lighting. Tudor brickwork is still evident on the south side, with a date plaque of 1563. Barry (who, with Pugin, famously built the House of Commons) managed to enlarge the church while still retaining its medieval village atmosphere. In the churchyard rest anti-slavery campaigner James Stephen (great-grandfather of author Virginia Woolf), and Alderman William Picket (the Lord Mayor of London in 1789).

577

CLISSOLD HOUSE

577   N16

1790s; 1820–30 J. WOODS

Grade II–listed Clissold Mansion was built in the 1790s
for an Irish Quaker and banker (whose bank later became
part of Lloyds Bank). In 1811, ownership passed to the
Crawshaw family (who made a fortune from iron making
in South Wales). It became Clissold Place when one of
the daughters married Reverend Augustus Clissold. This
liaison had been opposed by her father, who heightened
the garden wall to prevent their seeing each other and
threatened to shoot the go-between who carried their
love letters. Renamed Clissold Park in 1889, it opened
as a public park under the Metropolitan Board of Works.
This neo-classical house has a one-storey colonnade of
fluted Greek Doric columns approached by a ramped
courtyard. The three-storey brick villa, with its tall
windows, diamond-patterned railings, and many-potted
chimneys, overlooks a crescent-shaped lake, originally
part of the New River.

WHITE HART LANE ESTATE
578   N17

1904–12, 1921–28 W. E. RILEY AND G. TOPHAM FORREST

White Hart Lane is most famous as the home of the Tottenham Hotspur Football Club that moved here in 1899. In somewhat earlier times, 'Totenham' appears in the Domesday Book and soon became a rural village. The estate here was a vast undertaking at the turn of the century, when some 71 hectares (177 acres) were developed by the London County Council with the intent to create a garden city that met current ideals. Here, the inventive detailing of porch and brickwork, plus the projecting central bay, relieve the flat street frontage and, with the tidy small-paned windows, manage to achieve the romantic cottage look, albeit in suburbia.

579

LAUDERDALE HOUSE
579   N19

FROM 1580

Placed among the rolling acres of Waterlow Park, the relatively simple, late Georgian exterior of this house hides a much older Tudor manor—but only the masonry and one southeast room have survived from the 1500s. First built (and named) for a rich city merchant, the Earl of Lauderdale, this is said to have been the home of Charles II's most famous mistress, Nell Gwynn, and their baby son. Inside are a 1600s staircase and a lovely entrance hall with Corinthian columns. The park inspired poet Andrew Marvell to write 'The Garden' and later, poet Samuel Taylor Coleridge came to stroll and contemplate the sweeping views across the city. Today, restored Tudor gardens occupy the site of what was, at one stage, a private pleasure garden.

580

581

24–32 WINSCOMBE STREET
ROW OF HOUSES
580   N19

1966-68 NEAVE BROWN

These buildings were an early project for the
leading 1960s and '70s architect who went on
to create the renowned housing at Alexandra
Road (see page 400). His buildings all exhibit
his strong ideas about social structuring and
the need to interrelate all the elements into a
pleasing architectural and urban composition.
This neat row of houses have very well-
planned interiors with interesting use of
different levels as well as epitomising new
1960s architecture at the domestic level.

UPPER HOLLOWAY ROAD
ST JOHN THE EVANGELIST
581   N19

1822-26 SIR CHARLES BARRY

This brick church was designed by the young
Charles Barry—most famous now as the
designer of the Houses of Parliament.
Externally, it is a replica of his St Paul's in
Ball Pond Road. The extensive church is
in Perpendicular Gothic style, with a tiered
tower and roof pinnacles. It was raised among
the then-new development of houses and
villas along Upper Holloway Road. The rear
churchyard was destroyed when the Great
Northern Railway arrived in the 1840s, and
the church now stands next to Holloway Road
station. For a while, Upper Holloway was the
haunt of highwayman Claude Duval, until he
was executed at Tyburn in 1670.

582

ALEXANDRA PARK, WOOD GREEN

ALEXANDRA PALACE

582   N22

1875 J. JOHNSON

The epitome of opulent splendour, this ill-fated building opened as the People's Palace in 1873 but then, just sixteen days later, was destroyed by fire. It was rebuilt but the central section burned yet again in 1980. Completely rebuilt, it reopened in 1988. Its seven acres of palatial building are set within 196 acres of fine parkland with excellent views over London. Inside are museums, art exhibitions, an ice rink, a vast concert hall for 14,000 people, and the mighty Willis Organ—one of the largest in the world, driven by steam engines and huge bellows. The first public television transmissions were made from here in 1936.

NORTH WEST LONDON (NW)

This area sweeps through stunning Regent's Park, pretty Primrose Hill, and Somers Town—squeezed between Euston and St Pancras stations. It is served by the solid march of the ancient A5—that began life as Roman Watling Street, striding from Dover to Shropshire—as well as the North Circular road looping around the busy suburbs. The mighty M1 has carved its way into the landscape here, too, coming to an abrupt end near Hendon.

Hampstead is a tangle of roads, once a spa, with lovely vistas that attracted writers and artists. In Kentish Town, the River Fleet flows, albeit channelled out of sight; and at Gospel Oak, the custom of beating the parish boundaries used to culminate in biblical readings around the tree. Kilburn—once a northern outpost, has many Victorian and Edwardian houses. St. John's Wood, originally part of the

Great Middlesex Forest, was owned by the Knights of St John of Jerusalem and is home to Lords Cricket. Here are Abbey Road Studios where many 1960s Beatles's recordings were made, including *Abbey Road* with its sleeve depicting the pedestrian crossing—now a place of pilgrimage.

Golders Green, once fields and farmland, is today a solid middle-class suburb with a Jewish community, synagogues, and many substantial Edwardian family homes. Hampstead Garden Suburb, meanwhile, began as a utopian housing project in 1907, spearheaded by Lady Henrietta Barnett where (in theory) the several tiers of the rich, the middle-class professionals, and honest artisans would gain from closer contact. Whatever its achievements in merging social stratas, it is regarded as one of the finest examples of early 1900s domestic architecture and planning.

NW1

NW1 Regent's Park
NW2 Cricklewood
NW3 Hampstead
NW4 Hendon
NW5 Kentish Town
NW6 West Hampstead
NW7 Mill Hill
NW8 St John's Wood
NW9 Kinsbury
NW10 Willesden
NW11 Golders Green

583

ST PANCRAS STATION, HOTEL, AND OFFICES

583   NWI

1866–76 SIR GEORGE GILBERT SCOTT; W. H. BARLOW AND R. M. ORDISH

This splendid building, the terminus of the Midland Railway, is one of the engineering wonders of the Victorian Age. It has a vast 74-metre (243-foot) single span. The glass and iron train shed is 213 metres (689 feet) long with 55-ton ribs, and curves up to rise 30 metres (100 feet) above the rails at its apex. Its skeletal transparency is a masterpiece. An extension is being added to allow Eurostar trains to use the station as a terminus for the Channel Tunnel Rail Link and the station will be serve a shuttle service to the 2012 Olympic Games. The hotel used 60 million bricks and 9,000 tons of ironwork, and boasts polished granite and limestone columns, a beautiful, long curving dining room, a majestic staircase, and London's first smoking room for ladies. It was converted into offices (St Pancras Chambers) in 1935. In the mid-nineties, the exterior was restored at a cost of around £10 million.

ST MARY THE VIRGIN

1824 HENRY W AND WILLIAM INWOOD;
1888 EWAN CHRISTIAN

This Commissioners church was designed by
Henry W. & William Inwood in what is called
'Carpenter's Gothic' style. Its centre tower was
built in London stock brick and rises above a
symmetrical west front and bright blue doors
that open into a rich warm interior. This
church, so close to Euston Station, has been
called the 'Cabbies Church'—and has also
welcomed many Pearly Kings and Queens.
It was a focal point of the slum clearance
movement here, lead by Friar Basil Jellicoe.

MARYLEBONE STATION

1898-99 R. W. EDIS

This Victorian station is one of the smallest
of the railway terminals in London, and the
newest, apart from Waterloo International.
It has an elegant glass and iron structure that
spans the street to connect it with the Great
Central Hotel. When the station was opened
in 1899, it was the terminus of the Great
Central Railway's newly extended London main
line. It features in the British version of the
board game Monopoly, and several scenes in
the 1964 Beatles movie, *A Hard Day's Night*,
were filmed here. In the late 1980s, the station
was greatly improved with a multimillion-
pound facelift.

LISSON GALLERY

1992 AND 1996 TONY FRETTON ARCHITECTS

This renowned gallery in a beautifully
glazed contemporary design was built as two
buildings—each meant to retain its distinct
character and fulfil slightly different roles—
but now they have merged into a single entity.
The building is north facing, with good natural
light and windows with views of the city
beyond, as well as opaque and translucent
panels. Generous gallery spaces allow the
display of large-scale works. The art exhibited
here is by some of the most stimulating,
contemporary British artists.

PUBLIC LIBRARY

1939 SIR EDWIN COOPER

This is Georgian Marylebone at its best, Sir
Edwin Cooper having used a fine, smooth
Portland stone to create a building that looks
very clean and elegant. A linking structure that
resembles a modern 'Venetian Bridge of Sighs'
arches between the two buildings. In 1931,
this architect was awarded a gold medal by
the Royal Institute of British Architects (RIBA).

584

585

586

587

588

SUSSEX PLACE

588   NWI

1822 JOHN NASH

Sussex Place is the most unconventional terrace here with curved wings. Twenty-six houses have polygonal bow windows, octagonal domes, pointed cupolas along the roofline, and fifty-six Corinthian columns decorating the façade. This terrace is named after Augustus, the Duke of Sussex (George IV's younger brother). The view of the lake from the terrace is superb. During the 1960s, the terrace was rebuilt behind the original façade to serve as the premises for the London Graduate School of Business Studies, and the Royal College of Obstetricians and Gynaecologists is based at number 27.

589

BUILT ON A CRICKET GROUND

589   NWI

c. 1815

These houses rose on the site of Thomas Lord's first cricket ground, here from 1787 to 1811, and the square was named after the Duke of Dorset, who was an early patron of the game. Here, the well-preserved, late-Georgian houses retain individual features. On the eastern side are some fine cast-iron verandas, a feature that arrived in the wake of the British colonial experience, when many Eastern influences impacted on domestic architecture. The houses on the north side are more or less original. Number 1 was the Free French Headquarters in World War II, and a plaque remembers the brave men and women who set off from here to occupied France. Number 28 was home to George Grossmith, an actor and the co-author of *The Diary of a Nobody*.

590

ST JOHN'S WOOD CHAPEL

590   NWI

1813 THOMAS HARDWICK

Thomas Hardwick (1752–1829) was an eminent architect and the son of a master mason. Thomas's son Philip and grandson Philip Charles both held the post of surveyor to St Bartholomew's Hospital. Thomas Hardwick studied architecture under Sir William Chambers, and helped with the construction of Somerset House. He explored buildings in Paris, Lyon, and Rome, and this influenced his own neo-classical style. This church has a splendid Ionic portico. Inside, Tuscan columns support glazed galleries, while Ionic columns rise to the gentle curve of the ceiling. Hardwick, mainly a church architect, was also clerk of works at Hampton Court for King George III — and worked at Kew Palace and gardens. He advised J. M. W. Turner (one of his pupils) to concentrate on painting rather than architecture.

WESTMINSTER COUNCIL HOUSE, MARYLEBONE TOWN HALL

591   NW1

1914–21 SIR EDWIN COOPER

These classical Edwardian structures in Portland stone are both fine examples of public buildings. The town hall was built some twenty-five years after the Westminster Council House and now, a reflection of the changing roles of such places, has four complexes used for marriages: the Blue Marriage Room, the Yellow Marriage Room, the Purple Marriage Room, and the Reception Room. From the intricate detailing on the tower of the older building to the smoother lines of the newer one, the refining of the architect's style and the general direction of architecture is clearly demonstrated.

591

HANOVER TERRACE AND LODGE

592   NW1

1822–23 JOHN NASH; 1827 DECIMUS BURTON

This terrace was named after George III's other kingdom, Hanover. Twenty tall mansions have a continuous roofed gallery along the ground floor, with three decorated pediments. Mystery writer Wilkie Collins (1824–89) lived here and entertained artists and writers, including Charles Dickens. Today, number 10 is the office of the provost of University College. In 1827, Hanover Lodge was designed for Colonel Sir Robert Arbuthnot, a hero of the Napoleonic campaigns, and serves as an entrance to Regent's Park. The house is octagonal with a tall central chimney and steep pitched roof. From 1832-45, Admiral Thomas Cochrane resided here. Known as the Sea Wolf, this courageous and audacious Royal Navy commander used to harass enemy shipping in the Mediterranean.

592

LONDON CENTRAL MOSQUE

593   NW1

1978 BUILT BY SIR FREDERICK GIBBER AND PARTNERS

In 1944, King George VI gave several acres of land and a Victorian mansion to Britain's Muslims as a centre for worship and study. This huge mosque has a golden-copper dome and an elegant, tall, white minaret — the balcony of which provides a panoramic view of the courtyard and gardens, Regent's Park, and the lovely Nash terraces. Inside, there is a glorious chandelier, traditional Islamic blue mosaic patterns, and a great expanse of carpet in the huge hall, which can accommodate almost two thousand worshippers. A separate porch gives entrance to female worshippers, and a balcony for them overlooks the main hall. The cultural centre here has a library and reading room with a collection of books in all languages, including every book in English on Islam.

593

594

595

596

ASHMILL STREET
HOUSING IN MARYLEBONE
594   NWI

1984 JEREMY AND FENELLA DIXON

Here are fourteen houses in a small terrace on a fairly narrow slither of land. They have white stucco on the ground floor with brick above and interesting balconies—but the most striking features are the tall staircase window sections that rise up to roof level in a neat ladderwork pattern that stripes the terraced run.

35 PARK ROAD
RUDOLPH STEINER HOUSE
595   NWI

1926–37 MONTAGUE WHEELER

Rudolf Steiner (1861–1925) was an Austrian philosopher, literary scholar, architect, playwright, educator, and social thinker. He founded schools with new approaches to education, biodynamic agriculture, anthroposophical medicine, and new artistic approaches. Here, the Expressionist architecture sought to reflect its namesake by exploring Steiner's preference for curves over right angles. There are interesting double entrance doors.

OUTER CIRCLE AND ST ANDREW'S PLACE
ROYAL COLLEGE OF PHYSICIANS
596   NWI

1518; 1960–64 SIR DENYS LASDUN AND PARTNERS

This is the oldest medical institution in England, founded in 1518 when Henry VIII granted it a charter. The present building stands on the site of Someries House, an orphanage for adults, designed free of charge by John Nash for the daughter of clergymen and officers. With its white mosaic and bricks, and circular dome, it has, despite the straight lines at the base, an almost Asian appeal. The Council Chamber within has a vaulted roof and is flooded with daylight. The college has a huge collection of portraits and physicians' records, and a fine library with books on maths, physics, and law—plus a near-contemporary manuscript of Chaucer's *Canterbury Tales*.

1935 T. P. BENNETT AND JOSEPH EMBERTON

Situated next to the Marylebone Station, this wonderful example of Art Deco style consists of ten-storey interlocking blocks of apartments, with commercial establishments at its base. The living space ranges from one- to three-bedroom apartments, the size of their terraces and balconies proportional to the scale of the home. There is some pleasing vertical detailing on the brick walls, bay windows with French doors, curved corner decorative mouldings, and metal balustrades. The top stories are stepped back.

1823 DECIMUS BURTON

Clarence Terrace is one of the smallest terraces here, with just twelve houses. It was named after King William IV's earlier title, the Duke of Clarence. Wilkie Collins lived here in 1859, the year in which he launched *All the Year Round* and in which he published his most famous novel, *The Woman in White*. It has also been the home of actor William Charles Macready in 1848 and of poet Louis MacNeice from 1954–63. Following successive bomb blasts, the façade of number 2 is now a replica of the original.

1821–23 JOHN NASH WITH DECIMUS BURTON

Cornwall Terrace was designed by Decimus Burton, aged twenty-one, under the guidance of the John Nash, and was named after an earlier title of George IV, Duke of Cornwall. It was the first terrace built in the Regent's Park and consists of nineteen houses in a modern design for the period. After the damage done during World War II, this terrace was restored and is now the office of the British Land Company, a property-owning enterprise. In 1982, the British Academy occupied house numbers 21 and 22.

1824–26 JOHN NASH, JAMES BURTON,
AND WILLIAM MOUNTFORD NURSE

York Terrace was named after the younger brother of George IV, Frederick, the Duke of York. Each of the two terraces has twenty houses with York Gate, an entrance to Regent's Park and the route to St. Marylebone Church, situated between them. The design of the main entrance gives the impression that the terraces are actually two long palaces. Hugh Walpole occupied number 24 in 1922–23.

1822; 1910–11 SIR ERNEST GEORGE AND ALBERT B. YATES

When the first academy opened—in a house in Tenterden Street, Hanover Square—there were only twenty-one very young pupils, one being Charles Dickens's sister, Fanny. Today, this exalted academy for advanced musical training offers excellent amenities, including a wonderful concert hall, teaching rooms, recital hall, and library. Pupils have included Sir Arthur Sullivan, Sir Henry Wood, Sir John Barbirolli, and Simon Rattle. It is now a constituent college of the University of London.

1837 SIR J. PENNETHORNE;
1867 ALTERATIONS W. BUTTERFIELD

Christ Church is definitely one of the most asymmetrical architectural creations in London, with a massive doorway marked by two giant pilasters, and fort-like yellow masonry but a very graceful tower. Rossetti designed the glass window that depicts the Sermon on the Mount and this was executed by William Morris. The funeral service for George Orwell was held here in 1950; however, the author was actually buried in Gloucestershire.

597

598

599

600

601

602

603

604

ARLINGTON ROAD, FORMERLY ROWTON HOUSE
ARLINGTON HOUSE
603   NWI

ALBANY STREET
PARK VILLAGE EAST AND WEST
604   NWI

1905 H. B. MEASURES

Providing accommodation for over a century now, this building houses more than a thousand people and some sixty staff. Originally raised in a spirit of true Victorian philanthropy, it has a highly decorated Free Style front door and elaborate redbrick walls. Through the years it has been home to working men, soldiers, refugees, and many seeking work in London. The building requires renovation and there are ambitious plans for its future.

1829 JOHN NASH, J. PENNETHORNE

The buildings in these two delightful park villages, once separated by a branch of the Regent's Canal, are set along a winding road. Their style inspired many a Victorian builder who wanted to emulate their grandeur in suburbia. The pretty Tudor and Italianate exteriors in cream stucco have projecting eaves and black lattice pergolas. James Pennethorne, Nash's pupil, planned numbers 1–7 Park Village West. Renowned actor Edmund Kean lived at Bute Cottage; Dr James Johnson, a physician to William IV, at 12 Park Village West; and geographer James Wyld at number 8. Sadly, half of Park Village East was destroyed in 1906, when the Euston Railway cutting was enlarged, but the remaining houses have all been lovingly restored.

05

606

OUTER CIRCLE, REGENT'S PARK
ST KATHARINE'S HOSPITAL

605   NWI

1826 AMBROSE POYNTER

Founded in 1148 by Queen Matilda of England (wife of King Stephen), St Katharine's Hospital was started as a charitable body to treat thirteen poor people. It sat on the banks of the Thames near the Tower of London until 1825, when St Katharine's Dock was built and the hospital was relocated to the Regent's Park. In 1826, Ambrose Poynter designed a Tudor Gothic stone-and-brick chapel and a school for children of impoverished families—built adjacent to the hospital. This chapel was granted to her fellow Danes by Queen Alexandra in World War I. The 1600s wooden figures of Moses and John the Baptist were brought here from the old Danish church at Limehouse. Outside there is a copy of the rune stone erected in Jelling by Harald Bluetooth, the first Christian king of Denmark, in the year 980.

ALBANY STREET, FORMERLY THE WHITE HOUSE
MELIÁ WHITE HOUSE HOTEL

606   NWI

1936 R. ATKINSON

This sophisticated nine-storey star-shaped set of apartments, faced with beautiful cream faience tiles, is very elegant—and was a futuristic vision in the 1930s, its shops, restaurants , and leisure facilities all part of the scheme. It has sweeping curves and many interesting angles, and oozes sophistication. In 1975, it became a six-hundred-bedroom hotel, with apartments leased separately. The building complex was renovated and relaunched yet again in 2002 as another deluxe hotel.

607

608

609

610

611

612

FLATS AT ALBERT COURT

607   NWI

1963–66 PROPERTY AND DEVELOPMENT LTD,
MARTIN RICHMOND AND MALCOLM HIGGS

This building has a rather industrial and functional appearance for its Regent's Park setting but this is somewhat relieved by the fine trees around. It has broad windows and tidy lines. The principal entrance is at the back.

WILD HOUSE

608   NWI

1982 DAVID WILD

Designed by David Wild for himself, this interesting house seems to soar up. It has a two-storey portico, glass brick panels, some exposed concrete blockwork, and glazed screens. Trees and climbers soften the powerful lines of the building.

REDBRICK FLATS

609   NWI

1964 JAMES FRAZER STIRLING

Stirling, an important 1960s architect, often used colourful, geometric designs in unusual shapes. Here, however, there is symmetry everywhere, with an unusual entrance ramp placed centrally. Four identical redbrick blocks of flats are raised on columns above a car park—their living rooms facing the rear garden. Stirling was awarded the Pritzker Prize in 1981, and Britain's annual Stirling prize for architecture was named after him. Stirling's works include the Clore Gallery at the Tate Britain, and Number One Poultry.

KENT HOUSE

610   NWI

1936 CONNELL, WARD AND LUCAS

Incorporating many of the socialist ideals of early modern architecture, Kent House consists of two buildings (one a storey higher than the other) with white stuccoed walls, metal window frames, and cantilevered balconies that protrude like metal-caged theatre boxes. Its name is blazoned clearly on the front in large letters.

GILBEY'S OFFICES AND WAREHOUSES

611   NWI

1937 SERGE CHERMAYEFF

This is a large corner building in white stucco with interesting lines of windows, especially the vertical row of eight-paned glazing. It is raised on a reinforced concrete frame. The foundations were floated on thick cork insulation so that the wine stocks here would not be unsettled by the vibrations of trains in the nearby cutting, while air-conditioning helped to limit railway noise and grime.

ALL SAINTS, CAMDEN TOWN

612   NWI

1822–24 W. AND H. W. INWOOD

Originally known as Camden Chapel, All Saints is one of three chapels designed by William Inwood and his son, Henry William Inwood. The yellow stone building is now a Greek Orthodox place of worship that welcomes many Greek Cypriots. There is evidence of Henry's enthusiasm for Greek architecture, in the semicircular portico with Ionic columns and decorative Greek details, while the porch with a lantern is clearly a British feature.

GLOUCESTER GATE AND LODGE

EARLY 1800s JOHN NASH WITH RICHARD MOTT AND
JOSEPH JOHN SCOLES

Gloucester Gate was named after the Duke of Gloucester,
a brother-in-law to George IV. Joseph John Scoles
(architect on the site) did not care for Nash's façade so
he doubled the scale of the mouldings on the capitals.
Nash, preoccupied with his prestigious Buckingham
Palace project, merely commented that 'the parts looked
larger than he had expected.' The two-storey Gloucester
Lodge has a central portico and a three-bay pavilion.

CUMBERLAND TERRACE

1826–27 JOHN NASH AND JAMES THOMSON;
POST-WORLD WAR II, RECONSTRUCTED K. PEACOCK

This is a most magnificent structure, the longest and most
elaborate terrace here, situated on the eastern side of
Regent's Park. It is named after the Duke of Cumberland
(King George IV's younger brother). Three main blocks are
linked together with ornamental crescents and elegant
arches; their grandeur is theatrical. The pediment of the
central block is graced with statues, designed by George
Bubb, including Britannia—with the arts, sciences, and
trades that marked the achievements of her empire.

WORKING MEN'S COLLEGE

1905 W. H. CAROË

This rather austere Edwardian building has arched and
circular windows with 'Founded in 1854' clearly stated
high up on the wall. It was one of the first British adult
educational institutes and it moved here some five
decades after its inception. It was begun by a small group
of professionals; teachers and students were treated as
equal members of a community, and the focus was on
humanitarian studies and the furtherance of Christian
brotherhood and social justice. Renowned teachers
have included Tom Hughes (author of *Tom Brown's
Schooldays*), Charles Kingsley (of *The Water Babies*
fame), and artists Ruskin, Rossetti, and Burne-Jones.

613

614

615

616

617

618

619

1962–64 EDWARD CULLINAN

The two-storey house was designed by the architect for his own use and has many interesting constructional features. Cullinan built it in two years of weekends, with the help of his wife and two friends. The plan is very simple and hierarchic. The house is set at right angles to the mews. Over the plinth of bedrooms are the public rooms, and the garden is located on the first floor over the garage. The layout of the house reflects the architect's interest in inventive building construction. The house became a place of pilgrimage for 1960s students interested in new architecture.

1968–71 GEORGIE WOLTON

This multi-storey group of studios has a rendered exterior, painted white, and comprises a mixture of double-height studios and single-storey apartments. There is a lovely roof garden on top and much of the living accommodation looks out over another garden to the rear, with views beyond of the rise of Highgate ridge. Highgate Wood was once part of the ancient Forest of Middlesex and was declared 'an open space forever' by the Lord Mayor of London in 1886. The Cliff Road elevation is a painted concrete frame with glass bricks; and metal louvered doors can cleverly convert the inside space into a balcony.

313; 1000s; RESTORED 1848 ROUMIEU AND GOUGH

This is one of the oldest Christian places of worship in Europe, the first church built here as long ago as AD 313 or 314. A Saxon altar found here dates from about 600, and the chancel was rebuilt in about 1350. Fragments from the 1200s remain in the Norman doorways but the Grade II–listed building is now largely Victorian. Joseph Grimaldi, a clown, was married here in 1801 and, in 1814, poet Percy Bysshe Shelley and Mary Godwin declared their love for each other over her mother's grave. An attempt to create a railway tunnel in 1866 that would have disturbed the churchyard caused a huge public outcry, and the matter was discussed in the House of Commons. Today, the sombre Soane Mausoleum is Grade I–listed. Other people buried here include composer Johann Christian Bach, author John Flaxman, and many refugees from the French Revolution.

1964–72 TEAM FOUR
(INCLUDING NORMAN FOSTER, TOM KAY, AND RICHARD GIBSON)

Murray Mews is a good example of a London mews transformed into residential properties. This calm habitat is narrower and lower than many other mews. The north side was designed by Team Four and has a terrace with three houses, numbers 15, 17, and 19. In 1964, house number 22 was designed by Tom Kay. The ground floor has solid redbrick walls, and the glazed roof lets daylight flow into the living space on the first floor. The design followed the nineteenth-century studio tradition.

MAIDEN LANE

620   NW1

1976–81 LONDON BOROUGH OF CAMDEN;
ALAN FORSYTH AND GORDON BENSON

This large complex of over two hundred houses was built in the northern and eastern side of King's Cross and St Pancras stations. Maiden Lane houses two-storey row houses plus three- and four-storey apartments. With its terraced community centre, squash courts, meeting rooms and central plaza, and living spaces located on the top level, it was hailed in its day as a model new community with excellent public spaces and a good mix of dwelling types.

SAINSBURY'S SUPERMARKET

621   NW1

1988–90 NICHOLAS GRIMSHAW AND PARTNERS

The supports to the roof of this shopping mall are counterbalanced by the weight of the first floors—these, in turn, are held up by cables that project from the face of the building. The road façade clearly exhibits this complex structure. Sir Nicholas Grimshaw is noted for several modernist buildings, including the international railway terminal at London's Waterloo Station and the Eden Project in Cornwall. In 2004, he was elected president of the Royal Academy.

EUSTON STATION AND OFFICES

622   NW1

1968 BRITISH RAIL ARCHITECTS DEPARTMENT AND R. SEIFERT AND PARTNERS

The original Euston Railway Station was built in 1837 but this new station rose to meet the needs of expansion in railway operations and the electrification of routes. The lovely screen, portico, and Great Hall of the old station were swept away, and many regret, in particular, the loss of Philip Hardwick's magnificent Euston Arch from the 1830s. The statue of George Stephenson, however, was retained. The aim of the new station was to marry simplicity of form with modern function. The low building is faced with polished dark stone, complemented by white tiles, and plain glazing. There are now eighteen platforms, and the station is used by some 51 million people per year.

620

621

622

623

624

GOWER STREET

UNIVERSITY COLLEGE HOSPITAL

623   NWI

1828; 1834; 1897–1906 ALFRED WATERHOUSE

The University College Hospital first began as a dispensary in 1828 and was converted into a 130-bed hospital in 1834. In 1844, Joseph Lister (later Lord Lister) was a student here. In due course, he would become famous for his introduction of antiseptic surgery. In 1846, Robert Liston performed the first major operation (a leg amputation) under ether in Europe. Another renowned medic here was Sir William Gowers, a neurologist whose text book on the nervous system is still revered. Sir John Blundell Maple donated £200,000 towards a major rebuilding programme in 1897 and the number of beds increased to three hundred. The rather eccentric red terracotta building, with turrets and spires, is seven storeys high and occupies an X-shape, set diagonally across its square site.

EUSTON ROAD AND UPPER WOBURN PLACE

ST PANCRAS CHURCH

624   NWI

1819–22 H. W. AND W. INWOOD

This is a fine example of Greek revival architecture. Built in brick and faced with white Portland stone, it has a pretty octagonal bell tower that rises above a spacious Ionic portico. Two pavilions (that serve as vestries and also guard the entrance to the burial vaults) are supported by regal, draped caryatids made of terracotta—based on the caryatids of Erechtheum.

625

THE BRITISH LIBRARY

625   NW1

1974–98 SIR COLIN ST JOHN WILSON

This vast library comprises the British Museum Library, the National Central Library, and the National Lending Library for Science and Technology. 150 million items include 10 million books and a copy of every new British publication— in 625 kilometres (388 miles) of shelves. twelve kilometres (over 7 miles) are needed every year to hold 3 million new items—pamphlets, manuscripts, maps, charts, music scores, Egyptian papyri; government papers, newspapers, prints, drawings, patents, and 8 million postage stamps. Sixteen thousand people use them each day. A glass tower contains the King's Library, with 65,000 books, manuscripts, and maps collected by King George III.

626

CHARLTON STREET, PHOENIX ROAD, AND OSSULTON STREET

LEVITA HOUSE, CHAMBERLAIN HOUSE, OR WALKER HOUSE

626   NW1

1928 G. TOPHAM FORREST

This is rather upmarket local authority housing, with neat avenues of trees and the immaculate buildings set behind arched, internal courtyards. The architect, Topham Forrest, headed the London County Council Architects' Department from 1919 until 1935—a time of much municipal housebuilding—and so he was able to have a great influence over the character and development of many new London residential sites.

627

EUSTON ROAD AND MELTON STREET,
FORMERLY LONDON, EDINBURGH AND GLASGOW ASSURANCE

DEPARTMENT OF HEALTH AND SOCIAL SECURITY

627   NW1

1908 E. BERESFORD PITE

This is a magnificent Grecian-style building in Portland stone, which spans seven floors and is Grade II listed. The basement—that once housed company records—has very thick walls and steel bomb-blast-resistant doors. The main entrance hall is decorated with yellow and sage-green Doulton Parian ware. There is a magnificent mosaic floor with an astrological design, lovely tiled arches, and superb marble fireplaces in the boardrooms. Light floods down into the lower floors through skylights and five light wells, lined in white glazed brick.

EUSTON ROAD

FIRE STATION

628   NWI

1901–02 W. E. RILEY (LCC ARCHITECTS' DEPARTMENT)

This is a most unusual fire station, especially when set against today's high-tech, streamlined station buildings. It replaced the old Metropolitan Board of Works station and is a wonderful free-style Arts and Crafts mixture of gables, arches, and almost fairy-tale-like turrets and projections. Its four floors also provided accommodation for the fire station staff. When it opened, it housed…one station officer, one sub officer, seventeen firemen, three coachmen, three horses, one steam fire engine, one horsed escape, one motor staff car, and one hose cart.

628

EUSTON ROAD

KING'S CROSS STATION

629   NWI

1851–52 LEWIS AND JOSEPH CUBITT

The original King's Cross was a monument to King George IV. The terminus of the Great Northern Railways was built here to serve the Great Exhibition tourist rush—in solid cast iron and concrete. It had two large train sheds, eleven platforms, and a high central clock tower. Legends claim the Queen Boudicca of the Icene fought her last battle against the Romans near here, and that she was buried where platform 9 or 10 now serve the populace. And it is here, in more recent story-telling, that Harry Potter catches the Hogwarts Express at platform nine and three-quarters.

629

EUSTON ROAD

THE WELLCOME TRUST HEADQUARTERS

630   NWI

1999–2004 HOPKINS ARCHITECTS

This dramatic new headquarters houses over five hundred staff as well as serving as a research facility and education resource for any matter medical. It acts as a centre for conferences and exhibitions, and is freely open to the public. It is ten storeys high on its busy Euston Road side, with vertical service towers, but drops to a five-storey level on its southern aspect. Both the curved roof and walls are glazed on a steel frame—to stunning effect.

630

NORTH WEST (NW) **357**

631

632

633

FRIENDS' HOUSE

631   NWI

1925-27 HUBERT LIDBETTER

This rather regal, neo-Georgian redbrick building is the headquarters of the Religious Society of Friends (Quakers) in Great Britain. The large meeting house is surrounded by a ring of offices set around light wells on either side—and there is an impressive library (founded in 1673) that contains books on Quaker literature that include such treasures as George Fox's journal and documents relating to the founding of Pennsylvania.

PARKSIDE AND CLIFTON WAY

DOLLIS HILL SYNAGOGUE

632   NW2

1937-38 SIR OWEN WILLIAMS

Owen Williams produced a series of reinforced concrete buildings and is sometimes referred to as the king of concrete. This synagogue was, for its day, uncompromisingly modern. The roof is pre-stressed concrete; there are shield-shaped windows, reinforced concrete in folded slabs, and side walls that create a zigzag—dotted with hexagonal windows like a child's folded paper cut-out. Inside are cantilevered galleries. Williams specialized in the creation of highly functional buildings with decorative façades. He combined his energies as both an engineer and an architect, and helped to develop the first plan for Britain's motorway system and the famous Gravelly Hill Interchange (Spaghetti Junction) near Birmingham. Other works include the Boots Pharmaceutical Factory, the Dorchester Hotel, and the Daily Express Building.

NORTH END

WYLDES FARM

633   NW3

1600s

Part of a tract of land donated by Henry VIII to Eton College, this 1600s farmhouse is now the central section of a larger building. Famous former owners have included the painter John Linnell, who made it his home from 1792–1882, during which time the poet William Blake made many visits. Over the years, other guests have included artists George Morland and John Constable, and also writer Charles Dickens—who stayed here while mourning the death of his cherished sister-in-law, Mary Hogarth. The renowned architect and planner of Hampstead Garden Suburb, Sir Raymond Unwin, also lived at Wyldes while he was working on that prestigious undertaking, and it was he who oversaw the conversion of the lovely large barn into a home.

JACK STRAWS CASTLE

1700s; 1964 RAYMOND ERITH AND QUINLAN TERRY

This coaching inn was named after a leader of the Peasants' Revolt, Jack Straw, one of Wat Tyler's lieutenants. He is supposed to have taken refuge here, building an encampment from which he planned to march on London; but he was captured and hanged. The pub's patrons have included authors Wilkie Collins, William Thackeray, and Charles Dickens. Today, it takes the form of a timber-frame mock castle with castellations—all pre-fabricated and assembled on site. The fittings are original, however, and the pub has lovely views.

STUDIO HOUSE

1885 R. NORMAN SHAW

This pretty house was built for the renowned nineteenth-century children's illustrator Kate Greenaway, also known for her romantic liaison (unfulfilled and largely pursued through the exchange of letters) with the writer John Ruskin. She lived here from 1885 until her death in 1901. Shaw's designs proved a source of inspiration for many socially committed architects. Here, there is an overhanging tile-covered roof, a projecting two-storey front bay, and a canopy over the door.

ANNESLEY LODGE

1896 C. F. A. VOYSEY

Among all of Voysey's works in London, many consider this to be his best. It was built for his father in the suburbs of London. The L-shaped Art Nouveau house maximises the corner plot, its garden and front lawn neatly enclosed by two long wings. A path leads between these to the front door set centrally at the junction. Voysey's signature style is evident in the long, unbroken red tiled roof (buttressed at the corners), the tall chimney, white pebbledash walls, and the pretty heart motif on the front door.

BRICK HOUSES

1937 E. L. FREUD

This is a tidy complex of six semi-detached brick houses, built in an enclosed courtyard-like plan. There are large windows, dark redbrick walls—and straight lines everywhere. A brick band defines the upper-storey windows. The architect of this cluster, E. L. Freud, was the son of Sigmund Freud.

A FINE HAMPSTEAD HOUSE

1938 CONNELL, WARD AND LUCAS;
2000-3 RESTORED BY AVANTI ARCHITECTS

This Grade II–listed long, stucco building expresses le Corbusier ideals to perfection. Built in reinforced concrete, its straight lines and simplicity make a sharp contrast to the area's usual brick and Georgian architecture. By contrast, the rear is all interesting windows and glass. Its recent £1.5 million restoration has made it a state-of-the-art twenty-first-century home—and the architects responsible received the inaugural RIBA Conservation Award for their work in 2005.

JUST ONE HOUSE!

1967 JAMES GOWAN

This unusual tall building was designed by James Gowan—a partner of famous modern architect James Stirling—after the two had parted company. Built for a furniture manufacturer in a purple tone of brick, the piers are clearly defined by continuous strips of windows. Nearby, a glazed dome covers a circular swimming pool that was once but is no longer part of the property. The front lawn is raised on the garage rooftop.

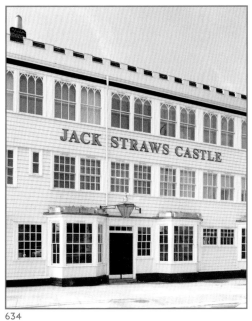

634

635

636

637

638

639

640

641

ELM ROW		NEW END SQUARE	
ELM LODGE		**BURGH HOUSE**	
640	NW3	641	NW3

EARLY 1700s

This row of houses rises above the street in an elegant composition somewhat hidden by high boundary walls. Number three is the former home of art patron and museum director, Sir Henry Cole, who lived here in 1879–80. Several of the houses here have fine features, including Elm Lodge, which has a pretty miniature, Palladian entrance stairway.

1703–4

Originally occupied by the Sewells, this grand property is now named after a vicar, the Reverend Allatson Burgh, who bought it in 1822. A fine Queen Anne mansion, it has been a militia headquarters and offices' mess—and home to a physician (who added the present wrought-iron gates which bear his initials), a professional upholsterer, a stained-glass designer and his twelve children, a miniature portrait specialist, and, in the 1930s, the daughter of Rudyard Kipling. It was bought by Hampstead Borough Council in 1946 and then Camden Council and, finally, run by a trust who sought to rescue it from demolition. A local museum and exhibition centre were established, and today is licensed for civil marriages—held in its panelled music room.

42

643

ELM ROW
FOLEY HOUSE
642   NW3

EARLY 1700s

Two mansions had been built here in 1698 and then this area developed quickly after the discovery of wells here. It had become a veritable spa by the 1700s. This rather magnificent dwelling is set back behind hedges and a walled entrance court—entered through a door set in a sturdy pointed arch. The building has an interesting angular projecting bay.

HAMPSTEAD GROVE
OLD GROVE HOUSE
643   NW3

1700s; 1730 STABLES AND COTTAGE WING ADDED

Old Grove House and New Grove House both date from the 1700s. Thirty years after the former was constructed, stables and cottages were added to this interesting building. It is built in brown brick with red dressings and has a very imposing Tuscan doorway with a charming circular window placed above. Artist and writer George du Maurier lived at New Grove House, 28 Hampstead Grove, from 1874–95.

644

645

GEORGIAN HOUSES

644   NW3

1700s–1800s

There are many Georgian houses in this vicinity, including good examples in Lower Terrace, Mount Vernon, Holly Walk, Holly Place, Hollyberry Lane, Benham's Place, and Prospect Place. Mount Vernon takes its name from General Charles Vernon who brought property hereabouts in 1785. This older, traditional part of Hampstead has many criss-crossing streets and alleys. Famous residents include the painter John Constable, who lived at 2 Lower Terrace. This is Holly Cottage, which seems rather tall for its name.

THE LAWN ROAD FLATS

645   NW3

1933 WELLS COATES

This Grade I–listed building represents one of the early experiments in collective living, a concept inspired by the early Modern movement. Walter Gropius, Moholy-Nagy, Adrian Stokes, Agatha Christie, and others lived here, while Jack Pritchard occupied the penthouse (he created mass-produced furniture, and the flats take their name from his factory). Hungarian architect Marcel Breuer stayed here and was invited by Pritchard to design furniture for his company. In 1969, the building was converted into thirty-four flats. In a 2003 restoration Camden Council, its present owners, created a public gallery to display the original interiors.

646

THE OLD BULL AND BUSH

646   NW3

1700s

The Old Bull and Bush pub is among the oldest vestiges of the hamlet of North End (where the 1776 home of Pitt the Elder can also be found). The bull of the pub's name derives from the fact that it was once also a farmhouse, and the bush, from the famous yew trees—supposedly planted by William Hogarth, who may have lived here once. Always popular with artists and writers, including with William Blake, it was made famous by Florrie Forde's song 'Down at the Old Bull and Bush.' In its current role as a contemporary bar and restaurant, its interiors do not really reflect the building's long history.

647

HAMPSTEAD LANE

KENWOOD HOUSE

647   NW3

1616 JOHN BILL; 1764–69 ROBERT ADAM, 1793–96 GEORGE SAUNDERS

Beautiful neo-classical Kenwood House is set back from the road in a park, and approached by a winding drive through thick woods. It was remodelled for the Earl of Mansfield in 1764 by Robert Adam, who is responsible for the magnificent portico and the library—considered one of his finest works ever. George Saunders added the lovely white brick wings that house the music and dining rooms. Kenwood still houses the significant art collection of Lord Iveagh, who bought the house in 1925 and bequeathed both art and house to Britain in 1927. There are works by Van Dyck, Gainsborough, Reynolds, Landseer, Rembrandt, and Turner.

648

BRANCH HILL

FORTY-TWO HOUSES

648   NW3

1970–77 LONDON BOROUGH OF CAMDEN ARCHITECTS DEPARTMENTS; GORDON BENSON AND ALAN FORSYTH

Here, forty-two dwellings, built by a local housing authority, stand on a steeply sloping site in the wealthier part of Hampstead. The plan follows the model of a Mediterranean hill town, raised up high and built into the slope, with the houses reached by flights of steps. It also borrows from the ideas of master Swiss architect and planner Le Corbusier.

SPANIARDS ROAD
THE SPANIARDS
649   NW3

1500s

This white, weather-boarded inn beside the heath has a lively history. This includes a duel unto death between its two Spanish proprietor-brothers over a woman, and the regular patronage of the 1700s highwayman, Dick Turpin—whose ghost, it is said, still frequents the Turpin Bar. Poets Shelley, Keats, and Byron, painter Sir Joshua Reynolds, and actor David Garrick all wet their whistles here. During the 1780 Gordon Riots, anti-Catholic rioters paused en route to Kenwood House, which they planned to burn down, but the wily publican plied them with free beer until the army arrived. A pair of muskets over the saloon bar may have been theirs.

649

9 FROGNAL WAY
SUN HOUSE
650   NW3

1935 E. MAXWELL FRY

One of the first really large, Modernist urban houses in London, Sun House sits on a slope with all the main rooms overlooking a quiet road. The clean lines of this painted, concrete building have been compared to Le Corbusier's Villa Stein. It relies on the play of alternating rectangular solids and voids, and the lightness of the design is reinforced by elegant balconies on slender columns and graceful steel railings. Sun House belonged to the Indian High Commission in the 1980s.

650

CHURCH ROW
HOUSES
651   NW3

1720

This is one of Hampstead's most beautiful streets. It is tree lined in the centre and bordered by redbrick-faced, double-storey houses that have changed little over the years. There is elegant wrought ironwork everywhere and neat Georgian sash windows. Authors Wilkie Collins, George du Maurier, and Compton Mackenzie lived here, plus H. G. Wells at number 17—and Thomas Park and his son John James who wrote the first history of Hampstead. The daughter of William Makepeace Thackeray, Anne, also a resident, described it as 'an avenue of Dutch red-faced houses, leading demurely to the old church tower that stands guarding its graves in the flowery churchyard.'

651

652

7 HAMPSTEAD HILL GARDENS
HOUSES FOR ARTISTS

652   NW3

1873 BATTERBURY AND HUXLEY

Hampstead Hill Gardens was built on a small estate, north of Pond Street, and their original proprietor was one George Crispin. The dwellings were intended for those with an artistic bent, and the first half dozen occupants who moved in 1873 were indeed 'gentlemen artists.' The houses have lovely brick ornamentation, arching over the windows. This property has a lovely arch over the front door.

6 ELLERDALE ROAD
HAMPSTEAD TOWERS

653   NW3

1875 R. NORMAN SHAW

Now an Italian convent, Hampstead Towers was built in 1875 by Shaw, for himself. Many features such as the tall chimneys and porthole windows are characteristic of his architecture and of the Queen Anne style. A decade later, he extended the house at the rear and, subsequently, other owners have made a few minor changes. Half of the house is higher than the other side; the main staircase divides the sections. The difference in elevation is also marked by one side being brick-faced and the other being stuccoed. Various types of windows make an interesting pattern on the exterior, and two long oriel windows stand out on the street side. The interior retains much of the original panelling.

653

654

655

656

EAST HEATH ROAD

PROBABLY 1770s JAMES WYATT

East Heath Road borders the southeast of Hampstead Heath. The lodge consists of two houses that share a large, south-facing platform and are marked by a blue plaque in recognition of distinguished resident, composer Sir Arthur Bliss. Built in brick with an arched entrance around the door, the building has a gently curving front bay and large shutters flank the other windows. Katherine Mansfield and her husband, John Middleton Murray, lived nearby—at number 17, a large grey house they called the Elephant.

KEATS HOUSE

1815–16; 1974–75 RESTORED

This two-storey, stuccoed house was originally a pair of semi-detached buildings. The smaller of the two became home to John Keats, when the writer Charles Armitage Brown invited the poet to move in here. This was where Keats was living when he became engaged to Fanny Brawne, the girl next door, and where he produced some of his most celebrated poetry, including 'Ode to a Nightingale'. Keats's health eventually compelled him to seek refuge in the more temperate climate of Italy, where he died in 1821, when aged only twenty-five. By 1839, the two houses had been combined into one by actress, Eliza Chester. It became a museum in 1925.

COTTAGE-STYLE HOUSES

c. 1815

Over the years, the attractive pretty little houses have appealed to many artists and writers seeking a more rural abode. Here, in Keats Grove, the mixed stucco and yellow brick houses have pretty front gardens, doors set into neat archways, sash windows, and lots of climbing plants scrambling over the brickwork to add to the rural feel.

A WHITE CUBE

657   NW3

1998 RICK MATHER ARCHITECTS

With a 1930s feel, this white stuccoed cube fronts a complex interior. There is an interesting corner window. Award-winning projects by Rick Mather include the renovation and extension of the Dulwich Picture Gallery, the Wallace Collection, the National Maritime Museum, and *The Times* newspaper headquarters in London's Docklands—as well as private residences, like this one, in Hampstead.

EAST OF HOLLY BUSH HILL

ROMNEY HOUSE

658   NW3

1797

A blue plaque identifies this large weatherboard house as one in which the painter George Romney lived. Here he created a gallery for pictures and sculpture and also enclosed half the garden under a timber arcade as a riding area. The house is set behind a walled courtyard, with a door (marked number 5) dwarfed by the vehicular entrance gates with trelliswork above.

ADMIRAL'S WALK, WEST OF HAMPSTEAD

ADMIRAL'S HOUSE

659   NW3

MID 1700s

Named after Admiral Matthew Barton who lived nearby (but never in this particular house), this building's first resident was a naval officer, Fountain North. He made a quarter deck on the roof, from whence, legends, claim, Admiral Barton would fire ceremonial salutes. The naval theme is reflected in the flagpole, railings, galleries, and roof conservatory. Sir George Gilbert Scott and Sir John Fortescue are two of the illustrious residents here, and writer John Galsworthy lived in the attached Grove Lodge from 1918–33. The house was depicted in a painting by John Constable.

CHURCH ROW

ST JOHN

660   NW3

1333; 1744–77 JOHN SANDERSON

A chapel to the Blessed Virgin Mary was here once. The present building (Hampstead's parish church) has been altered several times. The copper spire was added in about 1783. When its tower was threatened with demolition in the 1870s, a petition signed by notables such as William Morris, Anthony Trollope, and Sir Gilbert Scott put an end to the Victorian threat of destruction and rebuilding. The church has a fine pulpit, a balustraded gallery, and a bust of poet John Keats, who lived locally. John Constable and his wife, George du Maurier, Sir Walter Besant, Sir Herbert Beerbohm Tree, and Norman Shaw are buried here.

---

63 ETON AVENUE

VICTORIAN HOUSE

661   NW3

1880 H. B. MEASURES

This Victorian house has a high stepped gable, a sturdy porch and several long windows that emphasise its height. Some of the redbrick buildings in this row are said to resemble faces with doorway 'mouths,' porthole window 'eyes,' and the chimney thrusts looking like the bridges of rather sharp noses. All these buildings are highly ornamental with large bay windows, pretty porches, and brick gateposts. There are many variations on a theme here, with offset entrances, conical corner windows, and large and small bay windows.

VALE OF HEATH

WOODBINE COTTAGE

662   NW3

1780

This unusual rather rural-looking building is set in a charming, tightly knit hamlet of small streets and passageways. Many old buildings survived due to the 1871 Act of the Preservation of the Heath. In the 900s, the Vale belonged to the Westminster abbot and monks. By the 1700s, this marshland area, known as Gangmoor, was a popular haunt of paupers and thieves. When the malarial marsh was drained in 1777, the area was transformed into a fashionable address—renamed the Vale of Heath by 1802. Writer D. H. Lawrence, essayist and poet Leigh Hunt, and Indian poet Rabindranath Tagore have all lived in the Vale.

657

658

659

660

661

662

663

664

665

666

MALL STUDIOS

663   NW3

1872 THOMAS BATTERBURY

From the late 1920s, the seven cottage-style studios here buzzed with artists of international standing and, over the years, Barbara Hepworth, Ben Nicholson, and Herbert Read lived here—while Henry Moore was a regular visitor. The interiors were designed as double-height studios. There are monograms visible on the chimney pots of numbers 4 and 32. There are east-facing skylights and west-facing bull's-eye windows. Today, the storage balconies and model changing rooms have been converted into bedrooms and dining rooms.

A GRAND AVENUE

664   NW3

c. 1870–78 DANIEL TIDEY AND WILLIAM WILLET

The grand avenue of large, Italianate, semi-detached villas arrived during a period of extensive building in the area, driven largely by Daniel Tidey and then William Willet. The two obtained leases for the Belsize estates—the name comes from the sixteenth-century manor house and parkland that once stood on the site—developing a vast residential area. Huge bay windows are set into the uniformly white exteriors (in keeping with the landlord's stipulation) with grandiose bay windows.

ST MARY

665   NW3

1816

The need for a place of worship by French refugees who arrived in 1796 was fulfilled by St Mary, one of the first—and possibly one of the most diminutive—post-Reformation Roman Catholic churches to be built in London. Tucked away in the centre of a row of three-storey cottages, the pretty building was embellished with its stuccoed front and Tuscan doorway in the mid-1800s. A statue of the Virgin Mary (in Caen stone) is set in a recess above the door and there is a lovely open bellcote.

ST JOHN

666   NW3

1818 PROBABLY WILLIAM WOODS, REVD. JAMES CURRY AND EDWARD CARLISLE

Set in a garden bounded by ornamental early nineteenth-century iron railings, the neat square, white stucco chapel has a handsome portico, and bell turret rising above. Its late Georgian interior includes a gallery reached via beautiful staircases on both sides of the porch. There are neat umbrella stands on the pew doors. Although the identity of the architect is speculative, it is most probable that the trio of builder William Woods, the Reverend James Curry (a clergyman), and lawyer Edward Carlisle raised the chapel for the local residents. William Harness, the first minister here, was a life-long friend of Lord Byron, who had often protected him from bullies at Harrow school. Byron almost dedicated *Childe Harolde* to him but feared it might do the good man's reputation no service.

667

PRETTY GEORGIAN HOUSES

667   NW3

1700s

Hampstead is a treasure trove of eighteenth-century Georgian houses, and this is a very neat row with delicate wrought-iron rails and balustrades—and brick, arched patterns curving around the doors. At the end of Flask Walk is the Flask Inn, where the Kit-Kat Club met (founded in 1705 by Whig politicians and writers). In nearby Well Walk, the Great Room and Pump Room were renowned for their healing waters, concerts, and dances. It was demolished in 1822 and another spa rose here, patronized by Dr Johnson. Writers John Masefield, D. H. Lawrence, and J. B. Priestley lived nearby.

668

WYCHCOMBE STUDIOS

668   NW3

c. 1880 SIR THOMAS D BECKET

The builder's terracotta monogram is visible on the front wall of each of these six fine studios, which collectively form an L-shaped court at the end of a walled drive. This group of buildings were raised on land leased from the Eton College Estate and have high Dutch gables. Past occupants include Arthur Rackham (a most celebrated artist of children's books) who lived at number 6 in 1900.

669

ODEON CINEMA

669   NW3

1937 HARRY WEEDON

Harry Weedon was a pianist and a World War I pilot, as well as an architect. From 1932, he designed over three hundred Odeon cinemas. Now Britain's largest cinema chain, with many changes in ownership, it was launched by Oscar Deutsch and its original style was Art Deco, with *moderne* exteriors, and rich impressive interiors. The term Odeon may be an acronym of 'Oscar Deustch Entertains Our Nation.' Deutsch eventually sold out to film producer, J. Arthur Rank and, later, to Terra Firma Capital Partners; and over the years, many of the cinemas have been subdivided and have rather lost their glamour.

1–3 WILLOW ROAD
HOME TO GOLDFINGER
670   NW3

1940 ERNÖ GOLDFINGER

The design of these apartments was inspired by terrace houses from by 1700s and 1800s, but built with modern materials. The central house of this series of three (which look like one big villa) was lived in by the architect Ernö Goldfinger himself and later bought by the National Trust. A highly regarded architect, he emigrated from Hungary in the late 1920s, trained in the École des Beaux-Arts in Paris, and pioneered Modernism in England.

670

80–90 SOUTH HILL PARK
HOUSES FOR ARCHITECTS
671   NW3

1956 HOWELL AND AMIS

The architects designed this small terrace as homes for themselves. Set on a steeply sloping site, they have very narrow frontages with stark brick uprights. However, they go back deeply and have interesting garden façades, now overgrown with creepers. Some of the living rooms are of double height and attached to gallery bedrooms. The style is an example of English Brutalism, with continuous windows and with infill glass panels.

671

78 SOUTH HILL PARK
HOUSE WITH GLASS BRICKS
672   NW3

1968 BRIAN HOUSDEN

This unusual house is set in a concrete frame and has multiple panels of glass brick, set on an exposed concrete frame. There are interesting levels, and cantilevered floors and overhanging elements. The window frames were painted red. This was a house that Housden built for himself on a site that slopes down to the heath. His architecture was greatly influenced by the Dutch architect Van Eyck.

672

673

674

BOLTON HOUSE

673   NW3

1700s

Long gardens front a group of fine Georgian
houses that includes Volta House, Bolton
House, Windmill Hill House, and Enfield
House. This brown brick structure here is laced
with redbrick, and beautiful carved brackets
support the doors. Painter George Romney
(1734–1802) lived in Holly Bush Hill.

FENTON HOUSE

674   NW3

1693

Although the house was built in 1693, the
building's name originates from a merchant,
Philip Fenton, who bought it in 1793. The
National Trust was gifted this property in
1952 by Lady Binning, along with her
remarkable porcelain collection, furniture,
and paintings (including works by Constable
and Brueghel the Elder). Today, there is
also a display of early musical instruments
bequeathed by Major George Henry Benton
Fletcher—including a 1612 harpsichord
played by Handel. There are wrought-iron
gates on the south side, and an entrance in
Hampstead Grove.

LONDON ZOO

Set in Regent's Park, with Regent's Canal threading through it, the zoo opened in 1828 as a place for eminent scientists to study animals. In 1847, the public were allowed to visit, and it soon become one of the most famous zoos in the world. Its global 'firsts' include a children's zoo (1938), a reptile house (1849), a public aquarium (1853), and an insect house (1881).

The zoo incorporates many splendid pieces of architecture that have met unusual challenges. Many renowned architects have designed structures here and there are ten listed buildings. The Giraffe House (1836–37) is by Decimus Burton and is Grade II listed, with its scale designed to accommodate these tall creatures in a classical Roman design.

The Snowdon Aviary (1962-64) by Lord Snowdon, Cedric Price, and Frank Newby appears—like a bird—to be almost weightless. Its aluminium frame uses tension to support its structure and a giant net 'skin' is wrapped around a skeleton of poles.

Berthold Lubetkin was responsible for the Grade I–listed Round House (1932–23), one of the first British Modernist buildings. In cold weather a half-drum-shaped screen can be slid from within one half to enclose the other, and so protect the inmates—in this case, gorillas. Lubetkin also designed the Penguin Pool (1934), listed Grade I, a highly innovative, elegant piece with interlocking ramps—recently used to house porcupines.

The Elephant and Rhino Pavilion (1962–5) by Sir Hugh Casson and Neville Conder has a heavy structure that reflects the solidity of these African giants. Concrete ribs on its exterior imitate elephant hide while 'trumpeting trunks' on the roof act actually filter light into the interior.

The Grade II–listed Mappin Terraces (1913–14) for sloths and langurs are by Sir Peter Chalmers Mitchell and John James Joass, and imitate a mountain landscape—in reinforced concrete, then a comparatively new idea. The cavernous interior holds reservoirs of water, which is filtered and circulated into the aquarium below.

The Grade II–listed Clock Tower (1828) is based on Tudor designs, and was created by Decimus Burton. This is the zoo's oldest building. It was built to house llamas originally, but it now contains shops.

London Zoo had the first hippo seen in Europe since the Roman Empire, the largest elephant known in 1880, Jumbo—later sold to Phineas Barnum—and Winnie, a American black bear that inspired A. A. Milne's *Winnie the Pooh*. Goldie, a golden eagle, became a national celebrity in 1965 when he escaped, and flew around Regents Park for two weeks. Guy, the famous gorilla, lived at the zoo and stared back at curious visitors from 1947–78.

Today, the zoo participates in breeding programmes for many threatened species and is introducing new more naturalistic enclosures such as 'Into Africa' and 'Butterfly Paradise' (2006), plus the 'Gorilla Kingdom' and a South American rainforest exhibit that are both due to open in 2007.

675

ZENW3

675   NW3

1985 RICK MATHER ARCHITECTS

Designer of a number of Zen restaurants, here Rick
Mather introduced a rather startling design into Georgian
Hampstead, encouraged by his client, Laurence Leung.
Unlike the usual eating places that seek an intimate,
enclosed atmosphere, this blatantly exhibits its clientele
to the outside world through a clear glass frontage.
The simple stark white of its interior and cool aquatic
sculpture offer diners a soothing backdrop while they
discover Chinese (and now Japanese) cuisine.

676

1643

This pub was originally stables and a house — bought by artist George Romney in 1796 and later sold to the Hampstead Assembly Rooms. The stable block was sold in the early 1800s, to be converted into a kitchen and servants' quarters, and then later into a tavern. This has retained its vintage alehouse ambience, and reminds one that Dr Johnson, Boswell, and other London greats once drank — and intellectualized — here. A 1960s refurbishment has retained the open fireplace and gas lamps.

677

1981 SPENCE AND WEBSTER

Connected by a common courtyard, the two single-storeyed houses here were influenced by Mies van der Rohe's courthouse studies of the 1930s. They were built in fine steel and aluminium sections (used to create one home for each of the architects), and are set behind the wall of a large house. This rises high above them, emphasizing the simplicity (and scant height) of the square glass façades, each large section screened by blinds.

678

1961 DOUGLAS STEPHENS AND PANOS KOULERMOS

One of the early experiments in mixed commercial and residential use blocks, Centre Heights is all concrete and glass — increasingly popular building materials in the early 1960s. It was influenced by Le Corbusier and the Italian Rationalists of the time. There is an interesting stair tower, shops on the ground floor, and five floors of flats and maisonettes set above all this.

NEW END SQUARE, WELL WALK
WELLS TAVERN

679   NW3

1837

An old alehouse and a postman's cottage (where John Keats lived briefly) merged into Wells Tavern. Once dandies came to partake of the health-giving waters in the wells here and later 'Hampstead's last affordable pub' (as it claimed to be) was frequented by the staff of wealthy local inhabitants. In this smart street, lined with elms and lime-trees, lived John Constable and Tennyson's mother. Many of the tavern's original interior features have vanished but it retains a dignified exterior.

679

ROSSLYN MEWS
BLACKBURN HOUSE

680   NW3

1987–88 CHASSAY WRIGHT AND THE WILSON PARTNERSHIP

Another of London's surprises, the three-storeyed Blackburn House is a most unusual building. It was created to incorporate three elements—studio, home, and private art gallery. There are metal projections on the monumental white stuccoed exterior and a vast oriel window, set aslant. The interior, designed by Peter Wilson, has an even more pronounced air of bizarre fantasy. In this building, expect the unexpected!

680

2 LOWER TERRACE
A SUMMER HOME

681   NW3

1700s–EARLY 1800s

This sweet pair of cottages have pretty front doors with fanlights and arched curves around them. The windows have interesting shapes to their surrounds. John Constable lived at number 2 during the summers of 1821–22. While inspired by the countryide and landscapes that he loved most, this artist studied at the Royal Academy and spent many months in London, painting from his numerous sketches, and preparing for exhibitions.

681

682

682

LAMBLE STREET
ABSTRACT HOUSING
682   NW3

1973–81 LONDON BOROUGH OF CAMDEN ARCHITECTS
DEPARTMENT: ALAN FORSYTH AND GORDON BENSON

This series of nine terraced houses form
a simple, long, low run. (There is a similar,
even longer stretch, in Mansfield Road to
the north). Here, in Oak Village (to the south
of Mansfield Road), the run is linked by a
continuous storey at attic level. Though
externally the houses assume a simple
abstract form as they flow from one to
another, internally there are quite complex
split levels.

SHIRLOCK AND SAVERNAKE ROADS
ALL HALLOWS
683   NW3

1889 JAMES BROOKS; CHANCEL
1913 SIR GILES GILBERT SCOTT

The foundation stone of this (the last church
designed by James Brooks) was laid by Queen
Mary's mother in 1892. It was consecrated in
1901, the year of the architect's death. This
vast building has no spire, but the massive
buttresses supporting the aisle structure
create a sense of enormity (somewhat
diminished by the emergence of brick
houses around it). Inside, the aisles and the
monumental nave are of the same height.

683

1975 MICHAEL HOPKINS

Here, the architect's understanding of the powerful potential of using glass on a steel column and beam structure led him to adapt the techniques of impersonal spaces, such as offices and warehouses, into his creation of a most unusual building—combining home and office space. The dazzling two-storeyed house does not have a conventional entrance but is accessed by means of a metal bridge at first-floor level. This is a truly avant-garde building; its extensive glazing makes a dramatic impact.

2005 S. & P. ARCHITECTS

Here, 131 up-market apartments, duplexes, and penthouses—in various sizes and configurations—have been arranged over eleven floors, with sweeping views over Primrose Hill and Regent's Park. The building is stepped up from north to south, with the south façade 'inversely raked,' so that each floor overhangs the one below it. As well as state-of-the-art facilities, the amenities on offer include theatre-ticket booking, dining reservations, a twenty-four-hour concierge service, and even butler service—at a price; these rather exclusive apartments cost over £2 million each.

1964 SIR BASIL SPENCE, BONNINGTON AND COLLINS; 2000 RESTORED BY JOHN McASLAN AND PARTNERS

This was part of a much larger civic centre plan that was never fulfilled when Hampstead came under Camden borough; the library and swimming pool were the only buildings to be completed in 1964—and are now regarded as a landmark in British Modernist architecture. Sir Basil Spence's library houses the central facility of the public library service; an admirable restoration effort has sensitively adapted this classic library and it now implements modern hi-tech requirements. Meanwhile, the swimming pool is being replaced by a new leisure centre. The exterior has protective pre-cast concrete fins that act as sun protection.

2003 BENNETTS ASSOCIATES

This striking building has two storeys above ground and one below. The auditorium has been created in the shape of an ellipse, with flexible seating for up to 330 people. The auditorium is clad in matt zinc, set in a mainly transparent pavilion punctuated by timber slatting. The foyer areas, built in steel, concrete, and timber, are in an uncomplicated design, but one given great impact by the dramatic lighting. There is also a workshop, a studio theatre, administrative office, and dedicated rehearsal space.

84

685

586

687

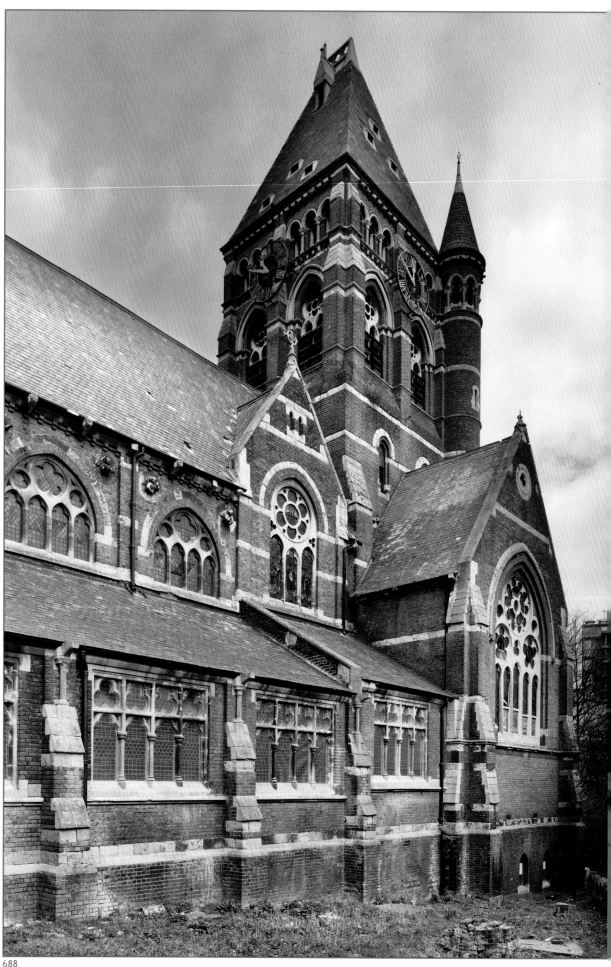

ROSSLYN HILL

ST STEPHEN

688   NW3

1869-71 SAMUEL S. TEULON

Having been declared redundant in 1977, this building then lay dilapidated for twenty-five years before being rescued. It is one of London's most striking nineteenth-century churches, now Grade I listed, with a huge, ornate tower and capped roof. A new crypt has been built, and the nave now serves as a community hall and classrooms for Hampstead Hill School.

689

690

691

692

693

694

THE SIR RICHARD STEELE

1870s

This pub was named after soldier, journalist, and playwright Sir Richard Steele, who heralded from Dublin and was co-founder of the *Spectator* and *Tatler*. His house was nearby (in Steeles Lane). This likeable rake married into a fortune, was widowed, knighted, spent the fortune, married again, and was widowed once more. A splendid stained-glass window in a corner depicts him as a rather more saintly figure than this history would suggest. Countless knickknacks inside include old photographs, bottles, enamel signs, vintage typewriters, toys, sewing machines, and a child's dogcart. A ceiling fresco includes images of politicians and pub regulars of yore.

FREEMASON'S ARMS

1800S; 1930S

This is an area of broad avenues, where elegant bow-fronted villas with balconies and bow windows are set behind wrought-iron railings. The pub was completely rebuilt after its original 1800s structure was declared unstable, partly due to a tributary of the Fleet River that flowed underneath. The new Freemason's Arms now has a handsome '1930s Regency' exterior and tasteful, immaculate décor inside—with an enormous continuous bar. A 'pell mell' court survived from the original pub; in this ancient game, a large, heavy wooden ball has to be rolled through iron hoops—rather like croquet but without the mallets.

HOUSES AND MAISONETTES

1967-77 LONDON BOROUGH OF CAMDEN ARCHITECTS DEPARTMENT: NEAVE BROWN

Here, near Belsize Park and Hampstead Heath, in a high-density but low-rise development, the buildings are set beside narrow pathways. A neat cross-section provides the residents with large balconies and communal gardens There are split-level maisonettes, good-quality interiors, and roof gardens, and the harder lines of the stairways have now been softened with climbing plants.

KENTISH TOWN HEALTH CENTRE

1973 LONDON BOROUGH OF CAMDEN ARCHITECTS DEPARTMENT: PETER WATSON

This local clinic was raised to relieve the pressure on hospitals and includes two group surgeries, a care centre for young children, and a teaching unit—all set around a central entrance. Two double-storey wings are set at right angles to each other and enclose a parking area. There is a lovely, long, glazed entrance canopy.

GOSPEL OAK

1954-80 METROPOLITAN BOROUGH OF ST PANCRAS SUCCEEDED BY LONDON BOROUGH OF CAMDEN ARCHITECTS DEPARTMENT

Gospel Oak is a suburb below Hampstead Heath; its name derives from an oak tree where parishioners gathered to hear annual gospel readings. Its landowners planned an elegant development in the mid-1800s but, when two railway lines arrived, the first buildings became cottages for navvies and shoemakers. Today's twin railway bridges were depicted on Sinead O'Connor's *Gospel Oak* record sleeve. This became a respectable area of terraced housing—demolished during post-war building of massive estates. Famous residents include ex-*Monty Python* star and travel writer Michael Palin.

GROVE TERRACE

1780-93

Close to Hampstead Heath and village, this attractive row of houses was built in the Georgian equivalent of ribbon development that spread along the roads leading out of London. Here the gracious Grade II–listed houses are set behind well-manicured lawns or pretty gardens and railings, and many have generous rear gardens. The buildings arrived when this area was open countryside—but now sell for over a million pounds each.

695

14 LEIGHTON CRESCENT	HOLMES ROAD

FLEXIBLE FLATS

POLICE STATION

695	NW5	696	NW5

1975–80 EDWARD CULLINAN ARCHITECTS

Edward Horder Cullinan, CBE, RA, RIBA, worked for Denys Lasdun, before setting up his own practice in 1959. He has been awarded five professorships and three honorary doctorates, as well as a CBE, and was elected a Royal Academician in 1989. In this Cullinan building, stairs and a central ramp rise above ground-floor gardens and lead to the front door of four houses—but the block of dwellings also includes twelve apartments. French windows open onto small balconies and add to the overall unity of the design. Meanwhile, the gallery style and mobile partitions of the interior allow for great flexibility in how the rooms can be arranged by individual owners.

1894–96 R. NORMAN SHAW

This is a very elegant 'cop-shop'! Architect Shaw revelled in baroque revival, and the three-storey yellow-brick building here benefits from his enthusiasm. It has many interesting stonework details, a wide archway that leads to a court behind, and a main street entrance set behind another smaller arch that is echoed in the arch over the steps and path.

96

697

698

5 CAVERSHAM ROAD

MIXED MARRIAGE

697   NW5

COUTTS CRESCENT, 23 ST ALBANS ROAD

HOUSING COMPLEX

698   NW5

1978 LONDON BOROUGH OF CAMDEN:
COLQUHOUN AND MILLER

Here some 1970s housing had to fill an
unlikely slot between nineteenth-century
buildings—with terraced housing on one
flank and semi-detached villas on the other—
without looking obtrusive. It has managed
to meet this difficult brief very successfully,
marrying into the missing half of a semi-
detached villa in Caversham Road while
remaining unashamedly modern and
clean looking.

1986–89 CHASSAY WRIGHT ARCHITECTS

This small crescent of eleven large four-
storey houses is set behind a walled yard.
The immaculate brickwork is arranged in very
pleasing stripes with various arrangements
of windows in squares and strips. The end
dwellings are like a turret with double-height
studio bedrooms and an attached curved bay.

699

700

699

24A YORK RISE

AWARD-WINNING HOUSE

699   NW5

KILBURN PARK ROAD

ST AUGUSTINE, KILBURN

700   NW6

1975–79 JO VAN HEYNINGEN AND BIRKIN HAWARD

This brick house is immaculately designed
to fit into a very small space. A double-height
conservatory links the lounge above to the
ground-floor kitchen with a glazed roof
and part-glazed wall creating interesting
triangles. The house was built for the
architects themselves—and won a 1980
Eternit International Architecture Award
for its clever design.

1870–98 J. L. PEARSON

St Augustine is a fine example of Victorian
church architecture and is one of the largest
churches in London, its crowning glory the
soaring spire that reaches 77 meters (254 feet)
in height. The church is in redbrick with many
pinnacles and a huge round window. Its fine
vaulted interior was the work of Pearson, the
renowned Gothic architect. Sir Giles Gilbert
Scott designed the altar in the Lady Chapel.

701

702

703

KINGSWOOD AVENUE

701   NW6

1875–87 AUSTIN, ROLAND PLUMBE
(CORPORATION OF THE CITY OF LONDON)

Thirty-acre Queen's Park was established on land bought from All Souls College, Oxford, with money left in the will of one William Ward. It had superb trees and a lovely cast-iron bandstand. The Victorian housing development here (that gave its name to the famous football club) provided two thousand homes for sixteen thousand residents. It was built by the Artisans' Labourers' and General Development Company. The early residents were mainly the families of railwaymen, policemen, artisans, and clerks. These are fine houses, with generous bays, white brick surrounds to the windows, and many elegant Gothic details.

PRINCE ALBERT ROAD

NORTHGATE MANSION

702   NW8

1910

St John's Wood has courtly origins. Granted by William the Conqueror to a lady called Eideva, the area belonged later to the Knights Templar and then the Knights of St John of Jerusalem in 1312, who gave the district its present name. Prince Albert Road first appears in the tax records in the 1820s and was called Albert Road until 1938, when it was renamed after the Prince Consort. Northgate is a large Edwardian redbrick mansion that occupies an entire whole block. It is highly ornate, with decorative balconies, lovely gables and turrets, and a superb view across Regent's Park.

BOUNDARY ROAD

RESIDENTIAL SUITES

703   NW8

1978 EVANS AND SHALEV

This building, with stepped terraces facing south, was created to provide a permanent home for thirty severely handicapped adults—incorporating residential suites with private outdoor space, a community hall, and a shared roof terrace.

704

705

LORD'S CRICKET GROUND, ST JOHN'S WOOD

MOUND STAND

704   NW8

1987 MICHAEL HOPKINS AND PARTNERS

This vast stand covers 5,505 square meters (6,584 square yards) and is built in steel-reinforced concrete. The stock brick arcade of an earlier open terrace was extended in a curve that now sweeps to the east. Meanwhile, a mast-supported membrane of white PVC-coated fabric stretches over the new white-painted steel structure to shelter the private boxes and cantilevered terrace below.

LORD'S CRICKET GROUND, ST JOHN'S WOOD

A NEW GRANDSTAND

705   NW8

1998 NICHOLAS GRIMSHAW AND PARTNERS

Lord's is owned by the Marylebone Cricket Club and is home to the Middlesex County Cricket Club. The annual Eton versus Harrow match was launched in 1805 (when Lord Byron played for Harrow) but the cricket club moved just a few hundred yards northwest to its current site in 1814, when the building of Regent's Canal arrived in its outfield. Over one hundred test matches have been played at Lord's since 1884. Today, an uninterrupted view of the pitch now regarded as 'the home of cricket' is provided in the new grandstand, which can seat two thousand spectators.

706

LORD'S CRICKET GROUND, ST JOHN'S WOOD

NATWEST MEDIA CENTRE

706   NW8

1998 FUTURE SYSTEMS

This centre of this dramatic curving, aluminium, state-of-art media centre was actually prefabricated by boat builders (Pendennis Shipyard) and the different sections were then welded together on site. Set high above the cricket ground, it offers a brilliant view for radio and television sports journalists. As well as a tiered seating area, the egg-shaped structure includes a restaurant and hospitality rooms. The cost of construction was about £5 million. Stirling Prize judges described the Media Centre as 'A breath of architectural fresh air … a wacky solution to a singular problem.'

707

ALEXANDRA ROAD HOUSING

707   NW8

1969–79 NEAVE BROWN

In this high-density public-housing scheme, more than five hundred row houses, flats, and maisonettes were built over an area of 16 acres. The dwellings occupy open rows of long terraces, with variations in height. Alexandra Road is the main terrace, built in stepped sections that rise to form an eight-storey wall against the mainline railway cutting behind. The front, however, faces south to enjoy this sunnier aspect rather than the view of passing trains on the Euston line.

708

ST JOHN'S WOOD

HAMILTON TERRACE

708   NW8

1829–30

Laid out in 1829 on the Harrow School estate, this long, broad terrace with trees and tall houses was named after a school governor—James Hamilton, Duke of Abercorn. Number 17 was the home of Sir James William Bazalgette —the civil engineer who created London's drainage system and the Victoria embankments. In 1900–21, artist William Strang lived at number 20. The houses are in stock brick and stucco. Just around the corner (at the junction of St John's Wood Road and Maida Vale), a Victorian gentlemen's public lavatory with polished brass staircase handrails has survived.

709

BROADLEY TERRACE

UNCONVENTIONAL OFFICES

709   NW8

1985 SIR MICHAEL HOPKINS AND PARTNERS

The architects responsible for this building run their business from this unusual building. Both walls and roof have been built with identical composite metal panels— in what is termed the Patera system—building blocks rise quickly on a steel base in the architectural equivalent to Henry Ford's T-Model motor-car construction. This is ideal for factories and offices, which can be built at great speed and low cost. Here, the walls mutate into the roof. The architects have won numerous design awards, including the RIBA's Royal Gold Medal in 1995, and Michael Hopkins has been knighted.

PRINCE ALBERT ROAD
VICEROY COURT

710   NW8

1937 MARSHALL AND TWEEDY

This fine building is yet another very elegant 1830s
apartment block in this prime location next to Regent's
Park. Here there are lovely curved corners, large
balconies, and wide windows that flow along the
building's contours. The architects also designed
classic cinemas.

710

WELLS RISE
NUMBERS 1, 3, 4, 6, 8 AND 10

711   NW8

1933 FRANCIS LORNE AND TAIT

The stuccoed terrace houses that have survived in
this once-Victorian street are reminiscent of the Dutch
movement in 1920s architecture. An interesting mix
of windows creates squares as well as horizontal and
vertical patterns on the buildings, which are all straight
lines. There are neat entrance canopies and various
surface colours.

711

55–56 PRINCE ALBERT ROAD
IMPERIAL COURT

712   NW8

1965

With its interesting mix of long, graceful balconies and
shorter, protruding 'boxes,' this building is rather like a
theatre auditorium, overlooking the scene of action in
Regent's Park. It is a more recent arrival than many of
its 1930s neighbours but has the same grandiose style.

712

713

714

---

44 GROVE END ROAD

HOUSE AND STUDIO

713   NW8

C. 1825; 1883 SIR LAWRENCE ALMA-TADEMA;
2006 RESTORED BLEIER ESTATES LTD

This rather splendid Grade II-listed building
was home to two famous artists—first
Jacques Joseph Tissot, a.k.a. James Tissot
(1836–1902), the French painter who
depicted social life in Victorian Times. Next,
Sir Lawrence Alma-Tadema (1836–1912)—a
Dutch-born English classicist painter—spent
several years, and a large part of the fortune
his paintings had earned him, refurbishing
the place. After two or three years' prodigious
labour, he had created a magnificent, triple-
height silver-domed studio with a vaulted
ceiling and apse, an atrium with a fountain,
and further artist's studios. He also added
many Greco-Egyptian embellishments.
After damage inflicted during World War II,
the house was converted into eleven
apartments, but has recently been
restored as a single residence.

PRINCE ALBERT ROAD

104–114 NORTHGATE

714   NW8

1936 MITCHELL AND BRIDGWATER

At the eastern end of Prince Albert Road,
many of the original pretty villas remain, but
elsewhere, these have been replaced by
impressive blocks of flats. Here, the large
seven-storey apartment buildings at the east
end of the Northgate complex comprise an
elegant redbrick building—with a central
curved bay where the sweep of windows
overlooks Regent's Park.

CENTRAL MIDDLESEX HOSPITAL PARK ROYAL
ACAD CENTRE
715   NW10

1995-2000 AVANTI ARCHITECTS

The ACAD (ambulatory care and diagnostic) centre at Central Middlesex Hospital (once the Willesden Workhouse) is designed for the diagnosis and treatment of patients who do not require a hospital bed. There is a spacious reception area and a two-storey treatment wing, with x-ray facilities and operating theatres. The consulting and treatment rooms are arranged around open landscaped courts. Stonework, brickwork, aluminium cladding, timber panelling, and glass blockwork have all been used. An internal double-height street, has bridged walkways, and oodles of top light.

HOOP LANE
GOLDERS GREEN CREMATORIUM
716   NW11

1905-38 SIR ERNEST GEORGE AND YATES

During the 1860s, as London's graveyards filled to overflowing, the Cremation Society strove to establish the adoption of cremation. The society built this crematorium and three chapels in redbrick Romanesque style. Ashes could be scattered in the memorial gardens—where the Philipson Mausoleum stands. More than a quarter of a million cremations have taken place here, including those of Sir Henry Irving, W. S. Gilbert, Anna Pavlova, Rudyard Kipling, Sigmund Freud, George Bernard Shaw, Kathleen Ferrier, Sir Alexander Fleming, Ralph Vaughan Williams, and T. S. Eliot.

TEMPLE FORTUNE, HAMPSTEAD GARDEN SUBURB
SHOPS AND FLATS
717   NW11

1907 RAYMOND UNWIN

Set on land originally given to Eton College by Henry VI, Hampstead Garden Suburb was founded in 1907 as a model of community life. Henrietta Barnett, a cosmetics heiress turned social worker, spearheaded the project, hoping to provide homes for the needy at the same time as saving Hampstead Heath from the fast-encroaching tube lines and march of terraced houses. On the edge of the estate, these two impressive redbrick blocks have a rather Germanic appearance, with their steeply pitched roofs, towers, and dormer windows.

HEATH CLOSE, OFF HAMPSTEAD WAY
WATERLOO COURT
718   NW11

1908-9 M. H. BAILLIE SCOTT

This multiple housing scheme was built to contain fifty flats for single working women. A timber-covered approach leads to a two-storey court with white-painted brickwork. There are sweeping arcades with fine semi-circular arches all around, and the simple but delicious central pavilion has a neat bellcote. Baillie Scott revelled in the whimsical and here the smooth, round-arched cloisters, deep roofs, and heavy timbers are a delight, with a theatrical, almost fairy-tale appeal.

ERSKINE HILL, HAMPSTEAD GARDEN SUBURB
ELEGANT SYMMETRY
719   NW11

1908-10 SIR EDWIN LUTYENS

The west side of Erskine Hill was designed by Lutyens in splendid 'Wrenaissance' style. The properties are built in grey brick with dormers and multiple white-painted window frames. Here number 9 rather resembles a country rectory—made formal for town with its straight lines and tall chimneys.

CENTRAL SQUARE, HAMPSTEAD GARDEN SUBURB
THE INSTITUTE
720   NW11

1909-20S SIR EDWIN LUTYENS

The Institute, built of small grey bricks with red dressings and stone trim, is an elegant public building with a fine steeple and clock raised high above its arched entrance. Its pretty small-paned windows overlook a paved courtyard. The Institute once served as a girls' school (the Henrietta Barnett School, named after the philanthropist described above left) and has long been an adult education and social centre, but new purpose-built accommodation is now being built to take over these roles.

715

716

717

718

719

720

721

722

SUBURB, SQUARE, AND CHURCHES

721   NW11

EARLY 1900s

At the turn of the last century, Golders Green changed from a country crossroads into an urban suburb—albeit one designed to feel like parkland, with lots of green areas. Today, it has expanded over the years to become 324 hectares (800 acres). The residential closes of country-style or neo-Georgian houses, pedestrian pathways, and winding roads are lined with privet hedges and flowering cherry trees. The central area has many terraces of houses and flats designed by Lutyens and he also designed St Jude's Church, one of two large churches on Central Square. Here, too, are the Free Church (shown here), formed in 1910 and with a lovely Lutyens dome, and a Quaker Meeting House.

COTTAGE-STYLE HOUSES

722   NW11

c. 1910 BAILLIE SCOTT

Here, the pebble-dashed cottage-style properties have steeple pitched roofs, and dormers—and are full of interesting and unexpected angles. Baillie designed numbers 6–10 Meadway as well as this property. All are rather romantic. Here there are flowing roofs, 'doll's-house' windows, and high 'Hansel and Gretel' gables.

SOUTH WEST LONDON (SW)

South West London is one of the city's most historic areas, thronging as it is with all the magnificent buildings in Westminster, such as the Houses of Parliament, Westminster Abbey, Westminster Cathedral, and the tower of Big Ben. There are numerous famous sights, including Buckingham Palace, Horse Guards Parade, St James's Palace, and Hyde Park Corner. Tate Britain is found in this region, as well as the wonderful store, Harrods, and the glorious Royal Albert Hall.

Kensington is home to a great concentration of magnificent museums, including the grandiose Natural History Museum with its incredible dinosaurs and Blue Whale, the fascinating Science Museum, and the treasures in the Victoria and Albert Museum. Belgravia and Chelsea are wealthy; Chelsea has been described as 'a village of palaces' but is also famous for Chelsea buns and Chelsea china—and was where Henry VIII

was rowed upriver to visit his chancellor, Sir Thomas More, in the 1500s.

Further south lie . . . Battersea, renowned for its power station and dog's home; Wimbledon, known for its common, the Wombles, and the tennis tournaments; and Crystal Palace (destroyed by fire in 1936), where the Great Exhibition of 1851 displayed 13,000 exhibits to over 6,200,000 visitors in a magnificent glass edifice—later transferred to Sydenham from Hyde Park. Tooting Bec and Streatham rose on a former Roman route linking Roman London with Chichester to the southwest—eventually the turnpike road from London to Brighton, and the forerunner of today's A23. South West London includes the Bishop's Palace in Lambeth, the largest open-air swimming pool in the United Kingdom in Tooting, and regal Victoria Station.

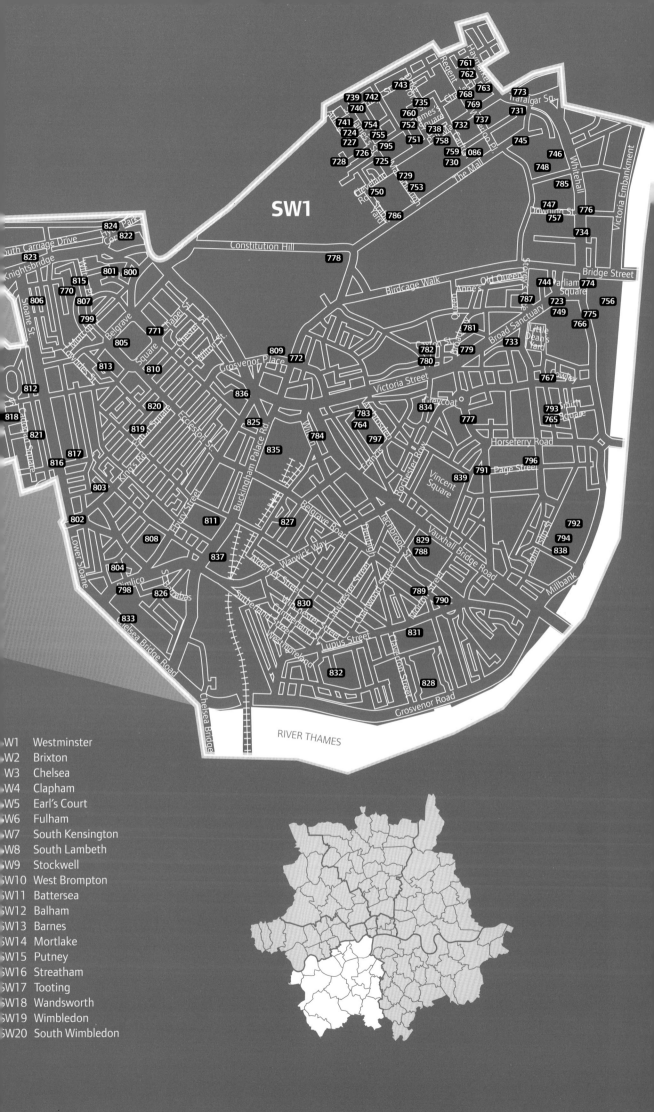

SW1

Constitution Hill

Birdcage Walk

The Mall

Whitehall

Victoria Street

Bridge Street

Parliament Square

Broad Sanctuary

Little Dean's Yard

Greycoat

Horseferry Road

Page Street

Vincent Square

Smith Square

Millbank

Belgrave Road

Vauxhall Bridge Road

Warwick Way

Lupus Street

Pimlico

Grosvenor Road

Chelsea Bridge

RIVER THAMES

South Carriage Drive

Knightsbridge

Sloane St.

Belgrave Square

Grosvenor Place

Lower Sloane

Chelsea Bridge Road

Kings Rd

Eccleston St.

Buckingham Palace Rd.

SW1 Westminster
SW2 Brixton
SW3 Chelsea
SW4 Clapham
SW5 Earl's Court
SW6 Fulham
SW7 South Kensington
SW8 South Lambeth
SW9 Stockwell
SW10 West Brompton
SW11 Battersea
SW12 Balham
SW13 Barnes
SW14 Mortlake
SW15 Putney
SW16 Streatham
SW17 Tooting
SW18 Wandsworth
SW19 Wimbledon
SW20 South Wimbledon

723

WESTMINSTER ABBEY

FROM 1066; 1245; 1375, HENRY YEVELE

Westminster Abbey can be found just to the west of
the Houses of Parliament. Reaching the grand scale
of a cathedral, this has been the traditional venue for
coronations, royal weddings, and many funerals of
English monarchs. Monks were living and working here
from AD 785; the scant remains of a Norman monastery
now house the Abbey Museum. Edward the Confessor
built a new church in 1065, and William the Conqueror
was crowned here on Christmas Day 1066. In the 1240s,
King Henry III decided to rebuild the abbey in its current
Gothic style. The exterior was constructed from soft
Reigate stone and has been refaced several times.
Master mason Henry Yevele demolished the nave and
constructed a replacement in keeping with the earlier
style. Until 1375, the abbey had a Gothic eastern end
and a Norman nave. In 1400, Geoffrey Chaucer was
buried here, and since then the remains of many authors
have been laid to rest in Poets' Corner, including
Sheridan, Browning, Tennyson, and Ben Jonson—buried
upright, at his own command, to conserve space. Actor
Laurence Olivier is also buried here. Today, in the centre
of the nave, the Grave of the Unknown Warrior is a
sombre reminder of those lost at war.

724

THE ECONOMIST PLAZA

25 ST JAMES'S STREET

724   SW1

1964 ALISON AND PETER SMITHSON

Here are the offices for *The Economist* newspaper, with a bank and apartments. The finely detailed towers, each built on a different scale, are clad in traditional Portland stone and set on upon a slightly raised plaza. The aim was to create a stimulating group of buildings yet one that fitted in with the historical surroundings. The reinforced concrete frame is clad with Portland stone. In 1990, the glazed lobby to the tower was enlarged and a canopy was added. The architects' policy was to make a detailed study of the needs of the people working in any building they designed.

725

PICKERING PLACE

OFF ST JAMES'S STREET

725   SW1

1731 WILLIAM PICKERING

Pickering Place is one of the smallest public squares in Great Britain. It is found through a narrow oak-paneled passageway that threads between two shops in St James's Street. The paved court is surrounded by four brick houses and is lit at night by original gas lamps. The houses were built by William Pickering, whose mother-in-law owned a grocer's shop on the site of number 3 James's Street. Along the passageway into the square is a door into the original shop. During the seventeenth century, the cul-de-sac was a common venue for dueling contests. Indeed, it is thought that the last duel in Great Britain may have been fought here.

726

WHITE'S CLUB

37-38 ST JAMES'S STREET

726   SW1

1787-88 JAMES WYATT; 1853 JAMES LOCKYER AND GEORGE SHARF

White's is a very grand gentlemen's club, first established in 1693 at White's Chocolate House, owned by an Italian, Francesco Bianco (hence the name White). Famous for their outrageous gambling, its list of members spans two and a half centuries and includes Prince Charles. Its Regency splendour incorporates splendid French-influenced relief panels, impressive first-floor windows flanked by Corinthian pilasters, and a bow window, installed in 1811, at the centre of the ground floor. Here was set the club's seat of privilege, taken by famous dandy Beau Brummel for many years. in 1853, a round-headed central window on the first floor and 'four seasons' decorations were added.

27 ST JAMES'S PLACE

SPENCER HOUSE

727   SW1

1752–54 JOHN VARDY; 1772 ALTERED BY SIR ROBERT TAYLOR

Spencer House is one the city's most regal eighteenth-century mansions, and a very early first example of neo-classical architecture. It was built in a Palladian design for the first Earl Spencer (an ancestor of Diana, Princess of Wales) as his London property. The façade facing the park boasts a rusticated ground floor with seven arched windows. The upper floor has seven bays split by Tuscan columns and is crowned by a pediment with a richly decorative central feature. Inside, accurate Greek detail gives an extra boost to the impressive presentation. In 1772, Sir Robert Taylor added a tunnel vault to the entrance hall.

727

26 ST JAMES'S PLACE

LUXURY FLATS

728   SW1

1958–60 SIR DENYS LASDUN

One of the first architecturally inspiring luxury blocks of flats to be built in London after World War II, this relatively small eight-storey building by Green Park was designed with clear horizontal bands that designate the different floor levels. The block uses sweeping granite facings for the bands, and the window frames are bronze. With graceful trees outside and Spencer House an elegant neighbour, this has been a prime place to live. The Royal Gold Medal for Architecture awarded to Lasdun acknowledged his stature, long recognized by his fellow architects. He once wrote, 'Every building has, at its heart, a generating idea, which must express itself through every part and in every detail.'

728

89 PALL MALL

ROYAL AUTOMOBILE CLUB

729   SW1

1908–11 MEWÈS AND DAVIS, WITH E. KEYNES PURCHASE

This building is an opulent Edwardian celebration of the motorcar by Mewès. It has a large Portland stone façade and a high entrance hall that leads on to luxurious club rooms, all in Louis XVI style. The basement houses squash courts, Turkish baths, a solarium, and a luxurious marble swimming pool with Moorish pillars faced in fish-scale mosaic. Spies Burgess and Maclean had lunch in the club before fleeing the country. A few years ago, one of the staff was actually murdered here—moreover, by someone who was not a member! An old gentleman spent every day in the library pretending to read: 'I have come here to die', he explained. 'I have had a busy life and I want to end it in peace.' He did so here.

729

THE MALL
CARLTON HOUSE TERRACE
730   SWI

1827–32 JOHN NASH

In Carlton House Terrace, blocks of Grade I–listed, white stucco-faced houses overlook St James's Park. They were constructed on the site of Carlton House, George V's residence before Buckingham Palace was built. All is in Roman classical style with short Doric columns on cast-iron platforms and a grand sweeping façades of taller Corinthian columns. Although now occupied mainly by businesses or organisations, over the years the houses have been home to several prime ministers—including Lord Palmerston (number 5, 1840–46), Earl Grey (number 13, 1851–57), and William Gladstone (number 11, 1857–75).

BETWEEN THE MALL AND TRAFALGAR SQUARE
ADMIRALTY ARCH
731   SWI

1906–11 SIR ASTON WEBB

Built in Portland stone, this giant Corinthian triple archway marks the first point of the royal route from Buckingham Palace to St Paul's Cathedral. The Grade I–listed building has three deep arches with splendid wrought-iron gates, the one in the centre opened only for ceremonial occasions. The triumphal arch incorporates offices and living quarters for senior navy officials, has served as a hostel for London's homeless, and is home to the Prime Minister's Strategy Unit. Since 2000, it has been used by the Cabinet Office. Commissioned by King Edward VII in memory of his mother, Queen Victoria, its Latin inscription translates as: *In the tenth year of King Edward VII, to Queen Victoria, from most grateful citizens, 1910.*

107 PALL MALL AND WATERLOO PLACE
THE ATHENAEUM HOTEL
732   SWI

1828–30 DECIMUS BURTON

The Athenaeum was founded in 1824 as a social club for London's intellectual elite. It was originally known simply as the Society, but was renamed when it moved to Pall Mall—named after the Athenaeum in Rome, a university for the study of science and literature. It is of classical revival design, with a front portico incorporating paired Doric columns. On the first floor, above the porch, is a gilded statue of Pallas Athene, a continuous balustrade, and a frieze copied from the Parthenon. The attic storey was added in 1899. The building was bought by Rank Hotels in 1971 and opened as the Athenaeum Hotel and Apartments in 1973—purchased by new owners in 1992.

730

731

732

733

METHODIST CENTRAL HALL

733 SWI

1905-12 LANCHESTER AND RICKARDS

This vast hall opened to mark the centenary of John Wesley's death. In 1898, a million Methodists were asked to contribute one guinea to the 'Million Guinea Fund.' In sumptuous style, it occupies an entire block in an almost square plan, surmounted by a huge dome. An ornate staircase leads to a landing, a statue of John Wesley, and the main hall that hosted the first meeting of the United Nations General Assembly in 1946. Here, the Suffragettes campaigned for the vote in 1914, Mahatma Gandhi addressed the Temperance movement in 1931, and General de Gaulle announced the foundation of the Free French movement in 1940.

734

VICTORIA EMBANKMENT; FORMERLY NEW SCOTLAND YARD

NORMAN SHAW BUILDING

734 SWI

1886-90 R. NORMAN SHAW

Part of the old Whitehall Palace was originally lodgings for Scottish kings. In 1829, when Sir Robert Peel created the new Metropolitan police force, Great Scotland Yard became their headquarters. This imposing red-and-white brick Victorian Gothic fortress has round towers inspired by Scottish castles and is 'a very constabulary kind of castle.' The granite facing was probably quarried by convicts on Dartmoor. Its original telephone number was the famous Whitehall 1212. The police moved out in 1967 but the name, New Scotland Yard, went with them. It was bombed by the Fenians in 1883, when a wall exploded. In 1888, a woman's torso was discovered in the cellar.

735

15 ST JAMES'S SQUARE

LICHFIELD HOUSE

735 SWI

1764-66 JAMES ATHENIAN' STUART; 1791-94 INTERIORS SAMUEL WYATT

This very elegant house was constructed in Portland stone with a graceful, Greek-influenced Ionic portico. It is thought that Wyatt made some alterations to the front of the house, including the stone balcony and copper railing—and, inside, he merged two rooms to form a library. Since 1856, Lichfield House has been occupied by the General Medical Society (now the Clerical, Medical and General Life Assurance Society) but its more exotic earlier residents included Frances, Duchess of Richmond. She was the model for Britannia on the old English penny, and was greatly admired by Charles II but denied him her favours.

THE MALL
THE CITADEL

736   SW1

1940 W. A. FORSYTH

The Citadel was one of the few new structures to rise during World War II—a fortress and bunker beside the Admiralty, providing bomb-proof protection with observation slits for gun emplacements. An underground shelter, six floors down, protected the nation's leaders during the Blitz. This was the centre of the Naval Intelligence Division and, in the event of a German invasion, would have served as a fortress. During wartime, all was bustle here, with officers and civilians rushing everywhere. It is still used by the Ministry of Defence but with a slightly less ominous appearance: its massive, black-and-beige, compressed pebble and flint block walls are now covered in Virginia creeper.

736

PALL MALL AND WATERLOO PLACE; FORMERLY UNITED SERVICES CLUB
INSTITUTE OF DIRECTORS

737   SW1

1827, 1842 JOHN NASH, DECIMUS BURTON

The Institute of Directors building rose on the site of the demolished Carlton House. Indeed, the interior incorporates the original staircase, a magnificent design, presented to the club by George IV. John Nash built the United Service Club building in 1827, but fifteen years later Burton remodelled the exterior to look more like the Athenaeum he had raised opposite at number 116. This Victorian Italianate exterior has a Roman Doric porch, cornice with balustrade, frieze, and fluted Corinthian columns on the upper portico. Burton incorporated nineteen lanterns around the exterior; they are still fully functional.

737

106 PALL MALL
TRAVELLER'S CLUB

738   SW1

1829-32 SIR CHARLES BARRY; 1952-53 RESTORED F. ROWNTREE

The Traveller's Club, founded in 1819, is the oldest of the Pall Mall gentlemen clubs. It was established as a reunion venue for gentlemen who had travelled abroad—at least five hundred miles in a straight line from London. It is built in the style of an Italian Renaissance palace (the Palazzo Pandolfino in Florence) around a central court. There have been two suicides on the premises. On both occasions a member shot himself in the billiards room. After the second death, the chairman, Colonel Baring, commented, 'I'll take damn good care he never gets into any other club I have anything to do with.'

738

PICCADILLY ARCADE

739   SWI

1909–10 THRALE JELL

This was an extension to Burlington Arcade. It runs under a building between Piccadilly and Jermyn Street, and is lined with twenty-eight bow-fronted shops. The upper floors were designed as offices and chambers and, in 1915, part of the upper accommodation became the Felix Hotel. The Portland stone Piccadilly front is a lively mix of columns, pilasters, cornice, frieze, and neat iron-railed balcony. Irena Sedlecka's life-size statue of Beau Brummell, the nineteenth-century English dandy, stands at the Jermyn Street entrance.

HIGHLY ORNATE OFFICES

740   SWI

1882 R. NORMAN SHAW

St James's Street arrived after Henry VIII acquired St James's Hospital and built St James's Palace here. It was an area renowned for its coffee- and chocolate houses and clubs. Shaw, the architect of these ornate offices, was extremely influential in the last decades of the nineteenth century, best known for his country houses and commercial buildings. This elaborate castle-like structure is a great example of his brick and gabled style—copied widely by others. He revelled in half timber and hanging tiles, projecting gables, and tall chimneys.

BROOK'S CLUB

741   SWI

FOUNDED 1764; 1777–78 HENRY HOLLAND

Brook's was a social rather than political gentlemen's club. In 1778, it moved to number 60 St James's Street, a residence under the management of wine merchant and money-lender William Brooks. Although it was the main social centre for the Whigs, it also acquired a reputation for heavy gambling. The frontage to the building is constructed from white brick, with three floors, tall Corinthian pilasters, and a cornice that spans the central four columns. Inside, are a glass domed ceiling and a stone staircase. In an upstairs room are the busts of Charles Fox and William Pitt, who were members.

ST JAMES'S

742   SWI

1676–84 SIR CHRISTOPHER WREN; 1700 SQUARE TOWER ADDED

Wren was especially proud of St James's, built as part of Henry Jermyn's development to the St James's Palace estate, in plain brick and Portland stone; the north and south elevations have elegant two-tiered windows. Its interior is one room with a vaulted ceiling, galleries on three sides and square pillars, the nave's barrel vault supported on sturdy Corinthian columns. Here, in 1865, explorer Sir Samuel Baker married his second wife, Florence Barbara Maria Finnin von Sass, the young woman he had bought at a slave auction in a Turkish bazaar—and who had been his companion on his journey up the river Nile.

THE RED LION

743   SWI

1821; 1870 REDESIGNED

The Red Lion was built on the site of another public house. Its style and decoration suggest the late Victorian period, when it was restored. It has a brick exterior above the heavy timber of the ground floor and boasts some ornate ironwork and lanterns. The interior has a plush and glittering air, with crystal chandeliers and lots of cut-glass mirrors sparkling in dark mahogany frames. It probably served the people who worked in the grand houses in the neighbourhood.

MIDDLESEX GUILDHALL

744   SWI

1868; 1906–13 J. S. GIBSON AND RUSSELL

Built on the site of a notorious slum, Parliament Square provided an open aspect for the 1870 Houses of Parliament. In 1926, it had Britain's first official roundabout and traffic lights. Behind Abraham Lincoln's statue, this medieval-style, Gothic hall has leering gargoyles and a 1600s doorway, a remnant of Tothill Fields Prison. Here was the Sanctuary Tower, where the oppressed sought refuge; Edward V was born here after his mother found sanctuary. The Grade II–listed building now houses Middlesex Crown Court, with seven courtrooms, some used during World War II by the Allies maritime courts. in 2008, it will accommodate the House of Lords Supreme Court.

739

740

741

742

743

744

745

746

747

WHITEHALL
ADMIRALTY SCREEN AND ADMIRALTY HOUSE
745   SWI

1759–61 ROBERT ADAM; 1786–88 S. P. COCKERELL

The Admiralty Screen was Robert Adam's first assignment, constructed in front
of the courtyard of Admiralty. Its Roman Doric design features a central arch
with seahorse decoration and flanking pavilions with sculptured pediments.
Admiralty House can be found to the south of Admiralty, and was built by
Cockerell as a residence for the First Lord of the Admiralty—a role it played
until 1964. It has also been the home of Members of Parliament, including Sir
Winston Churchill. It is a three-storey building in yellow brick. The front façade
has three bays, and to the rear, five bays face Horse Guards Parade.

WHITEHALL
DOVER HOUSE
746   SWI

1754–58; 1787 JAMES PAINE, HENRY HOLLAND

Although Dover House is essentially the work of two architects, it is still possible
to see the influence of both within the building. The main block and two-storey
wing running into Whitehall were built in Paine's distinctive Romanesque style,
while the façades show the mark of Holland's Greek-inspired work. At the front
of the building is a rusticated wall and Greek portico with Ionic columns. The
impressive entrance hall and rotunda is also Holland's. Dover House suffered
bomb damage during World War II and was restored in 1955. It was the London
headquarters of the Scottish Office until 1999. Architect James Paine is
depicted in a portrait in the entrance hall waiting room.

WHITEHALL
OLD TREASURY BUILDING
(AND CHURCHILL MUSEUM)
747   SWI

1733–36 WILLIAM KENT; 1824–27 SIR JOHN SOANE; 1844 SIR CHARLES BARRY

This outer façade is typical early Victorian, with stone rustication and a small
portico of Ionic columns. Inside there are impressive entrance halls and
fragments of Henry VIII's Whitehall Palace, including tennis courts and a
fireplace. Sir John Soane's addition proved too small and it was replaced by
Sir Charles Barry's design. World War II bombs inflicted serious damage, and
what we see now is mostly the work of the most recent architect. The building is
presently mostly occupied by the Cabinet Office. Here are the rooms from which
Churchill directed Britain's war effort during the darkest days of World War II,
often catching brief snatches of sleep here too, in the rooms below ground. The
Churchill Museum opened in 2005 to mark the fortieth anniversary of his death.

748

WHITEHALL

THE HORSE GUARDS

748   SW1

1745–55 WILIAM KENT, JOHN VARDY

A small guardhouse was built here in 1649 on the site of Henry VIII's tiltyard (a tournament ground). By the 1660s, a larger building had been constructed for both horse guards and foot guards. The current building was completed in the 1750s by John Vardy after the death of its designer William Kent, and is of Palladian design; it was originally the main entrance to Buckingham Palace. Its picturesque arches surround Venetian or pedimented windows. At the rear, away from the road, is the parade ground. Here, the Changing of the Guard ceremony happens daily in summer, and the Trooping of the Colour once a year. This custom of the latter dates back to Charles II's reign, when the colours of a regiment were used as a rallying point in battle: To ensure that every soldier would recognise the colours of his own regiment at a glance, they were trooped in front of the men every day.

PARLIAMENT SQUARE

HENRY VII'S CHAPEL, WESTMINSTER ABBEY

749   SW1

1503–12 SIR REGINALD BRAY

The Henry VII Lady Chapel can be found at the far eastern end of Westminster Abbey. Its architect was also a statesman—and one of the Henry VII's closest advisors. The chapel is an impressive presentation of Perpendicular architecture and one of the first buildings in Britain to be influenced by Renaissance design. Its best feature is the fan-vaulted roof with fine carved pendants. Statues of ninety-five saints surround the walls, and the large windows flood the interior with light. Henry VII originally planned to build the chapel as a shrine for his half uncle, King Henry VI— miracles were recorded as happening at Henry VI's tomb in Windsor, so Henry VII wanted to have him canonised. This never transpired however, and Henry VII was himself buried in the chapel in 1509.

49

CLEVELAND ROW, MARLBOROUGH GATE

ST JAMES'S PALACE

750   SW1

1530s HENRY VIII; FROM 1698 MODIFIED BY CHRISTOPHER WREN

Built by Henry VIII on the former site of a leper hospital, from 1698, this became one of the principal homes of England's kings and queens. Charles I spent his last night here. The building was mostly destroyed by fire in 1809. Whilst it was being rebuilt, George III chose to live at Buckingham House, now known as Buckingham Palace, which Queen Victoria made her royal home in 1837. This palace was constructed in a Tudor style, using redbrick, and designed around four interior courtyards. It is mostly the work of Christopher Wren, apart from the gatehouse and its octagonal turrets—part of the original building, and now includes the Prince of Wales's London residence.

750

80–82 PALL MALL

SCHOMBERG HOUSE

751   SW1

C. 1698

This Grade II–listed building was designed for the German Duke of Schomberg. The central section of its brown brick, red-trimmed façade juts out slightly and each end has tower-like projections. Home to portrait painter Thomas Gainsborough, the War Office, and a high-class brothel and gambling den, in 1771 it was the Temple of Health and Hymen. Here, infertile couples hoping to conceive slept in the Magnetic Celestial Bed—sometimes entertained by the 'Goddess of Health,' a young girl in a diaphanous robe; this was the future Lady Hamilton, and Horatio Nelson's lover. The 'Dr' Graham who ran this concern was eventually confined in a lunatic asylum!

751

4 ST JAMES'S SQUARE

THE NAVAL AND MILITARY CLUB

752   SW1

1726–28 EDWARD SHEPHERD

The original building here was owned by the tenth Earl of Kent, Anthony Grey. In fact, his descendants owned the land until 1908. The house burned down in 1725; rebuilt, it has remained relatively unchanged since then. The impressive Palladian frontage is five windows wide and three storeys high, with a deep band of brickwork above the first floor windows. This was once the home of Nancy Astor; Waldorf Astor, the second Lord Astor, lived here from 1912–42. Since 1999, the building has been house to the Naval and Military Club—founded in 1862 and one of the oldest clubs in London. The Libyan embassy in St James's Square was the site of the 1984 siege.

752

753

1623-27 INIGO JONES

This was first designed for the Infanta of Spain who was due to marry Charles I, but was finally built for Queen Henrietta Maria and refurbished for Catherine of Braganza, wife of Charles II. Inspired by Italian styles, it has stucco walls, Portland stone quoins, and a simple pediment. Inside is a coffered ceiling and England's first Venetian window, at the eastern end of the chapel. This is one of the two main Chapel Royals in England—the other one is also in St James's Palace. Chapel Royal originally referred to a body of priests and singers who served the sovereign, but it is now associated with a number of chapels used by monarchs over the centuries.

754

88 ST JAMES'S STREET

OFFICES AND FLATS

754   SW1

1903 R. NORMAN SHAW WITH ERNEST NEWTON

This Grade II–listed building is in rich Baroque style with wide arches over the entrance and windows, sweet curved balconies, and an intricate top storey with tall chimneys set beside and behind the gable end. English architect. Ernest Newton was apprenticed to R. Norman Shaw in 1873. In 1879, he left Shaw's office to form his own practice and in 1884, with W. R. Lethaby, E. S. Prior, and other young architects and artist-craftsmen, formed the Art Workers' Guild. Shaw, meanwhile, explored the classical style and influenced the emerging Edwardian Classicism of the early twentieth century and was elected to the Royal Academy in 1877.

755

74 ST JAMES'S STREET, FORMERLY CONSERVATIVE CLUB

HSBC OFFICES

755   SW1

1843 GEORGE BASEVI AND SYDNEY SMIRKE

The Conservative Club was founded in 1840, and its base at 74 St James's Street was built on the site of the Thatched House Tavern. The front façade is of Palladian design, with a rusticated ground floor, and Corinthian pilasters and pediments to the first-floor windows. At centre stage of the interior is a square room with an upper gallery and circular dome in the ceiling. Recent refurbishments have transformed the building into a £100 million high-tech banking facility.

756

PALACE OF WESTMINSTER

HOUSES OF PARLIAMENT

756   SWI

1835–60 SIR CHARLES BARRY; AUGUSTUS WELBY PUGIN;
1940s SIR GILES GILBERT SCOTT

The Palace of Westminster began life in 1042 as a royal
residence for King Edward the Confessor. The present
Houses of Parliament were built after a devastating fire
in 1834. Sir Charles Barry was largely responsible for the
neo-Gothic design of the exterior, and Augustus Pugin for
its ornamentation and the interior. Following damage by
bombing during World War II, the House of Commons
was rebuilt and some of Pugin's decorative features
were simplified. There are a thousand rooms, eleven
courtyards, eight bars, and six restaurants. It is dominated
by the famous clock tower, completed in 1858 and
commonly called Big Ben—but actually this is the name
of the bell. The Victoria Tower was finished in 1860, the
year of Barry's death (attributable in part to exhaustion
after this huge undertaking); his son supervised the final
stages. Pugin died in Bedlam (Bethlehem Hospital, for
the care of the insane) in 1852, just one the year after the
official opening of the Houses of Parliament. The cellars
are still searched by the Yeomen of the Guard before each
State Opening of Parliament, after Guy Fawkes and his
fellow conspirators plotted to blow up King James I and
his ministers on 'Remember, remember the fifth of
November' in 1605.

757

FAMOUS HOMES

757   SW1

1680–1766 SIR GEORGE DOWNING

Numbers 10, 11, and 12 Downing Street are the official residences of the Prime Minister, the Chancellor of the Exchequer, and the Chief Whip. The earliest known building on the site was a brewhouse at the beginning of the 1500s. A century later this came into the possession of Sir George Downing, who built a cul-de-sac of plain brick terraced houses here—of which only numbers 10, 11, and 12 remain. Links to the government date back to 1732, when King George II offered number 10 to Britain's first Prime Minister, Sir Robert Walpole; this is actually two houses. The one facing Downing Street is a seventeenth-century townhouse design, refronted and enlarged over the years. The building is actually made of yellow bricks, but these have been painted black. Rumour has it that the front door of the building can be opened only from the inside.

MARLBOROUGH COURT

1931 SIR EDWIN LUTYENS WITH ROMAINE-WALKER AND JENKINS

The Junior Naval and Military Club building here was demolished in 1930 to make way for this block of business premises and flats—a corner building, with a bank on the ground floor and flats above. Lutyens was responsible only for the elevations, and the final designs had to be approved by King George V, the Queen, and Prince of Wales. In Palladian style, it has a recessed portico on the north front and windows on the west, with simple columns and wide rusticated piers. The windows on the south wall overlook Marlborough House (the official residence of the Prince of Wales from 1850), and were filled with opaque glass.

STIRLING HOUSE

1998 SIR JAMES STIRLING

This Italian, palazzo-style building is approached through immaculate landscaped gardens and an impressive circular outer lobby veneered with European oak. Here, located on different storeys, are apartments, penthouses, and offices, the residential accommodation having its own exclusive entrance. The architect's aim was to create light and space, innovation and tradition. In former times, Carlton Gardens has been the address of Lord Kitchener, Palmerston, Curzon, de Gaulle, and Gladstone.

NUMBERS 9, 10, AND 11

ESTABLISHED 1670s; 1734 HENRY FLITCROFT

This was one of London's first and most fashionable squares. In its early days, it was surrounded by the houses of people who needed to live near St James's Palace–one of the principal residencies of royalty—including palace employees and two mistresses of James II at number 21. Number 10 is Chatham House. Flitcroft supervised its build and was most probably also responsible for its neighbours, numbers 9 and 11. Behind the Palladian façade, number 10 is now home to the Royal Institute for International Affairs, but over the years it has been occupied by prime ministers, such as William Pitt the Elder and William Gladstone.

THEATRE ROYAL

1720; 1831 RECONSTRUCTED JOHN NASH; 1994 REFURBISHED

The theatre's front façade boasts nine decorated windows above an impressive portico of Corinthian columns. In 1873, it was the venue for the first scheduled matinee show. During its £1.3 million refit in 1994, some 1,200 books of twenty-four-carat English gold leaf were used. Much of the stage machinery used today is original. Oscar Wilde's *A Woman of No Importance* (1893) and *An Ideal Husband* (1895) were first produced here. Buckstone, a friend of Charles Dickens's and manager of the Haymarket from 1853–79, still haunts the auditorium and dressing rooms, keeping an eye on his beloved theatre.

FANCY THAT OF LONDON

c.1760–70

This is the only surviving eighteenth-century building along Haymarket. It was built around 1760, and the double-bayed shop front was added in 1770. The shop was owned and occupied for 231 years by the tobacconists and snuff makers Fribourg and Treyer. They left the premises in the 1980s and it is now a gift emporium—and has spread next door. Around the mid-1600s, Haymarket was the site of a market for hay and straw—and later a twice-weekly market for sheep and cattle, but both markets were eventually relocated in an attempt to gentrify the area.

NEW ZEALAND HOUSE

1960 SIR ROBERT MATTHEW, JOHNSON-MARSHALL

Set in a part of London that has many eighteenth- and nineteenth-century buildings, this was one of the first office buildings here to be fully air-conditioned. It was built with vast sheets of glass, with opaque pleated curtains and thin horizontal slithers of stone added later. It stands on a broader base podium. Behind the glass façade is the New Zealand High Commission and the tourist board that offers a vast store of information for visitors to the antipodes.

758

759

760

761

762

763

DOMINE · JESU · REX · ET · REDEMPTOR
PER · SANGUINEM · TUUM · SALVA · NOS

764

WESTMINSTER CATHEDRAL, ARCHBISHOP'S HOUSE, AND CLERGY HOUSE

764   SW1

1895–1903 JOHN FRANCIS BENTLEY

Presided over by the Archbishop of Westminster, this is the headquarters of Britain's Catholic Church. Marshland was reclaimed by the Benedictine monks of Westminster Abbey and used as a market site. Here was held St Mary's Fair, and later a prison occupied part of the site. The Roman Catholic cathedral that stands here now is in Byzantine and Romanesque styles, inspired by Bentley's visits to Europe and Constantinople, and is built in redbrick with contrasting bands of Portland stone. There are several domes, over a hundred different marbles, mosaic cladding, plus Eric Gill's *Stations of the Cross* on the nave's main piers. The eight columns of dark green marble in the widest nave in England were hewn from the quarry that, back in the 500s, had provided the marble for St Sophia, in Istanbul. Pope John Paul II celebrated mass here in 1982.

A POLITICAL SQUARE

765   SWI

c. 1720 SIR JAMES SMITH

Smith Square was named after the man who developed the
square and its surrounding streets, Sir James Smith. Almost all of
the brick terrace houses on the north side are original, along with
their accompanying ironwork and lamp holders. The south side is
now filled with office blocks, however, which sprang up in the
aftermath of World War II damage. Two impressive examples
of neo-Georgian design stand on the square: number 36 by
Lutyens, and the house in the northwest corner by Oliver Hill.
The square has a strong political history: It has accommodated
the Conservative Party Central Office since 1958, and housed
the headquarters of the Labour Party between 1928 and 1980.

6–7 OLD PALACE YARD

HOUSE ON AN HISTORIC SITE

766   SWI

1756–60 JOHN VARDY

This lovely Portland stone house in Palladian style was designed
John Vardy, the Clerk of the Works at Whitehall and St James.
He was associated with architects such as William Kent and Inigo
Jones, and also designed furniture—he worked on pieces for
Lord Spencer at Spencer House, for example. This was once the
site of the palace of Edward the Confessor and, later, Chaucer
lived in a house on the north side. Old Palace Yard now serves as
a car park used by Members of Parliament. In 1606, however, this
was the site on which Guy Fawkes and his fellow plotters were
hung, drawn, and quartered. Explorer Sir Walter Raleigh was also
executed here in 1618.

LORD NORTH STREET AND COWLEY STREET

NEAT GEORGIAN STREETS

767   SWI

c. 1720

The houses in both these streets were constructed in brown brick,
with neat redbrick decoration around the windows and arches.
They are two of the most complete examples of early Georgian
streets in London. Both were developed in 1722, and are
extremely popular as elegant places to live for Members of
Parliament. Cowley Street was constructed in recognition of the
actor Barton Booth, who attended the local Westminster School
and is buried in Cowley, just outside London. At number 2 Lord
North Street is the Institute of Economic Affairs.

765

766

767

768

ROYAL OPERA ARCADE

768   SWI

1816–16 JOHN NASH AND G. S. REPTON

The Royal Opera Arcade was the first shopping arcade in London. It was built at the rear of Nash's Royal Opera House, which burnt down in 1867 and was replaced by Her Majesty's Theatre. On the eastern wall of the arcade were secondary entrances to the opera house, and so the bow-fronted shops span only the western wall, set into elegant, vaulted bays with glass domed crowns. Today, the arcade is home to a rather refined gentlemen's clothing shop, as well as a royal-appointed hunting, shooting, and fishing supplier.

769

100 PALL MALL

AN IMPOSING ADDRESS

769   SWI

1956–58 D. ARMSTRONG SMITH AND DONALD MCMORRAN

100 Pall Mall must rank as one of the most prestigious addresses, set in the heart of the St James's area and next door to the Royal Automobile Club. The Swedish Modern style swept in after World War II when this distinguished Grade II–listed building replaced the Carlton Club. Its six storeys are neo-Georgian, with set-back roof pavilions and the smooth lines associated with Scandinavian styles. The exterior was designed by Donald H. McMorran (later elected to the Royal Academy, in 1962) and the building as a whole was the responsibility of Armstrong Smith. Inside, there are interlocking ground floors, mezzanine levels, and imposing double-height areas.

770

53 KINNERTON STREET

THE NAGS HEAD

770   SWI

PRE-1820s

Kinnerton Street arrived in the 1820s, providing cottages for artisans and tradesmen in a tranquil mews, where the first landlords hired out horses. The wooden frontage of what was once the smallest pub in London resembles a Dickensian shop. It has a low ceiling and the stools are only chair height, but the floor behind the bar is lower and allows even tall staff to stand upright. Here, an antique pewter beer engine has little pink Chelsea Pottery hand-pulls. There are 1930s penny-in-the-slot machines, ice-skates, carpet beaters, a huge ancient cash register, and lots of prints. The Victorian bar-room has a grand 1820s cast-iron fireplace.

GROOM PLACE
THE HORSE AND GROOM
771   SWI

1864

Surrounded by narrow, cobbled Groom Place, and some of Belgravia's great houses, this former mews cottages once housed the grooms who gave the street its name. It is still a tiny, one-room, wood-panelled pub. It opened in 1864, to take advantage of the Beer Act that allowed householders to sell beer on payment of two guineas a year to the justices. During the 1960s, one regular here was Beatles manager Brian Epstein—and it is rumoured that a good deal of mescaline and LSD was indulged in here, too, as well as beer. Dedicated Beatles fans still make pilgrimages to the pub.

771

6 BUCKINGHAM PALACE ROAD
BAG-O-NAILS
772   SWI

1774; REBUILT 1830S

Opposite the Royal Mews, this was the local drinking spot for the grooms, coachmen, and stable boys employed at Buckingham Palace. It may have had its first license in 1774, but was rebuilt in the 1830s when the Grosvenor Estate expanded. Today, this old pub has a single bar, dark wood panelling, and framed sepia prints. Tradition claims that its name derived from bacchanals, ancient rites surrounding the grape harvest and the god Bacchus, which often invited great drunken revelry. It is just as likely that it derived from the sign of a nail-studded sack, symbolising an ironmonger's shop.

772

SUFFOLK STREET AND SUFFOLK PLACE
FROM HORSES TO HOUSES
773   SWI

1820 JOHN NASH, SIR REGINALD BLOMFIELD, AND OTHERS

These two surviving stretches of Nash's 1820s development show a Greek influence, and have elegant stuccoed façades and pretty ironwork balconies. In Suffolk Street, number 1 dates from 1906 and was designed in Parisian style by Sir Reginald Blomfield. Nash was responsible for number 7—a Roman Doric design, with an arched ground floor and portico. Numbers 18 and 19 stand at the back of the Theatre Royal. Suffolk Place takes its name from the Earl of Suffolk who had stables on the site in the early seventeenth century.

773

774

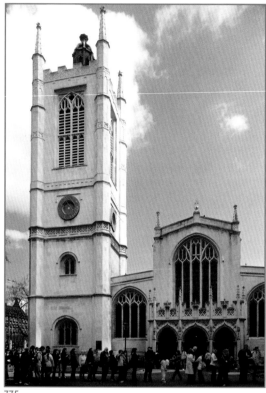

775

BRIDGE STREET

PORTCULLIS HOUSE NEW PARLIAMENTARY BUILDING

774   SW1

1997 (OPENED 2001) MICHAEL HOPKINS AND PARTNERS

This splendid building is named after the chained portcullis that symbolises the Houses of Parliament on letters and documents. Six floors of offices for members of parliament and staff are arranged around an atrium, with shops at ground floor level and an underground station below. The corners hang from the roof on massive steel beams. It has lovely sandstone and bronze window frames, and a steeply pitched roof—its tall, narrow ventilation ducts resembling Victorian chimney stacks. A thick slab of concrete separates the building from the station, possibly to defend against bomb attacks. There is a post office, an 'e-library,' conference suites, and committee rooms—named Betty Boothroyd, Harold Macmillan, Margaret Thatcher, Clement Attlee, and Harold Wilson. A formal restaurant is called the Adjournment, an informal cafeteria is the Debate, and a snack shop, the Despatch Box.

PARLIAMENT SQUARE

ST MARGARET'S WESTMINSTER

775   SW1

1120–40 FOUNDED; 1480–1523 REBUILT;
1735-37 TOWER REBUILT JOHN JAMES; 1758 APSE KENTON HOUSE;
1877 RESTORED GILES GILBERT SCOTT

Standing between Westminster Abbey and the Houses of Parliament, this has been the parish church for the House of Commons since 1614. In late perpendicular Gothic style, and encased in Portland stone, it still retains many ancient features. Founded in the 1100s to serve the lay people of the monastery, it ran in conjunction with Westminster Abbey for centuries. In the 1600s, its was the local Puritans' choice of place to worship and there have been parliamentary services here ever since. The richly coloured Flemish glass of the east window dates from 1509, and marks the betrothal of Catherine of Aragon to Prince Arthur, Henry VIII's brother. Other windows remember William Caxton—Britain's first printer, buried here in 1491, Sir Walter Raleigh, buried here in 1618 after his execution, and poet John Milton (1608–74), who was both buried here—and married, as were Samuel Pepys (1655) and Winston Churchill (1908).

776

777

WHITEHALL
RICHMOND TERRACE

776   SW1

1822–25 HENRY HARRISON;
1980s ENTRANCE WILLIAM WHITFIELD AND PARTNERS

This is now all government offices, primarily the Department of Health but, back in the 1820s, it was an understated brick terrace, built on the site of Richmond House. One of the houses here was home to the explorer H. M. Stanley (who died in 1904 at number 2), and the philanthropist Quentin Hogg lived at number 6 from 1873–77 and at number 4 from 1877–81. In the 1960s, the terrace was threatened with demolition; it survived, but the interiors had to be rebuilt in the 1980s. The neo-Perpendicular entrance, which can be seen from Whitehall, was added towards the end of the 1980s.

124 HORSEFERRY ROAD
CHANNEL 4 TELEVISION HEADQUARTERS

777   SW1

1994 RICHARD ROGERS PARTNERSHIP

A RIBA award–winner, this dramatic building uses lots of glass and steel, with curved pillars and two wings set each side of a convex corner entrance area. Two more wings enclose a central courtyard garden. There is plenty of the glass, pewter grey aluminium, and exposed structural steelwork that are the hallmark of Richard Rogers's brave designs, but this was a (relatively) budget-conscious exercise, with a £35 million cost limit. The entrance is approached by a bridge over what seems, at first glance, to be a glass pool but which, in fact, is the roof of a studio set underground. Inside, a concave atrium leads through to a staff restaurant with the lush, landscaped courtyard beyond.

WESTMINSTER

Composed Upon Westminster Bridge

EARTH has not anything to show more fair:
Dull would he be of soul who could pass by
A sight so touching in its majesty:
This City now doth, like a garment, wear
The beauty of the morning; silent, bare,
Ships, towers, domes, theatres, and temples lie
Open unto the fields, and to the sky;
All bright and glittering in the smokeless air.
Never did sun more beautifully steep
In his first splendour, valley, rock, or hill;
Ne'er saw I, never felt, a calm so deep!
The river glideth at his own sweet will:
Dear God! the very houses seem asleep;
And all that mighty heart is lying still!

William Wordsworth
September 3, 1802

Boswell, also inspired by this vantage point, claimed to have made love on Westminster Bridge!

Westminster has been the seat government for almost a thousand years; in 1066 William the Conqueror was crowned here—as was almost every English monarch since. Westminster Hall—built in 1097 by Willian Rufus (William the Conqueror's son) and the largest Norman hall in Europe—hosted the trials of Charles I, Guy Fawkes, and Sir Thomas More; the abdication of Edward I; and the deposition of Richard II. Whitehall, meanwhile, was the largest European palace in the 1500s; here were apartments for visiting kings of Scotland, and the name Great Scotland Yard derives from these.

Today's Parliament buildings have over a thousand apartments, covering more than 3 hectares (8 acres). When the old palace of Westminster had burned down in 1834, the new buildings were positioned so as to allow the river Thames to act as a natural barrier. Outside, a cast of Rodin's *The Burgers of Calais* depicts the brave men who surrendered as hostages to Edward III in 1347 during the Hundred Years' War.

Nearby is Westminster Abbey, founded in 616 on Thorney Island, with the stone abbey raised around 1045–50 by King Edward the Confessor. Here Chaucer was buried in 1400 (since which Poets' Corner has been the resting place of many writers) and one memorial marks the first man in London to carry an umbrella. William Caxton rented a shop in the precincts of Westminster Abbey and then set up his printing press by Chapter House.

BUCKINGHAM PALACE

778 SW1

1715; 1825–30 JOHN NASH; 1830–47 EDWARD BLORE;
1912–13 SIR ASTON WEBB

Buckingham Palace has been the official residence of
the monarch since 1837, when Queen Victoria moved
here. Built in 1715, it started life as a country house,
and, although George III bought it in 1762, it stayed in its
original role until 1820, when Nash was commissioned to
transform the building—one can still see evidence of his
French neo-classical work in the rear façade that faces the
garden. Nash was dropped from the project in 1830, and
Edward Blore succeeded him, building over the frontage
that faces the Mall. Queen Victoria's ballroom was once
the biggest room in London, measuring 37 by 18 metres
(122 by 60 feet). By 1913, the soft French stone of the
palace frontage was deteriorating, and so Sir Aston Webb
designed what we see now in Portland stone. The current
palace comprises more than six hundred rooms. The
forecourt, where the Changing of the Guard takes place,
was constructed in 1911.

NEW BASE FOR
NEW SCOTLAND YARD

779   SWI

1962–66 CHAPMAN TAYLOR PARTNERS, FAÇADES DESIGNED BY ADRIAN GALE

First built as a speculative venture, during the redevelopment of Victoria Street, these slab-like offices on a triangular site were occupied later by the Metropolitan Police, as their third headquarters, extending over eleven acres. They have impressive granite and aluminium-clad façades, twenty storeys, and nearly seven hundred offices. The most well-known feature is the revolving sign outside, which has appeared in countless news reports and television shows.

779

23 CAXTON STREET

BLUECOAT SCHOOL

780   SWI

1688 SCHOOL FOUNDED; 1709 BUILT

The school was founded around 1688 as a charity school for fifty poor boys of St Margaret's parish, and funded by local brewer William Greene. Its design could have been influenced by Sir Christopher Wren. The building was used as a school until 1939, with girls being admitted from 1713. During World War II, it was an army store, and then a centre for guides and youth clubs. It was bought by the National Trust in 1954. Now, squeezed between tall office buildings, its size shows how buildings have grown in scale over the centuries. A statue of a charity boy wearing a blue uniform and yellow stockings is set into the wall.

780

55 BROADWAY

BROADWAY HOUSE

781   SWI

1927–29 CHARLES HOLDEN

Built as new headquarters for London's Underground Transport, this cruciform-shaped, Art Deco building rises above St James's Park tube station. It was a very tall building in its day, at 53 metres (175 feet). The end of one wing rises above the entrance set on a corner and is stepped back towards a central clock tower. The ground floor contains a shopping arcade with many Art Deco details. Sculptures include works by Eric Gill, Henry Moore, and Jacob Epstein—who had to remove a couple of inches from the penis of his *Day* figure when the public protested loudly about the size of this feature.

781

782

FORMAL PATTERN BOOK HOUSES

782   SWI

FROM 1704

Both streets were developed at the same time, Old Queen Street being a narrow continuation of Queen Anne's Gate. They comprise a most complete example of houses from the beginning of the 1700s. The designs (from a formal pattern book) form regular brown brick and stone bands between the storeys. West along the street from Queen Anne's statue, the decorations to the buildings become slightly more elaborate, due to the fact that they were constructed before the formal pattern book was agreed. These more elaborate buildings are decorated with fun wooden canopies and pendants, arches, and friezes.

783

AMBROSDEN AVENUE

ARCHBISHOP'S HOUSE, WESTMINSTER CATHEDRAL

783   SWI

1895–1903 JOHN FRANCI BENTLEY

The Archbishop's House, providing accommodation for the current archbishop of Westminster Cathedral, adjoins the eastern end of the cathedral, in Ambrosden Avenue. It runs along one side of the striking cathedral complex and was also designed by John Francis Bentley (1839–1902), the accomplished Victorian church architect, who was appointed by Archbishop Herbert Vaughan (later Cardinal Vaughan) to undertake this task in 1892.

784

17 WILTON ROAD

APOLLO VICTORIA THEATRE

784   SWI

1929–30 E. WALMSLEY LEWIS

This very large theatre was once a striking, moderne Art Deco–style cinema with alternating horizontal bands of windows and striped spandrels, and splendid interiors. The New Victoria Cinema was taken over in 1979 by Apollo Victoria UK Limited and converted into a theatre for full-scale musicals. It has also staged concerts by Shirley Bassey, Cliff Richard, and Sammy Davis Jr. In 1981, the theatre presented a revival of *The Sound of Music* and later, for almost eighteen years, was home to Andrew Lloyd Webber's musical *The Starlight Express*—extensively redesigned to accommodate a multi-tier roller-skating arena. This huge theatre seats 2,208 people.

785

786

787

BANQUETING HOUSE

1619–22 INIGO JONES AND JOHN WEBB

This was originally planned as part of a new Palace of Whitehall and was the first purely Renaissance building in London. The façade visible from the street is faced in Portland stone and lined by two floors of columns, Ionic at ground level and Corinthian above. The lower of the two floors was used for the king's less formal parties. The upper was a more lavish room for masques and banquets. The roof is almost flat and framed by a balustrade. The superb ceiling painting in the gallery was executed by Rubens as a commission for King Charles I. Years later, in 1649, the same king was executed on a high scaffold set in front of the building. Although the event drew massive crowds, it was a controversial execution. The head executioner refused to wield the ax and his assistant could not be found. Eventually a hooded individual, whose identity was never revealed, executed the sovereign.

LANCASTER HOUSE

1825–40 BENJAMIN WYATT, SIR ROBERT SMIRKE, AND SIR CHARLES BARRY

Lancaster House was originally built for the Frederick Duke of York, the second son of King George III. It has been renamed many times, mutating from York House to Stafford House when it was bought by the Second Marquess of Stafford; and finally to Lancaster House, in 1912, when it came into the hands of Lancastrian soap-maker Sir William Lever. The Bath stone façades have three Corinthian porticoes. Sir Robert Smirke was originally commissioned to build the house, but the duke's brother, George IV, disliked the plans and Benjamin Wyatt replaced him. However, Wyatt died before the building was finished, and so Smirke and Sir Charles Barry returned to complete the work.

QUEEN ELIZABETH II CONFERENCE CENTRE

1979–86 POWELL MOYA AND PARTNERS

Built in white concrete and lead, this seven-storey, purpose-built venue encompasses conference rooms, accommodation for the press, and offices. An in-house team of audio-visual specialists assist with the staging of events. There are also caterers, a built-in wireless network, webcasting, online conference facilities, and all the latest technology to make a conference run smoothly. Up to a thousand delegates can be accommodated, with the Churchill Auditorium having the capacity to seat seven hundred—but many consider that a new London conference centre, able to cope with much greater numbers, is now sorely needed.

788

NOEL COWARD HOUSE

788   SW1

1961–70s DARBOURNE AND DARKE

Probably built on the site of Tothill Fort, this estate was an early attempt to break away from high-rise flats in high-density housing projects. The huge development aimed to house two thousand people, and to provide shops, surgeries, a community hall, pubs, and a library. It was not completed until the late 1970s and was made a conservation area in 1990, with certain elements listed Grade II. The relatively low-rise, redbrick buildings have cantilevered balconies and interesting roof angles. Outside are Mediterranean gardens, classic mixed borders, an exotic tender plant area, a sensory garden with a bubble fountain, and a secret wildlife garden.

789

ST GEORGE'S SQUARE

ST SAVIOUR

789   SW1

**1863–64 THOMAS CUNDY III (THE YOUNGER);
1913–14 VESTRY BY NICHOLSON AND CORLETTE**

This neo-Gothic church is set in the classical square. It has a tall tower and long, slender spire in a carefully crafted, pinkish stone. The church's west front, east window, and spire are orientated to face the square. There are some magnificent stained-glass windows.

790

ST GEORGE'S SQUARE

RIVER-FACING SQUARE

790   SW1

FROM 1850

This long, narrow, elegant square is set beside the Thames with views, from its south side, of the river flowing past towards Battersea—the only river-facing residential square close to central London. Some of the houses have bay-windowed houses and all have regal porches. The Perseverance Pub at the northeast corner dates from 1840, and the square has remained pretty much as it was since it was first built. Bram Stoker lived here (and died here, in 1912, from syphilis). Princess Diana was working in a playgroup nearby when the news of her relationship with Prince Charles hit the newspapers.

PAGE STREET AND VINCENT STREET
CHEQUERBOARD HOUSING

791   SW1

1928–30 SIR EDWIN LUTYENS

These large five- and six-storey modernist blocks of
flats were built first as artisans' apartments. Their large
U-shape wraps around a paved courtyard. A dazzling
chequered effect is created by alternating windows with
silver-toned brick and white Portland cement panels.
The balustrades of the galleries are faced in Portland
cement with brick piers. Decorated classical pavilions
between the blocks house shops. A freestanding, one-
storey pavilion at the south end of each courtyard serves
as an entrance gatehouse, while cast-iron fences and
gates give a view of the courtyard beyond.

791

MILLBANK; FORMERLY VICKERS TOWER
MILLBANK TOWER

792   SW1

1963 RONALD WARD AND PARTNERS

This visible landmark in the skyline has thirty-two storeys
set upon a podium and rising 118 metres (387 feet) high.
It marks the bend of the river between Vauxhall and
Lambeth. Before the 1997 General Election, the Labour
Party took over two floors for its general election
campaign centre, but the £1 million per annum rent
forced them out soon afterwards! The United Nations and
the Central Statistical Office (predecessor of the Office
for National Statistics) have also had offices here.

792

SMITH SQUARE
ST JOHN

793   SW1

1714–28 THOMAS ARCHER

St John was built at the same time as the square under
the Fifty New Churches Act of 1711. The aim of this act
was to halt Nonconformism in the Church of England.
The church is Baroque in style and boasts four towers
crowned with pineapples. On the north and south sides
are pediments and porticos to the entrances, and steps
up to impressive Tuscan columns. In the east and west
walls are large Venetian windows. The building has been
damaged over the years. It was burned down in 1742,
struck by lightning in 1773, and hit by a wartime bomb
in 1941. The church is now used widely as a concert hall
because of its good acoustics.

793

1897 SIDNEY SMITH; 1909 ADDITIONS ROMAINE WALKER;
1937 NEW SCULPTURE GALLERY J. RUSSELL POPE;
1971-79 EXTENSION J. LLEWELYN DAVIES, WEEKS, FORESTIER-WALKER & NOR;
1990-2000 JOHN MILLER AND PARTNERS

This gallery stands on the site of a vast prison. Sir Henry
Tate, the sugar magnate, after whom it is now named,
helped to fund the building and contributed his art
collection. There have been six additions; the central
cupola arrived in 1937. Art dealer Sir Jospeh Duveen paid
for a wing to house the Turner Collection (thousands of
watercolours and oil paintings). Later, his son paid for a
further extension for modern foreign works and helped
to build the long sculpture gallery in 1937. In 1979, the
gallery absorbed the old military hospital opposite. Then
a major reorganisation saw the shift of contemporary art
to the converted power station at Bankside. Tate Britain
explores work from the 1500s onwards, including pieces by
Hogarth, Gainsborough, Constable, the Pre-Raphaelites,
Stubbs, Blake, Turner, Moore, Epstein, and Hockney.

1765 JOHN CRUNDEN

In the 1700s, the London club developed from the
coffeehouse. First known as the Savoir Faire and then
named after its proprietor—Boodles is a pretty building,
designed in the style of Robert Adam by architect John
Crunden, also inspired by the Chippendale school. It has
neat brick façade with a central arched Venetian window,
flanking porches, and a fine interior. It began in 1762 as a
political club and soon became known as the club without
scandal—refined (stodgy even, some claimed). Here,
servants wore black knee-breeches, and coins were boiled
clean before they were handed to members. Archetypal
dandy Beau Brummell was one of its most famous
members and was regarded as London's oracle on matters
of sartorial elegance—it was alleged that he could reduce
a grown man to tears by criticising the cut of his coat!
Other members included Charles Fox and the fifth Duke
of Devonshire.

1991-2005 TERRY FARRELL & PARTNERS

After the high-rise office slabs occupied by the
Department of the Environment were demolished, a
series of distinct buildings rose here, separated by public
spaces, and aiming to integrate rather better into this
historic city site. Farrel's design provides space for three
thousand staff in three conjoined buildings—a central
block with a great, glazed screen on its grand entrance
and two end pavilions. A naturally lit internal 'street'
links them all.

1895-1903 JOHN FRANCIS BENTLEY

The site of the cathedral and adjoining Clergy House and
Archbishop's House was once all marshland—known as
Bulinga Fen. The land was reclaimed by the Benedictine
monks who built Westminster Abbey, and in the Middle
Ages it was used as the site for a market and an annual
fair. Following the Reformation, there was a maze here,
plus a pleasure garden and a ring for bull-baiting, but
much of it was still waste ground until the seventeenth
century. Then, a part of the land was sold by Westminster
Abbey and a prison was built here—later demolished and
replaced by an even bigger prison in 1834. The site was
acquired by the Catholic Church in 1884.

794

795

796

797

798

799

800

NAMED FOR A BISHOP

c. 1850

These semi-detached houses seem to have a much more recent style than their nineteenth-century origins, their louvered window setting and linear stripes unusual features for the period. The road was named after Charles James Bloomfield, who became bishop of London in 1828 and consecrated the church of St Barnabus in 1850.

PANTECHNICON

1830 SETH SMITH

The word *pantechnicon* was coined in English when a busy shop opened up on this site in 1830. The word derives from the Greek, meaning 'pertaining to all the arts or crafts.' The vehicles that moved the furniture to and from the shop were called pantechnicon vans, and the term 'pantech truck' or 'pantech van' is still used in Australia. The shop in Motcomb Street did not last for long, however. The building was turned into a furniture warehouse, and, even though it was constructed to be fireproof, burnt down in 1874—to be resurrected as the current building with its large Doric façade. Today, tailor-made clothing is sold here.

REGENCY HOUSES

1860 SETH SMITH, THOMAS CUBITT

Grosvenor Crescent connects beautiful Belgrave Square with Hyde Park Corner. Here are lovely sweeping curves of elegant terraced housing, those on the north side designed by Seth Smith. On the south side are individual houses created by Thomas Cubitt, and at the Hyde Park end is the Lanesborough Hotel (see page 461). No 1 Grosvenor Crescent is a superb house—a Grade II–listed Regency masterpiece, meticulously restored, with ornate panelling and plasterwork, and a magnificent central staircase. Previous residents in the area have included Britain's war minister, Sidney Herbert, and Florence Nightingale, whom he sent out to the Crimea.

801

802

18 WILTON ROW; FORMERLY THE GUARDSMAN
THE GRENADIER

801   SW1

SLOANE SQUARE
ROYAL COURT THEATRE

802   SW1

1826–7

This was once the unofficial officers' mess for
the Duke of Wellington's Regiment, and he is
said to have played cards here. The tall, late
Georgian cottage is full of military mementoes,
weapons (including sabres, bayonets, and flare
pistols), prints, and even a bearskin busby.
A polished pewter bar-top, an original feature,
is said to be the oldest of its kind. Outside are
stone steps with a sentry box at the bottom,
the remaining stone of the duke's mounting
block, and enormous carriage lanterns still lit
by gas. The pub is reputed to be haunted by
an officer who was flogged to death after
cheating at cards.

1888 WALTER EMDEN;
2000 RECONSTRUCTED HAWORTH TOMPKINS ARCHITECTS

In 1870 a Dissenters' chapel here was
converted into a small theatre. The first major
successes were the dramas of Sir Arthur W.
Pinero, in the 1890s—and then the works of
George Bernard Shaw. The theatre closed in
1932 for twenty years (except for a brief spell
as a cinema). It was bombed in 1940, rebuilt
in 1952, and then the English Stage Company
took it over in 1956. Many radical productions
followed—such as *Look Back in Anger, Chips
with Everything,* and *The Entertainer.* In 1980,
a rehearsal room became the 80-seater
Theatre Upstairs. Today, this is a leading force
in world theatre, producing new, innovative
plays, and described by the *New York Times*
as 'the most important theatre in Europe.'

803

22 EATON TERRACE
THE ANTELOPE

803   SWI

PROBABLY 1820s, PERHAPS EARLIER

Long ago, the Bloody Bridge crossed a swamp and the noxious river Westbourne here, and this was a notorious spot for thieves and highwaymen. When Cubitt and his building gangs moved into the area in the 1820s—to construct some of the finest houses in London in what would become Belgravia—this was an isolated country pub whose main customers were bandits. Some claim that it was purpose-built to serve the builders who created Belgravia—and then the servants who came to work here in the grand houses. It was originally divided into several bars, keeping the servants within their respective household ranks.
Today it has wooden settles, stripped floors, a matchboard ceiling, old panelling, and a rich oak floor.

804

29 PASSMORE STREET
FOX AND HOUNDS

804   SWI

1860

This tiny pub stands at the end of a terrace of artisans' cottages and generally served the local tradesmen—such as glaziers, plumbers, and chimney sweeps. It has a squat timber front and several narrow bars inside. Until 1998, it had the distinction of being London's last beer-only pub (the government once believed spirits to be harmful to the lower classes and restricted the number of full licences) and, until 1980, had only a single (outdoor) toilet. With its cottage-type furniture, old prints, and a very convivial atmosphere, it has long been a favourite with actors and staff from the Royal Court Theatre, which is just around the corner.

805

806

807

808

809

810

MANSIONS AND GRAND HOUSES

805 SWI

1820s THOMAS CUBITT, SIR ROBERT SMIRKE AND OTHERS

This was a focal point of Cubitt's vast development for Earl Grosvenor in the 1820s. The magnificent houses include elegant Sleaford House and several embassies. In the early 1900s, the buildings were occupied mainly by private tenants and their staff; coachmen and grooms lived in the mews houses. By the 1990s, most of the tenants were companies or organisations. Lady Sassoon lived here from 1929–42 and kept an open house for the troops during World War II, while part of the property was a supply depot for the Red Cross. The square's private garden has been restored to the 1867 layout with plane trees, roses, pergolas, wisteria, and many statues.

TREE-LINED SQUARE

806 SWI

1836; 1841; LEWIS CUBITT; 1931 MESSRS JOSEPH

This is a pretty, tree-lined square surrounded by old apartment buildings and embassies, including the Pakistan High Commission. Some of the houses have sweet balconies and delicate tympanums. Redbrick blocks of flats were built the west side in 1931. There have been several reports in the square of a white-haired old lady in a bath chair, who sits by the kerb and pulls faces at people. She is reputedly the ghost of an old woman whose daughter would wheel her out into the street on sunny days to watch the world go by. A stroke had left her unable to speak, so when she wanted to return inside, she would pull faces at passers-by until one of them rang the front door bell for her.

BELGRAVIA HOUSES

807 SWI

1827 W. H. SETH-SMITH AND THOMAS CUBITT

Built in 1827, the crescent makes a grand entrance to the surrounding Grosvenor estate. It was named after the owner of the land, the first Marquess of Westminster. The houses on the south side of the crescent are presented in typical Belgravia style, with stuccoed frontages and giant pilasters. The north side of the crescent was refaced with stone during the early 1900s. Notable buildings include the High Commission of the Republic of Singapore (number 2), the Embassy of the Republic of Argentina (number 9), and the Luxembourg Embassy (number 27). It has also been home to a large number of British Members of Parliament over the years.

GREEK REVIVAL FLATS

808 SWI

1830 J. P. GANDY-DEERING

Now residential flats, the former Literary Institute is in Greek Doric style, with its stuccoed frontage, columns, and portico looking like a veritable miniature temple set between taller buildings. Indeed, its designer, J. P. Gandy-Deering, was one of the few architects to promote Greek Revival style within this Mayfair estate area. In the sixteenth and seventeenth centuries, the manor of Ebury (from which the name Ebury Street derives) was leased by the monarchy to servants or favourites. The composer Wolfgang Amadeus Mozart wrote his *First Symphony* at nearby 180 Ebury Street.

ROYAL MEWS

809 SWI

1760 AND 1820 WILLIAM CHAMBERS

The Royal Mews (*mews* means 'stabling with living quarters') is home to the royal horses, plus carriages such as the Gold State Coach, and cars—eight state limousines, five Rolls-Royces (with no number plates), and three Daimlers. The first royal to travel in a motorcar was Edward VII, when he was still heir-apparent. A giant entrance archway is flanked by Roman columns and overlooked by a clock tower. The Riding House inside was built in the 1760s, sixty years earlier than the mews itself. It was decorated at the beginning of the nineteenth century with the acanthus frieze and a pediment, *Hercules Capturing the Thracian Horses*.

MARY SHELLEY'S HOUSE

810 SWI

1835

This long slender square has many elegant houses with cobbled mews set behind them. Novelist, biographer, and poet Mary Shelley (1797-1851) lived here from 1846–51 at number 24. Mary had her first poem published at the age of ten. When she was sixteen, she ran away to France and Switzerland with the poet Percy Shelley; they were married in 1816. It was Lord Byron who set Mary the challenge to write a good ghost story when she was eighteen. Mary was aged twenty-one when her story *Frankenstein; or The Modern Prometheus* was published.

VICTORIA COACH STATION
811   SW1

1932 WALLIS GIBERT AND PARTNERS

This transport terminal is in Art Deco style, its central tower
clearly named in bold capitals. It covers some 12,000 square
metres (three acres) and was opened in the 1930s for London
Coastal Coaches Limited—by 1968, a subsidiary of the National
Bus Company. Its ownership passed to Transport for London in
2000. It has separate arrivals and departures terminals, plus the
usual food outlets, shops, luggage storage facilities, and ticket
offices, and has recently been refurbished.

55 SLOANE STREET
DANISH EMBASSY
812   SW1

1977 ARNE JACOBSEN, DISSING AND WEITLING

The top two floors of these offices and flats are set behind a
dark brown curtain wall; the bottom two are split into five even
window bays and covered by ochre-coloured aluminium panels.
Jacobsen is Denmark's best-known international architect, but
the embassy is his sole piece of work in London. The architect
died in 1971 before its completion. Luckily, however, his detailed
designs could be followed by Dissing and Weitling to finish the
building as planned. Jacobsen's architecture can be seen
elsewhere in England—for instance, at St Catherine's College
in Oxford. He was also known for furniture design.

6 BELGRAVIA MEWS WEST
STAR TAVERN
813   SW1

EARLY 1800S

Set at the end of a quiet cobbled mews off Belgrave Square,
this late-Georgian pub once served the imbibing needs of
local tradesman and the domestic staff of many great houses
hereabouts. The pub was then divided into many rooms, each used
by a specific rank of those working 'below stairs.' Now it is big and
open, with two fireplaces in the largest room, scrubbed pine tables,
and comfortable benches. It has a lovely upstairs bar and possibly
the smallest gentlemen's toilets in London! During the 1960s,
this pub was the haunt of rich gangsters, aristocrats, and other
glitterati. Here pop stars, models, actors, and the Great Train
robbers drank—the robbery could well have been planned here.

811

812

813

814

87-135 BROMPTON ROAD
HARRODS
814 SW1

1849; 1889; 1901-05 STEVENS AND MUNT

In 1834, Henry Charles Harrod was a wholesale tea merchant. This famous store developed from a small Knightsbridge grocer's shop he bought in 1849. In 1883, the store burned down, but the current Mr Harrod still managed to dispatch all his Christmas orders. By 1889, the new store was bought for £120,000. When the first escalator in London was installed in 1898, an assistant stood had sal-volatile and brandy ready for nervous customers. It is now the largest store in Europe, covering 1.8 hectares (4.5 acres), with 5.5 hectares (13.5 acres) of floors and some five thousand staff. The superb food halls have mosaic friezes and tiles depicting hunting scenes. Its ornate, red, terracotta-tiled exterior looks spectacular when illuminated at Christmas with 11,500 lights. Today, 'Everything for Everyone Everywhere' Harrods is rated the third most popular London attraction for overseas visitors and, at peak times, has up to 300,000 customers each day. The lifts travel 50,000 miles a year. The present owner is Egyptian tycoon Mohamed Al-Fayed, who bought the store in 1985 for £615 million.

815

WILTON PLACE
ST PAUL'S CHURCH
815 SW1

1840-43 THOMAS CUNDY III

St Paul's parish was founded in 1843 as the first developments were being made in Belgravia, which is part of the Grosvenor Estate. A beautiful Grade II–listed Victorian building, the church was built from brick in perpendicular style. An impressive entrance has been created at the base of the castellated western tower. The church is split into three galleries, supported by cast-iron columns, with the exposed woodwork of the roof construction an attractive feature.

1935-38 W. CRABTREE WITH SLATER, MOBERLY, AND C. H. REILLY

This huge, upmarket department store gently curves around the corner. Its structure includes an excellent example of an early glass curtain wall. The glazing bars create a neat pattern and the top floor is set back, giving the impression of an ocean liner. Inside are triple-height shopping areas and a glazed spiral staircase. In 1864, a young Welshman, Peter Jones, arrived in London and, after learning his trade at a draper's, soon opened his first shop in Hackney, and moved to the Sloane Square site in 1877. He was one of the first to install electric lighting in a large store. In 2000, over £100 million was set aside for a renovation, completed by June 2004.

SLOANE STREET

HOLY TRINITY

817   SWI

1888-90 JOHN DANDO SEDDING

Poet Laureate Sir John Betjeman once described this church as the 'Cathedral of the Arts and Crafts Movement.' It has beautiful decoration in Italian and Gothic styles, stained glass by Morris and Company (including the work of Edward Burne-Jones), altar rails, a grille, and railings outside by Henry Wilson, woodwork by Harry Bates—and other contributions by Bainbridge Reynolds, Nelson Dawson, and F. Pomeroy. The use of different Italian marbles shows a Ruskin influence. The architect believed that a church should be 'wrought and painted over with everything that has life and beauty—in frank and fearless naturalism.'

4 CADOGAN SQUARE

REDBRICK HOUSE

818   SWI

1879 GEORGE EDMUND STREET

Cadogan Square was one of the first nineteenth-century developments to take on brick rather than stucco. Most of its buildings are designed in Queen Anne style, with the exception of number 4. Street was famous for his interest in Gothic architecture, and this house is a grand example. The redbrick building sits in the northeast corner, and boasts an impressive asymmetrical porch. Originally, it was designed for the daughters of the Bishop of Gloucestershire (James Henry Monk), for whom Street had worked on other earlier projects.

EATON SQUARE

DESIRABLE HOUSES

819   SWI

1826-53 THOMAS CUBITT

Here generously proportioned residential homes occupy classically designed terraces. Most are three bays wide and four or five storeys high, with an attic, basement, and a mews house set to the rear. The majority are faced with white stucco, with a few faced by brick. The square was built by the Grosvenor family and named after Eaton Hall, the Grosvenors' country house in Cheshire. It was the formal start to the route from St James's Palace to Hampton Court. Famous residents have included British Prime Minister Neville Chamberlain, businessman George Soros, actress Vivien Leigh, and the 1980s James Bond, Roger Moore.

EATON SQUARE

CHURCH OF ST PETER

820   SWI

1824-27 HENRY HAKEWILL

Set in a residential garden square in London's exclusive Belgravia district, the Church of St Peter stands at the northeast corner here and on the corner of Hobart Place. Designed in classical Greek Revival style, it boasts an impressive six-columned Ionic portico and a clock tower. Inside, the chancel was added and the nave enlarged between 1872 and 1875. Despite being gutted by fire in the 1980s, the chuch thrives today—as does its associated school.

68 CADOGAN SQUARE

AN ELEGANT PORCH

821   SWI

1887 R. NORMAN SHAW

One of three houses by R. Norman Shaw in the southwest corner of the square, this exhibits Shaw's favourite redbrick, gables, windows with leaded lights and white painted sashes. The porch is a very impressive, ornate affair and there are pretty details on the railings. Author Arnold Bennett lived nearby, at number 75, in 1924.

816

817

818

819

820

821

822

823

824

LANESBOROUGH HOTEL

822   SWI

1827-29 WILLIAM WILKINS

Lanesborough House was built on the site in 1719 by James Lane, Second Viscount Lanesborough. A three-storey plain brick building, at that time on the edge of countryside, it was taken over by St. George's Hospital in the 1730s. A rustic cottage close by was occupied by Huggitt, the cow-keeper, who supplied the hospital with milk. By the 1820s, there was demand for more accommodation, and a new structure was designed by William Wilkins — influenced by classical eighteenth-century architecture. The façade looking over Hyde Park Corner is Greek stuccoed, with a central porch of square columns and two side wings. The top floor is a later addition. Henry Gray, who penned the famous *Anatomy* (1858), worked here. The hospital left here in 1980, moving to Tooting in South London, and the building was redeveloped into the Lanesborough Hotel.

66 KNIGHTSBRIDGE; FORMERLY HYDE PARK COURT

MANDARIN ORIENTAL HYDE PARK

823   SWI

1889; 1999-2000 RENOVATED

This extravagant exterior resembles Harrods, with grand turreted redbrick and stone. Two huge, bronze Oriental dogs guard the entrance and mark its present Far Eastern ownership. Inside, everything is opulence and marble. This is a good spot from which to watch the royal horses riding off to change the guard at Buckingham Palace. Queen Elizabeth and Princess Margaret learned to dance in the ballroom, Prince Philip brought his children here for tea, and Queen Mary often visited. Queen Victoria, however, objected to its being referred to as a gentlemen's residence on her royal land, and insisted on the Hyde Park gate being locked — now opened only with royal permission when royalty or heads of state arrive. Its restaurant — frequented by celebrities such as Madonna, and where Baroness Thatcher held her eightieth birthday party — is entered via a crystal-like corridor lined with glass shelves and over five thousand bottles of wine.

NUMBER ONE LONDON, HYDE PARK CORNER

APSLEY HOUSE AND WELLINGTON MUSEUM

824   SWI

1771-78; 1828-29 ROBERT ADAM BENJAMIN AND PHILIP WYATT

Sitting on the southeast corner of Hyde Park, Apsley House was originally built by Robert Adam for Baron Apsley. However, its most famous resident moved into the property fifty years later — Sir Arthur Wellesley, the First Duke of Wellington. It was at this time, in the 1820s, that the property took on its neo-classical look. Benjamin and Philip Wyatt enlarged the original brick building with Bath stone facing, an extension to the western side, and a Corinthian portico. It was known as Number One London — the first property inside London's western tollgate. The 'Iron Duke' is best known for his 1815 battle victory against Napoleon Bonaparte at Waterloo, although he served as a politician as well as a soldier. The building opened as the Wellington Museum in 1952.

GROSVENOR HOTEL

825   SW1

1860 J. T. KNOWLES; 1892 AND 1899 REFURBISHED

One of the best examples of Victorian London architecture, this is also one of the first examples of 'Second Empire' style and is the only remaining building from the opening of the first Brighton line station in 1861. The first five storeys are cut from brick and Bath stone. It is crowned with two further storeys, inserted into a dormered roof with French pavilions at either end. Medallion portraits include images of Queen Victoria and her husband Prince Albert, set between the arched windows. The hotel was refurbished, as part of a larger reconstruction of the station—and a further annexe opened in 1907.

ST BARNABUS: SCHOOL AND HOUSE

826   SW1

1846–50 WILLIAM BUTTERFIELD

The small Gothic, Anglo-Catholic church in Kentish ragstone was designed by Thomas Cundy and was the first London church to incorporate the ideas of the Oxford Movement, thus playing its part in the build-up to the anti-papal riots of 1850. Butterfield's rather fine clergy house and school has pointed windows, turrets, and tall chimneys. There seem to be sharp triangles and angles, quoins, and different textures everywhere.

ONCE-GRAND HOUSES

827   SW1

1835 THOMAS CUBITT

Today, many of these once-opulent stuccoed houses have been turned into flats or bed-and-breakfast accommodation, and their grander past is a dim memory. Here, a low-lying swamp had been drained in the early 1600s and turned into a three-acre square by Thomas Cubitt—now replanted with shrubs, climbers, and roses—named after the Duke of Westminster's estate at Eccleston, in Cheshire. Matthew Arnold occupied number 3 in 1877. Later, Winston Churchill lived at number 33, where his son Randolph was born. This house was the headquarters of the Labour Party during the 1926 General Strike.

DOLPHIN SQUARE

828   SW1

1937 GORDON JEEVES

This large, redbrick, neo-Georgian building comprises 1,236 flats arranged around a central garden (with tennis courts, squash courts, and a Modern-style restaurant). There is a swimming pool and the grounds cover over seven acres (3 hectares). This is close to the centre of Westminster, and many of the apartments are owned by Members of Parliament. When it was built, it was the largest residential block in Europe and, during World War II, became the headquarters of de Gaulle's Free French Army.

ST JAMES-THE-LESS PARISH HALL AND SCHOOL

829   SW1

1858–61 GEORGE EDMUND STREET

This superb Victorian Gothic complex incorporates a church, hall, and infant school. Its pretty, detached tower with sharp pinnacles marks the Vauxhall Bridge Road entrance and is surrounded by railings decorated with iron arum lilies. It was built when the area was very poor, and *The Illustrated London News* described it as 'a lily among weeds.' All the buildings are in redbrick, with black brick detailing. It has generous granite columns inside and three wide bays decorated with black brick, and red and yellow wall tiles. G. F. Watts was responsible for the mural fresco placed above the chancel arch.

VICTORIAN TOWNHOUSES

830   SW1

c. 1850

Here are substantial houses in several spacious streets that make up a triangle of buildings. Today, the grand Victorian townhouses are mixed with 1970s council housing. Cambridge Street (named after the Duke of Cambridge) was home to artist Aubrey Beardsley, who lived at number 114 from 1893–95. Designer Laura Ashley lived at 83, and author Barbara Pym at 108. Post-war Pimlico was the setting of the story of the Ealing comedy film *Passport to Pimlico*, as well as Paul Dorval's detective series *The Pimlico Boys*.

825

826

827

828

829

830

831

832

833

PIMLICO SCHOOL

831   SW1

1966–70 GLC ARCHITECTS DEPARTMENT (DESIGNED BY SIR HUBERT
BENNETT AND MICHAEL POWELL WITH C. A. BELCHER AND F. HALLOWES)

This four-storey comprehensive school is a shining
example of 1960s new concepts for schools. It has a long
internal 'street' and a dramatic glazed exterior with many
interesting angles. The building won a RIBA award in
1972. Sir Hubert Bennett has created many school and
college buildings and other large-scale projects.

GROSVENOR ROAD, LUPUS STREET, AND CLAVERTON STREET

CHURCHILL GARDENS ESTATE

832   SW1

1946–62 POWELL AND MOYA

This enormous, thirty-acre housing estate was an
important post-war development. While some experts
have praised it as an exemplary estate—and it was an
award-winning scheme of apartments and maisonettes—
it remains rather bleak looking. It aimed to house 6,500
people, and the rooms were heated with hot waste water
piped under the Thames from Battersea Power Station
opposite. The complex includes a covered shopping
centre, a restaurant, four public houses, and an
underground car-park.

CHELSEA BRIDGE ROAD

CHELSEA BARRACKS

833   SW1

1960–62 TRIPE AND WAKEHAM

This long neat red-and-white-chequered structure has
been home to the Queens Guard, the ceremonial troops
of the Household Division, for some forty years or so. It
has served as offices and quarters for 1,284 people, and
its parade ground bustled with activity. Now the army
and all their trucks have moved to Woolwich. The five-
hectare (fourteen-and-a-half-acre) site is up for sale in
2007/2008 by the Ministry of Defence, with a price tag
of £150–£250 million.

834

GREYCOAT PLACE

GREYCOAT SCHOOL (HOSPITAL SCHOOL)

834   SW1

1701

Greycoat School was founded in 1695 as a school for forty boys and forty girls from poor backgrounds. It was set up by eight parishioners of St Margaret's, each investing 12/6 (65 pence). Not only did pupils receive an education, they were also found work when they left. They wore grey clothing, as the school's name indicates, and wooden statues in the grounds depict two of these young scholars. Originally the site of a seventeenth-century workhouse, the building was converted into accommodation for the pupils. The façade is the original, and, beyond the front door, there are still workhouse flagstones. There is also an old staircase showing traces of bomb damage from the war, and around the Great Hall are hung portraits of the school's benefactors.

835

VICTORIA STREET

VICTORIA STATION

835   SW1

1862 J. FOWLER; 1898–1908 PARTIALLY REBUILT; 1920s FRONTAGE ALFRED BLOOMFIELD

Victoria Station was built in two parts. The western side opened in 1862, comprising six platforms, ten tracks, and the vast Grosvenor Hotel. Another nine-track, wooden-fronted building operated next door. Both were occupied by different companies, and, although there was a partial rebuild at the beginning of the 1900s, it was only in 1924 that both buildings united. To the east, J. Fowler's building houses platforms one to eight. It is made up of two vaulted iron-and-glass structures, plus a segmental arched roof. The frontage is of Edwardian design with baroque elements. For the 1910 funeral of King Edward VII, an emperor and empress, seven kings, more than twenty princes, and five archdukes arrived at this station. Between 1914 and 18, the station witnessed the mass transport of troops to France.

836

837

GROSVENOR GARDENS

ELEGANT APARTMENTS AND OFFICES

836   SWI

BUCKINGHAM PALACE ROAD;
FORMERLY BRITISH AIRWAYS TERMINAL

NATIONAL AUDIT OFFICE

837   SWI

1870 THOMAS CUNDY III

Grosvenor Gardens and Grosvenor Place extend Victoria Street north west to Hyde Park Corner. The gardens are made up of two triangular sections, and the surrounding terraces are strongly influenced by French Renaissance style. These terraces used to be made up of apartment buildings and ground-level restaurants. In the main, however, the buildings have now been taken over by businesses and are being used as offices. A statue of General Foch (who lived at number 32 from 1915–30) is located in the southern garden.

1939 A. LAKEMAN

This stone building strove to represent airlines and a flying theme with a sharp 'nose' at the peak of the tall tower and its two wide, outstretched wings. It has a dominant clock at the top and a splendid sculpture of a pair of winged figures, by E. R. Broadbent, set above the entrance. The building was used by both BOAC and British Airways but now houses the National Audit Office.

CLORE GALLERY

838

SWI

1979-85 STIRLING AND WILFORD

This gallery is part of the Tate Gallery and is set at its east flank with a rather clever, glazed, 'house-shaped' entrance. Inside, as in other museums by these architects, a promenade leads to the galleries and, here, the main eight top-lit galleries maximise the natural light while meeting all the new conservation demands. It opened in 1987 and contains some three hundred oil paintings and about 19,000 watercolours and drawings by J. M. W. Turner.

THE LAWRENCE HALL
(THE ROYAL HORTICULTURAL SOCIETY)

839

SWI

1923-28 EASTON AND ROBERTSON

This hall was renamed the Lawrence Hall in the 1990s. Regular exhibitions and flower shows are held here — in a building that was designed in the most modern style of its time. A stone on the corner marks the architects and their RIBA (Royal Institute of British Architects) award, acknowledging the first use of curved reinforced concrete in England in its interior. Stepped-back glazing is set between these parabolic concrete arches. The society was founded in 1804 by a group of enthusiastic gardeners and botanists, brought together by John Wedgwood (eldest son of the famous potter); Prince Albert was their president in 1858.

PULLMAN COURT

840

SW2

1935 FREDERICK GIBBERD

The manufacturing base of the nineteenth century and the industrial revolution left a legacy of poor housing in overcrowded, polluted cities — a balance which many twentieth-century architects sought to redress. As the Modern Movement developed, reinforced concrete and steel were explored as mediums in their own right. In this very lively, early Modern English design, the aim was to make a light building with clean lines. Three- and seven-storey blocks of flats are set around a green with mature trees. This was a pioneering design, and one that proved highly successful. Gibberd believed that, by using flat roofs as terraces for gardens, it was possible to maximise the amount of open space available to residents; large communal parks would replace small, individual gardens. Here the structure is of reinforced concrete throughout. Exterior walls have a thick cork lining for thermal insulation.

838

839

840

841

842

843

844

845

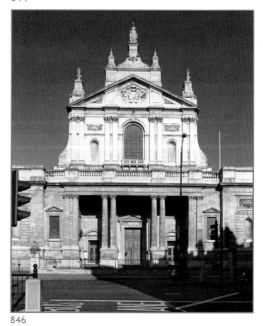

846

BRIXTON HILL
BRIXTON TOWN HALL
841   SW2

1908 SEPTIMUS WARWICK AND H. A. HALL

This Edwardian Baroque inspired design has a very tall
tower (with a pretty four-sided clock and pinnacles) rising
high above its corner site. The building was created by
two talented young architects, Septimus Warwick and
Herbert Hall, who submitted their winning design in the
shape of an A. It was opened by the Prince (later George V)
and Princess of Wales in 1908. In 1935–38, an assembly
hall was added and the building was raised by one storey.

BRIXTON HILL
ST MATTHEW
842   SW2

1822 CHARLES F. PORDEN

This Grade II–church, an enormous Victorian building,
is a 'Waterloo church.' Four were raised in the 1820s in
Lambeth. Some claim this was to celebrate the victory
over Napoleon a few years earlier but they were actually a
result of the Million Pound Act, which dedicated this vast
sum to building churches in expanding cities. It has a plain
but impressive Doric portico at the west end and a very
fine three-stage tower and steeple at the east end.
Converted in the 1970s and '80s, today much of the
interior has been cleared to serve as a community centre
as well as a place of worship. In 2002, St Matthew's
merged with the neighbouring parish of St Jude.

12 HANS ROAD
MIXED MOTIFS
843   SW3

1894 ARTHUR MACKMURDO

Architect Mackmurdo was inspired by many renowned
artists and architects (including William Blake and
Christopher Wren) and was able to draw upon these
influences in the creation of his buildings. He attended
drawing classes by John Ruskin and visited Italy in his
company. Number 12 displays a lively mixture of Queen
Anne–style motifs, plus other interesting inspirations
such as the oriel windows, derived from R. Norman Shaw.
Mackmurdo helped to set up of the Society for the
Protection of Ancient Buildings, where he met and was
inspired by yet another artist, William Morris.

95-100 CHEYNE WALK
LINDSEY HOUSE
844   SW3

c. 1674 REBUILT BY LUTYENS

This large country residence was built on the site of
Sir Thomas More's garden and has one of the finest
seventeenth-century exteriors in London—the only
surviving house of its date and scale in Chelsea. Its name
derives from Robert, the third Earl of Lindsey, who
purchased the property in the 1660s. In 1775, the three-
storey eleven-bay house was divided into five separate
dwellings. The engineers, Sir Marc Isambard Kingdom
Brunel and his famous son, Isambard Kingdom, lived here.
Artist James Whistler occupied number 96 from 1866–79;
he painted the renowned portrait of his mother here.

3-6 CHEYNE WALK
AUTHORS, DOCTOR, AND MISER
845   SW3

1708

The road derives its name from the Cheyne family—lords
of the manor of Chelsea from 1660–1712 when this was a
quiet riverside village. Many houses have fine gardens,
walls, and gates, with decorated gateposts and ironwork.
Numbers 3–6 have early Georgian features from about
1717. Painter William Dyce lived here and also novelist
George Eliot (then Mrs. Cross) from 1819–80. Number 5
was occupied by miser, John Camden Nield, who left his
fortune to Queen Victoria. Number 6, built by Sir John
Danvers in about 1718, was home to a Dr Domincetti
from 1765–82; he introduced medicated baths and
treated thousands of patients here.

BROMPTON ROAD
LONDON ORATORY
846   SW3

1880-93 HERBERT GRIBBLE; HOUSE BY J. J. SCOLES

This was the first large new Roman Catholic Church to
be built in London after the Reformation, its architect
and design chosen through a competition. The building is
vast. It has a fine concrete dome and vaulted side chapels.
There are Rex Whistler paintings of Sir Thomas More and
John Fisher, and many mosaics, and wood and stone
carvings. The glorious St Winifred's Chapel has a
magnificent high altar and Italian altarpiece inlaid
with precious stones, and marble statues of the apostles
from Siena cathedral. In 1892, the funeral of Cardinal
Manning was held here. Chevalliaud's marble statue
of Cardinal Newman was erected outside in 1896.

847

1891–94 C. F. A. VOYSEY

What had been respectable small houses degenerated into slums and, by the 1870s, Mr Harrod thought them dirty and dangerous; as his store prospered, the slums were gradually swept away. The houses on the west side were rebuilt in a far grander style and the street name was changed from Queen Street (after George III's Queen Charlotte) to Hans Road in 1886. Numbers 14–16 were built by Charles Voysey in 1891. With their clean lines of grouped windows and smooth, low porches, they represent some of his earliest works in London. The houses on the east side were demolished as Harrods was gradually extended between 1902 and 1911.

848

1890s C. R. ASHBEE

Only two houses remain of the eight that Arts and Crafts enthusiast Charles Robert Ashbee designed for Cheyne Walk. Number 39 was built as a speculative venture. Number 38, however, set behind street railings of black ironwork with ornamental gold balls, incorporated a studio for artist C. L. Christran. This was set in the top two storeys, behind the gabled façade with a pretty porthole window with an octagonal pattern. The lower floors have tall, narrow windows.

849

1692–4

William III once dreamed of a triumphal route between the Wren's Royal Hospital and Kensington Palace. Royal Avenue never quite achieved this vision but was planted with four rows of plane trees and connected the hospital to King's Road. Today the wide, leafy avenue is lined by nineteenth-century terraces and was the backdrop to the fictional home of James Bond. Here there are neat, brick facades on the upper storeys, with delicate wrought-iron balconies, pretty arched windows on the ground floor, and front railings with steps down the basement levels.

15-16 CHEYNE WALK
QUEEN'S HOUSE

850   SW3

1717-19 JOHN WIT AND RICHARD CHAPMAN

Numbers 15–16 are wonderful early Georgian houses. The largest in the terrace is Queen's (or Tudor) House and this is well preserved, with ornate ironwork at the entrance court. The initials on the beautiful iron gate are those of Richard Chapman, the builder. There is a large 1800s bay window in the centre bay. A. C. Swinburne and George Meredith lived here, as did the founder member of the Pre-Raphaelite Brotherhood, Dante Gabriel Rossetti—who kept a small zoo, including many noisy peacocks (since when leases for this building exclude the keeping of these birds). The house became a meeting place for poets and artists from 1871–81.

850

ROYAL HOSPITAL ROAD
ROYAL HOSPITAL

851   SW3

1681-91 SIR CHRISTOPHER WREN, NICHOLAS HAWKSMOOR, JOHN VANBRUGH

This was founded as a home for army veterans by Charles II, and James II. Built around three courtyards, it is still home to some four hundred ex-servicemen, the Chelsea Pensioners, and hosts the annual Chelsea Flower Show in the gardens. Inspired by Louis XIV's Hôtel des Invalides, the courts are open to face the river. Apart from minor alterations and the addition of stables, the building is largely unchanged. Tall, arched windows in the brick façades denote the most important rooms within—a central saloon, flanked by a gaunt hall and a grand chapel. In 1852, the Duke of Wellington lay in state here; two people died in the crush to file past his coffin.

851

35 GLEBE PLACE
CHELSEA HOUSE

852   SW3

C. 1869 PHILIP WEBB

This area was named after the glebe lands that belonged to Chelsea rectory. A small chapel was erected on the east side in about 1685 for the many immigrant Huguenots who settled in Chelsea then. In the 1800s, Glebe Place was (and still is) a veritable artists' colony, and there are many artist's studios here, including that of Charles Rennie Mackintosh at number 48. Number 35, by Philip Webb, is designed in Queen Anne domestic style, but was built in redbrick instead of the usual light or golden Georgian stock.

852

853

854

7–12 CHEYNE WALK	50 GLEBE PLACE
HOUSES BY THE RIVER	**GOTHIC HOUSE**
853	SW3	854	SW3

c. 1880s

Here, seeming to rise in layers from the river, can be found some three centuries of the finest domestic eighteenth-century architecture. Over the centuries, the houses were separated from the river by a shared garden frontage and a pavement planted with plane trees. Here were the homes of many famous artists, politicians, and other notables. Numbers 7–12 are lovely 1880s houses, with number 9 especially noteworthy. Number 10 was once the home of David Lloyd George from 1924–25 and, later, of Archbishop Lord Davison.

This pink Gothic extravaganza has a plethora of statues, balconies, and decorative wrought ironwork. There are chimneys in 'barley-sugar twist' style, a weather vane, an animal's head carved over the arched entrance—while a large oval decoration dominates the one surface that is otherwise featureless. Number 48, nearby, was Charles Rennie Mackintosh's studio house during the final years of his life, and a brickwork cottage (now number 51) is said to have been (but probably wasn't) a hunting lodge of King Henry VIII.

855

856

FULHAM ROAD

MICHELIN BUILDING

855   SW3

1905–11 FRANÇOIS ESPINASSE;
1984–88 REBUILDING AND RESTORATION BY CONRAN ROCHE YRM

This vivacious, white faience building was the Michelin's first permanent British headquarters. It is an exhilarating mix of Art Nouveau and Art Deco designs with tyres as a major decoration feature. Motorists used to have tyres speedily changed in fitting bays at the front of the building. A series of tile panels, on the ground floor and inside, explore motoring history and early racing cars. In the 1980s, the illuminated corner turrets (designed as a tyre stack) were restored, more office floors were added, and the Conran shop arrived (plus a new restaurant and bar)—named Bibendum, after the Michelin man. Inside, a brilliant mosaic depicts Bibendum raising a glass of nuts and bolts. Etchings of the streets of Paris on some of the first-floor windows reflect the Michelin mapping role.

TITE STREET

ARTIST'S HOUSES

856   SW3

1878–79 EDWARD WILLIAM GODWIN

This street was named after the Sir Wiliam Tite, architect and chairman of the Metropolitan Board of Works, who censored many of Godwin's designs and demanded ornamental mouldings before granting a building licence. The many artists who lived here included Whistler at number 35, his White House incorporated a teaching studio. Several of his friends followed him to Tite Street. In 1878, Godwin designed Chelsea Lodge for the Hon. Archibald Stuart-Wortley—sold, in 1879, to the Hon. Slingsby Bethell, amateur painter, and then to Edwin Abbey, RA. Keats House, at number 44, was home to Frank Miles and Oscar Wilde. Architect Godwin had an affair with the renowned actress Ellen Terry, and later married a young designer, Beatrice Birnie Philip; after Godwin's death, she married Whistler in 1888.

1930s HOUSE

857   SW3

1936 WALTER GROPIUS AND EDWIN MAXWELL FRY

The southern section of this street was once called Church Lane and its northern length was called the Road to the Cross Tree. Number 66 is 1930s architecture *par excellence*, designed by two leaders of modern functional architecture. After World War I, Gropius was made director of the Weimar School of Art, reorganizing it as the Bauhaus. Driven from Germany by the Nazi regime, he practised in London with Maxwell Fry and then went to America, where he headed the school of architecture at Harvard until 1952. Maxwell Fry was a Modernist architect in pre-war Britain who also pioneered the Modernist movement in the Third World.

10-34 CHEYNE ROW

THOMAS CARLYLE AND OTHERS

858   SW3

FROM 1708

Historian and philosopher Thomas Carlyle lived in number 24, where he and his wife entertained Tennyson, Ruskin, Darwin, Dickens, George Eliot, Browning, Thackeray, and Chopin—who played the piano in the parlour. This is now a museum, furnished with Victorian pieces and filled with Carlyle's books and pictures. Here Carlyle wrote *The French Revolution*, the work that made his name. Outside is a restored walled Victorian garden. Oscar Wilde lived just round the corner, potter William de Morgan lived at number 34 and had a warehouse and showroom nearby. A plaque at number 10 commemorates Margaret Damer Dawson, pioneer of women in the police force.

OFF FULHAM ROAD

SYDNEY CLOSE

859   SW3

c. 1850 BUILT BY SMITH CHARITIES

Sydney Place is named after one of the first Smith's Charities trustees. Here are fifteen mews studios built by Henry Smith, a local landowner, originally meant for the artists involved in the 1851 Great Exhibition. The studios are orientated so that they all receive good, stable, north light. The artist John Sargent was a resident of number 12, and it is said that Baroness Orczy wrote *The Scarlet Pimpernel* while living at number 10.

19-26 CHEYNE WALK

GEORGIAN TERRACE

860   SW3

1759-65

Numbers 19–26 form a fairly complete terrace of Georgian houses, built in the early 1760s on the site of a Tudor manor house built for Henry VIII (this had been demolished in 1753). It stood near the corner of Cheyne Walk and Oakley Street, and traces of it still remain in the basements of houses here, some of which are Grade II listed. Number 20 has a pretty wrought-iron entrance gate incorporating a lantern.

17 CHELSEA EMBANKMENT

SWAN HOUSE

861   SW3

1876 R. NORMAN SHAW

This stunning, original, graceful house on the Chelsea Embankment is considered by some to be the finest Queen Anne–revival domestic building in London. A pair of swans is depicted at the entrance. It has three gorgeous oriel windows at first-floor level and three, tall, narrow, oriel ones, alternating with slender windows, on the second floor. Above are smaller, matching windows and three dormers. Everything is beautifully proportioned. Richard Norman Shaw was one of the most influential British architects from the 1870s to the 1900s and became a member of the Royal Academy in 1877.

25 CADOGAN GARDENS

STUDIO HOUSE

862   SW3

1893-94 A. H. MACKMURDO

This studio house is in an Anglo-Dutch style and was designed for Mortimer Menpes—an artist and etcher who was a friend of Whistler's. It has wonderful double-height oriel windows and a Japanese-style interior with carved panelling made in Japan by over seventy craftsmen, under the supervision of Menpes. Doors, windows, carved friezes, and ceiling panels were packed in two hundred cases and shipped to London. Some of the lovely wooden panels resemble Japanese temples and the decor for each room was based upon a different flower.

857

858

859

860

861

862

863

864

865

866

BRAM STOKER'S HOUSE

863   SW3

1800s JOHN TOOMBS

The street's present name probably derived from Upton St Leonards in Gloucestershire, which was near to where builder John Tooms was born. This street was once called Green's Row after its earlier builder, a Westminster brewer. There are several pleasing eighteenth-century Georgian houses, some of which were rebuilt by Toombs, who raised some new houses here, too. A blue plaque at number 18 commemorates Bram Stoker, the author of *Dracula*, who lived here from 1896–1906. Actor Laurence Olivier lived at number 7 here.

KING'S HEAD AND EIGHT BELLS

864   SW3

ESTABLISHED 1580

Dwarfed by Carlyle Mansions (where lived writers Henry James, T. S. Eliot, and Ian Fleming) this comfortable early Victorian pub used to be on the riverfront with its own landing, called Feather Stairs—until the embankment and busy main road arrived. Artist J. M. W. Turner discovered the pub and introduced it to fellow artists Whistler and Augustus John (who was having an affair with Ian Fleming's mother). Welsh author and poet Dylan Thomas also visited often. There are some lovely pieces of Victorian glasswork.

COOPERS ARMS

865   SW3

1846; REBUILT 1874

The first mention of this Chelsea pub was in 1846, when Flood Street was called Queen Street. After Luke Thomas Flood of Cheyne Walk had willed a generous £3,000 to the parish, Queen Street was renamed Flood Street in his honour. The pub was rebuilt in 1874. By 1990, the Young's Brewery had taken over the pub and set about altering its mid-Victorian interior fairly drastically, turning it into a contemporary bar and introducing, amongst other bric-a-brac, a vast railway station clock. Denis and Prime Minister Margaret Thatcher used to live at number 19, just up the road.

MODERNIST HOUSE

866   SW3

1930s MENDELSOHN AND CHERMAYEFF

In this street, the oldest thoroughfare in Chelsea, Gropius and Mendelsohn introduced continental modernism to London, and number 64 is a very good example of 1930s architecture. In the 1920s, Erich Mendelsohn was one of the most prolific modern architects in Europe. He arrived in Britain in 1933, escaping Nazi Germany as Adolf Hitler became chancellor. His partner here was architect and interior designer (and a former ballroom dancer) Serge Chermayeff; he had come from Caucasia to study in the United Kingdom when he was twelve years old, changing his name from Sergei Ivanovitch Issakovitch. Later, in 1968, the stuccoed surfaces of these buildings would be refaced by Crosby Fletcher Forbes.

867

868

869

13 BRITTEN STREET
BUILDERS ARMS
867   SW3

1820s OR 1840

As its name suggests, this elegant Chelsea pub probably
originated as a place to eat, sleep, and drink for the workers who
were busy raising St Luke's Church opposite—by some called the
cathedral of Chelsea. This church building took from 1820–24,
and there are rumours of an underground passage linking the
pub to the church. Others claim that the pub arrived about
twenty years later—built in 1840 for Matthews and Cannings
Anchor Brewery. Inside are murals of Old Battersea Bridge and
Britten Street depicted in their nineteenth-century mode.

ROYAL HOSPITAL ROAD
STABLES, ROYAL HOSPITAL
868   SW3

1814 SIR JOHN SOANE

Soane was clerk of works to the Royal Hospital from 1807, and
the design of these stables incorporates many of his favourite
features. The simple, large, yellow, stock brick walls have no
mouldings or decoration but flow with arches, recesses within
recesses, plus arch-shaped, multi-paned windows—and the
building is crowned by chimneys with toadstool shapes perched
at the corners.

STAMFORD BRIDGE, FULHAM ROAD
EAST STAND, CHELSEA FOOTBALL CLUB
869   SW6

1975 DARBOURNE AND DARKE; FELIX SAMUELY AND PARTNERS, ENGINEERS

Old maps show Stanford Creek running along the route of what is
now a railway line at the back of the East Stand. In 1877, this was
an athletics track for the London Athletic Club but Chelsea's
football club have occupied this stadium, nicknamed, the Bridge,
since 1905. It has a capacity of 42,449. Its East Stand (capacity
11,253) is an imaginative sports building and was part of an
ambitious plan to cover all the spectator seating and create a
gallery under a cantilevered roof—a scheme, abandoned because
of financial constraints. A huge 13,500-seater West Stand
opened in 2001 and Stamford Bridge is now one of the largest
football stadiums in London. The year 2005 saw the opening of a
club museum to mark its centenary.

870

ROYAL ALBERT HALL

870   SW7

1867–71 CAPTAIN FRANCIS FOWKE, WITH MAJOR-GENERAL H. Y. D. SCOTT

The Royal Albert Hall of Arts and Sciences is dedicated to Queen Victoria's beloved consort, Prince Albert, who originally set about raising a cultural centre in Kensington with profits from the Great Exhibition. (The 50-acre site also houses the Imperial College of Science, Technology and Medicine, the Royal College of Art, the Victoria and Albert Museum, the Science Museum, the Natural History Museum, the Royal College of Music, and the Royal Geographical Society). With its vast elliptical dome of glass and iron, the Albert Hall is one of the best Victorian buildings in London, and opened in 1871 as the then-widowed Queen Victoria wept with emotion. A magnificent frieze encircles a building which has witnessed the first performance of Longfellow's *Hiawatha* (with music by black composer Samuel Coleridge-Taylor, who conducted it there in 1900), Wagner conducting six concerts, the first-ever gramophone concert, and Queen Elizabeth II's Coronation Ball. It is home to the largest pipe organ in the United Kingdom—and to the famous Sir Henry Wood's Promenade Concerts, held here since 1941.

EXHIBITION ROAD
HENRY COLE BUILDING
871   SW7

1863-73 LIEUTENANT-GENERAL SCOTT

This building is named after the first enthusiastic director
of the Victoria and Albert Museum, Sir Henry Cole. It now
serves as an extra wing to the museum and houses a new
archive, but was formerly occupied by the School of Naval
Architects, the Science School, and the Imperial College of
Science. The exterior is richly decorated with terracotta
panels with an Italianate arcade (loggia) running above
its seven splendid central bays. Inside, in the Manuscripts
Study Room, original documents can be explored with the
guidance of experts (a main point of focus is architecture)
and an education room is available for projects, workshops,
and seminars.

59-63 PRINCES GATE
1930s APARTMENTS
872   SW7

1935 GEORGE ADIE AND FREDERICK BUTTON

This was a famous, ultra-modern, functionalist block of
flats. Its two topmost floors are set back to form an attic.
Below, striped banding and the criss-crossed lines of
metal window frames flow across the rendered façade.
The building's cantilevered balconies and waffle slabs are
typical of the 1930s modern look. Architect George Adie
(1901–89) began by designing barracks and dormitories
for soldiers during World War II. From this unpaid work,
he went on to run a renowned Mayfair practice. An
accomplished and innovative architect, he sought the
new, while retaining a keen sense of living history and
the traditions of architecture.

170 QUEEN'S GATE
CEMENT-MAKER'S HOUSE
873   SW7

1887-89 R. NORMAN SHAW

Situated in leafy South Kensington, this graceful classical-
style Victorian house is a mix of Shaw's earlier free
composition and his later baroque revival. An elegant
door is set within an elaborate portico with columns,
flanked by multiple elongated windows and, at the
building edges, white quoins (dressed corners bricks). It
was built for a cement manufacturer and, six decades on,
purchased by Imperial College. It was named as a building
of special architectural or historic interest in 1958.

IMPERIAL INSTITUTE ROAD
IMPERIAL INSTITUTE
874   SW7

1887-93 THOMAS EDWARD COLLCUTT

The tall elegant Collcutt Tower (now called the Queen's
Tower), with its dome and balustrades, arches, and striped
façade, is the sole remaining feature of a building erected
after the 1886 Colonial Exhibition. Eighty-five metres
(280 feet) high, it was saved to become a freestanding
edifice in 1968. All around it, new Imperial Institute
buildings sprang up during the 1960s, so that now it
is surrounded by this redevelopment growth yet remains
a dominant and very pleasing feature.

PRINCE CONSORT ROAD
ALBERT COURT
875   SW7

c. 1890

Albert Court follows the sweep of the Albert Hall and is a
large and imposing seven-storey apartment building. It is
built in brick with many ornate features—multiple pillars,
tiered loggias, corner turrets, balustrades, and a veritable
march of tall Victorian chimneys. Leading through to the
Albert Hall area, an unusual 'internal street'—with light
wells that illuminate its passage—is resplendent with
huge fireplaces, minstrel galleries, post boxes, and even
grandfather clocks. This is Victoriana at its most lavish
'wedding-cake' best.

ONSLOW SQUARE
VAST HOUSES
876   SW7

1846 C. J. FREAKE

This elegant square was named after the Earl of Onslow
and has huge, Italianate stuccoed houses. Here in number
16 lived the Lutyens family with their thirteen children,
and where architect Edwin Lutyens was born in 1896.
Thackeray lived at number 36 in 1854–62 and wrote *The
Virginians* here. Admiral Robert Fitzroy, the meteorologist
and commander of the *Beagle* (in which Darwin sailed to
the Galapagos Islands), lived at number 38 from 1854;
and sculptor Carlo Marochetti, at number 34.

871

872

873

874

875

876

877

878

EXHIBITION ROAD

THE SCIENCE MUSEUM

877   SW7

QUEEN'S GATE

ST AUGUSTINE

878   SW7

1913 SIR RICHARD ALLISON

The London Science Museum has over ten thousand science, technology, and medicine exhibits, its earliest pieces drawn from the Royal Society of Arts and the Great Exhibition of 1857. More recently, work began on the museum's new Wellcome Wing in 1997. Once through the museum's somewhat austere entrance, visitors can see Whittle's first jet propulsion engine, Stephenson's *Rocket*, Arkwright's spinning machine, Edison's original phonograph, Babbage's 'difference engine,' and Crick's original DNA model. An impressive library holds many ancient manuscripts and books. All this is housed within an imposing structure, with its exterior modelled on an Edwardian office building and the interior on a department store. A roof-lit central well within is home to a display of large engines, and there are open galleries at the sides. This building is a fine example of Victorian Romanesque architecture.

1870–77 W. BUTTERFIELD

A curate, Richard Chope, raised an iron shed in his garden as a place to worship in Anglo-Catholic tradition in 1865. Ultimately, a parish was established four years later and was to be served by a new church, St Augustine. At first, the site had to be accessed from the back and so the church is set at an odd angle. The nave and aisles were built in 1871, and the sanctuary and chancel in 1876. Architect William Butterfield was obsessed with colour and every part of the simple interior was brightly decorated, but a 1928 whitewash covered much of his work. After a good deal of fund-raising, helped by the patronage of John Betjeman (later poet laureate), a 1980 restoration removed most of the whitewash to reveal Butterfield's favourite mix of multicoloured brick mosaics and diaper-patterns, coloured marble, and glazed tile murals.

879

880

ROYAL SCHOOL OF MINES

879 SW7

1909–13 SIR ASTON WEBB

The Royal School of Mines was founded over 150 years ago and today comprises the departments of Earth Science and Materials at Imperial College. Its origins lie in a 1851 establishment in Jermyn Street—a geology museum with minerals, maps, and mining equipment collected by Sir Henry de la Beche—director of the Geological Survey of Great Britain, who gave students the chance to study mineralogy and metallurgy. In 1863, it became the Royal School of Mines. Architect Webb was responsible for this early 1900s building, as well as the Victoria and Albert Museum and Imperial College. The school and the Bessemer Laboratory were completed by 1913, and the Goldsmith's Extension by 1915. Built of hard light stone, it has an impressive vast central entrance flanked by sculptures. Famous geologist Thomas Huxley is a notable past student.

VICTORIA AND ALBERT MUSEUM

880 SW7

1856–84 CAPTAIN FRANCIS FOWKE, GODFREY SYKES, AND OTHERS (MAIN QUADRANGLE);
1899–1909 SIR ASTON WEBB (CROMWELL ROAD FAÇADE)

This museum was part of Prince Albert's scheme to improve technical and art education, and was initially called the South Kensington Museum (renamed in 1899). Its first façade—with cast and corrugated iron resembling steam boilers lying side by side—was soon irreverently christened 'Brompton Boilers.' Francis Fowke's new 1869 buildings served as the main entrance until the opening of the Aston Webb façade in 1909. The museum acquired the collection of the East India Company's India Museum in 1880. During World War II, the V&A suffered a bomb blast but most of the works of art had been evacuated. Meanwhile, it served as a school for evacuees from Gibraltar and as a canteen for the Royal Air Force. Today, it exhibits paintings, ceramics, textiles, tapestries, furniture, costumes, jewellery, and other fascinating objets d'art from around the world.

881

THE NATURAL HISTORY MUSEUM

1873–81 ALFRED WATERHOUSE

Built to house the British Museum's growing collection of natural history specimens, this vast and impressive building has an amazing cathedral-like frontage with sculptures of plants and animals decorating its ornate façade. An iron and steel frame is set behind multiple arches and columns. Beyond the enormous arched entrance, a sweeping staircase leads to the upper galleries. There are four acres of exhibits in all, including the famous Blue Whale and the Diplodocus skeleton on view in the fine Central Hall—a gallery decorated with carved fauna details and a richly painted ceiling. Phase One of the Darwin Centre (see page 490) is now open, housing 22 million zoological specimens.

882

CROMWELL ROAD
DARWIN CENTRE

882   SW7

1992–2002 HOK INTERNATIONAL

This incredible research centre and museum
holds some 22 million zoological specimens
gathered over the last two centuries and
preserved in alcohol; some were brought from
Australia by Captain Cook in 1768. The
building serves as a store for these precious
specimens, laboratories for over a hundred
researchers and scientists, offices, and a
museum that offers fourteen guided tours a
day. Visitors can see the scientists at work from
the connecting walkways along the side of the
central atrium. This award-winning innovative
building is climate controlled and starkly
utilitarian—but very impressive.

883

196 QUEEN'S GATE, KENSINGTON
DUTCH-STYLE HOUSE

883   SW7

1875 R. NORMAN SHAW

Queen's Gate was built on land bought in 1855
by the Royal Commissioners for Prince Albert's
Great Exhibition, and they originally named
the street Albert Road. This house was built
for a rich young stockbroker and connoisseur,
J. P. Heseltine—and its style launched other
Dutch-inspired houses in Kensington. It is
reminiscent of many Renaissance townhouses
in Holland, with its tall narrow frontage; high,
curved, and stepped gable end; and redbrick
frontage with terracotta decorative panels.
Nearby are many splendid family homes in
Italianate style—and embassies.

884

885

IMPERIAL COLLEGE, EXHIBITION ROAD
TANAKA BUSINESS SCHOOL

884   SW7

15 SELWOOD TERRACE
ANGLESEA ARMS

885   SW7

2002–04 FOSTER AND PARTNERS

This new business school is part of a project to
undertake a radical reconstruction of the
college's main entrance. Some of the
postgraduate accommodation is contained
within a refurbished 1920s block, but this new
stainless-steel and gleaming glass façade
makes a dramatic new statement on Exhibition
Road. Behind the sheer glass are vast high
areas, stairwells, and facilities that include a
multi-purpose forum area, interactive lecture
theatres, study zones, and places where the
students can relax and eat. This new building is
yet another strand of the schemes set in
motion by Prince Albert back in the 1850s.

1825

This street has two names, one for each side of
the road. The pub stands on Selwood Terrace
(named after a former landowner here) but the
opposite side of the road is called Neville
Terrace! And once upon a time, this was all
Salad Lane, appropriately named for an area
full of market gardens. Houses were raised
here in 1830. The pub itself is named after a
general, Henry Paget, the Marquess of
Anglesey. He was riding next to the Duke of
Wellington when a cannonball hit him. 'By
God, sir,' he said to Wellington, 'I think I've lost
my leg.' 'By God, sir,' replied the Iron Duke,
'I do believe you have.' Paget had the leg
pickled and took it home to show family and
guests. Dickens once occupied number 11 and
his fiancée, Catherine, lived around the corner
in York Place. Author D. H. Lawrence resided
at number 9.

886

c. 1840 ELIAS GEORGE BASEVI

The lovely stuccoed houses were built by George Basevi in 1827–30 on the Smith's Charity Estate and named after Henry Thomas Pelham (the Earl of Chichester, a former trustee). The streets form a triangle here; there are three-storey houses with neat, front gardens while the large, sweeping crescent has houses with projecting porches. The famous actor-manager of Hammersmith's Lyric Theatre, Nigel Playfair, lived at number 26 from 1910–22. George Bavesi, a pupil of Sir John Soane, also designed the Fitzwilliam Museum in Cambridge but died when he was surveying Ely Cathedral and fell from the tower.

887

1962–73 H. T. CADBURY-BROWN, SIR HUGH CASSON

This was founded in 1837 as a school of design and practical art for manufacturing industries and was then next to the Victoria and Albert Museum. One of many institutions set up by Prince Albert, it aimed to supply British industry with trained designers. Workshops, a hall, and a library occupied these three later buildings—which seem to be all tall narrow windows. The structures are linked together and set around a courtyard, but the ground floor has been converted into exhibition space called the Henry Moore Gallery. In the 1950s and '60s, famous students included Peter Blake, David Hockney, and Eduardo Paolozzi—and the college became noted for modern art. Sir Hugh Casson's mainly glass-fronted 1973 building contrasts with the Victorian museums and colleges that are set all around.

888

1879–86 R. NORMAN SHAW

Facing Kensington Gardens, this massive sweep of six-storey, rich-redbrick apartments were the first to be designed in the new Queen Anne style—based on English and Dutch architecture of the early 1700s. A double-storey plinth supports the upper floors. These luxurious blocks—that wrap around and dwarf the Albert Hall—are topped by high broad chimneys and tall Dutch gables. They helped to launch a new vogue in Dutch styling. Architect Richard Norman Shaw based his plans on French apartments and included bathrooms, lifts, and wine cellars.

REGENCY FAÇADES

889   SW7

1818-37

Here, on this network of streets just south of Hyde Park, is a delightful cluster of Regency houses. With their elegant façades and railings, they would create the perfect backdrop for the *My Fair Lady* song, 'On the Street Where You Live.' Trevor Street was named for Sir John Trevor (a somewhat corrupt Speaker of the House of Commons) and was reputed to house the mistresses of the officers of the Household Brigade. The fictional character from Galsworthy's *The Forsyte Saga*, Soames Forsyte, lived at Number 62, Montpellier Square.

889

ALL SAINTS

890   SW7

1846-49 LEWIS VULLIAMY;
1892 WEST FRONT BY C. H. TOWNSEND

This unusual church, with its tall tower on one side, is a little 'slice of Italy,' for it is modelled on the eleventh-century basilica of San Zeno Maggiore, in Verona. It was once the Anglican parish church of All Saints—a daughter church of St Margaret's, Westminster—and the murals of biblical scenes and saints in the nave include Saint Margaret. The Arts and Crafts sgraffito decoration above the tall arches is by Heywood Sumner. The church was bought by the Russian Orthodox Church in 1979, and the doors of the icon screen before the altar were rescued from the chapel of London's Russian embassy after the 1917 Russian Revolution.

890

ROYAL GEOGRAPHICAL SOCIETY

891   SW7

1873-75 R. NORMAN SHAW

Set back behind an entrance court with a stable wing to the east, this Queen Anne–style house was built for MP William Lowther. It boasts many interlinked sections, elegant gables, and lovely brickwork. Tall chimneys and long windows lend the building height and stature. It was bought by the Royal Geographical Society in 1912, and a lecture hall was added in 1928–30 on the site of the stables. The Ondaatje Theatre, refurbished in 2001, was named after one Christopher Ondaatje—author and traveller, Olympic bobsleigh team member, millionaire, and benefactor to the society. This was founded in 1830 for the advancement of geographical science, and holds a collection of 2 million maps, photographs, books, and documents—covering five hundred years of geographical discovery and research.

891

892

ROYAL COLLEGE OF ORGANISTS

892   SW7

1875 H. H. COLE

This very pretty building was part of the scheme launched
by Prince Albert to sponsor places of education with
some of the £186,000 profits from his Great Exhibition
at Crystal Palace. Cream, maroon, and pale blue sgraffiti
by F. W. Moody decorate a very ornate three-bay building.
Considering that the college is now dedicated to organ
playing, it seems odd that its frieze of musicians contains
no organist, but the building began as the National
Training School of Music and was not confined to
organists until 1904. Sir Arthur Sullivan, of Gilbert and
Sullivan fame, was its first principal.

BATTERSEA POWER STATION

893   SW8

1929–55 HALLIDAY AND AGATE WITH SIR GILES GILBERT SCOTT;
S. L. PEARCE, ENGINEER

The iconic power station at Battersea is a power station
no longer—having been closed in 1983, when its old-
fashioned coal-fired generators could no longer meet
modern demands and health restrictions. The building
was originally commissioned in 1927 by the newly formed
London Power Company as a deliberately impressive
super power station, to forestall nationalisation of the
many small electricity-generation companies. Scott
designed a two-chimney station able to produce 400,000
kilowatts but even before construction was complete,
plans were drawn up to double the size and capacity—
by the simple expedient of building an identical copy
next door and so create the now-familiar, four-chimney
silhouette. Often described as the largest brick building
in Europe, this is, in fact, a steel-framed structure; the
brickwork is mere dressing.

894

895

896

897

BELGRAVE HOSPITAL FOR CHILDREN

894   SW9

1900-03 CHARLES HOLDEN

Charles Holden probably is best known for the design of London Underground stations and Senate House. He believed that, to deal with functional problems, contemporary architecture should, 'throw off its mantle of deceits; its cornices, pilasters, mouldings.' He was only twenty-five years old when he designed this hospital with delightful Arts and Crafts panel lettering, sturdy corner towers, and high gables. Holden twice declined the offer of a knighthood, believing that architecture was always a joint effort.

VILLAS

895   SW10

1850-60 GEORGE GODWIN

Here two partial crescents of large, semidetached Italianate houses face each other across a lens-shaped garden in the centre of which is placed a church. The concept was produced by architect George Godwin—who had been born less than a mile away and spent most of his professional life working on London housing, while indulging his unusual hobby of collecting chairs upon which famous people had sat. This development is generally considered to be his masterpiece, embracing so much that the Victorians admired in town planning.

BOULSFIELD SCHOOL

896   SW10

1955 CHAMBERLIN, POWELL AND BON

This school won an architectural award from the London County Council when it rather incongruously thrust its modern face into this genteel Victorian area. The design deliberately broke with that of the traditional urban school, by having a water jump instead of a fence at its entrance, and an open-air amphitheatre as well as viewing slots into the school from the pavement. The bare metalwork railings and brightly coloured panels were other features new to school design. Award or not, this school remains unique, as many structures that followed later reverted to a more traditional style and layout.

MONTEVETRO

897   SW11

1994-99 RICHARD ROGERS PARTNERSHIP

This impressive block of over one hundred apartments was constructed as a conscious attempt to reverse the trend of population loss in central London, by persuading people that even the most densely urban areas could be pleasant places to set up home. The block was built on the site of an old flour mill, and enjoys impressive views along the Thames to Battersea Bridge; each apartment has one floor-to-ceiling wall of glass overlooking the river. The luxurious (and enormous) penthouse apartments not only have glass walls on two sides, but also feature projecting rooms with glass floors. Overall it is a triumph of modern design.

30 VICARAGE CRESCENT
OLD BATTERSEA HOUSE
898   SWII

1699 POSSIBLY SIR CHRISTOPHER WREN

It is generally said that this house was designed by Sir Christopher Wren, although there is no real evidence to support the claim. At the time that the house was built, Battersea was a rural village—famous for its asparagus, grown on the drained marshes that had once made the village a virtual island. In 1930, the local council bought the house and grounds in order to flatten the lot and raise a large council housing estate. A local outcry meant that the house was saved, although the grounds were, indeed, built over.

LAVENDER HILL
ARDING AND HOBBS
899   SWII

1910 J. GIBSON

This building replaced an 1885 department store that was destroyed in a devastating fire of 1909. It was completed in the Edwardian Baroque style that dominated the public buildings and larger commercial structures of the time. The key feature is the cupola that tops the curved corner frontage on to Lavender Hill and St John's Road. This has been the most noticeable landmark in Clapham since it was built, and is now enhanced after dark by floodlighting. The overall effect is to dwarf the nearby commercial shops completed in more modest scale and style during Victorian times—which was no doubt the intention.

22 HESTER ROAD
ALBION RIVERSIDE: CURVES
900   SWII

1990 FOSTER ASSOCIATES

This unique development with sweeping sinuous curves was designed by Lord Foster. This eleven-storey building in aluminium and glass has 186 spacious apartments and penthouses (prices range from £250,000 up to almost £10 million) plus a restaurant, shops, art gallery, swimming pool, and gymnasium for residents. The sinuous lines of the balconies create a stunning impact.

HESTER ROAD
ALBION RIVERSIDE: STRAIGHT LINES
901   SWII

1990 FOSTER ASSOCIATES

This is Foster Associates own headquarters on a fine site looking out onto the Thames—housing over a hundred architects plus support staff. There are three buildings in all. The largest is the eleven-storey glass-fronted building that contains offices and luxury apartments. A second building is a more modest office block; this is the UK headquarters of Hong Kong developers Hutchison Whampoa. The third is a low-rise apartment building for the Peabody Trust (providing low-cost homes for the less well-off), with forty-five apartments for key workers. A wide riverside walk for the public runs along here from Battersea Bridge to Albert Bridge.

ROEHAMPTON LANE
HOUSING, ALTON WEST ESTATE
902   SW15

1955-59 LCC ARCHITECTS DEPARTMENT

Here, on 40 hectares (100 acres) near Richmond Park, this major 1950s project by the London County Council managed to retain the rolling Georgian landscape. Some 1,850 dwellings were raised, together with schools, shops, a library, and homes for the elderly. There are eleven-storey maisonettes, rows of three- and-four storey maisonettes, and twelve-storey point blocks—all built and clad in concrete, in a style reminiscent of Le Corbusier's Unite d'Habitation in Marseille, France. Generally, they lack interesting detailing or geometrical order, but perhaps the panoramic views of Richmond Park and southwest London compensate for this.

PORTSMOUTH ROAD
HOUSING, ALTON EAST ESTATE
903   SW15

1952-55 LCC ARCHITECTS DEPARTMENT

These early-1950s Alton Estates are now Grade II listed. Their Swedish-influenced modern style was one adopted by many local councils in the immediate post-war years. This estate on the edge of Richmond Park has tower blocks—with wide bands of concrete and multiple balconies—and terraced houses set among mature trees in a relatively rural setting of some 11 hectares (28 acres), housing 2,800 people. This East Estate was regarded as a 'sell-out' by hard-line Brutalists, who thought the painted window frames and coloured bricks were frivolous. There was no transport and few shops so the residents here were somewhat isolated.

898

899

900

901

902

903

904

905

ROEHAMPTON LANE

ROEHAMPTON HOUSE

904   SWI5

1710–12 THOMAS ARCHER;
ENLARGED BY SIR EDWIN LUTYENS

During the late 1200s, a village grew up
around a farm with many rooks—which led
to the name Roehampton. In time, this area
became a popular place for the very wealthy
to raise vast country villas. The Earl of
Portland, treasurer to Charles I, built Grove
House in 1630. The area became an even
more favoured residential suburb after Putney
Bridge opened in 1729. This Grade I listed
building was Thomas Archer's first London
work, built as a country house for Thomas
Cary. It has a grandiose entrance with pillars,
a fine deep-red brick façade, balustrades, and
multi-paned windows. During World War I,
soldiers were billeted here and it was
converted into Queen Mary's Hospital—
mainly to provide maimed soldiers with
artificial limbs and to help retrain them
in various trades.

ROEHAMPTON LANE

PARKSTEAD HOUSE

905   SWI5

1750–68 SIR WILLIAM CHAMBERS

Set in 14 acres, this is a simply splendid
example of a Palladian house, with an Ionic
portico and majestic domed ceilings and
archways. This Grade I building was raised for
the Second Earl of Bessborough, to entertain
his friends and house his collection of antique
sculpture. Since 2005, it has served as a
venue for conferences, weddings, and other
events. Sir William Chambers was also the
architect of Somerset House and the Pagoda
at Kew Gardens.

DIXCOT

906   SW16

Streatham and Tooting were originally Anglo-Saxon
settlements: Streatham means 'dwellings by the street'
and Tooting means 'the dwelling of the sons of Totas.'
They developed from villages to suburbs through the
1600s and 1700s, when merchants and other wealthy folk
set up their country homes here. Several large mansions
and elegant villas were built in the area as the population
of Tooting slowly expanded. These pretty buildings have
pointed gable ends, interesting strips of leaded windows,
and odd interesting angles everywhere.

POLLARDS HILL
APPLIED MATHEMATICS

907   SW16

1971 LONDON BOROUGH OF MERTON ARCHITECTS DEPARTMENT;
P. J. WHITTLE, DESIGN BY P. BELL, D. LEA, R. MACCORMAC, N. ALEXANDER

This low-rise high-density housing was, in essence, a
1970s version of the eighteenth-century London square.
It was inspired by 1960s research at Cambridge into how a
modern housing plan could implement the Fresnel Square
invented by Augustin Fresnel. (This French physicist, who
lived 1788–1827, studied light and optics, and devised
the square Fresnel lens used in theatre lighting and
lighthouses.) The result is this three-storey grouping of
houses set around an open public space approached by
steps and ramps. It all remains rather austere and empty,
despite its plantings, low walls, and the mathematical
inspiration—but there are dramatic views of South
London from Pollards Hill.

11–12 FROGMORE
THE ROCHE SCHOOL

908   SW18

1960 JAMES STIRLING AND JAMES GOWAN

Stirling and Gowan designed these two houses for
abandoned children in Putney. Built of brick, the home is
low key and unpretentious but very practical, the outside
play areas partially covered by the first-floor bedrooms,
while the stepped plan and corner windows add visual
interest. Stirling was renowned for his controversial
creations and was in partnership with Gowan, a Scottish
architect and teacher, from 1956–63. Together they
created some of the most important and influential post-
war buildings in Britain and became known for simple
functional modernist public buildings, often in brick and
rough-finished concrete. Stirling was knighted in 1992.

WIMBLEDON,
22 PARKSIDE

909   SW19

1970 RICHARD AND SUE ROGERS

Here two suburban buildings are set in an attractive
garden. They are unusual in that they exhibit many
building techniques usually reserved for larger
constructions. These include a single-span steel frame
and large sliding glass panes. A larger house is set behind
the smaller building, initially used as a guest house. Now
best known as the home of lawn tennis, Wimbledon's
famous residents have included Lord Horatio Nelson
and William Wilberforce. Parkside was home in the 1790s
to the Vicomte de Calonne, an exiled French statesman,
and today 54 Parkside is home to the Papal Nuncio
(ambassador) to Great Britain. When the Domesday Book
was compiled in 1087, Wimbledon was part of Mortlake
manor; it was held by the church until 1398 when it was
confiscated as crown property by Richard II.

906

907

908

909

SOUTH EAST LONDON (SE)

This area of London sweeps out from the Thames towards the Kent border and includes some of the greenest acres of the capital, such as Greenwich Park, Blackheath (where the Danes camped in 1012), Dulwich Park, and Peckham Rye Common.

The South Bank has long been equated with culture, with such gems as the National Theatre, the Royal Festival Hall (under scaffolding now and so, sadly, not in this edition), Tate Modern, and the New Globe Theatre.

Greenwich is steeped in history and home to the Queen's House, the Royal Naval College, and the *Cutty Sark*. Here, at the Greenwich Meridian Line at the Royal Observatory, East meets West

at 0 degrees longitude. This is also the home of Greenwich Mean Time (GMT)—upon which all the time zones in the world are based.

Nearby Deptford means 'deep ford' and is where the road from London to Dover crosses the Thames tributary over the river Ravensbourne. It was on the pilgrims' route to Canterbury and those in Chaucer's *Canterbury Tales* crossed the river here.

This area has associations with famous names like Sir Francis Drake and diarist John Evelyn. Back in 1513, King Henry VIII sited a naval dockyard here, where, in 1698, the young Russian tsar, Peter the Great, studied shipbuilding for three months.

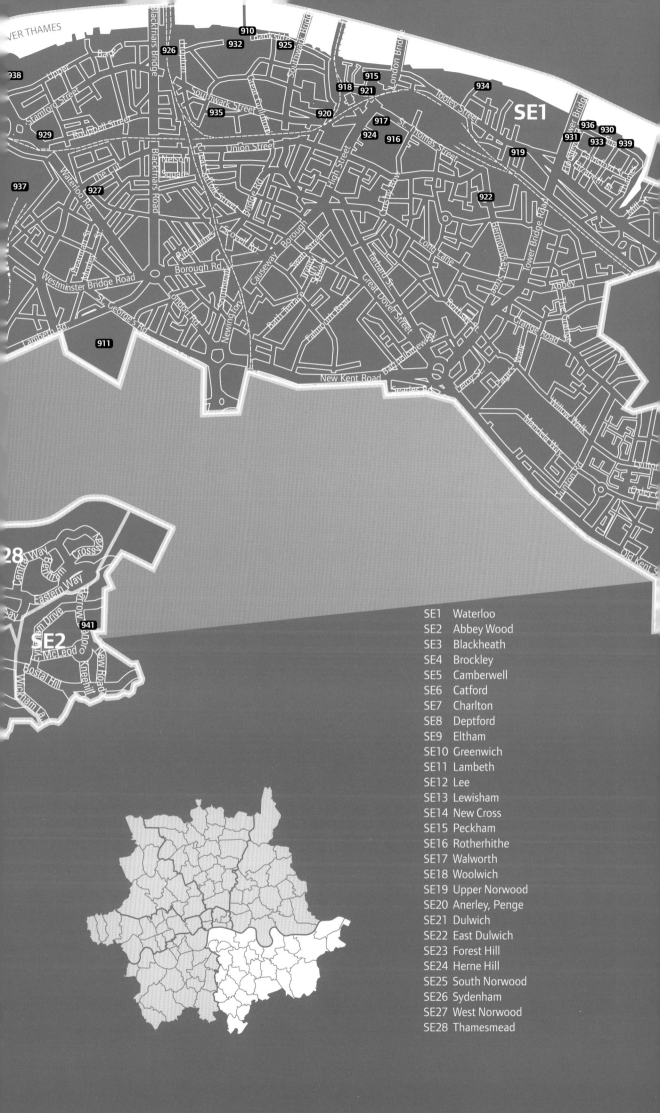

RIVER THAMES

938

929

937

Blackfriars Bridge
926
Bankside
910
932
925
Southwark Bridge
London Bridge
915
918 921
934
SE1

Stamford Street
Upper
Southwark Street
935
Blackfriars Road
Tooley Street
917
Tower Bridge
936 930
931 933 939

The Cut
927
Union Street
924 916
St Thomas Street
919

Waterloo Rd
Nelson Square
Great Suffolk Street
Bridge Rd
High Street
922

Borough Rd
Borough
Long Lane
Bermondsey Street

Westminster Bridge Road
London Rd
Newington
Bath Terrace
Great Dover Street
Abbey

St George's Rd
Causeway
Tabard St.
Grange Road

Lambeth Rd
911
New Kent Road
Bartholomew St

28
Central Way
Cross
Bentham Way
Eastern Way
Harrow
New Road
941
SE2
McLeod
Kneehill
Bostall Hill
Wickham La.

SE1	Waterloo
SE2	Abbey Wood
SE3	Blackheath
SE4	Brockley
SE5	Camberwell
SE6	Catford
SE7	Charlton
SE8	Deptford
SE9	Eltham
SE10	Greenwich
SE11	Lambeth
SE12	Lee
SE13	Lewisham
SE14	New Cross
SE15	Peckham
SE16	Rotherhithe
SE17	Walworth
SE18	Woolwich
SE19	Upper Norwood
SE20	Anerley, Penge
SE21	Dulwich
SE22	East Dulwich
SE23	Forest Hill
SE24	Herne Hill
SE25	South Norwood
SE26	Sydenham
SE27	West Norwood
SE28	Thamesmead

910

BANKSIDE; FORMERLY BANKSIDE POWER STATION

TATE MODERN

910   SEI

1947 AND 1963 SIR GILES GILBERT SCOTT;
1994-2000 HERZOG AND DE MEURON

The Bankside Power Station closed its doors to power
production in 1981, and was left unoccupied for almost
a decade and a half. During the mid to late 1990s, it
was transformed into the Tate Gallery's centre for
contemporary and international art, and it is now one
of London's most popular attractions. A great deal of the
building's former robust character has been maintained.
The entrance leads into what was once an immense
turbine hall, which housed the electricity generators of
the old power station; it is seven storeys tall, with vast
areas of floor space. Today, it is generally used for
specially commissioned large-scale projects. Elsewhere,
exhibits of international modern art from 1900 to the
present day include works by Dali, Picasso, Matisse,
Moore, Rothko, and Warhol.

IMPERIAL WAR MUSEUM

911   SE1

1812–15 J. LEWIS; 1839 SIDNEY SMIRKEP; 1989 ARUP ASSOCIATES

The Imperial War Museum building was once the site of the Bethlehem Royal Hospital, the world's oldest hospital for the insane. The term *bedlam* derived from the name of this dire place, where visitors once paid to view the crazed inmates chained in gallery cells. Sidney Smirke, brother of Sir Robert Smirke, added the Ionic portico and dome in 1838, but, despite the now-grand exterior, it was still grim inside. Architect Augustus Pugin was a patient here in 1852. In 1936, the building mutated into a war museum, and a 1989 renovation included the addition of a top-lit exhibition hall with a diagonally latticed, barrel-vault roof. This is a light steel structure, but original, heavy masonry walls remain. Exhibits here include everything from tanks and aircraft to ration books.

QUEEN ELIZABETH HALL

912   SE1

1964 LCC / GLC ARCHITECTS DEPARTMENT;
SIR HUBERT BENNETT AND JACK WHITTLE

Queen Elizabeth Hall is an example of 1960s Brutalism, and the passion then for multi-level constructions. The services and stairs are set around the exterior, leaving an uncluttered central core. The windows are almost invisible as they are set behind the line of the walls and roof. The venue was opened by the Queen in 1967 and, with seating for just over a thousand, it is used mainly for small orchestral concerts, chamber music, poetry readings, conferences, and film performances. The more intimate Purcell Room seats 372; soloists and chamber groups usually perform there. At ground and subterranean level, the concrete ramps have become hugely popular with local skateboarders!

HAYWARD GALLERY

913   SE1

1964 LCC / GLC ARCHITECTS DEPARTMENT;
SIR HUBERT BENNETT AND JACK WHITTLE

The Hayward Gallery is one of London's major venues for displaying contemporary art. Part of the South Bank Centre—which includes the Royal Festival Hall, Queen Elizabeth Hall, the Purcell Rooms, and the Poetry Library—this is another 1960s Brutalist design. Originally the building had a small foyer area, but a larger glass-fronted version was constructed in 2003. A new café with a glass pavilion was added at the eastern end of the building. The spindly Neon Tower on top of the gallery lift shaft was designed by Philip Vaughan and Roger Dainton. Made from coloured neon strips, it is activated by changes in the strength and direction of the wind.

LAMBETH PALACE

914   SE1

1297–1829

Lambeth Palace has been the official London residence of the archbishops of Canterbury since 1200. Located on the south bank of the Thames, the land here was low and sodden—known then as Lambeth Marsh. The palace comprises medieval, Tudor, and Jacobean buildings, and it would originally have been approached by river. Wat Tyler's rebels over-ran the palace in 1381, burning books, and smashing furniture and wine casks. The vaulted crypt under the chapel is thirteenth century, and Lollard's Tower dates from 1440. At the Tudor gatehouse (1486–1501), the Lambeth Dole was handed out three times a week to the poor until 1842. The palace was used as a prison during the British Civil War.

911

912

913

914

915

916

BOROUGH HIGH STREET	ST THOMAS STREET
SOUTHWARK CATHEDRAL	**GUY'S HOSPITAL**
915 SEI	916 SEI

1106-1420; 1822 TOWER RESTORED; 1838 NAVE REBUILT; 1890-99 NAVE REPLACED BY SIR ARTHUR BLOMFIELD

Southwark Cathedral, the earliest Gothic church in London, with many French-inspired details, developed from a priory—and then the Church of St Saviour and St Mary Overie. The current construction is the fourth holy building to have been built on this site; it became a cathedral in 1905. It is thought that the first building was constructed as early as the beginning of the seventh century. Traces of the third construction, the early twelfth-century Norman Priory church, still survive. In Elizabethan times, part of the church was leased as a bakery and even used as pigsties. A large nineteenth-century stained-glass window is dedicated to William Shakespeare. It depicts scenes from some of his plays; a nearby statue shows the writer holding a quill. John Harvard, the founder of Harvard University, was born in Southwark in 1607, and baptised in St Saviour's.

1722-80 AND 1780 W. JUPP; 1974 GUY'S TOWER

Guy's Hospital was founded in 1721 by religious publisher, MP, and sheriff of the City Sir Thomas Guy, who had made a 'killing' with South Sea stock. Set behind iron gates and railings, the ground floor of the frontage is rusticated and spanned by arched windows. Above three central arches, are columns crowned by a pediment—Jupp's Palladian addition of 1774. Behind the frontage are eighteenth-century courts and chapel. Famous 'Guy's' include Richard Bright (who pinpointed Bright's disease), Thomas Addison (Addison's disease), Thomas Hodgkin (Hodgkin's disease), plus poet John Keats, who was a student here. Guy's became the first hospital in London to appoint a dental surgeon, and it has been famous for dentistry ever since. The thirty-four-storey Guy's Tower was added in 1974. This makes the building one of the tallest in London, and the highest hospital anywhere—at 143 metres (469 feet).

ST THOMAS STREET

CHAPTER HOUSE, SOUTHWARK CATHEDRAL

917 SE1

1702–03

St Thomas's Hospital (founded in the 1200s) once stood here, and its chapel, built in Queen Anne's reign, evolved into the Chapter House of Southwark Cathedral. The hospital's old operating theatre is still in the tower. A group of houses arrived in the 1700s and this Georgian terrace became home to many connected with the hospital. This street also boasts the Gordon Medical Museum with many gruesome exhibits.

9 STONEY STREET; FORMERLY THE HARROW

MARKET PORTER

918 SE1

1638; c. 1890

There has been a pub here since 1638. This building is in Olde English Tudor style, with small-paned lead windows and lots of beams, panels, old partitions, a carved bar-back, stained glass, and open fires. The pub still has a market licence to serve the market porters, and is open for breakfast drinks. Its owner co-founded Bishop's Brewery. The pub was transformed into the 'Third Hand Book Emporium' in the film *Harry Potter and the Prisoner of Azkaban*, situated next to 'The Leaky Cauldron.'

TOOLEY STREET

ST OLAVE'S GRAMMAR SCHOOL

919 SE1

1571; 1893 E. W. MOUNTFORD

King Olave spread Christianity and fought paganism until he was killed in 1030. The street's name derived from 'Saint Oley's Street.' In 1896, St Saviour's and St Olave's schools (founded in 1562 and 1571 respectively) joined forces and eventually emerged as a prestigious school with excellent results. The redbrick and white stone decoration is typical of Victorian institutions. A statue of Elizabeth I from the original building is now holding court in the gymnasium. Notable alumni include the founder of Harvard University, John Harvard.

24 SOUTHWARK STREET

CENTRAL BUILDINGS AND THE HOP EXCHANGE

920 SE1

1867 R. H. MOORE

The Hop and Malt Exchange was a centre for hop growers, merchants, and dealers. Cast-iron hops entwine the front, and carvings depict hop gatherers pulling, picking, and packing the crop into wicker baskets or carts; many Londoners spent summer days hop picking in Kent's fields. Inside, this highly ornamental building has a spectacular atrium, dramatic high ceilings, and three floors of ornate galleries and balustrades. A 1920 fire destroyed the ornamental glass roof that allowed buyers to inspect the hops in daylight. The building has been restored—as offices and a venue for hire.

SHAD THAMES

COURAGE BREWERY

921 SE1

1787; 1891 REBUILT AFTER FIRE; 1980s CONVERTED

Originally built in 1787, the Courage Brewery operated for some two centuries, with nearby Anchor Terrace built for senior brewery employees in the 1830s. The brewery presents a massive bulk to the river, with its tall chimney, galleries, and a domed tower that all lend it great height and presence. Between 1985 and 1987, the brewery and adjacent boiler-house were converted into apartments.

BURMONDSEY STREET

MUSEUM OF FASHION AND TEXTILES

922 SE1

1995–2003 RICARDO LEGORRETA / ALAN CAMP ARCHITECTS

This is one of Mexican Ricardo Legorreta's few European projects and includes eight apartments—and a restaurant—as well as the museum. Fashion designer Zandra Rhodes, who inspired the museum, has the penthouse here. The exhilarating colours of shocking pink with vivid orange certainly make this building stand out, and the museum is the first of its kind to specialize in showcasing the talent of local and international fashion designers. Here, both vintage and modern fashions, as well as textile designs, can be discovered in ever-changing exhibitions.

917

918

919

920

921

922

GREENWICH

Greenwich (the green port) has a splendid, undulating park, markets, and vessels on the riverfront. It is home to the Millennium Dome, the Observatory and Maritime Museum, glorious Georgian, Regency, and Victorian housing, old almshouses, and artisans' cottages. Bronze Age tumuli and Roman coin hoards in Greenwich Park show that this place has been busy for three thousand years. Here, the Vikings made camp in 1012 on their way to conquer England, killing the Archbishop of Canterbury Alfege en route. Today, St Alfege's Church, designed by Nicholas Hawksmoor in 1714, marks the place where archbishop was murdered.

Henry VI and Margaret of Anjou honeymooned in 1445 at Greenwich Palace. Here, Henry VIII was born, Edward VI died, and Elizabeth I spent her summers. It was at Greenwich that Walter Raleigh spread his cloak across the puddle for his queen to step across. Inigo Jones designed the delightful Queen's House for James I, and Christopher Wren and Nicholas Hawksmoor raised the splendid hospital painted by Canaletto—later the Royal Naval College of Greenwich, and now the University of Greenwich and Trinity College of Music. Architect Sir John Vanbrugh lived in a house that he designed, overlooking Greenwich Park.

In 1694, the Government Powder magazine was located here and, in 1800, a huge tidal mill arrived. Alongside the busy wharves, guns and cannons were made—and ships. Then power stations, refineries, foundries, cable factories, and gas works arrived alongside tanneries. The Millennium Dome was built on a disused British Gas site here.

Now in dry dock at Greenwich, the sleek lines and enormous sails of the *Cutty Sark* made her the most famous fast tea clipper ever—and the only one to survive. Her figurehead is a beautiful witch wearing a short chemise or shirt (called a *cutty sark* in a Robert Burns poem). Here, too, is the *Gipsy Moth IV*, the vessel used by sixty-four-year-old Francis Chichester to circumnavigate the globe in the 1960s.

Back in 1675, when John Flamsteed was astronomer royal, a new observatory was built on Greenwich Hill. It would be another two centuries before Greenwich Mean Time was accepted around the world (in 1884) as a base meridian for longitude. In 1980, a small main belt asteroid (number 2830), discovered by Edward Bowell, was named 'Greenwich'—honouring this place's special importance in the field of astronomy. In 1997, maritime Greenwich was made a World Heritage site.

923

SOUTHEAST END OF WESTMINSTER BRIDGE

FORMER COUNTY HALL

923   SE1

1911–22; 1931–33 RALPH KNOTT

This riverside spot has long been a busy place and excavations to the site here revealed the remains of a Roman boat. The building's progress was interrupted by World War I, and County Hall was not finally opened by King George V until 1922. It was not until 1933 that the northern riverside façade was constructed, and it was 1963 by the time the whole block was completed. The size is impressive—a span of over 233 metres (765 feet)—with a colonnaded crescent and end pavilions. It is built in Edwardian Renaissance style—faced with Portland stone, but with a granite base. There are several internal courtyards. Today, County Hall is the site of Dalí Universe and the London Aquarium, as well as two hotels, plus several restaurants and apartments.

924

THE GEORGE INN

924   SE1

1676

The George is a galleried coaching inn—the only remaining example in London. Coaching inns, usually situated about seven miles apart, stabled horses for stagecoaches, replacing tired teams with fresh horses. It is thought that the original inn here dated back to the medieval period. The George was rebuilt in 1676 after a serious fire; the original building surrounded three sides of the courtyard but the central and northern wings were demolished in 1899 to make way for the railway. The Old Bar used to be a waiting room for coach passengers, and Charles Dickens mentions this inn in *Little Dorrit*. Shakespeare's plays are sometimes staged in the galleried inn yard.

925

1, 49, 50, AND 52 BANKSIDE

RIVERSIDE HOUSES

925   SE1

1700s

Here are a few surviving fragments of the 1700s. Provost's Lodgings, numbers 50 and 52, were gutted in World War II but then restored. The houses from 49 to 52 remained as homes, even during the recent development of the Globe Theatre. The busy Thames riverside was crammed with ale houses. The Anchor, on the corner, has existed here for over eight hundred years, but has been rebuilt several times. A plaque on number 49 claims that Wren lived here while designing St Paul's across the river (this may not be true). Samuel Pepys had watched the Great Fire of London across the river from here—seeking refuge in 'a little alehouse on bankside…and there watched the fire grow.'

926

HOPTON STREET

HOPTON ALMSHOUSES

926   SE1

1752

Almshouses provided charitable housing—usually maintained by charities or trustees—often housing the elderly from certain areas of former employment. Hopton Almshouses are named after Charles Hopton, a local fishmonger in the mid-eighteenth century. Here, the accommodation surrounds three sides of a square courtyard. The building with the pediment, at the far end of the two rows of houses, is used as the trust's committee room. Residents celebrated the 250th anniversary of the almshouses in 2002 with a service at Christ Church, Southwark, and by inviting Prince Charles to visit.

OLD VIC THEATRE WORKSHOP

927   SE1

1958 LYONS ISRAEL AND ELLIS WITH JOHN MILLER

A Grade II–listed building, this is the only architect-designed theatre workshop in Britain—and one of the earliest and purest examples of New Brutalism. At last, the company's scenery workshops, wardrobes, and offices were all gathered in one place. The exterior has minimal decoration. A double-height room inside can accommodate the construction and painting of large pieces of scenery. The Old Vic was the home of the National Theatre until 1976.

927

LAMBETH PALACE ROAD

ST THOMAS'S HOSPITAL

928   SE1

1106; 1860s; 1956 FOWLER HOWITT; FROM 1963 YORKE ROSENBERG MARDALL

This ancient institution was probably part of a priory. In the early 1400s, Lord Mayor Richard Whittington made 'a new chamber with eight beds for young women who had done amiss, in trust of a good amendment.' By 1566, the first physician received £13 6s 8d a year; in 1583, the cook earned an extra £1 per year as a gravedigger. The hospital moved here in the 1860s—built in the Italianate style approved by Florence Nightingale, who established the Nightingale Training School of Nursing and revolutionised the role of nurses, replacing degenerate (and often inebriated) slovens with caring hygienic professionals. After World War II, a new east wing was built; a north wing arrived in the 1960s.

928

WATERLOO ROAD

ST JOHN'S

929   SE1

1822-24 F. O. BEDFORD; 1885 RENOVATED SIR ARTHUR BLOMFIELD;
1924 NINIAN COMPER; 1950 RESTORED

Built (with three other churches) to commemorate the Battle of Waterloo, this church was designed in Greek Revival style and constructed on piles in Lambeth Marsh. It has six fine Doric columns on its portico, a three-level tower, and an obelisk spire. Unfortunately, World War II bombs caused enormous damage, but the walls, portico, steeple, and an eighteenth-century Italian marble font survived.

929

930

WAREHOUSES

1800s; 1980s RECONSTRUCTION CONRAN ROCHE

Today, Shad Thames is partly cobbled, and is flanked by many converted brick warehouses with original brickwork, winches, and Victorian signage. Now there are restaurants, shops, and offices at ground level, and domestic flats above. In Victorian times, this vast warehouse complex stored tea, coffee, and spices. High above the pavement, raised walkways criss-cross the path between the Butlers Wharf and Cardamom buildings. These would have been used to roll barrels between the warehouses. In *Oliver Twist*, Charles Dickens set Bill Sykes's den at the eastern end of Shad Thames. This area has been a film location for *Oliver!* (1968), *The Elephant Man* (1980), *The French Lieutenant's Woman* (1981), *A Fish Called Wanda* (1988), and *Mad Dogs and Englishmen* (1995).

931

932

GAINSFORD STREET, COPPER ROW,
HORSELYDOWN LANE, SHAD THAMES

HORSELYDOWN SQUARE

931   SEI

21 NEW GLOBE WALK

THE NEW GLOBE

932   SEI

1986-91 WICKHAM AND ASSOCIATES

With its Mediterranean colours of bright
ochres and reds, Horselydown Square makes
a cheerful contrast to its neighbours, the Shad
Thames warehouses. The buildings set around
the square are a mixture of domestic flats,
offices, and shops set into alcoves. The five-
and seven-storey buildings are a combination
of brick, metal, and glass, with interesting
windows, balconies, bays, and circular towers
that almost look like lighthouses.

1997 NORDEN AND HOLLAR

This exciting project seized the world's
imagination as Shakespeare's Globe Theatre
rose again beside the Thames. Today's
reconstruction of the playhouse (designed first
in 1599) is very close to the original site — now
partly covered by a listed Georgian building in
Anchor Terrace; a coloured brick semicircle
marks its exact location. Here, Shakespeare
acted and wrote many of his greatest plays.
In 1613, the theatre burnt down when a spark
from cannon set the roof alight during a
performance of *Henry VIII*. The Globe was
rebuilt in 1614, closed by the Puritans in
1642, and demolished two years later. Other
buildings, including a brewery, followed — but,
eventually, the site was deserted. This New
Globe was inspired by actor-director Sam
Wanamaker and raised on the Bankside after
over twenty years of determined effort. The
complex includes a pub, visitors' centre, and
exhibition hall. The New Globe has the first
thatched roof permitted in London since the
Great Fire, made of Norfolk reed (well fire-
proofed!), on a timber frame of green oak.
The open air arena (called the pit or yard)
has a raised stage surrounded by three tiers
of roofed galleries.

933

934

SHAD THAMES

REGENERATION AND CONVERSIONS

933   SE1

TOOLEY STREET

HAY'S WHARF AND ST OLAVE HOUSE

934   SE1

1994 MICHAEL HOPKINS AND PARTNERS

This is an area that has seen massive reconstruction. Everywhere, there are converted warehouses, a good number named after the commodities they once stored — such as Vanilla and Sesame Wharf, Cayenne Court, and Wheat Wharf. The scents of spices like ginger and cloves are said to still permeate the buildings. In between the conversions, are squeezed some replacement buildings. From the mid-1980s numerous architects have been involved in the redevelopment here, including Conan Roche, who designed Saffron Wharf in 1990. This is number 22 Shad Thames, the headquarters for the designer David Mellor. It has a robust concrete frame and lead panelling. In 1994, its design won a commendation in the Civic Trust Awards and a RIBA London Region award.

1651; 1932 H. S. GOODHART-RENDEL

Hay's Wharf is the longest and oldest wharf in the Port of London, started by merchant Alexander Hay in 1651, and rebuilt in 1932. This building was created for the Hays Wharf Company in 1928–32 as offices and warehousing — with a warehouse on the riverfront and an office block (St Olave House) facing Tooley Street — raised on columns to allow access to the river. Its steel frame is faced in Portland stone, and the river façade is decorated with beautiful sculptured panels with decorations by Frank Dobson that frame the board and common rooms. The Tooley Street façade has turrets, angled walls, and geometric patterning inside.

935

85 SOUTHWARK STREET

ALLIES AND MORRISON STUDIOS

935   SE1

2001–3 ALLIES & MORRISON

This is an elegant, glazed office development. The street elevation (facing north) is beautifully detailed, with bright yellow internal shutters. The south side is a stepped atrium, linking six storeys of office floors, while the ground floor incorporates a through route from Southwark Street. The interior uses high-quality exposed concrete with black granite and grey resin floors, and there is a magnificent metalwork staircase. The building's final flourish is a south-facing roof garden. This studio block won the RIBA London Building of the Year Award in 2004.

SHAD THAMES

COURAGE BREWERY

936   SE1

1787; 1891 REBUILT AFTER FIRE; 1980s CONVERTED

Originally built in 1787, the Courage Brewery operated for some two centuries, with nearby Anchor Terrace built for senior brewery employees in the 1830s. The brewery presents a massive bulk to the river, with its tall chimney, galleries, and a domed tower that all lend it great height and presence. Between 1985 and 1987, the brewery and adjacent boiler-house were converted into apartments.

936

937

938

939

WATERLOO INTERNATIONAL TERMINAL

937   SE1

1848; 1900-22; 1994 NICHOLAS GRIMSHAW AND PARTNERS

The original mainline Waterloo Station opened in 1848, named after the Battle of Waterloo in which Napoleon was defeated near Brussels. This station was also the terminus for London's daily funeral express to Brookwood Cemetery and transported many a coffin at 2/6d a single trip. The station was torn down at the turn of the last century and rebuilt. With Eurostar's Channel Tunnel services to France and Belgium, Waterloo International was linked to the mainline terminus in the 1990s, at a cost of £130 million. Its design, with a 400-metre (1,312-foot) glass canopy with bowstring arches, won several awards—but now the Eurostar service is moving to St Pancras in 2007. The station is linked to the South Bank by an elevated walkway.

ROYAL NATIONAL THEATRE

938   SE1

1967-76 SIR DENYS LASDUN AND PARTNERS

The idea for a Royal National Theatre had been debated for two centuries and, at last, this purpose-built theatre arrived on the South Bank. The idea to build a theatrical complex here was conceived by Sir Laurence Olivier in 1963, but it took a further thirteen years for Lasdun and Partners' designs to be realised. The first-ever production starred Peter O'Toole in *Hamlet*, directed by Sir Laurence. The building has three performance venues: the Olivier, the Lyttleton, and the Cottesloe. The building was updated in 1998, with the addition of a new entrance from the river Thames side and a paved square known as Theatre Square.

DESIGN MUSEUM

939   SE1

1989 CONRAN ROCHE

Inspired by 1930s buildings, this was an imaginative renovation and transformation of a 1950s warehouse, with 'cool' stuccoed surfaces painted sparkling white. Its calm spacious interior has galleries on the top two floors, and a neat exhibition display system. Exhibits include cars, tableware, telephones, radios and televisions, washing machines, office equipment, and furniture—arranged by theme. Temporary shows are sometimes held in the Collection Gallery. The top floor focuses on contemporary design, with everything from Nike trainers to an Aston Martin V12 Vanquish. The Blueprint Café enjoys extensive balconies, overlooking the Thames and Tower Bridge. The building was described by fashion designer Paul Smith as 'the natural home for everyone who has ever enjoyed or appreciated design.'

940

BUS STATION

2004 ARUP ASSOCIATES

Vauxhall is London's second busiest bus station; second only to Victoria. It is housed in a landmark structure with gleaming stainless steel everywhere. A long, wide stainless-steel ribbon, studded with photovoltaic cells, is angled towards the sun, and generates electricity for the station lighting. The undulating line this makes is designed to rise over the double-decker buses, and then drop down lower again to integrate rows of seating below. The building has lifts to the new Underground ticket hall, staff offices, and a police station. The whole structure is floodlit, while the underside of the canopy has parallel rows of lights that change to blue further up the roof tilt. This busy building sees 2,000 buses come and go each day, plus 712 tube trains and 730 main-line trains.

THAMESMEAD

941   SE2

FROM 1950s GLC ARCHITECTS DEPARTMENT

Vast marshes once covered this area—enclosed in the early thirteenth century by monks and used in the 1700s by the Woolwich arsenal. Weapons, missiles, and tanks were tested here during the 1800s and, north of Thamesmead, some of the arsenal's moated enclosures still survive. This estate was developed from the 1950s and was part of Thamesmead, a 'new town' suburb. There are twelve-storey blocks and medium-rise concrete buildings, with more recent additions in brick and in more traditional styles. Building continues, and there is still lots of water in the area—now an important resource, used in the parks and in inventive sewage processing works.

MORDEN COLLEGE

942   SE3

1695 POSSIBLY SIR CHRISTOPHER WREN AND EDWARD STRONG

This began as an almshouse founded by philanthropist Sir John Morden, a merchant who faced potential poverty when his ships were believed to be lost. In 1695, when the vessels had finally arrived safely, he built these homes, as a thanks offering—for 'poor Merchants. . . and such as have lost their Estates by accidents, dangers and perils of the seas or by any other accidents ways of means in their honest endeavours to get their living by means of Merchandising.' He is buried here, and there are statues of him and his wife in a double arch in a pediment above the west door. The building has a lovely colonnaded courtyard and is home to elderly people.

COLONNADE HOUSE

943   SE3

c. 1804 MICHAEL SEARLES; RESTORED BERNARD BROWN

This fine detached Georgian house, facing a small pond on the heath, belongs to the Trustees of Morden College. The elegant triangular composition of one, two, and three storeys is linked by a long Tuscan seven-bay colonnade. For many years, the building was a boarding house, but has been restored—and is now let as flats sharing a communal garden.

SUBURBAN HOUSES

944   SE3

c. 1825

There was rumoured to be a vast Black Death plague pit in Blackheath—hence the name. Here, Wat Tyler gathered his revels during the Peasants Revolt of 1381. The village began to spread in the 1820s, as more homes were needed for the middle classes who were moving into the area—a development that increased with the arrival of the railway in 1849. This early suburb of Victorian terraces and villas was built on the grounds of Sir Gregory Page's estate, and has a number of attractive houses in a variety of styles. The tree-lined avenues have now been infiltrated by more recent suburban housing.

TERRACED HOUSING

945   SE3

1957–59 ERIC LYONS (FOR SPAN)

Here in the Hall, the Keep, Corner Row, and South Row, two- and three-storey houses and apartments share well-planted common gardens. The houses are all in 'little-box' rectangular style with neat front porches and an interesting mix of tiles and textures on the surfaces.

THE PARAGON

946   SE3

c. 1795–1806 MICHAEL SEARLES; 1949–58 RESTORED CHARLES BERNARD BROWN

This crescent of large semi-detached Grade I–listed houses is set in a shallow semicircular sweep, with space for carriages, stables, servant's quarters, and large gardens. They were built provided no resident practised the 'art, mystery or trade' of various occupations, including school teaching or fishmongery. One early resident, Miss Eliza Robertson, ran up huge debts, and spent four years in Fleet Prison—still attended by her maid. Linked by single-storey Tuscan colonnades, with a lodge house at each end, they have Georgian windows with arched heads, mansard slate roofs, and vast, rear bay windows.

941

942

943

944

945

946

947

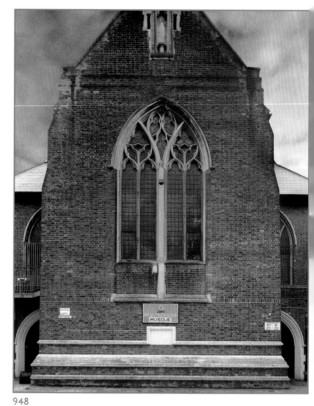

948

949

950

VANBRUGH CASTLE

947   SE3

1770-26 SIR JOHN VANBRUGH

An author of Restoration comedies, Sir John Vanbrugh was also an architect, renowned for his design of Castle Howard and Blenheim Palace. In 1716, he was appointed surveyor to Greenwich Hospital as Wren's successor, and built this edifice—England's first mock medieval castle, overlooking the Royal Hospital. It has Gothic-inspired narrow windows and turrets and false roofs, and was called 'the Bastille' by Vanbrugh—who had been imprisoned in the Bastille in 1692 on suspicion of being a spy. Only the centrepiece has survived redevelopment in the 1890s and 1900s. The Blackheath Preservation Trust purchased the site in 1976 and set about restoring the castle and converting it into four dwellings.

ST MARK

948   SE5

1879-1932 R. NORMAN SHAW

This church in a Victorian street was begun in 1879 and consecrated in June 1880—but was not completed until 1932. In Gothic style with some Queen Anne details, it has octagonal redbrick pillars, wooden vaulting, and a stone screen. It was damaged by bombing during World War II.

ST GILES CHURCH

949   SE5

1842-44 SIR GEORGE GILBERT SCOTT;
WEST FRONT SIR ARTHUR BLOMFIELD

In February 1841, the parish church of Camberwell was destroyed by fire. A competition to find an architect for a new church was won by the Scott & Moffatt practice. This replacement church, raised with the £14,500 insurance money, was consecrated in November 1844. Its central tower has a broach spire some 64 metres (210 feet) high; this has recently undergone a complete rebuild due to major structural defects. The large Kentish ragstone church is in Gothic style, but with some continental details; and its imposing porch has many decorative features. The church is now Grade II listed. An early 1300s church once stood on this site, and just a few remnants of this have been placed in the south wall of the present chancel.

SOUTH LONDON ART GALLERY

950   SE5

1896-98 MAURICE B. ADAMS

This contemporary art gallery has Victorian origins, being launched as part of the South London Working Men's College—whose principal was biologist Thomas Henry Huxley (grandfather of Aldous Huxley). The college (with its library) has relocated several times, but has remained under local authority control; it is now the responsibility of the New London Borough of Southwark. In 1953, to celebrate the coronation, the gallery added contemporary works (by artists such as John Piper and Christopher Wood) to its permanent collection and then acquired over five hundred twentieth-century prints. It presents many shows and events, including exhibits by renowned contemporary artists.

951

SCHOOL OF ARTS AND CRAFTS

951 SE5

1896–98 MAURICE B. ADAMS

Many apprentice craftsmen once learned their design skills through the forerunner of this institution, whose first president was William Gladstone. After 1908, fine art was taught, too. There were classes in architecture, cabinet design, embroidery, wood carving, wood block and stencil cutting, stone carving, plasterwork, house painting and decorating, drawing and design, life classes, and modelling. A new sculpture building opened in 1953. By 1968, painting, sculpture, graphic design, ceramics, metalwork, textiles, art history, and printing were taught in this redbrick, stone, and slate building. In 1986, the school became part of the London Institute.

952

BRUNSWICK PARK JUNIOR SCHOOL

952 SE5

1958–62 STIRLING AND GOWAN

Once upon a time, this was just a conventional junior Victorian school around which a sprawling housing estate developed—until the school was no longer large enough to serve its community. Developed by two quite influential architects, its new square plan is divided into four smaller squares. It has steep-pitched roofs with glazed façades on three sides so light pours inside, and locally it has been nicknamed the 'Butterfly Building.' The walls are in brickwork with some decorative redbrick banding. Large, steeply ramped grass banks add to the building's landscaping—its exciting angles emphasised by its proximity to the original Victorian school.

953

OLD PEOPLE'S HOME

953 SE7

1960 STIRLING AND GOWAN

The accommodation here was planned around an internal courtyard, and varies from one to three storeys. Here there is expressive use of brickwork with castellations, stepped sections, a high 'keep,' arches, and tall stepped strips enclosing window areas. This street is also home to the Cherry Orchard Primary School—so both ends of the age spectrum are well served in this neighbourhood.

CHARLTON HOUSE

954   SE7

1607-12 ATTRIBUTED TO JOHN THORPE

This is the only complete Jacobean house in Greater
London. It was built as a retirement gift for Adam Newton,
a tutor to James I's son—now a community centre and
library. The redbrick building has white stone quoins
and dressings, and forms an H shape. An orangery and
summerhouse here are probably the work of Inigo Jones.
The north wing was damaged in World War II and rebuilt,
but much else survived intact, including original ceilings,
fireplaces, the carved main staircase, wood panelling, and
stables. The ceilings have been restored using the original
mouldings. The oldest mulberry tree in England may be the
one planted here by James I in 1608.

954

LABAN DANCE CENTRE

955   SE8

1997-2003 HERZOG & DE MEURON

Here are vast, sweeping, semi-translucent glass façades,
especially impressive when lit at night. This unique
building was named after Rudolph Laban (1879–1958),
described as the father of modern dance. Purpose-built
for dance training, it claims to be the biggest and best-
equipped contemporary dance school in Europe. Internal
courts let natural light into the building—and allow views
across it. The interior is painted in strong colours and has
two black spiral staircases. Thirteen studios are arranged
around the perimeter; the centre houses a three-hundred-
seat theatre.

955

ST PAUL

956   SE8

1712-30 THOMAS ARCHER; 1975-76 RESTORED

This rather refined building is considered to be one
of the loveliest parish churches in the city and a royal
commission described it as one of London's best Italianate
Baroque buildings. The church has a splendid semicircular
Doric colonnade, crowned by a tall pointed steeple in
slender 'wedding-cake' tiers. Tablets commemorate John
Harrison, who founded the London Hospital and was a
surgeon there; while Margaret Hawtrees, a midwife, is
remembered in an inscription that reads:
'She was an indulgent mother, and the best of wives.
She brought into this world more than three thousand lives.'

956

957

958

TUDOR HOUSE

957   SE9

ELTHAM PALACE

958   SE9

Eltham developed along the old road from London to Maidstone. Its name may mean 'Homestead or river meadow frequented by swans' or, more likely, 'a man named Elta.' Later Tudor royalty preferred the riverside palace of Greenwich, but Sir John Shaw, supporter of Charles II's Restoration, built himself an elegant mansion here, Eltham Lodge. Famous locals include Bob Hope and Lee Ryan (born here), Frankie Howerd and Boy George (brought up here), and the daughter of Sir Thomas More, Margaret, and her husband, William Roper, who lived nearby at the Tudor Barn. Edith Nesbit (whose books include *The Phoenix and the Carpet* and *The Railway Children*) lived at Well Hall House. This particular building is a superb slice of Tudor architecture with its sturdy timberwork striping the gable end, dormers, superb leaded windows, and overhanging upper storeys.

1300S; 1479; 1931-37 RESTORED STEPHEN COURTAULD

In the 1000s, Odo, Bishop of Bayeux owned Eltham manor, but it was a royal palace from 1311—presented to the future Edward II; he extended it for Queen Isabella, who spent much time here. It was ever a convenient spot for monarchs travelling to and from their French territories. Later improvements and the building of a stone bridge over the moat were supervised by Geoffrey Chaucer, then clerk of works. Here, Henry IV was married by proxy to Joan of Navarre in 1402. The moat bridge and the great hall (built in the late fifteenth century) have survived. The hall boasts the third largest hammer-beam roof in England, constructed about 1479 by Edward IV. A new chapel was built in the reign of Henry VIII, who often called by. When Parliament seized it, after the execution of Charles I, the palace was used as a farm. It was soon reported to be 'much out of repair,' and by the 1660s, was in ruins—with the Great Hall used as a barn. It was not rescued until the 1930s, when the medieval palace was restored and a new house rose here, too, with a splendid Art Deco interior and a glass dome. At the entrance to the palace, in Court Yard, is Chaundrye Close, once home to Cardinal Wolsey.

959

960

GREENWICH PENINSULA

THE MILLENNIUM DOME

959   SE10

4–6 BALLAST QUAY; FORMERLY THE UNION TAVERN

CUTTY SARK

960   SE10

1997–2000 IMAGINATION (GARY WITHERS), RICHARD ROGERS PARTNERSHIP (MIKE DAVIES), BURO HAPPOLD (IAN LIDELL)

Built on the site of an abandoned gasworks, this vast umbrella structure is made of a double layer of lightweight coated fabric—92,900 square metres (1 million square feet) of it—and the roof is strong enough to support the weight of a jumbo jet. From the tips of steel tube masts (each set on a steel base), tensioned steel cables are anchored to the perimeter. The Dome's 'footprint' is ten times the size of St Paul's Cathedral and the area it covers (24,282 square metres, or 6 acres) is one hundred times larger than Stonehenge—bigger than the Great Pyramids, three times larger than the Colosseum, and twenty-five times greater than the Taj Mahal. The structure includes canopied walkways and a floating jetty. The enormous twenty-acre roof has a volume that could contain 1,100 Olympic-size swimming pools or 80,000 double-decker buses. If inverted under Niagara Falls, it would take ten minutes to fill. The exterior masts lean at three times the angle of the Leaning Tower of Pisa—and are forty metres (131 feet) taller. The Millennium Exhibition ended as the year did.

1805

Here, in a delightful row of elegant houses from the late 1700s and early 1800s, is this Grade II–listed tavern with a large bow window. There has been an inn here for nearly five hundred years. The present building (renamed after the famous tea clipper in dry dock at Greenwich), dates back to at least the early nineteenth century, but may well be much older. The ground floor bar is dominated by an enormous staircase, and there are nooks and crannies everywhere, stone and bare board floors, black oak beams, Victorian glass, ship timbers, brass lamps, and lanterns. The chairs are made out of barrels to reflect this nautical flavour. Outside, a riverside terrace is set beyond a narrow cobbled way.

ROYAL NAVAL COLLEGE

961   SE10

1694–1742 SIR CHRISTOPHER WREN, NICHOLAS HAWKSMOOR,
SIR JOHN VANBRUGH, JOHN WEBB, AND OTHERS

The King Charles Block was planned as a palace; the hospital arrived later, on the instructions of Queen Mary of Orange, who was concerned about the plight of wounded sailors. This magnificent retreat incorporated the Queen's House and King Charles Block into a grand symmetrical sweep. The buildings mirror each other, and create an 'avenue' leading to the river. The hospital closed to pensioners in 1869; the buildings were occupied by the Royal Naval College from 1873 until 1998—and have appeared in *The Madness of King George*, *Four Weddings and a Funeral*, *The Mummy Returns* and *Lara Croft: Tomb Raider*.

HOUSING

CREEK ROAD

962   SE10

1967 JAMES GOWAN

Scottish architect, teacher, lecturer, and author James Gowan began working in the New Brutalist style with his partner, Sir James Stirling, in the late 1950s and early '60s. Together, they created some of the most important and influential post-war buildings in Britain. Gowan liked to combine elemental geometrical forms with meticulous detailing; he explored new materials and how to use them expressively—especially brick and exposed concrete. This very simple brick housing in Greenwich has an interesting composition of tall, narrow elements, and is reminiscent of work by Dutch architect Willem Marinus Dudok.

TRAFALGAR ROAD

FOUR-STOREY MAISONETTES

963   SE10

1965–68 JAMES GOWAN

Here, tall maisonettes enclose an internal courtyard. They have redbrick façades and industrial metal windows, inspired by 1930s styling. A second-floor access gallery is cut into the surface, and there are neat bridges. From this angle, the simple façades of the blocks seem to slot into each other and create a geometric pattern—almost like a child's building block structure—with only a few windows visible.

GREENWICH HIGH ROAD AND ROYAL HILL

GREENWICH TOWN HALL

964   SE10

1939 E. C. CULPIN AND BOWERS

This style of this yellow stock-brick building seems to be a hybrid of factory and church parentage. It has a tall, stylish tower with a banner of windows at the top and a dominant clock. Inspired by Dutch and Scandinavian architecture, the interior has 'ocean liner' features. It is no longer a town hall, and is used by Greenwich Dance Agency.

7 COLLEGE APPROACH

ADMIRAL HARDY

965   SE10

1830

This tavern exterior remains more or less original with its formal stone frontage and narrow, deep sash windows. Inside is a stone floor, wooden panelled walls, a cast-iron fireplace, suitably nautical oil paintings, and tall lamps made from oars. The pub adjoins the covered market and at one time incorporated a grocery store, fishmongers, and a delicatessen. The tavern was named after the Hardy from whom Nelson received his dying kiss at Trafalgar. Captain Hardy served with Nelson in Egypt, Naples, Sicily, Copenhagen, Toulon, and the West Indies. He became the first sea lord of the admiralty but spent the last years of his life as governor of Greenwich Hospital.

ASHBURNHAM GROVE

THE ASHBURNHAM ARMS

966   SE10

c. 1850

Built to serve the local artisans, clerks, and tradespeople of Greenwich, this plain brown-brick pub is set in a quiet area of small brick cottages and villas in early-Victorian streets and terraces. It has a large L-shaped bar, a tiny snug, a spacious conservatory, and a beer garden beyond. The Coade stone lions now standing regally on the south side of Westminster Bridge used to be outside the gates of the Lion Brewery that owned this pub. It has featured in the campaign for Real Ale's *Good Beer Guide* for many years. Author Edgar Wallace was born in this street in 1875, at number 7.

961

962

963

964

965

966

967

968

969

QUEEN'S HOUSE

967   SE10

1616-35 INIGO JONES; 1637 JOHN WEBB

From the 1400s, nobility had enjoyed the Greenwich countryside (Henry VII and Elizabeth I were born there). The Queen's House was built as a potential home for two queens but neither lived here. In 1613, James I had given the existing Greenwich Palace to his wife, but the old rambling building was not to Anne of Denmark's taste, so Inigo Jones was instructed to build a new building where the old southern gatehouse stood. Anne died before this was complete and the building remained 'in limbo' until Charles I decided it might suit his wife. John Webb enlarged it and added further bridges along two fronts, but Henrietta Maria preferred Hampton Court and never moved in, either. The house became the home of the governor of the naval hospital. It has a beautifully proportioned Palladian-inspired façade and was a model for many later buildings.

CHAPEL

968   SE10

1600s CHRISTOPHER WREN AND THOMAS RIPLEY; 1789 JAMES 'ATHENIAN' STUART AND WILLIAM NEWTON

Wren's original chapel was gutted in 1779, when a fire spread from a tailor's shop below. Its restoration incorporated elaborate Baroque and Rococo styling with delicate plasterwork decorations and pastel colours. Two pairs of vast Corinthian columns flank Benjamin West's vast painting of St Paul's shipwreck near Malta. Decorative panels on the pulpit also depict St Paul, and there are excellent paintings by Italian artist Biagio Rebecca. A fine bust depicts Admiral Sir Thomas Hardy (of 'Kiss me, Hardy' fame), who commanded the Victory at Trafalgar. The huge organ, set in a gallery with fluted, marble Ionic columns, was made by famous organ-builder Samuel Green. Above the entrance, rises a great domed tower with eight bays and three tiers of windows.

ENERGY-SAVING SAINSBURY'S

969   SE10

1996-2000 CHETWOOD ASSOCIATES

This store is all curves, glass and timber. Daylight pours through an arching glass and steel roof into this pioneering low-energy building with superb insulation. Air is drawn from under the earth banks and warmed by under-floor heating pipes, while earth at the sides of the building insulates and shelters it, and reduces wind turbulence. Thick concrete side walls support a dramatic arched roof. Many features contribute to this energy-saving structure that uses only half the energy of a standard store. Even the entrance mats were made from recycled bus and aeroplane tyres, and the panels in customer toilets from recycled plastic bottles. The signs are illuminated with electricity generated by a wind turbine and solar panels.

ST ALFEGE
970   SE10

POST-1012; 1200s; 1712–18 NICHOLAS HAWKSMOOR JOHN JAMES; 1730 WESTERN TOWER JOHN JAMES; 1952 RESTORED SIR ALBERT RICHARDSON

A slab in the chancel pavement commemorates the 1012 murder by Danes of St Alfrege, Archbishop of Canterbury, after he refused to sanction a demand for ransom. The first church arrived soon afterwards. Henry VIII was baptised here. A window commemorates composer Thomas Tallis, buried here in 1585. The present church (financed by a coal tax) is a splendid example of Hawksmoor's distinctive design, with columns and pediments surmounted by urns. The original wrought-iron altar and gallery rails are attributed to Jean Tijou, a Huguenot refugee and renowned craftsman. General Wolfe was buried here in the family vault in 1759, and General Gordon, hero of Khartoum, was christened here in 1833. Ruskin Spear created the stained glass of the east window, and in 1956, designed the aisle windows, which depict local historical scenes.

PARK ROW
TRAFALGAR TAVERN
971   SE10

1837 JOSEPH KAY; 1965 RESTORED

The old George pub was replaced with this grand tavern, renamed to commemorate the lying-in-state of Nelson's corpse (preserved in a barrel of brandy) in the nearby hospital in 1806. People used to take a cruise upriver to enjoy a whitebait supper here—inspired by member of Pitt's cabinet who entertained his colleagues at his Greenwich house with this delicacy. Liberals held their whitebait dinners in the Trafalgar's grand saloon with eight chandeliers—now called the Nelson Room. Gladstone used to arrive in a Royal Navy barge. Later, it became a seamen's mission, then a working men's club. Its award-winning restoration covered several stately saloons, a grand ballroom, ornate fireplaces, oak panelling, moulded plasterwork, and a main bar lined with naval prints. Customers have included writers Thackeray, Wilkie Collins, and Dickens—who set the scene of a wedding feast in *Our Mutual Friend* here.

MONKTON STREET
LAMBETH COMMUNITY CARE CENTRE
972   SE11

1985 EDWARD CULINIAN ARCHITECTS

This is located in a quiet back street of nineteenth-century, small terraced houses mixed with sprinkling of small industrial premises. Here a community centre provides physiotherapy, occupational therapy, dentistry, and social work—as well as places to eat and relax. The main staircase is placed in a conservatory that links the two floors. Short-stay accommodation upstairs serves twenty patients, with a sitting room and a staff room opening out onto a south-facing terrace above the garden. This building has won the RIBA Regional Award 1988, the PA Award for Innovation 1988, and the Civic Trust Award 1987.

COURTENAY SQUARE
REGENCY-STYLE HOUSES
973   SE11

1914 ADSHEAD AND RAMSAY

Just a few buildings remain of a model estate built on the Duchy of Cornwall Estate as part of a slum-clearance scheme. The houses are in brick with delicate timber trellis porches—this pair sharing a curving porch roof that looks almost Asian. These pretty two-storey terraced houses have lovely arched windows on the ground floor, their curves echoed by the railings in front of them.

970

971

972

973

974

KENNINGTON PARK ROAD

A PARK LODGE

974   SE11

1851 HENRY ROBERTS

Kennington Common was a site of public executions until 1800, and witnessed many a grisly hanging. More cheerfully, this has ever been a place for great cricket matches, long before the Oval cricket ground arrived. Later, when John Wesley spoke here in 1739, he addressed a crowd of some 30,000. In 1852, the common was enclosed after the unruly Chartists had gathered here in 1848. Charlie Chaplin grew up locally and is possibly met his first girlfriend in the park. This building eventually became the lodge for Kennington Park; it looks like a single entity but in fact was designed to comprise four small Tudor-style homes—two on each storey. The building was first seen at the 1851 Great Exhibition, as an example of Reformist housing. Then, with its multi-coloured brickwork, elegant gables, and central balcony, it was rebuilt here.

NEW CROSS ROAD

DEPTFORD TOWN HALL

975   SE14

1900-03 LANCHESTER, STEWART AND RICKARDS

The architects for this Grade II–listed town hall, one of Deptford's most renowned buildings, were chosen through a competition. Their work was instrumental in the classical revival and founding of Edwardian Baroque. This magnificent, seven-bay stone façade has many nautical features, including statues of admirals and a clock tower with a sailing-ship weathervane. A sea battle is depicted in the tympanum and, inside, behind this jolly façade, are marble columns, more sculptures, and a domed lantern. The building was given a much-needed facelift after Goldsmiths College acquired it in 2000.

975

976

977

978

979

980

981

CAROLINE GARDENS

976   SE15

1827–28 HENRY ROSE

Nearly two hundred almshouses were erected here between 1828 and 1866 to provide homes for retired members of the licensed victualling trade, and a chapel sprang up, too, in six acres of grounds. While the chapel in the centre has a handsome Doric portico, these plain yellow-brick façades face an undecorated court and have scant embellishment. In 1959, the property was turned into retirement homes. The buildings were renamed Caroline Gardens to honour a nineteenth-century local, Caroline Secker, the widow of James Secker, who had served with Nelson at the Battle of Trafalgar.

ST MARY'S ROAD
PIONEER HEALTH CENTRE

977   SE15

1934–36 SIR OWEN WILLIAMS

This, the 'Peckham experiment,' was founded to provide a place where families could discuss their health problems, seek the advice of trained staff, and enjoy excellent sporting and recreational facilities—including a large swimming pool with a glazed roof, a gymnasium, and theatre. This three-storey building was built in concrete and glass with six bay windows, cork floors to encourage people to walk about barefoot, and inner partition walls of glass. During World War II, the building was taken over by a munitions company, and today provides a rather more conventional adult education centre, a doctor's clinic, and housing.

ST MARY CHURCH STREET
ST MARY ROTHERHITHE

978   SE16

1282; 1714 JOHN JAMES; 1739 STONE SPIRE. LAUNCELOT DOWBIGGIN SPIRE; 1876 RESTORED WILLIAM BUTTERFIELD

The first church here, served by Catholic priests from Bermondsey Abbey, became a Puritan church. In 1714, parishioners and local craftsmen rebuilt it 'which standing very low and near the banks of the Thames, is often overflowed, whereby the foundation . . . is rotted and in great danger of falling.' Some medieval stone blocks remain. The piers are ship masts, encased in plaster. The Bishop's Chair is of timber salvaged from a battle of Trafalgar gun ship. A plaque commemorates Prince Lee Boo, son of a cannibal chief, who rescued shipwrecked sailors in 1783 and was brought to visit Rotherhithe.

265 ROTHERHITHE STREET
NELSON HOUSE

979   SE16

c. 1770

Nelson Dock is the only dry dock left in London. This very pleasing five-bay house with its beautiful wrought-iron gates and an elegant, white central section was the original dock owner's home—and a very rare example of the style used for merchant ship owners during the 1700s. It is now part of a Hilton Hotel complex that incorporates the original wharf buildings here. Nearby is *La Dame de Serk*, a full-size replica of a three-masted French barque that now houses a bistro called Traders.

ONEGA GATE, REDRIFF ROAD
FINLAND QUAYS WEST

980   SE16

1989 RICHARD REID ARCHITECTS

Greenland Dock is the oldest of London's riverside docks—a trading post for the import of softwoods (many from Scandinavia) with berths for over a hundred merchant ships. Now the busy dockside scene has been replaced with offices, luxury homes, and leisure facilities. Here, seven different house formats are linked along the old Greenland Dock, the name an echo of earlier whaling days. The first enclosed dock appeared in this area in 1697. Rotherhithe was the fictional birthplace of Jonathan Swift's character Lemuel Gulliver, of *Gulliver's Travels* fame, and here the *Mayflower* cast off for the New World. Now the waters are more like a quiet lake.

PLOUGH WAY
SUTTON DWELLINGS

981   SE16

1967 FREDERICK MACMANUS AND PARTNERS, DESIGNED BY JEREMY DIXON

A massive building programme took place in this dockland area during the late 1980s and early 1990s. Some 5,500 new homes were built, including individual houses, apartment complexes and shopping centres. Here, forty-eight large family flats share a lift, a raised garden above the parking area, a workshop, and a day-care nursery. It is close to South Dock—which now has the largest marina in London—and the impressive water-sports centre on Greenland Dock.

LIVERPOOL GROVE

ST PETER WALWORTH

982   SE17

1823–25 SIR JOHN SOANE; 1953 RECONSTRUCTION T. F. FORD

This is one of the loveliest of Soane's churches and the first to be designed by him. The Grade I–listed building has an Ionic portico into which its four columns fit very neatly–supporting a frieze with immaculate Greek decoration. There are tall arched windows set each side of the portico and a high, slender two-stage tower rises above. The church was built as part of wave of new churches, especially in poorer areas, that authorities hoped would address the spread of non-conformity and dissent. During World War II bombing, eighty-four people were killed while sheltering in the crypt.

103 WOOLWICH NEW ROAD

ST PETER THE APOSTLE

983   SE18

1843 AUGUSTUS WELBY NORTHMORE PUGIN

St Peter's has no tower and its chancel was added later. Pugin was the son of a French architect who came to England to escape the French Revolution. He designed both Anglican and Catholic churches here and abroad. His father had taught him to draw Gothic remains and, from fifteen years old, he was designing Gothic-style furniture for Windsor Castle. Later, he worked with Sir Charles Barry to complete the plans for the Houses of Parliament. Pugin produced a 'mediæval court' at the Great Exhibition of 1851 but died suddenly after a mental collapse. Queen Victoria granted his widow a pension of £100 a year. He was the father of Victorian architect E. W. Pugin.

85–91 GENESTA ROAD, PLUMSTEAD

HOUSING PROJECT

984   SE18

1935 B. LUBETKIN AND A. V. PILICHOWSKI

This was the first British housing project completed by Lubetkin—a most prominent architect in the British Modernist movement. This Modernist terrace, is a unique row, said to have been built for workers at a local factory. The houses have been awarded an English Heritage Grade II listing for exceptional design and historic importance. The simplicity is relieved by projecting window areas above street level and unusual balconies. A spiral central staircase cuts through the core of the house. Outside, the gardens have circular lawned tiers and views over London to the Thames and Canary Wharf.

GRAND DEPOT ROAD

GARRISON CHURCH OF ST GEORGE

985   SE18

1863 T. H. WYATT

Renamed after a visit by King George in 1928, St George's Church was the garrison church of the Royal Artillery but, sadly, was largely destroyed in 1944 by a German VI flying bomb. Now it survives only as a restored ruin set in a commemorative garden, but it still presents an elegant façade. The Lombard porch, columns, fragments of mosaic, and a few elements of its early Romanesque basilica remain. The Royal Artillery Victoria Cross memorial is in the form of a fine Italian mosaic depicting St George. Today, the ruins are still consecrated, as a memorial church.

BERESFORD SQUARE

ROYAL ARSENAL

986   SE18

1717–20 SIR JOHN VANBRUGH

Woolwich is an historic riverside site linked to both dockyard and weaponry since Henry VIII raised the first arsenal in 1512. In 1671, the Crown bought an old mansion (Tower Place), to use as an ordnance storage depot, and soon ammunition, fuses, and gunpowder were made here, too. This brick entrance is magnificent, with robust piers, lions set on pedestals, and a high central semicircular arch. In 1716—after an accident at the city's Moorfield foundry caused seventeen deaths—the government built its own foundry at Woolwich, designed by Sir John Vanbrugh. It is still much as it was then but today is home to a fascinating museum on firepower and artillery.

CASTLEWOOD, OFF SHOOTERS HILL ROAD

SEVERNDROOG CASTLE

987   SE18

1784 W. JUPP

In the 1500s, Shooters Hill was a beacon hill for signal bonfires. Here, rising above the trees of Castlewood, this triangular Gothic tower is an attractive folly with castellated hexagonal turrets and lancet windows. It was raised by Sir William James's widow (whose house was in the valley below) to celebrate her courageous seafaring husband's 1755 capture of its namesake, a pirate fortress in India. Ironically, a pirate radio station attempted to put its antenna on the roof of this Grade II–listed building. The castle rises 19 metres (63 feet) high but needs repair and, in 2004, was featured in the BBC *Restoration* series.

982

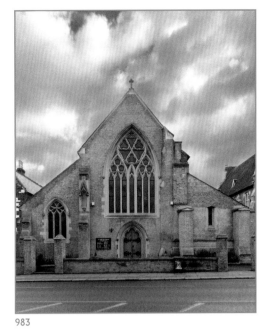

983

984

985

986

987

988

989

ROYAL ARTILLERY BARRACKS

988   SE18

1775–1802

Woolwich has been the home of the Royal Artillery since 1716 but the Master General of the Ordnance has equipped British campaigns from here since 1671. In 1805, the Royal Carriage Factory, Royal Laboratory, and Royal Foundry were amalgamated into the Royal Arsenal. Its splendid façade is the longest (323 metres, or 1,060 feet) continuous single piece of architecture in London. It has a white triumphal arch in the centre, with the three-storey brick barracks linked by elegant white colonnades. Today the Queen is Captain-General of the Royal Artillery. Woolwich has a few other claims to fame. General Gordon of Khartoum was born at 29 Woolwich Common and educated at the Royal Military Academy, diarist Samuel Pepys lodged in Woolwich during 1665 to escape the plague, and the United Kingdom's first ever McDonald's arrived here in 1974.

ACADEMY ROAD, WOOLWICH COMMON

WOOLWICH GARRISON

989   SE18

1805–8 J. WYATT

The former Royal Military Academy was launched in 1741 to instruct 'raw and inexperienced' recruits and, some sixty years later, this building was raised next to Woolwich Common—to replace the original school within the Arsenal. A brown and yellow brick façade in Gothic Revival style, it overlooks the parade ground with its centrepiece and domed corner turrets based on the Tower of London. The end pavilions are a later addition. It is still possible to see soldiers from the nearby Royal Artillery Barracks training on Woolwich Common. The Woolwich garrison is now home to a thousand infantry soldiers who are mainly engaged in ceremonial duties.

990

DULWICH MUSEUM, MAUSOLEUM AND PICTURE GALLERY

990   SE21

1811–14 SIR JOHN SOANE

England's oldest public art gallery was built for Dulwich College in simple classical lines. Unfussy and elegant, it houses a collection of paintings originally intended for the king of Poland but left to Sir Francis Bourgeois, whose bequest funded the college. Here are almshouses and, at the heart of the Gallery, a small mausoleum— possibly based on an Alexandrian catacomb—where the founders still lie. The buildings were renovated in 1953 after the mausoleum had suffered a direct bomb hit in 1944. The art gallery houses a collection of masterpieces by Canaletto, Gainsborough, Poussin, Rembrandt, Rubens, and Watteau.

991

POND COTTAGES

991   SE21

1700s

Here in prosperous Dulwich is a fascinating mix of twentieth-century suburbia, Victorian houses, clusters of cottages, and fine Georgian buildings. In the traditional village centre is the world-famous Dulwich Picture Gallery—England's oldest. Near the Mill Pond, by Dulwich College playing fields, are these delightfully rural, weatherboard and brick Pond Cottages, where the miller and tile-kiln workers once lived. Further down the road, a working toll-gate is the only one still in operation in London. Charles I came here to hunt stags but it was not always so peaceful. Two highway robberies occurred within an hour in 1800, and the common was often the site of a bloody duel.

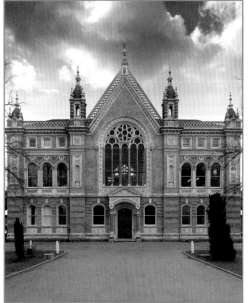

992

DULWICH COLLEGE

992   SE21

1866–70 CHARLES BARRY JUNIOR

An Elizabethan actor who had earned extra income licensing bears, bulls, and mastiff dogs bought Dulwich manor and founded a school for twelve poor boys in 1619. During the Civil War, Roundheads melted its organ pipes to make bullets, and quartered troops here. These new buildings were designed by the son of Sir Charles Barry in ornate Palladian, Italian Renaissance, and Gothic styles—in redbrick and terracotta. P. G. Wodehouse (of Jeeves and Wooster fame) attended school here, as did writer Raymond Chandler and explorer Ernest Shackleton. Its archives include a William Shakespeare folio, original poems by John Donne, and the lifeboat in which Shackleton made his courageous voyage to Elephant Island. It still serves as an independent, fee-paying school.

100 LONDON ROAD, FOREST HILL
HORNIMAN MUSEUM

993   SE23

1896–1901 C. H. TOWNSEND; 2002 NEW EXTENTION

Designed by an Arts and Crafts architect, this museum has a massive clock tower. Its top-lit galleries house the collection of F. J. Horniman —a prosperous tea trader in the late 1800s—and include musical instruments and curios such as an orang-utan's foot and Arabian shoes with flaps to scare off scorpions! The collection began in his home but, by 1898, Horniman had commissioned this museum. The exterior is in smooth stone with relief ornament and a large mosaic façade, *Humanity in the House of Circumstance* by Robert Anning Bell. The exterior is free style; interiors are simple and functional, but the Victorian atmosphere pervades. A lecture hall and library were added in 1910. There are sixteen acres of gardens and an aquarium.

993

CRESCENT WOOD ROAD
SIX PILLARS

994   SE26

1935 VALENTINE HARDING AND BERTHOLD LUBETKIN

As a student, Lubetkin had witnessed the Bolshevik revolution in Russia. He said that this was a defining moment and that architecture was another kind of politics: it should change people's lives. Lubetkin found others to join his radical practice, Tecton, aiming to bring Modernism to Britain. Grade II–listed Six Pillars was built for the headmaster of Dulwich preparatory school. An understated blend of concrete and London-stock brick, it has a high roof terrace and, of course, six pillars. At the back, large windows run the length of the rooms; in the ground-floor drawing room, a huge window-wall spans half the length of the house. There are multi-level roof terraces, a promenade balcony, and a wall of glass blocks with a 'cockpit' study set high above. The emphasis is on space and light.

994

KNIGHT'S HILL, NORWOOD HIGH STREET
ST LUKE

995   SE27

1822 F. O. BEDFORD

Set on a pleasing elevated site, this is one of the four Commissioner's churches in South London named after Matthew, Mark, Luke, and John. They were built with funds granted by Parliament as thanks for victory against Napoleon, and so are sometimes called the Waterloo churches. Unusually, this one was built by a female contractor, one Elizabeth Broomfield. It is in restrained Corinthian style with acanthus (a thistle-like plant) motifs. The interior was remodelled in 1878 by G. E. Street in Italian Romanesque style.

995

CLOSE TO LONDON

London is a huge city, and the previous sections of this book have concentrated on the more central areas because there is so very much to explore there. However, the capital's fringes have many fascinating treasures. Through the centuries, old Roman and drovers' roads turned into routes for horse and cart and coach; then railways, main roads, and motorways arrived—as they did, bringing more people into the city, the opportunities to escape from the centre also multiplied. This selection is only a taste of what can be discovered just a little farther out—and looks in particular at Kew. Other places within easy reach include Windsor Castle and Hampton Court (see page 556).

St Albans, for example, is only twenty-odd miles north of central London and has an abbey, cathedral, old town hall, market place, medieval clock tower, and Roman Verulamium—this was a major city in AD 130. To the west, Wembley boasts one of the world's most famous football stadiums, the English national football ground since 1923—where a new state-of-the-art stadium is presently rising. In the southwest, Richmond Park was enclosed by Charles I in 1637, and has red and fallow deer that are descendants of the original herd stocked by Henry VIII; the town has lovely Georgian dwellings. To the east, Romford has been a market town since 1247, and since mediæval days has had rights that stopped its neighbour Ilford from holding a market until the 1990s. It grew along the old Roman road to Colchester, named after a ford over a small stream called the Rom.

Meanwhile, the city of Rochester in Kent developed from a tiny Saxon village and Roman town (in AD 43). Charles Dickens lived here for a while and many of his novels included references to Rochester. Here, in the 1000s, busy Bishop Gundolf constructed a stone castle on the remains of the old Roman fort, a magnificent cathedral (the second oldest in the country,) and a leper hospital—as well as raising Maidstone cathedral and 'commuting in' to build the Tower of London.

TW9   Kew, Richmond
DA6   Bexleyheath
DA18 Thamesmead

DA17

DA18 1000

Eastern Way

Yarnton Way

Abbey Rd.

Bronze Road

West St.

Erith Rd.

Fraser Rd

Manor Rd

DA8

Bexley Road

Colyers La.

DA16

Lodge

Okehampton Cr.

Brampton Road

Long Lane

DA7

Parkside Ave.

Thames Road

Wickham

Upper Wickham

Bellegrove Rd.

Park View

Crook Log

Broadway

Albion Rd

Mayplace

Bob Dun

Westwood

Danson

999

Union Rd

Watling

Old Rd

London

Perry St

Iron Mill La

Crayford Way

Burnham Rd.

Blackfern Road

East Rochester Way

Danson Rd

DA6

Graveney Road

Crayford

Dartford West

DA1

DA15

Halfway Street

Hurst

Road

Parkhill Rd.

Bourne

Shepherd's Lane

Heath Lane

Prince

Longlands

Faraday Av

Bexley La

North Cray Rd.

Dartford Rd

Old Bexley

Oakfield

Parsons La

Station

DA14

DA5

Summer House

Broad La.

High Road

Main Road

Rectory La.

Sidcup Hill

Birchwood Road

DA2

Barn

Shire

Sidcup Bypass

Cray Rd

Maidstone Road

996

996

PALM HOUSE

996   TW9

1844–48 DECIMUS BURTON AND RICHARD TURNER

Prince Frederick, the son of George II and Queen Caroline, leased the Kew estate in the 1730s—and it was after his death in 1751 that his widow began the first true botanic garden here. Sir Joseph Banks was the first director of the royal gardens from 1772. He had sailed with Captain James Cook, on the HMS *Endeavour* (naming Botany Bay, Australia, in 1770) and collected many exotic plants. In due course, these were housed in Botany Bay House (1788–1856); 1841 is generally regarded as the foundation of the Royal Botanic Gardens when Sir William Hooker founded the museum, library, and herbarium. In 1848, the Palm House was added. This Grade I–listed building, a glass and iron palace for plants, is one of the world's finest surviving nineteenth-century glasshouses, and was the largest in the world when it opened. It was created specifically to house the collection of exotic palms and its structure was based on shipbuilding techniques, the design like an upturned hull. In 1984, it was emptied to be rebuilt and restored (see page 554—a photograph taken when this work was complete and the glasshouse was open for a week before being refilled with plants). Undoubtedly this helped it to survive the severe gales in 1987. It reopened in 1988, and today its toughened safety glass is held by sixteen kilometres (ten miles) of stainless-steel glazing bars.

ROYAL HOMES:
WINDSOR CASTLE
AND HAMPTON COURT

The towers and battlements of impressive Windsor Castle rise above the old town, with its timbered buildings, to make a defiant stand against the sky. The first castle, built by William the Conqueror in 1070, fell to a siege in 1193—led by Prince John, brother to Richard the Lionheart, and king some six years later. This is the largest occupied castle in the world and the oldest in continuous occupation—a royal home and fortress for over nine hundred years, except for Roundhead occupation during the Civil War. Its State Apartments ooze treasures from the Royal Collection, including paintings by Holbein, Rubens, and Van Dyck, fine tapestries, porcelain, sculpture, armour—and drawings from the Royal Library, including works by Leonardo da Vinci, Hans Holbein, and Canaletto in the Drawings Gallery. A special treat here is Queen Mary's Doll's House—a palace in miniature, built to a scale of one to twelve in the 1920s. Its miniature lights illuminate both state rooms and servants' quarters. St George's Hall was completely restored after a fierce fire in 1992 and is where the Queen holds banquets and receptions. Beautiful Gothic St George's Chapel dates back to the 1300s; ten sovereigns are buried here.

Hampton Court Palace is set in vast acres of gardens and is famous for its maze, built in 1714. The first buildings here were raised for the Knights Hospitallers in 1236, but in 1514, Thomas Wolsey, chief minister to Henry VIII, was granted the lease. He transformed it into a magnificent residence with new kitchens, courtyards, galleries, and gardens—all in due course seized by his sovereign when Wolsey fell from royal favour—largely because of his opposition to Anne Boleyn. Within a decade, the king had lavished an enormous sum (over £62,000) on this opulent home. Henry married Jane Seymour just eleven days after Anne Boleyn was despatched by a French swordsman, and Jane gave birth to the future King Edward VI at Hampton Court in 1537—but died just twelve days afterwards. She was buried at Windsor Castle; and in 1547, Henry was laid to rest beside her.

997

ORANGERY

997   TW9

1761 SIR WILLIAM CHAMBERS; RESTORED 1959 AND 2002

This elegant Grade I–listed structure has high ceilings, sweeping archways, and vast impressive windows. It was built for Princess Augusta in 1761 and filled with citrus trees. In 1863, it became a museum, but was restored in 1959 to once again hold citrus plants, before mutating into a gift shop and tea-room by the 1980s. The armorial bearings of Prince Frederick and Princess Augusta on the front are a reminder of its royal associations. In 2002, it reopened as a fine restaurant and entertainment venue—and now has a new outdoor terrace in York and Portland stone.

PAGODA

998   TW9

1762 SIR WILLIAM CHAMBERS

In the mid-1700s, chinoiserie was highly popular in English garden design. This ten-storey octagonal structure is nearly 50 metres (163 feet) high and was the tallest reconstruction of a Chinese building in Europe at that time. It tapers, with each floor slightly smaller than the one below, and has neat red-painted fencing around each tier. The roofs were covered with varnished iron plates, and originally had eighty carved wooden dragons on the corners—gilded with real gold—but these fiery fellows have not been replaced in recent restorations. Two hundred and fifty-three steps lead to the top and spectacular views across the gardens to London, with the London Eye, the new Wembley Stadium, and Canary Wharf visible—both here and as a 360-degree panorama online. Below, Pagoda Vista is lined with paired broad-leaved trees and evergreen plantings, including a superb juniper collection.

998

999

RED HOUSE LANE, BEXLEY HEATH

RED HOUSE

999   DA6

1859 PHILIP WEBB

Commissioned by William Morris in 1859, this Gothic building in warm redbrick has a steep, medieval-style, overhanging redtiled roof, both long and circular porthole windows, and a toadstool-style structure beside the arched entrance. Its interior retains many pieces of furniture designed by Morris and Webb, as well as wall paintings and stained glass by Rossetti and Burne-Jones. This has been a family home for a century and a half and epitomises countryside escapism.

1000

MODERN ART GLASS LIMITED

1000   DA18

1973 SIR NORMAN FOSTER

This spectacular building is particularly apt for a company dealing with glass and served as a prototype for some of Norman Fosters's later glass edifices. The warehouse exterior is in blue stove-enamelled corrugated steel sheet taken over the top of a neat steel framework. With reflections pooling into its glass façade, the frontage almost disappears into images of sky and chasing clouds.

GLOSSARY

A

Apse Semicircular area at the end of a church's central aisle; altar is usually here.

Arcade Series of arches or a roofed passageway.

Arch Curved construction that spans a recess or opening.

Architrave Bottom section of an entablature, resting on a column or pilaster.

Art Deco Style popular in the 1920s and '30s. It began in France and spread through Britain and America.

Arts and Crafts Movement Major English aesthetic movement in the late 1800s that influenced British decorative arts and architecture.

Attic Room just below the roof, usually with sloping ceilings.

Ashlar Stone dressed for building by hewing or squaring.

B

Baluster Short upright column or urn-shaped railing support.

Balconet Pseudo-balcony—a low ornamental railing which projects slightly beyond a windowsill.

Balcony Platform projecting from the wall of an upper storey, enclosed by a railing or balustrade, with an entrance from a window.

Balusters Upright supports in turned shapes, usually wider at the base.

Balustrade Series of balusters.

Barrel vault Semi-cylindrical ceiling, like an extended arch.

Bas-relief Slightly projecting carving, embossing, or casting.

Bay window Windows projecting outward around an alcove.

Beaux-Arts Classical style emanating from France's École des Beaux-Arts.

Blitz Intensive aircraft attack—in this book, during World War II on Britain.

Block of flats An apartment building.

Boss Ornamental knob or projection at intersections of a ribbed vault.

Bracket Support for a projection, such as a cornice, often scroll shaped.

Brutalist Movement in Modern architecture, emphasizing stark forms and raw surfaces—often concrete.

Bungalow One-storey house.

Buttress Projecting structure supporting a wall.

C

Cantilever Projection supported at only one end.

Capital Decorated top or crowning feature of a column or pilaster.

Cartouche Ornamental panel that bears an inscription.

Castellated Built to resemble a castle with turrets and battlements.

Cast iron Hard, brittle iron that has been shaped in a mould.

Cement Mixture of clay and limestone.

Classical Reflecting the styles of ancient Greece and Rome.

Clerestory Upper part of church wall (above aisle roofs) and its windows.

Coffer Sunken panel in a ceiling or dome or under an arch.

Colonnade A row of columns supporting an entablature and usually one side of a roof.

Column Round vertical support.

Concrete Mixture of crushed stone or gravel, sand, cement, and water that hardens as it dries.

Corinthian Slender, ornate classical Greek order of columns.

Cornice Projecting part of an entablature.

Course Horizontal layer of masonry.

Crocket Projections carved in the shape of stylised leaves to decorate the edges of gables and pinnacles.

Crossing Space at the intersection of the nave and the transept.

Cupola Light structure rising above a roof or a dome.

Curtain wall Exterior wall with no structural function.

D

Detached Independent building structure, not attached to another.

Dome Convex roof or ceiling.

Doric Heavy fluted column with plain saucer-shaped capital and no base. (Roman Doric columns are more slender; they may have bases and no fluting.)

Dormer Projection built from a sloping roof.

E

Eaves Underside of a sloping roof, projecting beyond the wall of a building.

Entablature In classical architecture, the top horizontal area, divided into cornice, frieze, and architrave, supported by a colonnade.

F

Façade Exterior face of a building, usually the front, and often decorative.

Faience Glazed ceramic material.

Fenestration Arrangement of windows to provide interior light; decorative window elements in a façade.

Fire, the Great Fire of London, 1666.

Frieze Middle horizontal section of an entablature between the architrave and the cornice.

Flying buttress Arch or half-arch that carries the thrust of a vault or roof from the upper part of the wall to an outer buttress and from there down into the ground, usually in Gothic-style architecture.

G

Gable Front or side of a building enclosed to mask the end of a pitched roof.

Gargoyle A carved or cast decoration shaped like a grotesque animal, devil, or human figure.

GLC Greater London Council.

Gothic Pointed arch style from about 1100–1500.

Grade I and **Grade II** Listings begun in Britain in 1950, classifying and protecting (now 500,000) buildings of interest—through age, rarity, architectural merit, or historic interest: *Grade I* buildings are of exceptional interest; *Grade II* (some 90 per cent) are important.

Greek Revival Architectural style based on that of ancient Greece, often used for banks and official edifices.

Groin Cross vault formed by joining two barrel vaults at right angles.

H

Half timbered Wall with the timber frame exposed and the space between filled with brick or stone.

Hammer-beam roof Roof with trusses that transmit its weight and thrust into the supporting walls.

Hipped roof A roof that has four sloped sides.

I

International style Modernist architecture from 1925–65, using modern materials, especially the heavy use of windows and minimal decoration.

Ionic Classical Greek order with fluted columns and prominent swirled capitals.

Italianate A style based on the Italian architecture.

K

Keystone Wedge-shaped top stone on an arch.

L

Leading Glass pieces held in place by thin strips of lead.

Lintel Heavy horizontal beam of wood or stone over a door or window opening to support the weight above.

LCC London County Council.

M

Maisonette Apartment with more than one floor; often two or more occupy a single house.

Marquee Rooflike shelter extending above a doorway.

Mansard Roof with a steep lower part and shallower upper part.

Modern movement Launched by International (Bauhaus) styles; buildings have scant ornamentation.

Mortar Mixture of sand, lime, and water used to cement stones and bricks together.

Mouldings Rectangular or curved strips, either above or below the surface, that enhance light and shade.

Mullion Thin strips that separate window panes in a series.

N

Nave Central church area, from the entrance to the crossing; where the congregation sit.

Newell Upright post supporting the handrail at the top or bottom of a stairway.

Niche Recess in a wall; may hold statuary.

P

Palladian Neo-classical Italian style.

Pavilion Projecting part of a structure, often in a garden or park.

Pediment Triangular section over a doorway or window, often decorated.

Pier Heavy rectangular projection from a wal,l decorated like a column.

Pilaster Rectangular shallow column, projecting only slightly from a wall.

Pinnacle Small turret or spire, often crowned by a pyramid or cone; can mean an apex or high point.

Portico Porch or covered walk, often a roof supported by columns.

Polychrome Use of colour to decorate a building or statuary.

Q

Quatrefoil Four-lobed circle shape in windows or arches.

Queen Anne An elaborate style, as in English manor houses.

Quoin Dressed stones or bricks at the corners of buildings, laid so that their faces are alternately large and small. Adds strength to the masonry wall and is a decorative feature.

R

Reredos Screen behind a church altar.

RIBA Royal Institute of British Architects.

Ribbed vault Framework of diagonal arches, that project from the surface and carry the sections.

Rococo Last phase of Baroque decoration—light in weight and style.

Romanesque Style inspired by pre-Gothic buildings.

Rustication Cut stone in a wall channelled with deep grooves.

S

Semi-detached Pair of linked dwellings, sharing one wall.

Setback Moving back the upper storeys of tall buildings to allow more light to reach the street.

Soffit Exposed underside of an arch or beam.

Spire Tall, slender pointed structure that rises from a tower, turret, or roof.

Steeple Tower and spire combined.

Strapwork Decoration made by interlaced strips—applied or carved in wood, stone, or plaster.

String course Horizontal band of masonry extending across a façade.

T

Terracotta Fired clay, usually brownish red, used for roofing, tiles, or decoration; brick red colour.

Tie beam Horizontal timber joining two opposite rafters to prevent their spreading.

Tracery Ornamental stonework in a Gothic window around the glass.

Transept The 'arms' of the cruciform shape across a church nave.

Trefoil Three-lobed circle or arch shape in windows or arches.

Turnpike Barrier across a road that acts as a tollgate.

Turret Small tower, often on the corner of a building.

Tympanum Triangular space enclosed by a pediment, usually carved; or a curved space bounded by an arch.

Tuscan Simplest classical Roman order with unfluted columns, unadorned capitals and bases.

V

Vault Arched structure of stone, brick, or reinforced concrete, forming the support for a ceiling or roof.

W

Whitewash Lime and water mixture, or whiting (powdered chalk, size, and water).

Wrought iron Tough but malleable iron, easily welded and forged.

INDEX

Mathews, E. D. Jefferis, 240
Mathews, J Douglass, 240
Matilda, Queen, 207, 345
Matisse, 507
Matrix Chambers, 124
Matthew, Robert, 428
Matthews and Cannings
    Anchor Brewery, 481
Maugham, Somerset, 52, 54
Maurier, George du, 363, 367,
    372
Maximilius, Emperor, 222
May E. J., 71
Mayfair, 10, 24, 47–52, 56,
    453, 484
Mayfair Conservation Area, 21
Mayflower, The, 545
Mayor (London's first), 195
Mayor of London, 296, 302
McAlpine, Sir Robert, 54
McAslan, John, 386
McAslan, Troughton, 293
McCann-Erickson, 109
McCartney, Paul, 17
McCartney, Stella, 123
McDonald's, 549
McKenzie Revd, M., 126
McManus, Frederick, 30, 545
McMorran and Whitby, 191,
    323
McMorran, Donald, 191, 256,
    323, 434
Meadway, 407
Measures, H. B., 344, 372
Mecklenburgh Square,
    110–11
Mecklenburg-Strelitz,
    Princess of, 111
Melba, Dame Nellie, 174
Melbourne House, 37
Melbourne, Lord, 37
Melbury Road, 97, 99
Melcombe Street, 336–37
Meliá White House Hotel, 345
Mellor, David, 521
Melton Street, 356
Members of Parliament, 21,
    432, 453, 462
Mendelsohn and Chermayeff,
    479
Mendelsohn, Erich, 479
Mendelssohn, 211, 255
Menpes, Mortimer, 476
Menuhun, Sir Yehudi, 314
Mercantile Marine Memorial,
    226
Mercer's Hall, 200
Meredith, George, 473
Mermaid Inn, 317
Mermaid Theatre, 177
Messel, Oliver, 54
Messiah, The, 22, 138
Messrs Joseph, 453
Methodist Central Hall, 416
Metropole, 133
Metropolitan, 416
    Association for Improving
    the Dwellings of the
    Industrial Classes, 280
    Board of Works, 328, 357,
    475
    Borough of Finsbury, 163
    Borough of St Pancras,
    391

Police, 440
Railway, 231
Water Board, 165
Meuron, De, 507, 533
Mewès, Charles, 201, 209,
    219, 413
Mewès and Davies, 46, 146,
    201, 209, 219, 413
Michelangelo, 27, 147
Michelin Building, 475
Microwave Telephone Radio,
    32
Middle Temple and Hall,
    267–69
Middlesex
    County Cricket Club, 398
    Crown Court, 418
    Guildhall, 418–19
Midland Bank, 197, 215
Midland Railway, 335
Milbank, Anne Isabella, 28
Mile End, 292
Mile End Road, 274–75
Miles, Bernard, 177
Miles, Frank, 475
Milk Street, 160
Mill Pond, 550
Mill, John Stuart, 83–84
Millbank, 445, 446–47,
    468–69
Millbank Tower, 445
Millennium Dome, 80, 514,
    535
Millennium Exhibition, 535
Miller, John, 446, 517
Miller, Owen, 49
Millers Court, 277
Million Pound Act, 471
Milne, A. A., 380
Milner Square, 306–07
Milton, John, 196, 249, 436
Ministry of
    Defence, 133, 417, 465
    Health, 47
    Information, 115
    Supply, 142
    Works, 32
Minories, 223, 225
Miss Pinkerton's Academy, 67,
    68
Missions to Seamen, 243
Mitchell and Bridgwater, 403
Mitchell, Sir Peter Chalmers,
    380
Mitchum, Robert, 215
Mitford, Nancy, 73, 313
Mithras, 160, 200
Mitre Court, 264
Mitre Tavern, 264
Mitre, The, 64
Model Dwellings, 118, 280
Modern Art Glass Limited, 559
Modern International, 77
Moholy-Nagy, 365
Monet, Claude, 144
Monger, Henry, 285
Monk, James Henry, 458
Monkton Street, 540–41
Monmouth, Geoffrey de, 256
Monopoly, 336
Monroe, Marilyn, 54
Montagu Square, 16–17
Montagu, Lady Mary Wortley,
    24, 52

Montagu, Mrs Elizabeth, 17
Montague
    Hotel,122
    House, 120
    Place, 114–15
    Street, and Garden, 122
    William, 202
Montevetro, 496–97
Montfort, Simon de, 280
Montpellier Square, 493
Monty Python, 316, 391
Monument Street, 233
Monument, The, 215, 232,
    233
Moody, F. W., 494
Moonstone, The, 17
Moor Lane, 184, 188–89
Moore, Henry, 47, 239, 375,
    440, 446, 507
Moore, R. H., 512
Moore, Roger, 458
Moorfields, 546
Moorgate, 160, 181, 202
Morden College, 528–29
Morden Road, 528–29
Morden, Sir John, 528–29
More, 195
More, Margaret, 534
More, Sir Thomas, 122, 155,
    194–5, 408, 438, 471, 534
Moreton Street, 462–63
Morgan, Guy, 317
Morland, George, 359
Morning Post, 146
Morris and Company, 296,
    458
Morris, John, 288
Morris, William, 31, 79, 80, 85,
    122–23, 182, 296, 297,
    342, 372, 471, 558
Mortlake, 502
Morton House, 67
Mossbourne Community
    Academy, 284–85
Motcomb Street, 448–99
Mott, Richard, 348
Mound Stand, 398
Mount Row, 49
Mount Royal Hotel, 21
Mount Street, 48, 49
Mount Vernon, 365
Mountford, E. W., 257, 512
Mountford, Edward, 165
Mountfort Court, 308
Mousetrap, The, 100
Moya, John Hildago, 443,
    465
Mozart, Wolfgang Amadeus,
    453
Muirgold Limited, 59
Mummy Returns, The, 536
Murray Mews, 350–51
Murray, John Middleton, 371
Museum of
    Childhood, 280–81
    Fashion and Textiles, 512
    London, 188–89, 199
    Mankind, 43
    Methodism, 181
Museum Tavern, 119
Musick House, 165
My Fair Lady, 493
Myddleton, Sir Hugh, 301,
    307

Myers, Val, 27
Mylne, William Chadwell, 325

N
Nags Head, The, 434
Nagy, László Moholy, 44
Napoleon, 59, 83, 85, 471,
    525, 551
Nash, John 10, 12, 26–29, 36,
    38, 46, 132–33, 141, 156,
    338–44, 348, 414, 417,
    428, 434–35, 439
National Audit Office, 467
National Bus Company, 454
National Central Library, 356
National Employers House,
    221
National Gallery, 51, 129,
    130–31
National Hall, 98
National Health Society, 49
National Hospital of
    Neurology, 115
National Lending Library for
    Science and Technology,
    356
National Maritime Museum,
    372
National Museum, 19
National Portrait Gallery,
    130–31
National Provincial Bank, 41,
    197, 207
National Theatre, 279, 504,
    517
National Training School of
    Music, 494
National Trust, 377, 379, 440
National Westminster, 201,
    208
National Westminster Bank,
    41, 197, 201, 207, 209
Natural History Museum, 408,
    482, 488–89
NatWest Media Centre, 399
NatWest Tower, 32, 208
Naval and Military Club, 424
Navarre, Joan of, 534
Neal Street, 127
Nefield Fire Brigade, 240
Nelson Dock, 545
Nelson House, 544–45
Nelson Room, 540
Nelson, Lord Horatio, 24,
    253–55, 424, 502, 536,
    540, 545
Nelson's Column, 100
Neon Tower, 508
Nesbit, Edith, 534
Neville Terrace, 491
New Bond Street, 47
New Bridge Street, 259
New Cavendish Street, 28
New Connaught Rooms, 19
New Covent Garden Market,
    136–37
New Cross Road, 542–43
New End Square, 362, 383
New Globe theatre, 504, 520
New Globe Walk, 520
New Grove House, 363
New Model Army, 185
New Oxford Street, 122, 126
New River, 301, 307, 313,

325, 328
New River Company, 325
New Scotland Yard, 416
New Southgate, 298–99
New Square, 153
New Street, 205
New Victoria Cinema, 441
New York Times, The, 450
New Zealand High
    Commission and House,
    428–29
Newby, Frank, 380
Newcastle, Duke of, 28
Newgate Prison, 126, 160,
    174–75, 189, 256, 302
Newgate Street, 175
Newman, Cardinal, 471
Newman, Paul, 278
Newton Road 62–63,
Newton, Adam, 533
Newton, Ernest ,38, 425
Newton, Sir Isaac, 86, 147,
    148
Newton, William, 159, 539
Nicholas Nickleby, 37, 111
Nicholson and Corlette, 444
Nicholson Inn, 36
Nicholson, Ben, 47, 374–375
Nickleby, Ralph, 37
Nield, John Camfield, 471
Nightingale Training School of
    Nursing, 517
Nightingale, Florence, 147,
    449, 517
Nine Elms, 136–37
Nisbet, Arthur, 249
Noble Street, 190
Noel Coward House, 444–45
Norden and Hollar, 520
Norfolk, Duke of, 252
Norland Square, 96
Norlands Estate, 96
Norman Conquest, 327
Norman Shaw Building, 416
North Audley Street, 20–21
North Circular, 332–33
North Drive, 502–03
North End, 358–59, 366
North End Way, 360–61
North Finchley, 298–99
North Hill, 318–19
North Road ,318–19
Northampton Institute, 165
Northampton Square, 164–65
Northampton, Marquess of,
    164, 313
Northern Inn, 124
Northern Line, 134
Northgate, 402–03
Northgate Mansion, 396–97
Northumberland Avenue, 133
Northumberland, Earl of, 227
Norwood High Street, 550–51
Notting Hill, 10–11
Nottingham House, 83, 91
Novello, Ivor, 138
Now and Zen, 128
Number One London, 460–61
Number One Poultry, 347
Nurse, William M., 342
Nutford Place, 18
Nye, David, 207

O

ACKNOWLEDGEMENTS

Thanks are due to the following organizations that have kindly granted permission to photograph buildings and to reproduce these in this book and/or given their assistance in various ways:

The London Cremation Company for permission to photograph Golders Green Crematorium.

Masters of the Bench of the Honourable Society of the Middle Temple for permission to photograph the Middle Temple and to reproduce these in this book.

Sarah Eastel Locations for organising access to Chiswick House and Eltham Palace.

Clare Skinner, Press and Public Affairs Officer, MCC, Lord's Cricket Ground, for permission to take photographs and to reproduce these in this book.

The Royal Botanic Gardens, Kew, for permission to photograph the buildings and glasshouses and to reproduce these in this book.

Helen Walker, Arts and Planning Manager, Pitzhanger Manor Gallery and House, for permission to photograph the buildings.

The inclusion of a building in this book does not mean that its interior (or exterior) is accessible. Readers are requested to please respect the privacy of those living in the buildings.

The author would like to thank the following for their help in research:

Lorraine Lees, Acting Assistant Librarian, West Library, London Borough of Islington.

Elizabeth Green, IT and Searchroom Officer, Hackney Archives Department.

Roz Sherris, Museum of London.

Tina Corry, Marx Library, British Library.

Lynn Fowkes, Kensington United Reform Church.

John Reynolds would like to thank Linda Macpherson for her legal advice on the rights of UK photographers.

Playne Books Limited and Playne Design Limited would like to give special thanks to Laura Ross of Black Dog and Leventhal, and Iris Bass, for their great assistance in the creation of this book.

The following photographs were taken by David Playne:

Page 317, building number 558, Catacombs at Highgate Cemetery.

Page 554, building number 996, Interior of Kew Gardens Palm House, empty of plants in 1986.

While every effort has been made to verify all of the factual information contained within this book, to seek permission to use the photographs taken by John Reynolds, and to identify the architects and dates of the buildings, the publishers wish to apologise for any inadvertent errors or omissions. They will be glad to rectify these in future editions if Playne Books Limited are notified of the relevant information by e-mail to playne.books@virgin.net or in writing to:

Playne Books Limited
Park Court Barn
Trefin
Haverfordwest
Pembrokeshire
SA62 5AU
United Kingdom